D0146737

ENCYCLOPEDIA OF ADDICTIONS

Volume 1
A–N

Kathryn H. Hollen

GREENWOOD PRESS
Westport, Connecticut · London

Library of Congress Cataloging-in-Publication Data

Hollen, Kathryn H.
Encyclopedia of addictions / Kathryn H. Hollen.
     p. ; cm.
  Includes bibliographical references and index.
  ISBN 978-0-313-34737-5 (set : alk. paper)—ISBN 978-0-313-34739-9
(vol. 1 : alk. paper)—ISBN 978-0-313-34741-2 (vol. 2 : alk. paper)
  1. Substance abuse—Encyclopedias.   2. Compulsive behavior—Encyclopedias.   I. Title.
  [DNLM: 1. Behavior, Addictive—Encyclopedias—English.   2. Substance-Related
Disorders—Encyclopedias—English. WM 13 H737e 2009]
  RC563.4.H65 2009
  616.86003—dc22   2008034529

British Library Cataloguing in Publication Data is available.

Library of Congress Catalog Card Number: 2008034529
ISBN: 978-0-313-34737-5 (set)
ISBN: 978-0-313-34739-9 (vol. 1)
ISBN: 978-0-313-34741-2 (vol. 2)

First published in 2009

Greenwood Press, 88 Post Road West, Westport, CT 06881
An imprint of Greenwood Publishing Group, Inc.
www.greenwood.com

Printed in the United States of America

∞™

The paper used in this book complies with the
Permanent Paper Standard issued by the National
Information Standards Organization (Z39.48-1984).

10 9 8 7 6 5 4 3 2 1

Dedicated to the mighty Howell sisterhood.

CONTENTS

LIST OF ENTRIES

GUIDE TO RELATED TOPICS

Abused and Addictive Drugs

Amphetamines
Anabolic Steroids
Anxiolytics
Barbiturates
Benzodiazepines
Bidis and Kreteks
Butorphanol
Cannabis
Chloral Hydrate
Cigarettes
Cigars
Cocaine and Crack
Codeine
Depressants
Designer Drugs
Dextroamphetamine (Dexedrine)
Dextromethorphan (DXM)
Dextropropoxyphene (Darvon and
    Darvocet)
Ecstasy (MDMA)
Ephedrine and Pseudoephedrine
Fentanyl
Flunitrazepam (Rohypnol)
Gamma Hydroxybutyric Acid (GHB)
Gateway Drugs
Ghutka
Hallucinogens
Hard Drugs vs. Soft Drugs
Hard Liquor vs. Soft Liquor
Hash (Hashish) and Hashish Oil

Hemp
Heroin
Hydrocodone
Hydromorphone
Ibogaine
Inhalants
Ketamine
Khat
Levo-alpha-acetyl-methadol (LAAM)
Lysergic Acid Diethylamide (LSD)
Marijuana
Meperidine
Meprobamate
Mescaline
Methadone
Methamphetamine
Methcathinone
Methylphenidate
Mini Cigars
Morphine
Nicotine
Opiates
Opium
Oxycodone
Oxymorphone
Pentazocine
Phencyclidine (PCP)
Prescription Drugs
Psilocybin and Psilocin
Shisha
Smokeless Tobacco
Snus

Stimulants
Substance Addiction
Tobacco
Tramadol

Addiction and Society

Addiction
Behavioral Addictions
Costs of Drug Abuse and Addiction
Drug Administration
Drug Nomenclature
Drug Screening/Testing
Drugged Driving
Gateway Drugs
Hemp
Hookah
Insurance Coverage and Addiction
Monitoring the Future
Paraphernalia
Pornography
Predatory Drugs
Prevention
Prohibition
Pseudoaddiction
Secondhand Smoke
Substance Addiction
War on Drugs
Women, Pregnancy, and Drugs

Biology and Chemistry of Addiction

Acetaldehyde
Agonists
Anhedonia
Antagonists
Behavioral Sensitization
Brain and Addiction
Conditioning
Craving
CREB (cAMP Response Element-Binding)
   Protein
Cross-Addiction and Cross-Tolerance
Delta FosB
Drug Classes
Drug Interactions
Drug Nomenclature
Genetics of Addiction

Long-Term Potentiation
Mesolimbic Dopamine System
Neuroadaptation
Neurotransmitters
Presynaptic Cell
Tolerance
Withdrawal

Compulsive, Impulsive, and Addictive Behaviors

Alcoholism
Anorexia Nervosa
Behavioral Addictions
Binge and Heavy Drinking
Bulimia Nervosa
Caffeine Addiction
Codependency
Compulsions and Impulses
Compulsive Computer Use
Compulsive Shopping or Spending
Cybersex Addiction
Denial
Dependence
Drug Administration
Eating Disorders
Exercise Addiction
Food Addiction and Obesity
Hypersexuality
Impulse Control Disorders (ICDs)
Intermittent Explosive Disorder
Kleptomania
Obsessive-Compulsive Disorder (OCD)
Online Gaming
Paraphilias
Pathological Gambling Disorder
Pipe Smoking
Pornography Addiction
Problem Drinking
Pyromania
Relationship Addiction
Self-Injury, Self-Mutilation
Sexual Addiction
Substance Addiction
Television Addiction
Trichotillomania
Work Addiction ("Workaholism")

Contributory Causes and Diagnosis

Abuse
Addiction
Addiction Liability
Addictive Personality
Anxiety Disorders
Conduct Disorders
Diagnostic and Statistical Manual of
*   Mental Disorders*
Disease Model of Addiction
Dual Diagnosis
Mental Disorders

Effects of Drug Use

Addiction
Alcoholism
Anhedonia
Behavioral Sensitization
Craving
Denial
Flashbacks
Hangovers
Intoxication
Long-Term Potentiation
Reward Deficiency Syndrome

Individuals

Begleiter, Henri
Blum, Kenneth
Carpenter, Karen
Famous Addicts
Ford, Betty
Jellinek, Elvin Morton
Jung, Carl
Mann, Marty
Nation, Carrie Amelia

Peele, Stanton
Rush, Benjamin
Silkworth, William D.
Smith, Robert Holbrook ("Dr. Bob")
Tiebout, Harry
Volkow, Nora
Wilson, William G. ("Bill W.")

Regulation of Drugs

Controlled Substances Act (CSA)
Decriminalization
Drug Screening/Testing
Prohibition
War on Drugs

Treating Addiction

Addiction Medications
Addiction Medicine
Alcoholics Anonymous
Alternative Addiction Treatment
Buprenorphine (Buprenex, Suboxone,
    Subutex)
Cocaine Anonymous
Compulsive Eaters Anonymous
Gamblers Anonymous
Ibogaine
Intervention
Medical Marijuana
Methadone
Minnesota Model
Prometa
Recovery
Serenity Prayer
Sexual Compulsives Anonymous
Synanon
Treatment
Twelve-Step Programs

PREFACE

How can I explain that obsession . . . the desperate hunger, the consuming thirst, the unbearable craving, the furious yearning, the excruciating need that . . . overrides the need for food, for water, for sleep, for love.

—William Cope Moyers

Broken: The Story of Addiction and Redemption

Over 22 million Americans abuse or are addicted to drugs—3.2 million abuse both alcohol and illicit drugs, 3.8 million abuse illicit drugs but not alcohol, and 15.6 million abuse alcohol but not illicit drugs. At least 70 million Americans are addicted to nicotine. Somewhere between 8 and 38 million Americans are believed to suffer from impulse control disorders, otherwise known as "behavioral addictions," like pathological gambling and compulsive shopping. Although eating disorders are not included in these figures, they are sometimes considered behavioral addictions and afflict another 8 million Americans. Direct and indirect costs of drug use alone to U.S. society are over $500 billion per year, with illicit drugs draining the nation's economy by an estimated $181 billion, alcohol by $185 billion, and nicotine-associated expenditures by $157 billion. The costs to individual families in terms of human suffering and tragedy are incalculable. Moreover, the federal government's Substance Abuse and Mental Health Services Administration (SAMHSA) estimates that only a small percentage of those needing treatment ever receive it.

Although not everyone who abuses drugs is an addict, abuse is a precursor to addiction, and part of the obligation of this encyclopedia is to make a clear distinction between the two. In language targeted to the nonscientific general reader, these volumes define addiction based on criteria laid out by the American Psychiatric Association (APA) in its *Diagnostic and Statistical Manual of Mental Disorders* (*DSM*), the authoritative reference used by mental health professionals in the United States to identify and diagnose mental illness. In most respects, the *DSM*'s criteria mirror those found in the World Health Organization's *International Statistical Classification of Diseases* (*ICD*), a worldwide standard.

From alcoholism to pathological gambling to dependence on illicit or prescription drugs, the encyclopedia contains approximately 200 text entries that discuss symptoms, causes, prevalence, prevention, and treatment as well as associated terms such as compulsion, tolerance, denial, and withdrawal. It explains why the current edition of the *DSM* uses the term "dependence" instead of "addiction" and why the APA seems likely to revert to the use of "addiction" in the upcoming fifth edition due for publication in 2012. In most cases, standard *DSM* diagnostic criteria are included as well as self-assessment questionnaires that, while not intended to be diagnostic, can help readers determine if their drug use or behavior is veering into dangerous territory. Also included are frequently asked questions, lists of facts, statistics, or a combination of these to give readers a comprehensive overview of the individual addiction. Many entries include lists of publications or Web sites for further reading.

Approximately 200 more entries cross-reference addictive drugs and medications by both generic and trade names, and Appendix B contains an index of street names by which many of the drugs are also known. For example, the encyclopedia entries for OxyContin and Percocet refer the reader to the entry for the generic drug oxycodone, where the full discussion of the opiate can be found, and Appendix B shows that common slang terms for the drug include "blue babies," "hillbilly heroin," or "killer." The cross-referencing entries for pharmaceuticals direct the reader to the "Addiction Medications" entry, where the medications are categorized by type, or to Appendix B, where their therapeutic potential as anxiolytics, agonists, antagonists, or preventive vaccines is explained more fully.

Hundreds of psychoactive substances are subject to abuse, and new ones, both legal and illegal, are being produced every day. In some cases varying from one another by as little as a single molecule, each of these substances—based on its chemical makeup and effect on the brain and body—falls into one of seven specific categories. Because some of these, such as ordinary household chemicals that users sniff or "huff," do not have individual entries, they have been addressed in the context of their overall category—in this case, "Inhalants."

In addition to those entries focusing specifically on drugs, behavioral compulsions, and the mental disorders like anxiety and depression that frequently co-occur with addiction, the encyclopedia includes biographies of pioneers in the field such as Bill Wilson, the founder of Alcoholics Anonymous (AA), and Benjamin Rush, an 18th-century physician who first pronounced alcoholism a disease. It also explores the science of addiction within the limits of current understanding. Including basic brain anatomy and neurotransmitter function, the text and accompanying illustrations show how the brain's chemical messengers operate to influence feelings, sensations, and behavior. It identifies the likely seat of addiction as the mesolimbic dopamine system (MDS), the so-called reward circuitry that produces pleasure when an organism engages in activities that support survival—such as eating or having sex. These pursuits stimulate an outpouring of dopamine and other neurotransmitters that program the brain to seek the life-sustaining stimuli again and again, thus ensuring that the species survives and reproduces itself. Psychoactive drugs overwhelm the reward pathway, triggering a euphoric reaction commonly referred to as a "high" or "rush" that is far more intense than the pleasure produced by natural stimuli. In the classic model of addiction, this phenomenon hijacks the brain by teaching it to prefer the drug-induced rewards, and as the brain adapts to the increased stimuli by reducing its own production of feel-good neurotransmitters, the addict requires more of the drug to produce the desired effect. As this neuroadaptation evolves, the addict begins to need the drug to feel normal, compelling him to engage in increasingly dangerous drug-seeking and drug-using behavior. Scientists believe this explains in large part how addicts come to neglect their responsibilities or their families, and how many reach the point of rejecting food or sleep in their desperate, single-minded pursuit of drugs.

The fierce debate about whether addiction is a disease or a choice is ongoing, having serious implications for prevention and treatment. The encyclopedia discusses the disease and choice models from both current and historical perspectives and addresses related public health issues. Although there seems to be consensus that genetics plays as strong a role as environment in the development of addiction, at this juncture opinions begin to diverge. Proponents of the disease model, including the Director of the National Institute on Drug Abuse and many other prominent experts, believe that some people are so susceptible to the neurological effects of even casual drug use that they become physiologically unable to control subsequent use. This is especially true in adolescents; even young people with no genetic predisposition are exquisitely vulnerable to drug-induced neurological remodeling because their brain circuitry is still under development. Yet critics of the disease model contend that, no matter how profoundly drugs affect the brain, addicts consciously choose to use the substances and that, with appropriate behavioral modifications, they can learn to use them moderately or not at all. This philosophy underlies many treatment approaches that stress short-term behavioral therapy instead of the "Minnesota model" of rehabilitation typified by many 28-day residential programs. Regardless of what experts call it or how they treat it, they agree that addiction has a devastating impact on brain development, personality, and overall mental health.

Since illicit drugs are subject to federal regulatory controls, some of them severe, Appendix A explains the U.S. Drug Enforcement Administration's Controlled Substances Act that groups drugs by schedules depending on their effect on the user. It itemizes penalties for the possession or use of the scheduled drugs and many of the chemicals that are used in their manufacture.

Appendix B is a Drug Index that shows how drugs of abuse are grouped into categories, provides an in-depth explanation of how various medications treat addiction, and lists the generic and trade names as well as the street and traditional names of many abused drugs.

In the case of marijuana—which is illegal under federal law—a wide variety of state laws impose penalties ranging from mild to severe for its use, possession, or distribution. Appendix C has been included to provide a comprehensive breakdown of these state laws as they appeared on the legislative books in the spring of 2008.

Several agencies of the U.S. government collaborate to accumulate detailed data on substance use, particularly among America's youth. They track much more than the number of people who use a specific substance; they also evaluate data such as age at first use, gender differences, ethnic breakdowns, geographic trends, and the degree to which prevention strategies or perceptions of risk affect use. Although specific entries such as "alcoholism" or "eating disorders" include relevant statistical information, more comprehensive information can be found in Appendix D. As SAMHSA obtains more current information, it will be updated on the agency's Web site at http://www.oas.samhsa.gov.

Because much of the statistical data and scientific research cited in the encyclopedia was obtained from agencies of the federal government, which uses acronyms widely, a list of these has been provided in Appendix E along with other abbreviations that appear throughout. Examples of these include the National Institute on Drug Abuse (NIDA), Centers for Disease Control and Prevention (CDC), and AA.

Avoiding drug use during adolescence and young adulthood seems to be key to preventing substance addiction, even if the person experiments with highly addictive drugs later in life. Compelling evidence suggests that individuals who reject drugs during crucial developmental years are protected in two ways. First, they are more likely to develop healthy coping skills rather than depending on drugs to balance mood and emotions; second, their fully developed brains are not as vulnerable to the structural changes that underlie abuse and addiction. To address critical prevention measures, the NIDA has prepared a guide to prevention programs for youth that can be found on its web site. Examples of some of these programs are shown in Appendix F.

Appendix G contains comprehensive lists of groups and organizations to which readers may turn for assistance or further information. A bibliography of sources and a general subject index appear at the back of the encyclopedia.

Acknowledgments

Writing this encyclopedia would not have been possible without the help of my husband, Brian. Not only was he a first-rate research and editorial assistant but he also produced the illustrations, graphics, and figures while juggling his many other business-related duties. Even more crucial was his support at home where he good-naturedly served as housekeeper, chef, and errand person so I could concentrate fully on the task at hand. Giving up numerous social and leisure activities while tolerating my intense preoccupation cannot have been easy for him, but he never complained and somehow managed to stay cheerful throughout. I am completely indebted to him.

I want to thank my family and friends for their patience during the past months, and my sisters, Jean and Martha, for their intellectual interest in my work, which has benefited from their comments and questions. I am very grateful to Mary Gustafson for the generous care and affection she showered on Jodie when I could not, and to Ben Goldberg, who regularly supplied me with organic chocolate "incentive" and always managed to make me laugh. Debby Adams at Greenwood Press also deserves my appreciation for the considerable effort she put forth to make this project feasible.

Finally, I owe a very special thanks to Lily and Jodie, who preserved my sanity simply by being themselves.

A

Abuse The terminology of drug use can be confusing. Although the word *abuse* is sometimes used interchangeably with *addiction*, and indeed there are significant similarities, critical distinctions must be made. According to the American Psychiatric Association, both involve a dysfunctional pattern of substance use that leads to impairment or distress manifested by intermittent failure to fulfill responsibilities at work or school; dangerous behavior while under the influence, such as driving a car; and negative consequences of continued use of the drug(s), such as legal or personal problems. What distinguishes addiction from abuse is the addict's lack of control over the frequency or amount of use, preoccupation with using, the development of tolerance to the substance, and the presence of withdrawal symptoms if the substance is discontinued. Though a hangover is in itself not a sign of alcoholism, frequent hangovers or a history of hangovers due to excessive drinking are strongly suggestive of addiction. The former director of the National Institute on Drug Abuse, Alan Leshner, has stated that, unlike abuse, addiction has moved the addict out of the realm of having free choice as his or her use of the substance has become compulsive.

Biological, genetic, and environmental factors influence an individual's vulnerability to addiction, just as the **addiction liability** of the substance in question affects the individual's response. Although many people can abuse substances for years without crossing over the line that separates abuse from addiction, **cocaine** and **heroin**, which are highly addictive, are more likely to addict someone than **marijuana**. Although these variables make it impossible to predict who will become addicted and who will not, there is no question that continued use heightens risk.

Further Reading

American Psychiatric Association. *Diagnostic and Statistical Manual of Mental Disorders*, 4th Edition, Text Revision. Washington, DC: American Psychiatric Association, 2000.
Erickson, Carlton K. *The Science of Addiction: From Neurobiology to Ttreatment*. New York: Norton, 2007.
Hoffman, John, and Froemke, Susan, eds. *Addiction: Why Can't They Just Stop?* New York: Rodale, 2007.

Acetaldehyde Acetaldehyde is the byproduct of oxidation that takes place in the liver as it metabolizes the ethyl alcohol consumed in an alcoholic beverage. If acetaldehyde is allowed to build up in the body, it can provoke toxic reactions, but the liver, under normal circumstances, breaks it down immediately into harmless substances. However, in certain Asian populations whose genetic heritage leaves them lacking appropriate enzymes, acetaldehyde builds up in their bodies to produce extreme discomfort—rapid flushing, dizziness, nausea, and vomiting. To produce the same effect in alcoholics to discourage them from drinking, a drug called Antabuse (disulfiram) that blocks their enzymes from processing acetaldehyde is often prescribed. As long as an alcoholic takes the prescribed dose of Antabuse, he or she will become violently ill if he or she drinks. The medication is a powerful motivator to abstain from alcohol, but compliance in taking it can be a problem.

In recent decades, some researchers have presented evidence that alcoholics are born with a metabolic quirk that causes them to process acetaldehyde differently. Unlike Asian populations that inherit a protective acetaldehyde-related gene, alcoholics inherit a variant that triggers addictive drug-seeking behavior in the **brain**. In such people, according to this theory, acetaldehyde stimulates an overabundance of chemicals called tetrahydroisoquinolines, or TIQs (also, THIQs). These are considered addictive in themselves because they interact with other **neurotransmitters** to impart a high level of stimulation to the reward pathway. This produces pleasurable feelings that compel the alcoholic to drink excessively to recapture them. Although not disproved, this theory has fallen into disfavor among many experts and has been replaced in recent years by research clarifying other mechanisms by which drugs and neurotransmitters affect the brain.

Acetylcholine. *See* Neurotransmitters.

Acomplia. *See* Medical Marijuana.

Actiq. *See* Fentanyl.

Adderall. *See* Dextroamphetamine.

Addiction Addiction is a complex disorder whose principal diagnostic feature is a repeated compulsion to take a certain substance or indulge in a certain behavior despite negative consequences. As an addicted person increasingly begins to rely on the object of addiction for physical or emotional gratification, he or she tends to neglect other, healthier aspects of life. It is generally agreed that there are two types of addiction: physical, when people become addicted to substances like drugs or alcohol, and psychological or behavioral, when people become addicted to activities like gambling or shopping. A **behavioral addiction** may also be called a "process" addiction. Although there is some disagreement over whether behaviors can be addictions in the same sense that drugs can be—some prefer to call such behaviors **impulse control disorders** or **obsessive-compulsive disorders**—the addict's need to indulge in them despite adverse consequences has led to their popular identification as addictions.

Both types of addiction initially provide some sort of pleasure, excitement, or gratification—often a combination of these. Addictions may range from mild to severe in degree; mildly addicted people may respond quickly to **treatment** and have relatively little difficulty refraining from the substance or behavior, whereas severely addicted people may be unable to recover.

Scientific advances over the past 30 to 40 years have revealed that addiction is based on neurochemical changes that take over or hijack a critical chemical pathway in the

mesolimbic dopamine system of the **brain**. Known as the reward pathway, this area is programmed to respond to certain stimuli such as food or sex with feel-good **neurotransmitters**, primarily dopamine. Scientists believe that the pleasure these stimuli produce is how organisms learn to repeat behaviors important for survival, such as eating and reproduction. In the case of addictive substances, however, this mechanism can backfire.

When someone ingests an addictive drug or engages in addictive behavior, the affected neurons are overstimulated to produce an excess of dopamine that the brain perceives as a significantly more pleasurable experience than that provided by life's natural rewards. With repeated exposure to the psychoactive stimulus, the brain compensates by reducing its neurotransmitter output and producing fewer cellular receptors to receive and transmit dopamine along the reward pathway. As **tolerance** develops, the individual begins to require more of the drug stimulus to achieve the initial effect. Eventually, his or her use or behavior takes on a compulsive quality as the individual finds him- or herself compelled to indulge more frequently—not to feel good but to avoid feeling bad. In spite of this, the person is likely to deny the problem and claim that usage or behavior falls within normal boundaries. A clear indication that the individual's judgment is impaired, this **denial** becomes a nearly automatic reflex with which one justifies pathological use or behavior. If the person is unable to indulge, he or she may undergo **withdrawal**, the physical and psychological distress that arises as the brain attempts to adjust to the absence of drugs.

Although behavioral addictions generally do not produce the more severe physical manifestations of withdrawal sometimes seen in **substance addictions**, individuals suffering from them may experience a certain level of agitation, restlessness, and depression if they cannot satisfy their need. Many drugs, such as certain antidepressants, cause physical **dependence** in the sense that they rebalance the brain's neurotransmitters, and their abrupt withdrawal can lead to distressing symptoms, but these drugs are not addictive because they do not trigger compulsive use and loss of control.

What Is Addiction?

A consensus exists among most scientists that addiction is the process during which the brain's neural pathways—primarily in the mesolimbic dopamine system—are hijacked by the artificial reward of drugs. It is not clear how certain combinations of genetic, biological, and environmental factors allow this to happen in some people and not others; what is known is that, for many, a drug-induced release of dopamine and other neurotransmitters overrides the brain's response to normal rewards that support survival, such as food or sex. This reaction leads to changes in the actual structure of axons and dendrites and alters synapse formation, a dysregulation that begins to affect the addicts' behavior outside of their conscious awareness. Although it is not completely understood how this physiological remodeling occurs, the distorted neurochemical messages it transmits affect learning, motivation, and memory. In time, addicts no longer respond to the drug with the same pleasure but find, instead, that they require the drug to feel normal. As their ability to enjoy other pleasures decreases and their need for the drug increases, many addicts gradually cease to care about families, homes, work, school, or health in their single-minded pursuit of the drug.

Indulging in addictive substances or behaviors does not have to occur on a daily basis for addiction to exist; weekend drinkers or those who go on monthly binges with days of remission between episodes can be addicted, just as heavy drinkers who have several cocktails every night for years are not necessarily addicted if their drinking does not produce negative consequences and if they are able to stop without difficulty.

Recent research on mice has revealed that dopamine-releasing cells in the brain seem to learn and remember their hypersecretion of dopamine in response to addictive drugs. Called **long-term potentiation**, this cellular memory remains active for some time and may be part of the basis for **craving**. Researchers also made the intriguing discovery that although psychoactive *nonaddictive* drugs like antidepressants do not potentiate the cells in the same way, acute stress does. Although stress does not cause addiction, this finding raises questions about how the relationship of drug exposure and stress could affect the brain's chemical threshold for prolonged potentiation and increased vulnerability to addiction. It may also help explain why stress is one of the most powerful threats to abstinence and **recovery**.

The American Psychiatric Association (APA), in its ***Diagnostic and Statistical Manual of Mental Disorders*** (*DSM*) published in 2000, presents criteria widely used by mental health experts to diagnose addiction and distinguish it from **abuse**. Although the *DSM* uses the term *dependence* in an effort to remove the stigma associated with the word *addiction*, this practice has led to considerable confusion, and increasing pressure is on APA editors to revert to the term addiction in the next edition of the *DSM*. Some experts, however, insist that addiction is a vague, clinically inaccurate term that does not properly distinguish between the medical disease that true addiction represents and the overindulgence of drugs or other substances that represents abuse, not addiction. They believe that the term dependence remains appropriate, especially if clear distinctions are made between chemical

---

Signs of Substance and Behavioral Addictions

- Anticipating the substance or behavior with increased excitement
- Feeling irritable or restless when prevented from indulging in the substance or behavior
- Devoting increasing amounts of time preparing for the substance use or activity or recovering from the effects
- Neglecting responsibilities at home, school, or work
- Indulging in the substance or behavior to manage emotions
- Thinking obsessively about the activity
- Seeking out the substance or activity despite the harm it causes (deterioration of health, complaints from family or coworkers)
- Denying the problem to self and to others despite its obvious negative effects
- Hiding the use or behavior from others
- Suffering blackouts—memory losses while under the influence or an inability when sober to remember behavior that occurred when under the influence
- Becoming depressed; often a contributory factor in the development of an addiction, depression is also a result
- Having a history of anxiety or other mental disorder, psychological or physical abuse, or low self esteem
- Experiencing some form of sexual dysfunction
- Feeling remorse or shame over use of substance(s) or activities associated with use

dependence and physical dependence. Despite this argument, there are indications that the APA will revert to addiction in the fifth edition of the *DSM* due to be published in 2012.

Evidence suggests that behavioral addictions tend to occur later in life but substance addictions usually have an earlier onset stemming from drug or alcohol use during adolescence. Some studies cite instant-onset addiction, when users report that their initial exposure makes them feel normal for the first time in their lives. Whether this phenomenon represents actual addiction or an unusual reaction to the drug is not yet clear. Late-onset addictions may occur in adulthood, although the National Institute on Drug Abuse (NIDA) reports that the likelihood of addiction is much greater among adolescents and very young adults due to the plasticity of their developing brains.

The Teen Brain on Drugs

According to the National Institute of Mental Health and other scientists studying the impact that drug abuse has on the brain, adolescents are more vulnerable than adults to the deleterious effects of drugs for three reasons: drugs increase the likelihood of risky behavior; they prime vulnerable areas of the brain for the development of addiction; and, in the long term, they can permanently impair mental capacity.

Once a child reaches puberty, the brain begins to thin out excessive brain-cell connections made when the child was younger and the brain was growing at a rapid rate. This thinning-out process also helps build longer chains of neural networks that are required for the more critical analytical thinking that adults require throughout their lives. The pruning can be likened to how a gardener trims out a bush to remove weaker, ineffective branches to allow the stronger limbs to develop fully so the bush will thrive. A similar process in the brain of someone roughly 11 to 25 years old represents a crucial stage of neurological development.

The final area of the brain to mature is the prefrontal cortex, where higher cognitive functions and judgment reside. With so many structures in the teenage brain set to "accelerate" mode, the inhibitory reasoning part of the prefrontal cortex might not engage well enough to adequately guide behavior. Even in their late teens, adolescents are more impulsive, aggressive, and likely to engage in novel or risky activities than people in their mid to late 20s. By the time adolescents outgrow their impulsive youth and more reckless behavior, it may be too late to reverse addictive patterns already laid down in the brain or to undo permanent damage to cognitive abilities.

Addictions for the most part are chronic, progressive, and highly destructive. Long-term drug users develop physical health problems, and interpersonal, social, and occupational relationships break down as well. The ingredients in some drugs that cut or alter the substance can be toxic; snorting—inhaling powdered forms of a drug—can erode nasal tissues; **stimulants** can cause heart attacks or respiratory arrest; and contaminated needles can transmit HIV and other serious diseases such as malaria, tetanus, blood poisoning, or deadly bacterial infections. Drugs can trigger aberrant or violent behavior, and accidents are common, particularly automobile accidents. About one-half of all highway fatalities involve alcohol alone.

Behavioral addictions such as **eating disorders** or **sexual addictions** that carry a risk of sexually transmitted diseases seriously compromise health. Others, such as pathological gambling, are devastating in other ways. Gambling addicts can squander a lifetime's accumulation of assets as they chase the next win, neglecting eating, sleeping, families, school, and work as their lives unravel.

Although their addictive potential varies widely, legal and illegal addictive substances are generally considered to be narcotics, stimulants, **depressants**, *Cannabis*, **hallucinogens**, **inhalants**, **anabolic steroids**, **nicotine**, alcohol, and **caffeine**. Aside from their inherent chemical properties, factors that affect their addictive liability include the method of administration as well as the addict's genetic and environmental background. Addictive behaviors can arise from normal activities such as gambling, computer usage, sex, shopping and spending, and exercising, or from aberrant practices like **kleptomania** (stealing), **trichotillomania** (pulling out of one's hair), **self-injury** (cutting behaviors), and **pyromania** (starting fires).

History of Addiction

The identification of certain activities as behavioral addictions is a comparatively recent event. Substance addiction has always been recognized, ever since humans began using mind-altering substances. In the 4th century B.C.E., Aristotle (384–322 B.C.E.) referred to drunkenness as an organic disorder, and discussions of **opium** addiction have appeared in medieval documents. Historical references to addiction focus on its negative aspects, although cultural attitudes about the more controlled use of some addictive drugs have been mixed. At one time, **cocaine**, **marijuana**, **methamphetamines**, and even opium were routinely prescribed for various conditions, and other drugs, such as peyote, are still in legal use among certain religious groups. Today, controlled substances such as **codeine** are prescribed for pain relief, and **Ecstasy** is being studied for the treatment of posttraumatic stress disorder.

Until the middle of the 20th century, addicts were usually shunned by the public or incarcerated in prisons or mental institutions. To some degree, modern attitudes have not changed: Many people avoid or ignore homeless addicts on the streets of U.S. cities. Others view addiction and the deterioration that accompanies it as behavioral aberrations that should be addressed with cognitive techniques administered through widely available social programs. Still others, increasing numbers of laypeople and professionals alike, have come to regard addiction as an illness. These differing attitudes are reflected in present-day disagreements over whether illegal drug use is best addressed with criminal, behavioral, or medical measures, or a combination of all three.

Since the 18th century, three models of addiction have emerged to explain the basis of addiction and to guide treatment strategies to address it: the moral model, the disease model, and the choice model. The disease model has received the most widespread acceptance in modern times, although many continue to support aspects of the moral and choice models.

In the United States, **Benjamin Rush** (1745–1813), a prominent physician, was the among the first to publicize the addictive potential of alcohol and to suggest that **alcoholism** was a disease, countering prevailing attitudes that drink was a nutritious tonic that promoted health. Although Rush did not necessarily favor abstinence, he suggested that excessive use of distilled spirits as opposed to beer and wine could lead to aggressive and immoral behaviors. The moral model of addiction arose partly out of this awareness, which posited that a robust sense of personal responsibility and devotion to spiritual matters were bulwarks against addiction. The underlying theme of the moral model was that the person who abused or was addicted to substances was a bad person deserving punishment. In the 1800s, the moral model helped drive the formation of early temperance societies that advocated abstinence and stigmatized those who were unable to adhere to their strict guidelines.

In 1825, the Reverend Lyman Beecher (1775–1863) of Litchfield, Connecticut, an early proponent of temperance, gave a sermon that bridged the gap between morality and medicine, linking the crime to the disease. In 1830, prominent physician Samuel Woodward (1787–1850) suggested that drunkards be housed in special asylums for treatment of their "physical disease." William Sweetser (1797–1875) argued in 1829 that intemperance affected all the organs of the body, and he was an early believer in the idea not only that alcoholism involved a physical craving that robbed the individual of choice but also that the disease was defined by the whole series of physical and social problems it produced. T. D. Crothers (1842–1918), an editor of the *Journal of Inebriety* published during the 1870s, argued that the disease presented itself in many manifestations that required highly individualized treatment to address one's "constitutional proclivity" toward excessive drug use. He claimed that inebriety was one of a family group of diseases, of which heredity was a prominent cause—although "bad surroundings" and "brain shocks" could be contributing factors. The American Association for the Study and Cure of Inebriety, an organization that pioneered in recognizing alcoholism as a disease, took a position very much in evidence today: that drunkenness was defined by a pathological need evolving primarily out of biological causes.

The work of these individuals and organizations helped drive the development of franchised chains of institutes claiming to cure addiction. The very cures they promulgated through their bottled medicines, however, often contained alcohol or opium. Moreover, cultural views of drug use and addiction developed racist overtones due to the influx of opium-using Chinese immigrants in the latter half of the 1800s; the U.S. practice of eating opium was considered a disease whereas the Chinese method of smoking it was labeled a vice, fueling rising public disagreement about the nature of all excessive drug use.

The moral model of alcoholism remained entrenched, however, despite the growing movement to define alcoholism as a disease. In 1874, one of the leaders of the Franklin Reformatory for Inebriates in Philadelphia renounced the disease concept and called drunkenness a habitual crime, suggesting that alcohol use was blasphemous. This same idea was earnestly promulgated by evangelical Christians who placed heavy emphasis on sin and vice as a cause of drunkenness.

By the beginning of the 1900s, the disease model was overshadowed once again by the belief that temperance was the best way to eliminate the evils of drugs and reform the people who used them. In 1914, society's efforts to marginalize "dope fiends" resulted in the Harrison Act, which brought narcotics under the control of physicians. In so doing, legislators unwittingly drove drug distribution underground and produced a criminal element more than happy to supply illegal drugs to a demanding public. Even though many physicians continued to support the **disease model of addiction**, suffering addicts were stigmatized with labels such as "carriers" that implied they were passing along dreaded contagion. **Prohibition**, a legislative act established with the 18th Amendment to the U.S. Constitution and in force by 1920, was based on the belief that total abstinence was the only way to deal with the corrupting influence of alcohol on society, and it banned alcohol entirely in the United States. Although Prohibition's failure led to its repeal in 1933 by passing of the 21st Amendment to the U.S. Constitution, the moral model still underlies many cultural attitudes toward addiction that encompass the belief that drug use is a criminal rather than a medical matter.

In the last half of the 19th century, the state of Minnesota recognized alcoholism as a disease and even instituted some tax strategies to help pay for a treatment center for alcoholics.

The disease model received a further seal of approval by **E. M. Jellinek** (1890–1963) in the *Disease Concept of Alcoholism* published in 1960.

Today, as accumulating data and brain-imaging studies reveal more about how addictions start and ultimately affect the brain's neurochemistry, the disease model has become widely accepted. The American Medical Association (AMA) declared addiction a disease in 1956; the NIDA defines it as a progressive, chronic, relapsing—and treatable—brain disease; and organizations such as the APA, the American Psychological Association, the American Society of Addiction Medicine, and the National Council on Alcoholism concur. They agree that although underlying physical or mental illness, genetics, and environmental factors coalesce in complex ways in the development of addiction, almost anyone can become addicted when compulsive behaviors or substance abuse continue long enough. In many people, especially those with a genetic predisposition, brains repeatedly exposed to the addictive substance undergo changes that leave users incapable of making the rational judgments needed to moderate addictive behavior, and so the disease worsens. Fortunately, some of the newer medications that target addiction-related neurochemistry in some cases can help restore the brain to normal functioning and reduce or eliminate craving, a major threat to recovery.

The choice model rejects this aspect of the disease model and suggests that the addict can adopt a cognitive, or rational, approach in weighing the consequences of addictive behavior. This model does not necessarily insist on abstinence, taking the view that substance use can be incorporated into new patterns of behavior that rationally balance a healthy reward system with the destructive one triggered by drugs. It promotes individually tailored approaches that combine treatments like medication and acupuncture to address unique issues facing each addict. The premise is that educating addicts about self-management techniques and providing other critical support can empower them to overcome addiction successfully. Disease proponents question why someone who is addicted would choose to repeat addictive behavior that results in such harm and suffering. **Nora Volkow** (1956–), a neurologist and director of the NIDA who firmly adheres to the disease model, has observed that the choice concept is already embodied in the disease model; her implication is that arguments in support of a separate choice concept are redundant. In 2007, she noted that many diseases are facilitated by behavioral choices, and addiction is no different—just as diabetics facilitate their diabetes by indulging in sugar, addicts facilitate their addiction by indulging in the addictive substance.

In recognition of the ongoing debate, some specialists have proposed a broad disease concept that would (1) portray addiction as a group of disorders arising from multiple causes that vary significantly, (2) define the interrelationship between addiction and other disorders to develop integrated models of care, (3) delineate the role of personal responsibility and human will in overcoming the disorder, (4) acknowledge a variety of treatment approaches, and, (5) champion chronic disease management techniques rather than acute care models. In this way, the disease model can embrace new findings in addiction science, public health priorities, and the lessons learned from clinical and recovery experience.

Causes of Addiction

One of the most puzzling aspects of addiction is why some people become addicted and others do not; what is clear is that no one can become addicted to a drug unless he tries it first. A child who takes a few sips of a parent's beer may like the pleasurable feelings that result, but the overwhelming reason most young people indulge in drugs or alcohol

---

Addiction Is a Disease—Comparing Addiction with Type II Diabetes

Many addictions specialists compare addiction with Type II diabetes to illustrate why addiction is considered a disease. Although Type II diabetes is related to imbalances in the body's insulin production, it shares key characteristics with addiction in terms of behavioral and neurological factors.

Characteristic	Addiction	Type II Diabetes
Early Onset	Although certain forms of addiction, such as alcoholism, may not manifest discernible symptoms until adulthood, addiction usually begins with childhood or adolescent use or abuse	Although the disease may not manifest symptoms until adulthood, it is associated with obesity and poor eating habits developed in childhood or adolescence
Poor Lifestyle Choices	Excessive consumption of substances of abuse	Excessive consumption of poor food selections and lack of appropriate exercise
Compulsive Behavior Arising from Alterations to Brain's Reward Pathway	Persistent use triggers powerful neurological responses	Persistent consumption of inappropriate foods triggers powerful neurological responses
Chronicity	A lifelong condition requiring careful management to prevent relapse	A lifelong condition requiring careful management to prevent relapse

Source: Hanson, Glen R. http://uuhsc.utah.edu/uac

---

for the first time is peer pressure. Friends urge them to "just try it." Despite adverse reactions like nausea or dizziness that many first-time users experience, the disinhibitory and euphoric effects of the drugs encourage adolescents struggling with emotional or peer issues to experiment with them again and again. Some substances are more addictive than others—**heroin**, more addicting than alcohol, triggers a greater flood of pleasure-giving neurotransmitters. Age and gender are factors—males are more susceptible, as are young people between the ages of 15 to 25. A child or teen is statistically much more likely to escalate usage into addiction. In fact, according to the NIDA, it is rare for anyone over the age of 30 to become addicted to alcohol; an alcoholic over age 30 is most likely to have acquired the disease as a young person, even if primary symptoms do not become apparent until the addict is older. Although young brains are still developing and therefore able to recovery more readily if the disease is not too advanced, they are also more vulnerable to the effect of drugs and more likely to develop an addiction.

The tendency of addictions like alcoholism to run in families gave rise to theories for a genetic basis for the disorder, and subsequent studies have borne these out. In fact, although vulnerability to addiction varies among individuals, a multigenerational history of addiction can increase someone's risk 4 to 5 times that of general population. The ability of modern science to map the human genome has allowed researchers to pinpoint "candidate genes" with genetic variations that are implicated in the disorder. How they are switched on or triggered by environmental stimuli is not yet clear, but isolating them

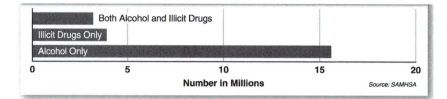

Substance Dependence or Abuse in the Past Year among Persons Aged 12 or Older: 2006

could allow scientists to develop drugs that modify their activity and mitigate their contribution to the disease. These findings show that, far from earlier explanations for the origin of addiction that focused on moral weakness and deficient will power, biology seems to account for at least half of a person's predisposition to addiction and environmental influences largely account for the rest. The latter, particularly among teenagers struggling with social status and self-image, include peer pressure, family dysfunction, issues with school or work, social demands, and a permissive culture.

As many as 40 percent of addicts suffer from co-occurring mental illnesses such as **anxiety disorders**, depression, or posttraumatic stress syndrome. Affected individuals tend to self-medicate with substances like alcohol to relieve distressing symptoms or, in more severe cases, to function at all. Individuals who are compelled to use psychoactive drugs as medicine are at higher risk for addiction than those who use them solely for recreational purposes. Besides those with **mental disorders**, scientists have been able to determine that certain personality types are more susceptible to addiction—most likely those with antisocial personality disorders or **conduct disorders**. In addition, it has been shown that the more quickly a given substance enters the bloodstream, the greater its initial effect; the greater its effect, the lower the low that follows, and the sooner the addict is using again.

Examples of Risk and Protective Factors

Risk Factors	Setting/Domain	Protective Factors
Early aggressive behavior	Individual	Impulse control
Poor social skills	Individual	Positive relationships
Lack of parental supervision	Family	Parental monitoring and support
Substance abuse	Peer	Academic competence
Drug availability	School	Antidrug use policy
Poverty	Community	Strong neighborhood attachment

Prevention

Many of the factors that lead to substance abuse and addiction take root in childhood and erupt during adolescence when puberty and access present opportunities for teens to experiment with mood-altering substances. After decades of failed attempts to deal with this fact through morality-based approaches based on punishment and ostracism, researchers began to develop what are called science-validated programs that are

---

Risk Factors

Any of the following may increase the risk of becoming addicted to drugs or alcohol:

- Having parents or siblings who are addicted to drugs or alcohol
- Being diagnosed with a conduct disorder or exhibiting aggressive behavior that might indicate a lack of self-control
- Having an untreated attention deficit or hyperactivity disorder
- Being depressed or anxious
- Having experienced trauma, such as exposure to violence or physical or sexual abuse
- Experiencing a stressful life transition, such as leaving home for the first time, losing a job, getting divorced, or losing someone close to you
- Having experienced conflict at home with parents, siblings, spouse, or children
- Being exposed to drugs and alcohol and peer pressure to use them
- Using drugs and alcohol before age 14

Source: Hoffman, 2007.

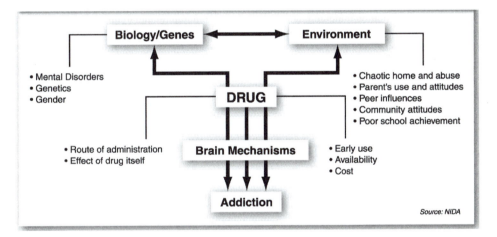

Multiple Risk Factors Can Lead to Addiction

producing positive results. Such programs work to balance preventive factors against risk factors for drug use by educating and working with young people, both those who use psychoactive drugs and those who have not yet begun to experiment with them. Designed to target various age groups in the school and in the home, science-validated programs have proved to be effective in reducing teen drug use and consequently are being adopted throughout the United States.

The NIDA reports that adolescent use of illicit drugs declined by 23.2 percent from 2001 to 2006, due in part to these educational approaches. As the perceived risk rose, use tended to decline. Since teens sometimes feel that drugs and alcohol are their only coping

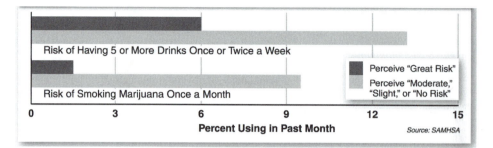

Past-Month Binge Drinking and Marijuana Use among Youths Aged 12 to 17, by Perceptions of Risk: 2006

mechanisms, the NIDA states that it is essential to find ways to prevent them from abusing the very substances that will warp brain development and derail their ability to mature physically and emotionally. Protective factors that can reduce the risk of addiction include parental supervision and support, academic success, and local **prevention** policies. Early **intervention** is critical; by the time most addicts enter treatment, they have been sick for 20 years. Not only is it tragic for addicts to lose years of emotional and intellectual growth to their addictions but it also allows the disease to progress.

In a person with a multigenerational history of drug and alcohol abuse, vigilance and a sensible lifestyle are the best preventive measures. Such individuals should avoid addictive substances just as someone with diabetes should avoid sugar.

Treatment

As a chronic disease, addiction requires lifelong management. Treatment approaches vary in both methods and philosophy, due largely to the centuries-old debate about whether addiction is a disease or a choice. Despite this, most treatment specialists agree that combining medical, behavioral, and motivational techniques tailored to the specific needs and profile of the individual addict is best. Active participation in groups like **Alcoholics Anonymous** (AA) or Narcotics Anonymous helps some addicts avoid relapse and sustain recovery for life.

With severe substance addiction, initial detoxification and withdrawal must sometimes be accomplished under medical supervision. Maintenance medications such as **methadone** or antianxiety drugs (**anxiolytics**) may be used to help ease the symptoms of withdrawal and craving, especially since studies have shown that painful withdrawal can increase an addict's potential for relapse. The use of other drugs such as naltrexone and disulfiram can also be helpful because they block the brain's receptors from responding to the addictive substance or make the addict very ill if he or she uses drugs.

Behavioral therapy is generally rendered as cognitive behavioral therapy (CBT), the development of practical, day-to-day tools to help improve immediate functioning, and in this regard differs from psychological therapies that focus on long-term causes. CBT may encompass medication, counseling, and training to help motivate the addict to change behavior and to develop coping strategies to solve problems, identify harmful patterns of behavior, and manage situations that could trigger addictive use or behaviors. On a less formalized basis, these same strategies could arise out of **12-step programs**, which tend to

Common Myths about Addiction

1. Addiction occurs because of a lack of willpower. Although much addiction treatment involves behavioral therapy, the area of the brain affected is not under conscious control.
2. Addicts should be punished, not treated. Addicts can recover if they receive treatment for the neurochemical imbalances in their brain and the altered function that results. Statistics show that punitive measures do not work.
3. People addicted to one drug are addicted to all drugs. Addicted people may become more easily addicted to drugs that are chemically similar to one another, but not necessarily to all drugs.
4. Addicts cannot be treated with medications. Many new medications that target specific brain receptors can curb craving and boost the effectiveness of other therapy.
5. Since addiction can be treated with behavioral modification techniques, why isn't it just a behavioral problem? Behavioral treatments don't simply change behavior; brain scans show that they also change the brain, whose chemistry and function play essential roles in the development of addiction.

Source: Adapted from Hoffman, 2007.

Statistics

The following drug-use statistics are courtesy of the U.S. Substance Abuse and Mental Health Services Administration (SAMHSA) 2006 surveys of drug use and health. For more statistics, see Appendix D.

Substance Dependence, Abuse, and Treatment

- In 2006, an estimated 22.6 million persons (9.2 percent of the population aged 12 or older) were classified with substance dependence or abuse in the year prior to the survey based on criteria specified in the 4th edition of the American Psychiatric Association's *Diagnostic and Statistical Manual of Mental Disorders* (*DSM*). Of these, 3.2 million were classified with dependence on or abuse of both alcohol and illicit drugs; 3.8 million were dependent on or abused illicit drugs but not alcohol; and 15.6 million were dependent on or abused alcohol but not illicit drugs.
- Between 2002 and 2006, there was no change in the number of persons with substance dependence or abuse (22.0 million in 2002, 22.6 million in 2006).
- The specific illicit drugs that had the highest levels of past-year dependence or abuse in 2006 were marijuana (4.2 million), followed by cocaine (1.7 million), and then pain relievers (1.6 million).

have greater spiritual focus and adhere to the 12 steps outlined by **Bill Wilson** (1895–1971) and Dr. Bob **Smith** (1879–1950), who founded AA in 1935.

Experts stress that it can take at least 90 days of treatment before therapy shows significantly positive results. The NIDA recommends that places to start seeking treatment are the family physician; a psychologist or psychiatrist who specializes in addiction; a pastor; an employee assistance program; 12–step programs; or county mental health centers.

See also Genetics of Addiction; Pseudoaddiction.

Further Reading

American Psychiatric Association. *Diagnostic and Statistical Manual of Mental Disorders*, 4th Edition, Text Revision. Washington, DC: American Psychiatric Association, 2000.

Califano, Joseph A., Jr. *High Society: How Substance Abuse Ravages America and What to Do About It*. New York: Perseus Books, 2007.

Engs, Ruth C., ed. *Controversies in the Addiction Field*. Dubuque, Iowa: Kendall-Hunt, 1990.

Erickson, Carlton K. *The Science of Addiction: From Neurobiology to Treatment*. New York: Norton, 2007.

Grant, Jon E., and Kim, S. W. *Stop Me Because I Can't Stop Myself: Taking Control of Impulsive Behavior*. New York: McGrawHill, 2003.

Halpern, John H. Addiction Is a Disease. *Psychiatric Times*, October 2002: 19(10), 54–55.

Hanson, Glen R. *Substance Abuse Disorders: Diseases of the Mind*. Online presentation, The Utah Addiction Center Web site, July 2007. Retrieved from http://uuhsc.utah.edu/uac

Hoffman, John, and Froemke, Susan, eds. *Addiction: Why Can't They Just Stop?* New York: Rodale, 2007.

Home Box Office (HBO). In partnership with the Robert Wood Johnson Foundation, the National Institute on Drug Abuse, and the National Institute on Alcohol Abuse and Alcoholism. *Addiction: Why Can't They Just Stop?* Documentary.March 2007.

Hyman, S. E., and Malenka, R. C. Addiction and the Brain: The Neurobiology of Compulsion and Its Persistence. *Nature Reviews Neuroscience* 2001: 2(10), 695–703.

Kalivas, Peter, and Volkow, Nora. The Neural Basis of Addiction: A Pathology of Motivation and Choice. *American Journal of Psychiatry* August 2005: 162(8), 1403–1413.

Kaminer, Y., Bukstein, O., and Tarter, R. The Teen Addiction Severity Index: Rationale and Reliability. *The International Journal of the Addictions* 1991: 26, 219–226.

Kauer, Julie A. Addictive Drugs and Stress Trigger a Common Change at VTA Synapses. *Neuron* February 2003: 37(4), 549–550.

Ketcham, Katherine, and Pace, Nicholas A. *Teens Under the Influence: The Truth About Kids, Alcohol, and Other Drugs*. New York: Ballantine Books, 2003.

Lemanski, Michael. *A History of Addiction and Recovery in the United States*. Tucson, AZ: See Sharp Press, 2001.

Lewis, D. C. A Disease Model of Addiction. In Miller, N. S., ed., *Principles of Addiction Medicine*. Chevy Chase, MD: American Society on Addiction Medicine, 1993.

Miller, Shannon C. Language and Addiction. *American Journal of Psychiatry* 2006: 163, 2015.

Moyers, William Cope. *Broken: The Story of Addiction and Redemption*. New York: Penguin Group, 2006.

National Institute on Drug Abuse. *The Science of Addiction: Drugs, Brains, and Behavior*. NIH Publication No. 07-5605, February 2007.

Nestler, Eric, and Malenka, Robert. The Addicted Brain. *Scientific American*, September 2007. Retrieved from http://www.sciam.com/article.cfm?chanID=sa006&colID=1&articleID=0001E6 32978A1019978A83414B7F0101

Nurnberger, John I., Jr., and Bierut, Laura Jean. Seeking the Connections: Alcoholism and Our Genes. *Scientific American* April 2007: 296(4), 46–53.

Ozelli, Kristin Leutwyler. This Is Your Brain on Food. *Scientific American* September 2007: 297(3), 84–85.

Pawlowski, Cheryl. *Glued to the Tube.* Naperville, IL: Sourcebooks, 2000.

Peele, Stanton. Is Gambling an Addiction Like Drug and Alcohol Addiction? . *Electronic Journal of Gambling Issues*, February 2001. Retrieved from http://www.camh.net/egambling/issue3/feature/index.html

Peele, Stanton. *7 Tools to Beat Addiction.* New York: Three Rivers Press, 2004.

Potenza, Marc N. Should Addictive Disorders Include NonSubstanceRelated Conditions? *Addiction* 2006: 101(s1), 142–151.

Schaler, Jeffrey A. Addiction Is a Choice. *Psychiatric Times* October 2002: 19(10), 54, 62.

Tracy, Sarah, and Acker, Caroline Jean, eds. *Altering American Consciousness: The History of Alcohol and Drug Use in the United States, 1800–2000.* Amherst, MA and Boston: University of Massachusetts Press, 2004.

Trimpey, J. *Rational Recovery: The New Cure for Substance Addiction.* New York: Pocket Books, 1996.

U.S. Department of Health and Human Services. *Morbidity and Mortality Weekly Report: Surveillance Summaries.* Centers for Disease Control and Prevention, Youth Risk Behavior Surveillance—United States. 2005.

U.S. Department of Health and Human Services. *Results from the 2006 National Survey on Drug Use and Health: National Findings.* Substance Abuse and Mental Health Services Administration, Office of Applied Studies. DHHS Publication No. SMA 07-4293, 2007.

U.S. Department of Health and Human Services, National Institute of Dental and Craniofacial Research (NIDCR), February 2008. Retrieved from http://www.nidcr.nih.gov

U.S. Department of Health and Human Services, National Institute of Mental Health (NIMH): http://www.nimh.nih.gov

U.S. Department of Health and Human Services, National Institute on Alcohol Abuse and Alcoholism (NIAAA), July 2007. Retrieved from http://www.niaaa.nih.gov

U.S. Department of Health and Human Services, National Institute on Drug Abuse (NIDA), June 2007. Retrieved from http://www.nida.gov

U.S. Department of Health and Human Services, Substance Abuse and Mental Health Services Administration (SAMHSA), August 2007. Retrieved from http://www.samhsa.gov

U.S. Department of Justice Drug Enforcement Administration (DEA), March 2008. Retrieved from http://www.usdoj.gov/dea

Vaillant, George. *The Natural History of Alcoholism Revisited.* Cambridge, MA: Harvard University Press, 1995.

White, William. Addiction as a Disease: Birth of a Concept. *Counselor Magazine* October 2000: 1(1), 46–51, 73.

White, William. Addiction Disease Concept: Advocates and Critics. *Counselor Magazine* February 2001, 2(1), 42–46.

White, William. A Disease Concept for the 21st Century. *AddictionInfo.com*, June 2007. Retrieved from http://www.addictioninfo.org/articles/1051/1/
A Disease Concept for the 21st Century/Page1.html

White, William. *Slaying the Dragon: The History of Addiction Treatment.* Bloomington, IL: Chestnut Health Systems, 1998.

Winters, Ken. *Adolescent Brain Development and Drug Abuse.* Philadelphia, PA: Treatment Research Institute, 2008.

Addiction Liability Addiction liability refers to the likelihood that a given substance will create chemical dependence. The higher the addiction liability, the greater the likelihood of addiction, although each individual brings unique variables of environment, behavior, and genetics into the mix. For example, although heroin has, on average, a high addiction liability compared to **marijuana**, its potential to addict may be much higher than average for individuals with a genetic predisposition and environmental risks, and significantly lower than average for a mature person from a stable socioeconomic background with no genetic vulnerability. Addiction liability combined with individual susceptibility helps explain why some people develop instant onset addiction at their first exposure while others can experiment to some degree without becoming addicted.

The complexities of addiction and the many variables that lead to it caution against rigid assessments of drug's innate addictive potential. However, most experts agree, all things being equal, that the most addictive drugs are **cocaine**, **amphetamines**, **nicotine**, and **opiates** like **heroin**; second are alcohol, **barbiturates**, and **benzodiazepines**; third are **marijuana** and **hashish**; and the least addicting are **hallucinogens** and caffeine. Differences lie within each of these categories as well; for example, some tranquilizers are more potent than others.

Addiction Medications Although there are currently no medications available that prevent or cure addiction, many help reduce the cravings, obsessive thoughts, anxiety, and withdrawal symptoms that promote abusive drug use. Researchers are becoming excited about the possibilities that vaccines offer and the potential drugs that will help mediate the "executive functions" in the prefrontal cortex of the brain that affect judgment, self-control, and behavior. A **cocaine** vaccine will be entering trials in humans in 2008, and some believe it could be available within 2 or 3 years. Vaccines for **methamphetamines**, **heroin**, and **nicotine** are also in development that will mobilize the immune system to detect and shut down the activity of the drugs. Unlike other medications that work by preventing receptors in the brain from reacting to the addictive stimuli, vaccines work by preventing molecules of the addictive drug from reaching the brain at all. Not only might vaccines help treat addiction in new and important ways but they might also prevent it in the first place. Vaccine therapy is not currently under consideration as a treatment for behavioral addictions.

Among other new developments is a formulation called **Prometa** that, combined with nutritional supplements and therapy, is touted by the manufacturer as a remarkably effective treatment in removing the cravings associated with alcohol, cocaine, and methamphetamine addiction. Not suitable for addiction to **opiates** or **benzodiazepines**, Prometa has been used by some criminal justice systems and private treatment centers to address methamphetamine **abuse**. However, the formulation is still under investigation. Some therapists have significant reservations about its safety and effectiveness, and some are highly critical of the lack of controlled studies to evaluate its benefit.

Many of the newer drugs approved by the Food and Drug Administration to treat certain conditions are often prescribed off-label, which means that physicians, at their own discretion, can prescribe them to treat disorders for which they were not originally formulated. Medications specifically designed or prescribed off-label to prevent or treat various types and stages of addiction generally fall into one of several categories:

- Antidepressant/antiobsessional drugs
- Opioid partial **agonists**
- Opioid **antagonists**
- Mood stabilizers (anticonvulsants)
- Atypical neuroleptics (antipsychotics)
- Vaccines

Other drugs sometimes used off-label to treat addictions include disulfiram (Antabuse), a drug that interferes with alcohol metabolism but may help in cocaine addiction, and **methylphenidate** (Ritalin), an addictive **stimulant** that can be safely used to treat certain **impulse control disorders** if they co-occur with attention-deficit disorders. With increasing frequency, researchers are finding that many new drugs developed to treat one type of addiction are effectively treating others. This is not too surprising because all addictions are seated, at least in part, in the same mesolimbic area of the brain, so drugs affecting that area of the brain are likely to have a broad effect.

Both behavioral and **substance addictions** respond to treatment with antidepressants, which modulate serotonin and other **neurotransmitter** activity. Usually prescribed to treat obsessive-compulsive or mood disorders such as depression, they have been shown to be helpful in mediating the **impulses**, cravings, and dysfunctional behaviors seen in addictions. In the case of impulse control disorders, therapists have achieved the best results by combining an antidepressant with a neuroleptic or mood stabilizing medication. Commonly prescribed antidepressants include:

- Bupropion (Wellbutrin)
- Citalopram (Celexa)
- Clomipramine (Anafranil)
- Escitalopram oxalate (Lexapro)
- Fluoxetine (Prozac)
- Fluvoxamine (Luvox)
- Nefazodone (generic versions only available in the United States)
- Paroxetine (Paxil)
- Sertraline (Zoloft)
- Venlafaxine (Effexor)

Medicating Impulse Control Disorders

In addition to antidepressants, therapists have found other drugs, used alone or in certain combinations, to be remarkably effective at reducing or eliminating the impulsive urges associated with behavioral addictions. Patient responses to these medications are highly individual, and it may take several weeks of therapy with different formulations or combinations before positive results are seen. However, the results can be dramatic. Many patients are freed of their impulsive urges for the first time in years, and, with counseling, can begin to resume normal lives.

See also Appendix B.

Medicating Substance Addictions

Like symptoms of impulse control disorders, some symptoms of substance addictions respond to antidepressants, but they can also be treated with specifically formulated medications. In many cases, such drugs have proven to be effective in treating addiction to a class of drug other than the one for which they were designed. Topiramate, for example, can be used to treat alcoholism as well as addictions to nicotine and other stimulants. In most cases, these medications are used in conjunction with behavioral therapy, which is considered an essential counterpart. Otherwise, if the motivating factors that fueled the drug addiction in the first place are not removed, the behavior is likely to re-emerge

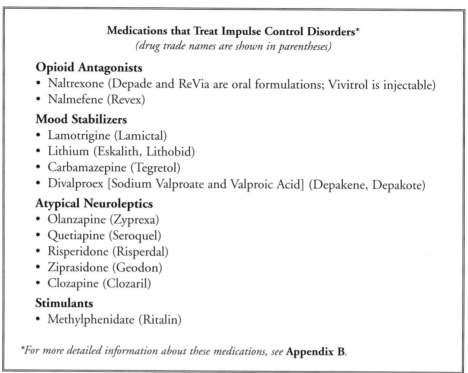

Medications that Treat Impulse Control Disorders*
(drug trade names are shown in parentheses)

Opioid Antagonists
- Naltrexone (Depade and ReVia are oral formulations; Vivitrol is injectable)
- Nalmefene (Revex)

Mood Stabilizers
- Lamotrigine (Lamictal)
- Lithium (Eskalith, Lithobid)
- Carbamazepine (Tegretol)
- Divalproex [Sodium Valproate and Valproic Acid] (Depakene, Depakote)

Atypical Neuroleptics
- Olanzapine (Zyprexa)
- Quetiapine (Seroquel)
- Risperidone (Risperdal)
- Ziprasidone (Geodon)
- Clozapine (Clozaril)

Stimulants
- Methylphenidate (Ritalin)

*For more detailed information about these medications, see **Appendix B**.*

when the medication is discontinued. Most of the following medications are prescribed off-label, that is, for a purpose other than that for which they were officially approved. Disulfiram, for example, has traditionally been used to treat **alcoholism**, but it is sometimes prescribed to help cocaine addicts.

Further Reading

Erickson, Carlton K. *The Science of Addiction: From Neurobiology to Treatment*. New York: Norton, 2007.
Grant, Jon E., and Kim, S. W. *Stop Me Because I Can't Stop Myself: Taking Control of Impulsive Behavior*. New York: McGraw-Hill, 2003.
Hoffman, John, and Froemke, Susan, eds. *Addiction: Why Can't They Just Stop?* New York: Rodale, 2007.

Medications That Treat Substance Addictions*
(drug trade names are shown in parentheses)

Cannabis

- None

Depressants

Alcohol

- Acamprosate (Campral)

- Anxiolytics
- Baclofen (Kemstro, Lioresal)
- Disulfiram (Antabuse)
- Memantine (Namenda)
- Nalmefene (Revex)
- Naltrexone (Depade and ReVia are oral formulations; Vivitrol is injectable)
- Ondansetron (Zofran)
- Prometa
- Rimonabant (Acomplia)
- Topiramate (Topamax)
- Varenicline (Chantix)

Benzodiazepines

- None

Hallucinogens

- None (vaccines are in clinical trials)

Inhalants

- None

Opiates (Narcotics)

Partial Agonists

- Buprenorphine (Buprenex, Suboxone, Subutex)
- Methadone (Dolophine)

Antagonists

- Nalmefene (Revex)
- Naloxone (Narcan)
- Naltrexone (Depade and ReVia are oral formulations; Vivitrol is injectable)

Vaccine (in development for heroin addiction)

Stimulants

Cocaine

- Baclofen (Kemstro, Lioresal)
- Diltiazem
- Disulfiram (Antabuse)
- Gabapentin (Neurontin)
- Modafinil (Provigil)

- Prometa
- Topiramate (Topamax)
- Vaccines (in clinical trials)

Methamphetamine

- Prometa
- Vaccine (in development)

Other Stimulants

- None
- Vaccine (in development)

Nicotine

- Bupropion (Zyban)
- Nicotine replacements
- Rimonabant (Acomplia)
- Topiramate (Topamax)
- Vaccines (in development)
- Varenicline (Chantix)

*For more detailed information about these medications, see **Appendix B**.

Addiction Medicine Although early pioneers like **Benjamin Rush** (1745–1813) had proposed in the late 1700s that alcoholism was an illness rather than a manifestation of weak character, it was not until the middle of the 20th century that addictions like alcoholism became widely recognized as something other than moral lapses. By that time, **Carl Jung** (1875–1961), **William Silkworth** (1873–1951), **E. M. Jellinek** (1890–1963), **Harry Tiebout** (1896–1966), and others in the research and scientific communities had lent support to the work that **Bill Wilson** (1895–1971) and "**Dr. Bob" Smith** (1879–1950) were doing to define alcoholism as a physical, mental, and spiritual illness. In the latter half of the 20th century, Alcoholics Anonymous (AA) and psychiatrists provided the bulk of addiction treatment, followed by inpatient treatment that had evolved from punitive incarceration measures into therapeutic 28-day stays in rehabilitation centers based on the Minnesota model. By the 1980s and 1990s these facilities had become the standard of care for addictions of all kinds, and they continue to flourish today.

Along the way, researchers and medical professionals came to understand that chemical and **behavioral addictions** were unique, complex diseases requiring a multidisciplinary approach to address not only the psychological components but also the physiological issues surrounding detoxification, damage to the body's organ systems, and secondary infections such as HIV, hepatitis, or tuberculosis that sometimes resulted from addictive behavior. As advances in neurological research and brain-imaging techniques began to reveal how certain people react to addictive stimuli and how they develop characteristically dysfunctional behavior, newer pharmacological and behavioral approaches were adopted to complement traditional treatment programs. In time, physicians and other treatment professionals came to recognize that a new medical specialty needed to be created to respond to the unique challenges that the treatment of addiction required.

Over the last decades, medical societies have sought to address this need. Among them have been the American Medical Association (AMA), the American Medical Society on Alcoholism (AMSA), the American Society of Addiction Medicine (ASAM), the Association for Medical Education and Research in Substance Abuse (AMERSA), and the American Academy of Addiction Psychiatry (AAAP). Currently, the only board-certified specialty offered in addictions medicine is for addiction psychiatry, but the ASAM is seeking recognition from the American Board of Medical Specialties to create an addiction medicine specialty for physicians other than psychiatrists.

Some therapists advertise themselves as addictionologists, that is, specialists in "addictionology." This so-called specialty is not generally recognized. Instead, to receive the proper credentials for specializing in treating addictions, psychiatrists can take an examination to receive a certificate in "Added Qualifications in Addiction Psychiatry" from the American Board of Psychiatry and Neurology, and general physicians can qualify for a certificate from the ASAM.

See also Disease Model of Addiction.

Addiction Potential. *See* Addiction Liability.

Addictionology. *See* Addiction Medicine.

Addictive Personality experts do not generally use the term "addictive personality"; it is a vague, nonscientific term in popular usage intended to describe someone who overindulges in different substances. For example, a person who smokes, drinks, and eats sugary foods to excess, even if he does not suffer from a diagnosable alcohol addiction or **eating disorder**, may be regarded by friends and associates as having an addictive personality. Other people who have a combination of biological, genetic, and environmental factors associated with increased vulnerability to addiction might also be viewed as having addictive personalities, but that description has no predictive value.

Some scientists acknowledge that the term can refer to someone with a collection of certain diagnosable **mental disorders** that predispose him or her to addiction. An example is a person suffering from an **anxiety disorder** who would be more likely to self-medicate with alcohol or other drugs to alleviate his or her emotional and psychic discomfort. There is also evidence that people with antisocial or **conduct disorders** are more likely to become alcoholics or **abuse** other drugs to such a degree that addiction could easily develop. Nevertheless, the scientific community prefers to describe them as vulnerable to addiction or at higher risk for addiction than to claim that such people have addictive personalities.

Adipex. *See* Stimulants.

AET. *See* Psilocybin and Psilocin.

Agonists Drugs that enhance the action of natural **neurotransmitters** are agonists. If the natural neurotransmitter triggers specific activity at a receptor, an agonist increases that activity; if the natural neurotransmitter inhibits certain activity at a receptor, its agonist further inhibits that activity. Agonists do this one of three ways: by increasing production of the natural neurotransmitter; by interfering with the recycling or reuptake of the neurotransmitter so it stays in the synapse where it continues to activate the receptor cell; or by replacing the natural neurotransmitter and binding directly to the receptor cell. Antidepressants are agonists of serotonin, and stimulants like **cocaine** and **methamphetamine** are agonists of dopamine and norepinephrine.

A partial agonist like **buprenorphine** (Buprenex, Suboxone, Subutex) or **methadone** has a similar but less potent effect on the **brain**; by partially binding the receptors, it competes with agonists. For example, methadone binds to the same opiate receptors to which **heroin** has an affinity, thus preventing heroin from binding the receptors and producing the characteristic euphoria. Although methadone is an addictive drug, it is not a drug of **abuse** because it does not produce the same euphoria associated with heroin.

See also Antagonists.

Alcohol. *See* Alcoholism.

Alcohol-Related Birth Defects, Alcohol-Related Neurological Disorder. *See* Women, Pregnancy, and Drugs.

Alcoholics Anonymous Uniting its members in fellowship to share experience, strength, and hope in a common desire to abstain from alcohol is the fundamental purpose of Alcoholics Anonymous (AA). By attending frequent meetings, adhering to AA's 12 steps, extending help to other alcoholics, and refraining from drinking "one day at a time," millions of formerly hopeless alcoholics have regained their sobriety and sanity. A self-supporting organization, AA emphasizes the anonymity of its members both to protect their privacy and to ensure that no individual's personality or station outside of AA distorts the peer relationship among members; this is a critical underpinning of the organization's philosophy. Today, the organization has about 2 million members around the world.

History

AA was formed in 1935 by **William Wilson**, known fondly within the organization as "Bill W.," an alcoholic who had been a member of the Oxford Group, an evangelical religious movement that embraced a philosophy of anonymity and service to others. During a period of hospitalization and detoxification under the care of **William Silkworth** (1873–1951), a pioneer in the belief that **alcoholism** represented a disease, Wilson underwent a spiritual experience that convinced him **recovery** lay in turning his will over to God. On his release, and with Silkworth's encouragement, Wilson began to spread his philosophy of recovery. Joining forces with a desperately struggling alcoholic named **Bob Smith** (1879–1950), a physician from Akron, Ohio, Wilson began hosting meetings at his home that focused on mutual support among attendees, acceptance of their powerlessness over alcohol, and their need to yield control of their lives to a higher power—conceived as God by most members.

By 1937, when Wilson and Smith had shown that their program had helped 40 alcoholics become sober, they decided to formalize their message. Two years later, in an effort both to raise operating funds and to publicize their successful program more widely, Wilson began writing the official text of their fledgling organization. Originally titled

Alcoholics Anonymous, the book is more familiarly known as *The Big Book* and is widely read and discussed in AA meetings worldwide. It contains stories of former alcoholics and lists the 12 steps to recovery developed by Wilson and Smith. It also states that the sole requirement for membership in AA is the desire to quit drinking.

Rather than a simple prescription for recovery, the 12 steps are principles that guide members through their lives and seek to address their spiritual, mental, and physical health. The strong focus on spiritual growth, which for some is a religious journey, is embodied in AA's philosophy of reaching out to other addicts through fellowship and service, a process that is considered critical to recovery. Exploring the 12 steps and sharing common experiences have been shown to create a solid framework on which members can attain sobriety and begin to rebuild their lives.

By 1941, public awareness of AA had spread widely and was boosted greatly by an article published in *The Saturday Evening Post*, a mainstream magazine of the era found in

---

The 12 Steps of Alcoholics Anonymous*

1. We admitted we were powerless over alcohol—that our lives had become unmanageable.
2. Came to believe that a Power greater than ourselves could restore us to sanity.
3. Made a decision to turn our will and our lives over to the care of God as we understood Him.
4. Made a searching and fearless moral inventory of ourselves.
5. Admitted to God, to ourselves, and to another human being the exact nature of our wrongs.
6. Were entirely ready to have God remove all these defects of character.
7. Humbly asked Him to remove our shortcomings.
8. Made a list of all persons we had harmed, and became willing to make amends to them all.
9. Made direct amends to such people wherever possible, except when to do so would injure them or others.
10. Continued to take personal inventory and when we were wrong promptly admitted it.
11. Sought through prayer and meditation to improve our conscious contact with God as we understood Him, praying only for knowledge of His Will for us and the power to carry that out.
12. Having had a spiritual awakening as the result of these steps, we tried to carry this message to alcoholics, and to practice these principles in all our affairs.

*The Twelve Steps and Twelve Traditions are reprinted with permission of Alcoholics Anonymous World Services, Inc. (AAWS). Permission to reprint the Twelve Steps and Twelve Traditions does not mean that AAWS has reviewed or approved the contents of this publication, or that AA necessarily agrees with the views expressed herein. AA is a program of recovery from alcoholism only—use of the Twelve Steps and Twelve Traditions in connection with programs and activities which are patterned after AA, but which address other problems, or in any other non-AA context, does not imply otherwise.

Source: Alcoholics Anonymous. http://www.alcoholics-anonymous.org

---

many U.S. homes. Written by Jack Anderson, the article was highly favorable of the organization's ability to help alcoholics quit drinking. Membership grew rapidly, and by 1946 it had become clear that some sort of governing body was required to lay out guiding principles for the organization. Because Wilson and Smith felt that handing over leadership or management of AA to an individual would undermine its egalitarian philosophy—all alcoholics were equal in their suffering and their desire to quit drinking—they resisted the establishment of a management hierarchy. Instead, they developed a governing structure whose framework is defined by 12 traditions:

The 12 Traditions of Alcoholics Anonymous*

1. Our common welfare should come first; personal recovery depends upon AA unity.
2. For our group purpose there is but one ultimate authority—a loving God as He may express Himself in our group conscience. Our leaders are but trusted servants; they do not govern.
3. The only requirement for AA membership is a desire to stop drinking.
4. Each group should be autonomous except in matters affecting other groups or AA as a whole.
5. Each group has but one primary purpose—to carry its message to the alcoholic who still suffers.
6. An AA group ought never endorse, finance, or lend the AA name to any related facility or outside enterprise, lest problems of money, property, and prestige divert us from our primary purpose.
7. Every AA group ought to be fully self-supporting, declining outside contributions.
8. Alcoholics Anonymous should remain forever nonprofessional, but our service centers may employ special workers.
9. AA, as such, ought never be organized; but we may create service boards or committees directly responsible to those they serve.
10. Alcoholics Anonymous has no opinion on outside issues; hence, the AA name ought never be drawn into public controversy.
11. Our public relations policy is based on attraction rather than promotion; we need always maintain personal anonymity at the level of press, radio, and films.
12. Anonymity is the spiritual foundation of all our traditions, ever reminding us to place principles before personalities.

*The Twelve Steps and Twelve Traditions are reprinted with permission of Alcoholics Anonymous World Services, Inc. (AAWS). Permission to reprint the Twelve Steps and Twelve Traditions does not mean that AAWS has reviewed or approved the contents of this publication, or that AA necessarily agrees with the views expressed herein. AA is a program of recovery from alcoholism only—use of the Twelve Steps and Twelve Traditions in connection with programs and activities which are patterned after AA, but which address other problems, or in any other non-AA context, does not imply otherwise.
Source: Alcoholics Anonymous. http://www.alcoholics-anonymous.org

---

In 1955, with AA expanding internationally, Wilson recognized that the organization needed a personnel staff to serve the growing needs of local groups by replying to questions, providing literature, and addressing problems. AA's General Services Office was established to deal with these issues, and a corporation, AA Grapevine, Inc., was formed to manage the publication and distribution of AA's monthly journal, the AA *Grapevine*. The officers of these organizations serve only as temporary trustees of AA's basic principles and as a link to local groups, and they rotate frequently to avoid the possibility that an individual or group of individuals might exercise undue influence on the autonomy of local AA groups. Unlike members of the individual self-supporting groups, the General Service officers receive salaries funded by the sale of AA books and pamphlets.

AA meetings are held every day, day and night, in church basements and other public venues throughout the United States and worldwide. As the AA Traditions explain, a meeting can consist of any two or three people who assemble with the common goal of becoming sober. Depending on the wishes of the meeting attendees, some meetings are closed to everyone but alcoholics; others are open to interested members of the public. Some may consist of a few people, others of hundreds. Some are for everyone; women or men only; straight or gay people; smokers or nonsmokers; or couples or singles. Some may be conducted by a guest member who gives a talk to the group about his or her experience; others may consist of members reading selected passages from *The Big Book*. Although the meetings are free, nominal "coffee and cookie" dues are asked of those who have the means. New members are urged to find a same-sex AA sponsor, a fellow alcoholic with a sustained period of recovery who becomes an as-needed personal mentor.

AA meeting schedules can be obtained on the Internet or by calling AA service offices listed in local telephone books.

Controversies

Despite the positive impact AA has had on millions of alcoholics and their families, criticism of the organization is widespread. Many feel that its insistence on total abstinence is too rigid and ignores problem drinkers who can learn to moderate their alcohol use and better manage their lives. Others complain that the religious "groupthink" approach to **treatment** discourages the kind of maturity and personal growth that is fundamental to recovery. The medical community and other alcoholism treatment professionals contend that AA's tendency to reject medication and behavioral therapy is outmoded and destructive. Some believe AA's insistence that alcoholism is a disease diminishes the role willpower, discipline, and personal responsibility should have in the alcoholic's efforts to overcome his or her disorder. Still others claim that AA is cult-like, fostering dependent relationships in which long-term members exploit newer, vulnerable members.

Despite efforts to evaluate the success rate of AA's approach to alcoholism treatment, no firm statistics have emerged. Part of the difficulty is that people quit drinking for different reasons, and even long-term alcoholics have been known to quit permanently and entirely on their own. People who join AA may be more highly motivated than those who do not join; even if the quit-rate of members is higher than that of nonmembers, it may simply be due to motivational factors rather than the AA membership.

AA and other **12-step programs** have touted success rates as high as 70 to 90 percent, but most experts are sharply critical of these claims. They cite dubious methods of collecting data; use of short-term measures of outcome; failure to calculate the effect of relapse on overall successes; and similar factors that can skew data and render it unreliable. They also point out that some statistics show that no treatment is as effective as AA membership. In 1992, the National Institute on Alcohol Abuse and Alcoholism conducted a survey called the National Longitudinal Alcohol Epidemiologic Survey (NLAES) to evaluate alcoholics' responses to treatment. Its startling finding confirmed that in the long-term there was little difference in recovery rates between the 2 groups. Nevertheless, most rehabilitation centers and counselors strongly recommend AA attendance for newly sober alcoholics, especially in the weeks and months after their discharge from treatment facilities when they are struggling to reestablish stable lives.

As researchers have learned more about the neurobiology of **addiction**, the entrenched, one-size-fits-all approach to alcoholism treatment that AA represents has been changing. The proven effectiveness of medications combined with cognitive behavioral therapy tailored to each individual's situation has convinced many in the alcoholism treatment field that AA and similar 12-step programs are not necessarily the only approach—or whether they should be part of treatment regimens at all. Millions of alcoholics, however, credit AA with saving their lives and believe that its teachings are the only true path to recovery.

Those who reject AA's religious focus might find a more comfortable place in secular organizations like Secular Organizations for Sobriety (SOS) and Self Management and Recovery Training (SMART) that are modeled on AA, although they are less likely to find the number and variety of meetings that AA offers in their area.

Further Reading

Cheever, Susan. *My Name Is Bill. Bill Wilson: His Life and the Creation of Alcoholics Anonymous.* New York: Simon & Schuster, 2004.

Jellinek, E. M. *The Disease Concept of Alcoholism.* New Haven: Hillhouse Press, 1960.

Johnson, Vernon E. *I'll Quit Tomorrow.* Revised Edition. New York: Harper-Collins, 1980.

Ketcham, Katherine, and Asbury, William. *Beyond the Influence: Understanding and Defeating Alcoholism.* New York: Bantam Books, 2000.

Vaillant, George. *The Natural History of Alcoholism Revisited.* Cambridge, MA: Harvard University Press, 1995.

White, William. The Rebirth of the Disease Concept of Alcoholism in the 20th Century. *Counselor Magazine* December 2000: 1(2), 62–66.

Wing, Nell. *Grateful to Have Been There: My 42 Years with Bill and Lois, and the Evolution of Alcoholics Anonymous.* Revised Edition. Center City, MN: Hazelden Foundation, 1998.

Alcoholism Alcoholism is an addiction to ethanol, the intoxicant in alcoholic beverages. Also known as ethyl alcohol, it is the byproduct of fermentation, a chemical interaction between yeast and sugar. Approximately 10 to 15 percent of people who drink alcohol become addicted to the drug. Social drinking or moderate drinking (1 to 2 drinks a day for men, 1 for women) is not considered harmful for most adults and may benefit cardiovascular function. A drink is defined as 5 ounces of wine, 12 ounces of beer, or 1 to 3 ounces of distilled spirits. Due to their significantly greater vulnerability to addiction and the permanent changes in brain function that alcohol can cause, people ages 12 to 20—the underage population—should not use alcohol at all. Acute alcoholism is characterized by episodic bursts of intoxication; chronic alcoholism is manifested in a deteriorating pattern of long-term use.

Although there is ongoing disagreement about whether alcoholism is a behavioral problem, a symptom of **mental disorders** such as anxiety or depression, or a primary disease that arises on its own, it is generally regarded as a progressive disorder characterized by early, middle, and late stages that can ultimately destroy the drinker's life. When the disease is advanced, an untreated alcoholic can die from the immediate effects of intoxication or from related complications such as dementia, heart failure, or cirrhosis of the liver. Despite continuing controversies about the exact nature of alcoholism, both the National Institute on Alcohol Abuse and Alcoholism (NIAAA) and the National Institute on Drug Abuse (NIDA) consider alcoholism to be a disease of the brain. In their view, anyone can become an alcoholic, although those with a genetic predisposition or those who drink heavily for a long time are at significantly greater risk. So, too, are teenagers whose developing brains are more vulnerable to alcohol's effects. As the brain's circuitry becomes corrupted in service to the addiction, one's judgment, learning, memory, and control over deteriorating behavior become increasingly impaired and cause the alcoholic to pursue the irrationality of continued drinking.

Chemically, alcohol is a **depressant** that suppresses central nervous system activity. When it enters the stomach, most of it goes to the small intestine, but some enters the bloodstream where it finds its way to the brain. There, it triggers the release of the feel-good **neurotransmitters** dopamine, serotonin, and norepinephrine, which activate the brain's reward pathway to produce pleasant sensations. It also releases gamma-aminobutyric acid (GABA) that inhibits the brain's excitatory responses and allows feelings of calm and relaxation to prevail. As the amount of alcohol in the body increases and the central nervous system is further depressed, reflexes and coordination slow and speech may become slurred. Further toxicity leads to vomiting and can be complicated by choking or suffocation if the drinker inhales his or her own vomit. In more severe cases, alcohol poisoning will result in respiratory depression, coma, and death.

Depending on the stage of the disease, an alcoholic undergoing **withdrawal** will experience a whole range of symptoms that occurs from 12 to 48 hours after he or she stops drinking. In milder forms these include sleep disturbances, thirst, sweating, headache, and anxiety; in more severe forms, hallucinations, seizures, and even death. There is increasing evidence that the brain's glutamate system is involved in producing some of these symptoms; drug therapies that target this system and reduce withdrawal symptoms offer promise.

In the United States, it is illegal for minors—anyone under the age of 21—to possess or, in most cases, buy or consume alcoholic beverages. In many other countries, the legal age is 18 or even younger. Despite its legality, it is considered one of the most dangerous drugs to society and exacts high personal and social costs.

Incidence

About a third of Americans **abuse** alcohol; of these, about 14 million are addicted and only about 24 percent of those receive **treatment**. Because it is legal and its use socially acceptable, alcohol is the drug of choice among adolescents, particularly high school seniors; the average age at which a teenager takes a first drink has declined from 17 to 14. About half of all teenagers report that they drink alcohol, and over half of those report that they have participated in binge drinking. Eighteen percent of college students have clinically significant alcohol-related problems. Some engage in extreme drinking during which they consume more than double the amount of alcohol they would consume if bingeing. Exacerbating the problem is availability; underage drinkers can easily obtain beverages containing alcohol, and "alcopops" and "malternatives" are marketed in fruity concoctions that teens enjoy. In Europe, distilled spirits are appearing in flavored beverages that appeal to younger palates.

How Much Is Too Much?

Alcohol can damage the entire body, especially the brain. It slows mental activity and impairs the drinker's focus, attention span, and organizational skills. In adolescents, alcohol abuse may decrease the size of the hippocampus, which affects memory and learning. Acute intoxication can lead to visual and auditory hallucinations, seizures, and poisoning, while chronic alcoholism can destroy entire organ systems.

Alcohol is metabolized in the liver at the rate of 0.25 or 0.5 ounces per hour. If alcohol is consumed faster than the liver can metabolize, it builds up in the bloodstream and brain and intoxication occurs.

These levels of blood alcohol (blood level concentration, or BAC) produce the following symptoms:

- .02–.03%: relaxation and mild mood elevation; the person feels less inhibited
- .04%: warmth, impaired reaction time, concentration and coordination become impaired
- .08–.10%: the legal drunk limit in most states; euphoria occurs; muscle coordination and reflexes are impaired; the drinker may do or say things he or she later regrets
- .15%: gross difficulty with balance and coordination; the drinker may weave and memory suffers
- .20–.25%: emotions veer out of control; the person walks with a staggered gait and may vomit or pass out
- .30–.40%: alcohol level is toxic, blood pressure drops; the drinker may go into a coma with respiratory depression and death
- .40–.50%: a lethal level for most people; alcoholics with high tolerance may be able to go to .60% BAC before reaching the lethal level

A standard drink contains about 0.6 fluid ounces or 1.2 tablespoons of ethyl alcohol. Different types of beverages vary in actual alcohol content. The following table shows the amount of alcohol in a number of standard drinks served in the United States. Moderate drinking for men under age 65 is 4 to 14 standard drinks per week; for women, 3 to 7 standard drinks per week. Pregnant women or those with certain health problems should not drink at all. All alcohol is equal: one ounce of ethanol in hard liquor is no more potent than one ounce of ethanol in beer.

Type of Beverage	Size	Number of Standard Drinks
Beer, contains ~5% ethanol	12 oz.	1
	16 oz.	1.3
	22 oz.	2
	40 oz.	3.3
Table wine, contains ~12% ethanol	5 oz.	1
	25 oz.	5
Hard liquor, contains ~40% ethanol	1 to 3 oz.	1 to 3
	16 oz.	11
	25 oz.	17
	59 oz.	39

Beginning in 1975, the NIDA began sponsoring a program that conducted ongoing studies among secondary school students, college students, and young adults in the United States. Called **Monitoring the Future**, it assesses various trends in drug use in this age group. Although alcohol use appears to have declined slightly in the last 2 or 3 years, **prescription drug** use has increased. Further, because many varieties of legal and street drugs are widely available, young people frequently use two or more in combination, and alcohol is almost always one of them. The NIDA reports that finding an alcoholic under the age of 35 who is not cross-addicted to a drug like *Cannabis* or **cocaine** is becoming increasingly rare.

The patterns of alcohol abuse and alcoholism vary across the major ethnic groups in the United States—Asian/Pacific Islander, Caucasian, African American, Native American/Alaska Native, and Hispanic. Factors such as socioeconomic background, education level, gender, age, marital status, community demographics, and religion, as well as accessibility to various treatments, skew drinking patterns and complicate statistical analysis. Further, different nationalities within ethnic groups exhibit different patterns. Hispanic Americans from South America consume less alcohol than Mexican Americans; Caribbean Blacks consume less than North American Blacks; and Korean Americans consume less than Japanese Americans. In general terms, overall statistics indicate that Caucasians—especially of Northern European heritage—have higher rates of alcoholism than other ethnic groups, and, of these, males are at higher risk than females. Trends also indicate that among high school students, alcohol use is higher among Caucasian and Hispanic youth than among African Americans. In terms of gender, females—due to complex differences in their physiology and emotional makeup that make them more sensitive to drugs—become addicted to alcohol and drugs more easily and suffer greater ill effects.

On average, an 8- to 10-year gap exists from when an individual begins abusing alcohol to the time he or she seeks treatment. This is a particularly critical issue for teenagers who drink. They may develop an earlier and quickly crippling form of the disorder because their young brains are more susceptible to the highly damaging effects of ethanol. Research shows that in teens who abuse alcohol extensively, the hippocampus is reduced in volume 10 to 35 percent. Since it is the seat of memory, this could cause serious deficits. The NIDA has reported fewer individuals developing the disease after the age of 30; alcoholism nearly always starts at a younger age even though clear symptoms may not manifest until later. The U.S. Substance Abuse and Mental Health Services Administration (SAMHSA) reports that of the 14 million adult alcoholics currently in the United States, over 90 percent reported that they starting drinking before age 21. Citing statistics showing that drinking as a teenager multiplies the risk of serious alcohol problems later in life by a factor of five, the Acting Surgeon General of the United States issued a Call to Action in 2007. The appeal urges renewed efforts to pinpoint the causes and extent of underage consumption, pursue further research studying how alcohol affects the developing brain, and adopt better surveillance strategies for preventing alcohol use among the nation's youth.

Diagnosis

How to characterize alcoholism—the consequence of an impaired sense of personal responsibility, a deficit of willpower, a vice, a symptom of another disorder, or a primary disease—has been debated for centuries and has complicated attempts to diagnose it.

Statistics

The following alcohol use and abuse statistics are courtesy of the U.S. Substance Abuse and Mental Health Services Administration's (SAMHSA) 2006 surveys on drug use and health. For more alcohol statistics, see Appendix D.

Alcohol Use

- Slightly more than half of Americans aged 12 or older reported being current drinkers of alcohol in the 2006 survey (50.9 percent). This translates to an estimated 125 million people, which is similar to the 2005 estimate of 126 million people (51.8 percent).
- More than one fifth (23.0 percent) of persons aged 12 or older participated in binge drinking (having 5 or more drinks on the same occasion on at least 1 day in the 30 days prior to the survey) in 2006. This translates to about 57 million people, similar to the estimate in 2005.
- In 2006, heavy drinking was reported by 6.9 percent of the population aged 12 or older, or 17 million people. This rate is similar to the rate of heavy drinking in 2005 (6.6 percent). Heavy drinking is defined as binge drinking on at least 5 days in the past 30 days.
- In 2006, among young adults aged 18 to 25, the rate of binge drinking was 42.2 percent, and the rate of heavy drinking was 15.6 percent. These rates are similar to the rates in 2005.
- The rate of current alcohol use among youths aged 12 to 17 was 16.6 percent in 2006. Youth binge and heavy drinking rates were 10.3 and 2.4 percent, respectively. These rates are essentially the same as the 2005 rates.
- Underage (persons aged 12 to 20) past-month and binge-drinking rates have remained essentially unchanged since 2002. In 2006, about 10.8 million persons aged 12 to 20 (28.3 percent of this age group) reported drinking alcohol during the month prior to the survey. Approximately 7.2 million (19.0 percent) were binge drinkers, and 2.4 million (6.2 percent) were heavy drinkers.
- Among persons aged 12 to 20, past-month alcohol use rates were 18.6 percent among blacks; 19.7 percent among Asians; 25.3 percent among Hispanics; 27.5 percent among those reporting two or more races; 31.3 percent among American Indians or Alaska Natives; and 32.3 percent among whites. The 2006 rate for American Indians or Alaska Natives is higher than the 2005 rate of 21.7 percent.
- Among pregnant women aged 15 to 44, binge drinking in the first trimester dropped from 10.6 percent in combined data from 2003–2004 to 4.6 percent in combined data from 2005–2006.
- In 2006, an estimated 12.4 percent of persons aged 12 or older drove under the influence of alcohol at least once in the year prior to the survey. This percentage has decreased since 2002, when it was 14.2 percent. The 2006 estimate corresponds to 30.5 million persons.

In the 1970s, three criteria emerged that most experts agreed could be used to diagnose alcoholism: (1) large quantities of alcohol had been consumed over a period of years, (2) alcohol use had led to diminished health or social status, and (3) a loss of control over the amount and frequency of use had become evident. These criteria have changed since then. Now only a loss of control is regarded as a definitive symptom, although **tolerance** and withdrawal are considered by some to be classic signs. The U.S. medical community usually bases formal diagnosis on the criteria published by the American Psychiatric Association (APA) in the 4th edition of the ***Diagnostic and Statistical Manual of Mental Disorders*** (*DSM*). Other countries generally rely on the criteria laid out in the World Health Organization's *International Classification of Diseases, 10th Revision* (ICD-10), which are similar to those of the *DSM*. Although the NIDA reports that heavy drinking is a risk factor for developing alcoholism, the disease is not defined by the amount someone drinks. Each person metabolizes alcohol differently, so what may be an excessive amount for one is not too much for another. Women, in general, are more affected by alcohol than men; what would be a moderate amount for a man could be an intoxicating or even dangerous amount for a woman, especially if she is pregnant.

A problem many experts have with the *DSM* criteria is that they describe a late stage of alcoholism when the disease is advanced and the alcoholic is very ill. Many sufferers die from complications before they reach end-stage disease. Since most experts agree that

---

DSM Criteria for Diagnosing Alcohol Dependence

The following criteria used for diagnosing alcohol *dependence* have been adapted from the 4th edition of the American Psychiatric Association's *Diagnostic and Statistical Manual of Mental Disorders* (*DSM*) criteria for diagnosis of substance addiction and abuse. The manual's editors use the word dependence in this edition as a synonym for addiction. Mounting pressure is on the Association to revert to addiction in the next edition.

The person should exhibit 3 or more of the following symptoms arising out of an abusive pattern of alcohol use within a 12-month period:

1. developing tolerance, manifested by a) the need for more alcohol to obtain the desired effect, or b) a noticeably diminished effect with continued use of the same amount of alcohol;
2. undergoing withdrawal, a) by showing classic symptoms of restlessness, tremor, sleeplessness, and anxiety, or b) by needing to drink to relieve those symptoms;
3. drinking more frequently or in greater quantities than was originally intended;
4. making frequent but unsuccessful attempts to control alcohol use;
5. spending more time to obtain alcohol, to drink, or to recover from hangovers;
6. neglecting social, academic, occupational, or recreational activities or responsibilities;
7. continuing to use alcohol in spite of negative consequences associated with its use, such as the development of physical or psychological problems.

Source: Adapted from American Psychiatric Association, 2000.

alcoholism is progressive, they seek ways to identify the early stage of the disorder and intervene to prevent its continued development. This can be difficult because early warning signs are not always easy to detect; if they do appear, the alcoholic—or friends and family—can easily deny their significance. Other critics worry that too many high-functioning alcoholics—those whose ability to function normally at home, work, and school has not yet begun to deteriorate in apparent ways—evade diagnosis even though their drinking patterns meet the appropriate criteria.

In early efforts to identify the different faces of alcoholism, **E. M. Jellinek** (1890–1963), a Yale University-sponsored researcher, published *The Disease Concept of Alcoholism* in 1960 in which he specified 5 types of the disorder, noting that many alcoholics might easily fit more than one category. According to Jellinek, alpha alcoholics, or Type I, drank heavily to relieve anxiety or depression but did not exhibit signs of withdrawal or loss of control. Beta alcoholics, or Type II, showed none of the mental obsession or physical **dependence** associated with drinking but developed organic damage in the form of cirrhosis of the liver or pancreatitis. Gamma alcoholics, or Type III, were those who could abstain for days or weeks but quickly lost control once they began to drink; they exhibited the progressive form of the disease. Delta alcoholics, or Type IV, drank all day and evening, topping off as necessary; while they seldom became acutely intoxicated and could withdraw from alcohol entirely for a day or two, they were seldom completely sober. Epsilon alcoholics, or Type V, engaged in intense binges during which they might inflict considerable damage on themselves or others. In the United States today, alcoholism experts and **Alcoholics Anonymous** (AA) view gamma alcoholism as the embodiment of all 5 types.

Other experts subscribe to a system of categorizing alcoholics that divides drinkers into two categories: Type I are those who have fewer risk factors for the disease, develop drinking problems later in life, lean toward psychological rather than physical addiction, and have a better prognosis. Type II are those who have a genetic predisposition and other risk factors making them more vulnerable to alcoholism, who drink more compulsively and are predominantly male; their prognosis is less favorable. Most physicians and other diagnosticians do not rely on these classifications, however. Instead, they are likely to diagnose alcoholism based on criteria laid out in the *DSM*.

Stages of Alcoholism

The initial stage of alcoholism can be easy to miss because the symptoms resemble normal drinking patterns. Some alcoholics report a subjective difference between themselves and normal drinkers in the heightened pleasure that they take from drinking from the beginning. They often develop a greater capacity for alcohol than their counterparts and find themselves arranging opportunities to drink or continuing to drink after everyone else has quit. Another danger sign is concealing the amount consumed, keeping extra stores of alcohol hidden or becoming irritable or preoccupied when alcohol is not available.

The middle stage is marked by more frequent and severe **hangovers** that may include gastrointestinal distress, shakiness, excessive perspiration, agitation, and feelings of guilt and shame. The drinker may begin to suffer from longer memory lapses and find he or she regrets impulsive behaviors he or she engaged in while intoxicated. Withdrawal symptoms become worse, sleep may be disrupted by restlessness or vivid dreams, and the individual will increasingly find him- or herself drinking or using other substances to recover from the effects of previous excesses. Complaints from family or friends, psychological or nutritional problems, and difficulties at school or work start to pile up.

In late stages, not only has the alcoholic's behavior and social structure deteriorated, but serious physical symptoms arise from accumulated assaults to the brain and the body as well. Withdrawal can provoke tormented **craving** and intense psychological discomfort; irritated stomach and intestines can produce nausea and diarrhea; neurochemical imbalances can result in mental confusion, hallucinations, even seizures. An elevated heart rate, rapid breathing, disorientation, and blackouts can be life threatening, and if severe delirium tremens develops, then death can result. If alcoholics stop drinking before that point, many can return to health if they receive appropriate medical treatment and continue to abstain from alcohol.

Evaluating Alcohol Use

A variety of questionnaires have been developed in recent decades to help determine a drinker's potential for alcoholism or whether addiction has already occurred. They are useful both for treatment professionals and for concerned drinkers to help recognize dangerous drinking patterns. These tests should not be considered diagnostic, but how an individual answers them can be a powerful indicator of whether his or her use has reached dangerous levels.

The Cage Questionnaire*

This test is used nationally and internationally to help primary care physicians and other treatment specialists establish a diagnosis of alcoholism. Answering 2 or more of these questions "yes" is considered clinically significant.

1. Have you ever thought you should **C**ut down on your drinking?
   ☐ Yes ☐ No
2. Have you ever been **A**ngry if criticized about your drinking? ☐ Yes ☐ No
3. Have you ever felt **G**uilty about your drinking? ☐ Yes ☐ No
4. Have you ever had an **E**ye opener (a drink first thing in the morning to treat hangover symptoms)? ☐ Yes ☐ No

Source: Adapted from Ewing, 1984.
*Note: A variation on this questionnaire is the CUGE, in which question #2 is replaced by "Have you ever driven a vehicle **U**nder the influence of alcohol?"

The Michigan Alcohol Screening Test (MAST)

The Michigan Alcohol Screening Test (MAST) is a widely used self-administered test. Scoring is indicated at the end.

1. Do you feel you are a normal drinker? ("normal"—drink as much as or less than most people) ☐ Yes ☐ No
2. Have you ever awaken the morning after drinking the night before and could not remember a part of the evening? ☐ Yes ☐ No
3. Does any near relative or close friend ever worry or complain about your drinking? ☐ Yes ☐ No
4. Can you stop drinking without difficulty after 1 or 2 drinks?
   ☐ Yes ☐ No
5. Do you ever feel guilty about your drinking? ☐ Yes ☐ No

---

6. Have you ever attended a meeting of Alcoholics Anonymous (AA)?
   ☐ Yes ☐ No
7. Have you ever gotten into physical fights when drinking? ☐ Yes ☐ No
8. Has drinking ever created problems between you and a near relative or close friend? ☐ Yes ☐ No
9. Has any family member or close friend gone to anyone for help about your drinking? ☐ Yes ☐ No
10. Have you ever lost friends because of your drinking? ☐ Yes ☐ No
11. Have you ever gotten into trouble at work because of drinking?
    ☐ Yes ☐ No
12. Have you ever lost a job because of drinking? ☐ Yes ☐ No
13. Have you ever neglected your obligations, your family, or your work for 2 or more days in a row because you were drinking? ☐ Yes ☐ No
14. Do you drink before noon fairly often? ☐ Yes ☐ No
15. Have you ever been told you have liver trouble such as cirrhosis?
    ☐ Yes ☐ No
16. After heavy drinking have you ever had delirium tremens (DTs), severe shaking, visual or auditory (hearing) hallucinations? ☐ Yes ☐ No
17. Have you ever gone to anyone for help about your drinking? ☐ Yes ☐ No
18. Have you ever been hospitalized because of drinking? ☐ Yes ☐ No
19. Has your drinking ever resulted in your being hospitalized in a psychiatric ward? ☐ Yes ☐ No
20. Have you ever gone to any doctor, social worker, clergyman or mental health clinic for help with any emotional problem in which drinking was part of the problem? ☐ Yes ☐ No
21. Have you been arrested more than once for driving under the influence of alcohol? ☐ Yes ☐ No
22. Have you ever been arrested, even for a few hours, because of other behavior while drinking? ☐ Yes ☐ No (If Yes, how many times? _____)

Scoring:

Score 1 point if you answered the following:

1. No
2. Yes
3. Yes
4. No
5. Yes
6. Yes
7. through 22: Yes

Add the scores and compare to the following score card:

0 – 2: No apparent problem
3 – 5: Early or middle problem drinker
6 or more: Problem drinker

Source: Adapted from Selzer, 1971.

AUDIT (Alcohol Use Disorder Identification Test)

This test is widely used to screen heavy and addictive alcohol use and indicate when to consult a health professional. "Alcohol" includes all alcoholic beverages.

1. How often do you have a drink containing alcohol?
   - ☐ Never (0)
   - ☐ Monthly or less (1)
   - ☐ 2 to 4 times a month (2)
   - ☐ 2 to 3 times per week (3)
   - ☐ 4 or more times a week (4)

2. How many drinks containing alcohol do you have on a typical day when you are drinking?
   - ☐ 1 to 2 (0)
   - ☐ 3 or 4 (1)
   - ☐ 5 or 6 (2)
   - ☐ 7 to 9 (3)
   - ☐ 10 or more (4)

3. How often do you have 6 or more drinks on one occasion?
   - ☐ Never (0)
   - ☐ Less than monthly (1)
   - ☐ Monthly (2)
   - ☐ Weekly (3)
   - ☐ Daily or almost daily (4)

4. How often during the last year have you found that you were not able to stop drinking once you had started?
   - ☐ Never (0)
   - ☐ Less than monthly (1)
   - ☐ Monthly (2)
   - ☐ Weekly (3)
   - ☐ Daily or almost daily (4)

5. How often during the last year have you failed to do what was normally expected from you because of drinking?
   - ☐ Never (0)
   - ☐ Less than monthly (1)
   - ☐ Monthly (2)
   - ☐ Weekly (3)
   - ☐ Daily or almost daily (4)

6. How often during the last year have you needed a first drink in the morning to get yourself going after a heavy drinking session?
   - ☐ Never (0)
   - ☐ Less than monthly (1)
   - ☐ Monthly (2)
   - ☐ Weekly (3)
   - ☐ Daily or almost daily (4)

7. How often during the last year have you had a feeling of guilt or remorse after drinking?
   ☐ Never (0)
   ☐ Less than monthly (1)
   ☐ Monthly (2)
   ☐ Weekly (3)
   ☐ Daily or almost daily (4)

8. How often during the last year have you been unable to remember what happened the night before because you had been drinking?
   ☐ Never (0)
   ☐ Less than monthly (1)
   ☐ Monthly (2)
   ☐ Weekly (3)
   ☐ Daily or almost daily (4)

9. Have you or someone else been injured as a result of your drinking?
   ☐ No (0)
   ☐ Yes, but not in the last year (2)
   ☐ Yes, during the last year (4)

10. Has a friend, relative, doctor, or other health worker been concerned about your drinking or suggested you cut down?
    ☐ No (0)
    ☐ Yes, but not in the last year (2)
    ☐ Yes, during the last year (4)

Add the scores and compare to the following:

0 – 3: No apparent problem
4 – 7: Drinking should be a matter for concern
8+: Drinking has reached unhealthy levels.
16+: Seek professional help

Source: Adapted from World Health Organization.http://www.who.int/substance_abuse/publications/alcohol/en/index.html

The American Academy of Pediatrics (AAP), recognizing that the manifestations of alcoholism in children and adolescents can vary from those in older people, has broken down the progression of the disorder into 3 stages in young people. Stage 1 is the experimentation stage during which teens indulge with their friends occasionally, perhaps on weekends only, and only as a recreational pursuit. Stage 2 occurs when teens actively try to obtain alcohol, especially when it is to relieve stress or deal with negative emotions of some kind. Stage 3 involves a preoccupation with alcohol, an inability to control its use, and significant physical dependence that can result in severe withdrawal symptoms if alcohol use is discontinued.

The physical damage alcohol causes can be a diagnostic tool. In earlier stages, injuries and accidents may increase. In later stages, poor nutrition, high blood pressure, the appearance of a spidery network of facial veins, weakened bones, heart arrhythmia or congestive heart failure, anemia, and a host of other serious ailments may develop. Chronic alcoholism is responsible for over 20 percent of patients going to see their physicians, and 50 percent of emergency room visits are reported to involve alcohol. Evidence also suggests that people genetically predisposed to alcoholism may be more vulnerable to severe forms of organ damage that drinking can cause.

History of Alcoholism

The term "alcoholism" did not exist until 1849 when the Swedish physician Magnus Huss (1807–1890) called its group of chronic symptoms "Alcoholismus chronicus." The word did not achieve widespread use in the United States until after the Civil War. Previously, the condition was often referred to as "habitual drunkenness," "intemperance," "dipsomania," or "inebriety." The latter two terms were in most frequent use at the end of the 19th century, but the disorder itself has been documented since early recorded history. Aristotle (384–322 B.C.E.) was not the first to refer to alcoholism as a significant problem for the affected individual and for society, but he was one of the more prominent early figures to do so. Dipsomania, coined in 1819, initially referred to binge drinking punctuated by periods of abstention whereas inebriety was defined as an addiction to any intoxicating or mind-altering substance such as alcohol or cocaine. Alcoholism gradually began to replace these terms during the final quarter of the 19th century, and by the time **Prohibition** was repealed a few decades later, the term had become synonymous with alcohol addiction.

Understanding the nature of alcoholism has been more problematic. Despite records dating to ancient times referring to it as a disease, drunkenness was also defined for many centuries in moral and religious terms as a sin that arose out of licentiousness and depravity. Moderate alcohol use was viewed differently, however. In the 1600s, colonial settlers, who were accustomed to substituting alcohol for the polluted water found in the public supplies of their native country, tended to drink a great deal. Although they viewed drunkenness as the work of the Devil, they regarded alcohol as a nurturing substance provided by God, which they used freely and nearly every day. Unfortunately, the settlers also passed on a taste for alcohol to Native Americans, whose genetic heritage and culture had not prepared them for its devastating effects. The early temperance reform in the United States may have begun with Native Americans struggling with addiction within their population, but **Benjamin Rush** (1745–1813) has been the person most closely associated with the U.S. temperance movement. In 1790, countering the prevailing view that alcohol offered healthful benefits, the physician argued that excessive consumption of alcohol, especially distilled spirits, could lead to disease. He even linked alcohol addiction to heredity and proposed that special hospitals be constructed to house inebriates. Although his position was that the enjoyment of moderate quantities of beer and wine was a wholesome pleasure, many viewed his warnings about the use of **hard liquor** as justification for the moral model of addiction that rejected all alcohol use; this model received wide support, especially among evangelicals. In his 1825 sermons later published as "Six Sermons on the Nature, Occasions, Signs, Evils and Remedy for Intemperance," the Reverend Lyman Beecher (1775–1863) of Connecticut not only proclaimed the evils of alcohol but called for prohibiting its sale or manufacture. An early proponent of prohibition, Beecher also helped fuel the birth of temperance societies that supported abstinence. The first, conceived in 1826, was the American Society for the Promotion of Temperance. Renamed the American Temperance Union in the 1830s, it was formed by evangelical clergymen and was the forerunner of numerous reform movements that proliferated during the first half of the 19th century. Among these were the Sons of Temperance, founded in 1842, and the Washingtonians, a group organized by several alcoholics who took the pledge to abstain from alcohol. In 1829, *The Philanthropist*, the U.S.'s first newspaper devoted to promoting temperance, began to spread word of the movement's growth. Women, who usually suffered the most from their husbands' alcoholic excesses, were the most fervent supporters of temperance, and by the middle of the 1830s they had helped temperance groups spread throughout the United States. When moral persuasion did not appear to convince alcoholics to stop drinking, many of these groups disbanded. Some of their founding principles—creating the idea of anonymity, providing material goods to impoverished alcoholics, and encouraging members to reach out to suffering nonmembers—were reborn in later years in the Salvation Army and AA.

Although the influence of temperance societies waned in the latter half of the 19th century, the message that alcohol was no health tonic had reached Americans; per capita consumption declined from an average of 6 gallons per year to about 2.5 gallons per year, roughly where it stands today. About this same time, the disease concept of alcoholism gained wider acceptance particularly within the medical community and led to the creation of several inebriate asylums designed to house suffering alcohol addicts and gain further insights into what was viewed as a "constitutional susceptibility" to the disorder. The American Association for the Study and Cure of Inebriety, founded in 1870, sponsored the creation of many of these institutions. In 1880, Lesley Keeley (1832–1900) opened the first of more than 30 private sanatoriums in the nation dedicated to treatment.

Despite this widespread support for a physiological basis of addiction, many remained committed to the belief that the alcoholic was a sinner whose only redemption lay in divine grace. Zealous temperance proponents advised penitent alcoholics to attend gospel meetings and pray for their deliverance via miraculous cures. Taking a more moderate view, scientists argued that alcoholics must restore weakened bodies and heal poisoned minds before their moral perspective could be expected to return. To bridge the two viewpoints, many physicians recommended a combined approach that focused on healing the physical body and bolstering the addict's moral foundation with less fervently religious means.

Nevertheless, temperance efforts prevailed. The Salvation Army formed in 1865 by William Booth (1829–1912) in London, England, arose primarily as a Christian-inspired "army" to engage in spiritual warfare against poverty and other ills of society, including alcoholism, which Booth regarded as a disease of indulgence. The Army's mission of charity, its philosophy of personal redemption through God's salvation, and its advocacy of a disciplined life of morality and abstinence from alcohol and **tobacco** were early models for other groups promoting temperance. One such group, the Women's Christian Temperance Union (WCTU) formed in 1874, lobbied for the closing of liquor establishments. Although a movement to establish a Prohibition Party failed to materialize, temperance gathered momentum and the WCTU, which doubled its membership during the 1880s, became a powerful supporter.

As the United States struggled to deal with cultural pressures emerging from industrialization and immigration, temperance groups often succeeded in linking these phenomena to the problems associated with "Demon Rum." Industrialists like Henry Ford and Pierre du Pont supported both the formation of the Anti-Saloon League in 1895 and the revival of the prohibition movement. The League gained power during the next few years and successfully shut down drinking establishments during the early 20th century. About the same time, **Carrie Amelia Nation** (1846–1911), who claimed to have been called on by God to destroy with a hatchet local bars, deepened religion's influence in the cause. So too did William Jennings Bryan (1860–1925), a prominent lobbyist for the Anti-Saloon League who also urged that the fight be taken directly to the saloons. These measures

WOMAN'S HOLY WAR.

Women, who often suffered the most from their husbands' excessive drinking, became very active in the temperance movement during the 1800s. This 1874 political cartoon depicts crusading women clutching hatchets similar to the one famously wielded by Carrie Nation.

succeeded in publicizing the cause of temperance and helped reduce alcohol use. The restrictions imposed on the use of grain during World War I drove down production of alcoholic beverages, further contributing to the suppression of alcohol consumption. Not long after Congress passed the Harrison Anti-Narcotic Act of 1914 to restrict the availability of certain drugs, a receptive public proved willing to support new laws that culminated in Prohibition.

Although the Anti-Saloon League proposed the legislation, it was guided through Congress by a zealously religious congressman from Minnesota named Andrew J. Volstead and became known as the Volstead Act. Voted in as the 18th Amendment to the U.S. Constitution in October 1919, the bill was vetoed by President Woodrow Wilson and returned to Congress where the veto was promptly overridden. The amendment was ratified by the states and Prohibition became law on January 20, 1920. The legislation underlying Prohibition defined "intoxicating liquors" and prohibited their sale, manufacture, and transport within the United States.

Prohibition was a failure. Although alcohol use fell off dramatically at first, the U.S. public proved unwilling to give up alcohol use entirely. As efforts to obtain the substance through illegal means expanded in the face of inadequate government funding allocated to enforce the legislation, an industry of corruption began to flourish, outmaneuvering and overwhelming any attempts to curtail it. Illegal, or "bootlegged," liquor smuggled into the United States and diluted with water or even toxic additives sloshed through supply networks established by organized crime. Liquor-making instruction manuals were in wide circulation, and in rural pockets of the United States, private stills produced moonshine that people concealed from authorities in hip flasks and hollowed-out canes. Although law enforcement officials generally drew the line at searching the homes of private individuals using alcohol strictly for their own use, their property, where liquor could be manufactured, was fair game. Almost three-quarters of a million stills were seized during the first 5 years of Prohibition, but loopholes in the law that allowed industrial use of grain alcohol and permitted churches to buy unlimited quantities of wine nurtured a California grape industry that gladly supplied its product to a thirsty public. When the U.S. stock market crashed in 1929, Americans suffering the economic crisis wrought by the Great Depression lost their enthusiasm for punitive laws restricting alcohol use. After President Franklin Delano Roosevelt cut funding for enforcing Prohibition, the 21st Amendment repealed the act entirely in 1933.

As the temperance movement flickered out with the failure of Prohibition, alcoholism again came to be viewed as a disease to be regarded in more compassionate terms. One group that attempted to do so was the Craigie Foundation. Evolving out of the Emmanuel Movement in 1909, which originally focused on group and individual therapy, the Craigie Foundation espoused treatment that combined religion and psychotherapy in church meetings conducted by clergy and staff. In an attempt to help addicts break the addictive cycle, support was offered by peer group members to help alcoholics with employment and other day-to-day matters. Although the movement represented a breakthrough by addressing psychology, medicine, religion, and social issues in its overall approach, it relied too heavily on Freudian psychoanalytic theory rather than behavioral modification to help alcoholics regain normal functioning.

The Oxford Group, originally established as an evangelical religious movement by the Reverend Frank Nathan Daniel Buchman (1878–1961), would embrace a philosophy that would become the foundation of many modern treatments models. One of its members, **Bill Wilson** (1895–1971), broke away from the group in 1937 along with another alcoholic named **Bob Smith** (1879–1950), but not before forming AA in 1935. Rejecting some of Buchman's more controversial practices but adopting several core principles from the Oxford Group—focusing on service to others, taking moral inventory, embracing the concept of powerlessness, and turning over control of one's life to God—they wrote the famous 12 steps that underlie many treatment programs and published *Alcoholics Anonymous* in 1939, which codified their beliefs and presented stories of other alcoholics that

AA members continue to read for inspirational support. A core figure involved in the early evolution of AA was **William D. Silkworth** (1873–1951), a physician who had treated Bill Wilson and became an early proponent of the disease theory of alcoholism; rejecting compulsive drinking as a moral issue, Silkworth likened alcoholism to an allergy.

Although the disease concept had originated outside of AA, members now use the term to refer to the physical, mental, emotional, and spiritual impoverishment that alcoholism produces. Viewing the disorder as a primary disease, the organization differs from many specialists who believe that alcoholism is symptomatic of other psychological problems, particularly underlying **anxiety disorders**, depression, or posttraumatic stress disorders, and that its management relies both on behavioral modification and on mental health therapy.

The Modern Alcoholism Movement

In the early 1940s, several organizations were involved in emerging campaigns known as the modern alcoholism movement that sought to establish alcoholism as a disease. In 1944, **Marty Mann** (1904–1980), an alcoholism researcher affiliated with Yale's Center of Alcohol Studies who cofounded the National Committee for Education on Alcoholism (NCEA) with E. M. Jellinek (1890–1963), was especially influential in the movement. The first female member of AA, she declared unequivocally that alcoholism was a disease, although Jellinek was more cautious. Other scientists of the time like **Harry Tiebout** (1896–1966), a psychiatrist who identified alcoholism as an illness, were fearful that such a characterization was oversimplified. Nevertheless, through their involvement with NCEA, Mann and Jellinek as well as AA's Bill Wilson, an advisor to the NCEA, endorsed both the disease concept and the value of AA as a therapeutic approach. Treatment programs based on AA's philosophy would form during this period at the Pioneer House, Hazelden, and Willmar State Hospital in Minnesota, which would become known as the **Minnesota model**. For a time, Mann and Jellinek enjoyed the prestige afforded by their association with Yale University, but this relationship ended in 1949 when the new director of Yale's Center of Alcohol Studies objected to their lack of scientific data to support their **disease model of addiction** and alcoholism.

During the 1950s, an increasing number of organizations joined AA in defining alcoholism as a disease. In 1954, Ruth Fox (1895–1989) founded the American Society of Addiction Medicine (ASAM), which echoed AA's principles and sought, as it does currently, to have **addiction medicine** included in the pantheon of bona fide medical specialties. The American Medical Association (AMA), the American Hospital Association (AHA), and the World Health Organization (WHO) endorsed the disease concept during this period, and, in 1961, the National Institute of Mental Health (NIMH) and what was then the Department of Health, Education, and Welfare (DHEW) jointly sponsored a commission recommending the establishment of a national forum for studying alcoholism. Both AA and Marty Mann of the NCEA, whose name changed to the National Council on Alcoholism and Drug Dependence (NCADD) in 1990, supported this effort, which resulted in 1970's Comprehensive Alcohol Abuse and Alcoholism Prevention, Treatment and Rehabilitation Act. Known more commonly as the Hughes Act, the legislation created the National Institute on Alcohol Abuse and Alcoholism (NIAAA) that provides federal funding for studies of treatment-related programs. Many private-sector individuals contributed financial and other resources to the cause, including R. Brinkley Smithers (1907–1994), an heir to the founder of International Business Machines (IBM).

By the 1970s and 1980s there was increasing acceptance of the disease concept and growing support for education, **prevention**, and treatment approaches. A courageous decision by First Lady **Betty Ford** (1918–) to publicize her struggle with alcoholism was influential in removing much of its stigma and educating the nation on the complex issues that surround it. Hospital- and rehabilitation center-based programs as well as private counseling increasingly came to be covered by major health insurers as alcoholism, and drug addiction in general, entered the realm of public health.

There have been some notable critics of this trend. In 1988, the U.S. Supreme Court challenged the AMA's definition of alcoholism as a disease, referring to it instead as "willful misconduct," but this may have resulted from imprecise definitions of alcoholism centered on heavy drinking rather than true dependence. Herbert Fingarette (1921–), a WHO consultant on alcoholism and addiction who published *Heavy Drinking: The Myth of Alcoholism as a Disease* in 1988, rejected decades of research suggesting a biological basis for the disorder. He challenged the loss-of-control concept that characterized a defining symptom of alcoholism by suggesting that circumstance and motivation affected the level of control someone could exert over his or her drinking. He also observed that support for the disease model was fueled by a political and economic agenda; powerful lobbies controlled funds allocated to treatment institutions that had been founded on the disease principle, and it was in their interest to maintain the status quo. In addition, Fingarette suggested that the disease model excused society from addressing the more complex economic, sociological, and psychological causes of alcoholism and allowed alcoholics—who often served as lay staff at rehabilitation centers and were the very heart of AA—to justify the powerlessness that was at the core of their **12-step** philosophy. Another prominent alcoholism researcher, George Vaillant (1934–), Professor of Psychiatry at Harvard Medical School, took a more balanced view in his 1995 *The Natural History of Alcoholism Revisited*. Although he asserts the belief that alcoholism is a disease, he disputes some of the founding principles of the AA position—that it is necessarily progressive or that in the early stages it cannot be controlled. In countering Fingarette's arguments, he acknowledged that although alcoholism was a deviant behavior that must be addressed, the fact that alcoholics have a mortality rate 2 to 4 times higher than the average person placed the disorder into the disease category and required that it be treated medically.

The debate continues into the 21st century; as the scientific community finds new evidence to support the disease model, skeptics present compelling arguments to refute it. Nevertheless, the perception that alcoholism is a disease, at least in many respects, has become firmly entrenched and drives most modern treatment approaches.

Causes

Most researchers believe the causes of alcoholism lie both in biology and in environmental factors, and some cite convincing evidence that the former plays the more significant role. Biology and genetics underlie metabolic disorders, ethnic susceptibilities, certain prenatal influences, and networks of neurotransmitters and neuromodulators in the brain, all of which subtly contribute to a person's vulnerability to alcoholism. Studies conducted to distinguish genetic from environmental influences found that adoptees who had an alcoholic biological parent were 2 to 3 times more likely to become alcoholic regardless of whether either adoptive parent was an alcoholic. On the other hand, studies also confirm that the absence of alcoholism in an adoptive family can help reduce the impact of genetic risk. Nevertheless, comparisons in the incidence of alcoholism in twins showed that if one identical twin is an alcoholic, the likelihood of alcoholism afflicting the other twin—who shares the same genes—is significantly higher than in fraternal twins, who have different genes. Twin studies have also suggested that the more severe forms of alcoholism are more heritable and the less severe forms are less so.

Among certain Asian populations, a variant of the *ALDH1* gene interferes with alcohol metabolism in such a way that even small amounts of alcohol can make the drinker violently sick. Although rare in people of European descent, this variant is present in a third to half of Asians and is protective in this population because its effect is such a powerful deterrent to alcohol use.

During the 1970s, a researcher named **Kenneth Blum** (1939–) at the University of Texas conducted experiments that convinced him and many of his associates that neurotransmitters like serotonin, GABA, and glutamate have critical roles in alcoholism. During the 1980s as his investigations led him to molecular genetics, his work with Ernest Noble (1929–), the former director of the National Institutes of Health's NIAAA, revealed the significance of the dopamine D2 allele in the disease. This confirmed the association of certain genes with alcoholism and helped launch a series of investigations within the scientific community as a whole into the **genetics of addiction**.

In addition to molecular studies that allow researchers to pinpoint variants in DNA common only to alcoholic family members, researchers are looking at measurable, internal physical traits called endophenotypes that may help assess an individual's risk. Brain activity is an example. Observing and recording how the brain reacts to excitatory stimuli such as alcohol can tell researchers about the balance or imbalance between excitatory and inhibitory processes in the brain. This biological activity may prove to be as reliable a marker as genetic variants in predicting one's risk for alcoholism. Recent studies of differences in brain activity between alcoholics and nonalcoholics reveal that the former have a muted response to certain stimuli in comparison to the reaction measured in nonalcoholics. Known as the P300 response, this significantly weaker reaction has been measured even in abstinent alcoholics and in the children of alcoholics, suggesting that it is a functional difference in brain biology that not only predicts risk but may also be one of the causes of the disease.

However, over half of all children born to alcoholics do not become alcoholic. Environmental issues cannot be tested as neatly as patterns of inheritance and DNA, but environmental variables can significantly affect risk. Customs in a given culture or religion, the accessibility of alcoholic beverages in industrialized countries, academic or occupational stress, peer pressure, family discord, and the degree of parental supervision over adolescent behavior can influence whether or not someone develops alcoholism or whether he or she drinks alcohol at all. Age and gender increase risks that biology and environment pose—some statistics state that males are 5 times more likely than females to become alcoholics—and so does smoking. Children who begin smoking before age 13 are at a significantly higher risk; researchers are not sure why, but some believe it is related to personality. Others believe this tendency is based in biology—the same neural pathway rewarded by the use of **nicotine** responds to alcohol. Those who are drawn to higher-risk behaviors are more likely to smoke, drink alcohol, and engage in other dangerous activities.

Within the broad categories of heredity and environment are individual traits associated with heightened risk. Medical experts have noted a powerful link between alcoholism and psychological factors such as excessive shyness, depression, a tendency to isolate, hostility, and self-destructive impulsivity. Although heavy drinking is not necessarily a sign of alcoholism, excessive long-term alcohol use dramatically increases risk. So do other patterns

Table 8. Tobacco Product and Alcohol Use in the Past Month among Persons Aged 12 to 17, by Gender: Percentages, 2002–2006

GENDER/SUBSTANCE	2002	2003	2004	2005	2006
Total					
Tobacco Products[1]	15.2[b]	14.4[b]	14.4[b]	13.1	12.9
Cigarettes	13.0[b]	12.2[b]	11.9[b]	10.8	10.4
Smokeless Tobacco	2.0[a]	2.0	2.3	2.1	2.4
Cigars	4.5	4.5	4.8[b]	4.2	4.1
Pipe Tobacco	0.6	0.6	0.7	0.6	0.7
Alcohol	17.6[a]	17.7[a]	17.6[a]	16.5	16.6
Binge Alcohol Use[2]	10.7	10.6	11.1[a]	9.9	10.3
Heavy Alcohol Use[2]	2.5	2.6	2.7	2.4	2.4
Male					
Tobacco Products[1]	16.0[b]	15.6[b]	15.3[a]	14.2	14.0
Cigarettes	12.3[b]	11.9[b]	11.3[a]	10.7	10.0
Smokeless Tobacco	3.4[a]	3.7	4.0	3.7	4.2
Cigars	6.2	6.2	6.6[b]	5.8	5.5
Pipe Tobacco	0.7	0.9	0.9	0.8	0.9
Alcohol	17.4	17.1	17.2	15.9	16.3
Binge Alcohol Use[2]	11.4	11.1	11.6	10.4	10.7
Heavy Alcohol Use[2]	3.1	2.9	3.2	3.0	2.8
Female					
Tobacco Products[1]	14.4[b]	13.3[b]	13.5[b]	11.9	11.8
Cigarettes	13.6[b]	12.5[b]	12.5[b]	10.8	10.7
Smokeless Tobacco	0.4	0.3	0.4	0.4	0.4
Cigars	2.7	2.7	2.8	2.5	2.7
Pipe Tobacco	0.4	0.3	0.5	0.4	0.4
Alcohol	17.9	18.3[a]	18.0	17.2	17.0
Binge Alcohol Use[2]	9.9	10.1	10.5	9.4	9.9
Heavy Alcohol Use[2]	1.9	2.3	2.1	1.8	1.9

[a]Difference between estimate and 2006 estimate is statistically significant at the 0.05 level.
[b]Difference between estimate and 2006 estimate is statistically significant at the 0.01 level.
[1]Tobacco Products include cigarettes, smokeless tobacco (i.e., chewing tobacco or snuff), cigars, or pipe tobacco.
[2]Binge Alcohol Use is defined as drinking 5 or more drinks on the same occasion (i.e., at the same time or within a couple of hours of each other) on at least 1 day in the past 30 days. Heavy Alcohol Use is defined as drinking 5 or more drinks on the same occasion on each of 5 or more days in the past 30 days; all heavy alcohol users are also binge alcohol users.
Source: SAMHSA.

of drinking. At one time, predictions were that only people with a genetic predisposition were likely to cross the line between normal and alcoholic drinking. In more recent years, experts are finding that more people with no genetic link are becoming alcoholics. They attribute this to adolescent binge drinking and teens' tendency to combine alcohol with other drugs.

Effects of Alcohol

Aside from intoxication and the potentially destructive behavior it promotes, the most frequently reported short-term effects of alcohol use are hangovers. These vary depending

Table 9. Tobacco Product and Alcohol Use in the Past Month among Persons Aged 18 to 25, by Gender: Percentages, 2002–2006

GENDER/SUBSTANCE	2002	2003	2004	2005	2006
Total					
Tobacco Products[1]	45.3[a]	44.8	44.6	44.3	43.9
Cigarettes	40.8[b]	40.2[b]	39.5	39.0	38.4
Smokeless Tobacco	4.8	4.7[a]	4.9	5.1	5.2
Cigars	11.0[b]	11.4	12.7	12.0	12.1
Pipe Tobacco	1.1	0.9[b]	1.2	1.5	1.3
Alcohol	60.5[a]	61.4	60.5[a]	60.9	61.9
Binge Alcohol Use[2]	40.9	41.6	41.2	41.9	42.2
Heavy Alcohol Use[2]	14.9	15.1	15.1	15.3	15.6
Male					
Tobacco Products[1]	52.1	51.7	51.7	51.6	51.0
Cigarettes	44.4[b]	44.2[a]	43.5	42.9	41.9
Smokeless Tobacco	9.4	8.9[a]	9.5	9.7	9.9
Cigars	16.8[b]	17.3[a]	19.7	18.3	18.7
Pipe Tobacco	1.7[a]	1.4[b]	2.1	2.3	2.2
Alcohol	65.2	66.9	64.9	66.3	65.9
Binge Alcohol Use[2]	50.2	51.3	50.1	51.7	50.2
Heavy Alcohol Use[2]	21.1	21.2	21.2	21.7	21.0
Female					
Tobacco Products[1]	38.4	37.8	37.4	36.9	36.8
Cigarettes	37.1[a]	36.2	35.5	35.0	34.9
Smokeless Tobacco	0.3	0.4	0.4	0.5	0.4
Cigars	5.2	5.5	5.8	5.6	5.5
Pipe Tobacco	0.4	0.4	0.4	0.6	0.5
Alcohol	55.7[a]	55.8[a]	56.0[a]	55.4[b]	57.9
Binge Alcohol Use[2]	31.7[b]	31.8[a]	32.3[a]	31.9[a]	34.0
Heavy Alcohol Use[2]	8.7[b]	9.0[a]	8.8[a]	8.8[a]	10.0

[a]Difference between estimate and 2006 estimate is statistically significant at the 0.05 level.
[b]Difference between estimate and 2006 estimate is statistically significant at the 0.01 level.
[1]Tobacco Products include cigarettes, smokeless tobacco (i.e., chewing tobacco or snuff), cigars, or pipe tobacco.
[2]Binge Alcohol Use is defined as drinking 5 or more drinks on the same occasion (i.e., at the same time or within a couple of hours of each other) on at least 1 day in the past 30 days. Heavy Alcohol Use is defined as drinking 5 or more drinks on the same occasion on each of 5 or more days in the past 30 days; all heavy alcohol users are also binge alcohol users.
Source: SAMHSA.

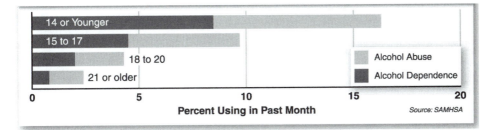

Alcohol Dependence or Abuse in the Past Year among Adults Aged 21 or Older, by Age at First Use of Alcohol: 2006

Clues to Alcohol Abuse among Adolescents

The following behaviors and symptoms are warning signs that children or teens are in crisis. They may be signs of serious emotional problems or they may be directly related to alcohol abuse. A teenager exhibiting several of these symptoms may need to be evaluated by a physician or mental health professional.

- Increased risk-taking behavior: driving under the influence, engaging in unsafe or promiscuous sex, fighting, or violence
- Problems at school: poor grades, suspension, decreased attendance
- Isolation or rejection of old friends for a different set of associates
- Impaired communication with family, increased secrecy
- Running away from home
- Depression—sleeping or eating difficulties, mood swings, excessive sadness or suicidal feelings, lethargy, weight loss
- Anxiety, restlessness, agitation, excessive sweating
- Changes in personal hygiene, clothing styles, grooming
- Bloodshot eyes and/or wearing sunglasses at odd times to disguise eyes
- Money problems
- Distrustfulness, paranoia, resentment
- Insomnia
- Smelling of alcohol
- Cigarette use; adolescents who smoke are more likely to use drugs
- Vomiting in bed
- Evidence of drug use (pop-tops, burnt matches, paraphernalia)

---

on the quantity of alcohol consumed and the duration of the drinking period; initially, the headaches and gastritis they produce are not serious. Blackouts, that is, short periods of memory lapses, are commonly seen in heavy drinking but are not necessarily signs of addiction. With repeated alcohol use, hangover symptoms worsen and may involve nausea and distressing psychological symptoms. With longer-term abuse, people may lose some sensation in their hands and feet as a result of peripheral neuropathy and are likely to experience some confusion or memory problems linked to shrinkage of the brain, particularly the hippocampus, which is considered the seat of memory. Although altered brain anatomy can return to normal during abstinence, prolonged assaults on brain cells can produce permanent damage. Eventually, cells subjected to the effects of heavy use will die, resulting in dementia. Incalculable damage can be done to other people as a result of an alcoholic's behavior from automobile accidents to emotional and physical abuse directed at the alcoholic's spouse, children, coworkers, or friends.

The following are some of the serious effects associated with excessive alcohol use. Some of these can be reversed to some degree with abstinence; others are permanent.

Alcohol poisoning is the result of ingesting more alcohol than the liver can process; the drinker can die from alcohol poisoning if he or she cannot eliminate it from his or her system through vomiting or through medical intervention to pump the stomach.

Alcoholic psychoses are a wide range of disorders characterized by severe brain dysfunction that includes auditory and visual hallucinations, dementia, irrational behavior, or amnesia. These are medical emergencies. Treated in time, in a hospital or clinic setting with appropriate medications, most patients can recover as long as all alcohol consumption stops.

Bone growth slows in heavy drinkers; teens may have stunted growth and adults may develop osteoporosis.

Brain shrinkage occurs in chronic heavy drinkers, especially the areas of planning, reasoning, balance, and certain kinds of learning.

Cancer: Long-term heavy drinkers have an increased risk of head and neck, esophageal, lung, bladder, colon, and liver cancers. The likelihood of these cancers is increased if the drinker also smokes.

Delirium tremens (DTs) represent a psychotic state, an extreme reaction that an alcoholic has to the withdrawal of alcohol. It begins with anxiety attacks, frightening dreams, and deep depression and progresses to a medical emergency when the person exhibits a high pulse, elevated temperature, disorientation, and terrifying hallucinations. It should be managed medically and will begin to resolve within 12 to 24 hours, although it might take as much as 1 to 2 weeks for symptoms to subside entirely.

Dementia is a brain dysfunction marked by personal and intellectual deterioration, and stupor. It may be a permanent result of chronic alcoholism.

Depression is often cited as a cause of alcoholism and it can be the result as well.

Esophageal varices are inflamed veins in the esophagus from chronic irritation due to alcohol use; they are related to liver deterioration and result in bleeding into the esophagus. Esophageal varices are a serious medical condition requiring immediate attention and permanent abstinence.

Fetal alcohol spectrum disorders: Pregnant women who drink are feeding alcohol to their unborn babies, which can cause serious birth defects and neurological problems. Fetal alcohol syndrome is the most common of these disorders and is a lifelong condition in which the child has abnormal features and retarded development.

Gastrointestinal problems associated with alcohol use include inflammation of the esophagus, stomach, and intestines, and excess acid reflux from the stomach (gastroesophageal reflux disease, or GERD) or bleeding. Gastritis, inflammation of the stomach lining, arises from a weakening of the mucous membrane that lines and protects the stomach from digestive acids, and it can produce a series of symptoms and disorders such as bloating, nausea, indigestion, internal bleeding, stomach and intestinal ulcers, and colitis.

Hangovers, the body's reaction to withdrawing from recent alcohol use, tend to become progressively severe as drinking patterns intensify and worsen. Symptoms include physical discomforts such as headaches or nausea; early-morning awakening accompanied by pounding heart and sweating; dehydration; and the "shakes." Psychological effects include anxiety, agitation, and depression. To avoid a hangover, drinkers should keep their blood alcohol level below 0.05 percent, although this varies slightly from person to person.

Heart disease: Alcohol can damage the heart so that it is unable to pump effectively. This can produce a range of serious problems such as congestive heart failure, cardiomyopathy (death of the heart muscle), abnormal heart rhythm, shortness of breath, and high blood pressure.

Hepatitis, inflammation of the liver, is common with heavy alcohol use, occurring in about 20 percent of drinkers.

Hypoglycemia is low blood sugar caused by damage to the liver, adrenal glands, pancreas, and central nervous system, which all monitor blood sugar levels. Low blood sugar levels can produce anxiety, depression, phobias, suicidal tendencies, confusion, exhaustion, and irritability.

Korsakoff's syndrome is a serious brain dysfunction, often the result of malnutrition, characterized by amnesia or memory distortions.

Liver disease (cirrhosis): Alcohol causes a fatty buildup in the liver that chokes out normal cells and leaves scar tissue that interferes with the liver's ability to work efficiently. Ultimately fatal, cirrhosis can be reversed in early stages with proper diet and abstinence from alcohol.

Malnutrition, in alcoholism, is caused by the liver's increasing inability to make nutrients and the alcoholic's tendency to neglect proper nutrition. Alcohol blocks the body's ability to absorb certain vitamins, causing deficiencies that result in damage to organ systems.

Olfactory sense is deadened in some heavy drinkers and they can lose their sense of smell.

Pancreatitis is an inflamed pancreas that can produce excruciating abdominal pain, nausea, and vomiting. In acute cases, such as those resulting from binges, shock and falling blood pressure can be life threatening. In chronic cases, scarring and thickening of the pancreas can result in cell damage and subsequent diabetes.

Polyneuropathy, inflammation in and damage to the body's peripheral nerves, may lead to numbness, especially in the hands and feet, and even paralysis. This can be a complication of malnutrition.

Psychological problems are related to depression, anxiety, and other neurological imbalances caused by alcohol abuse.

Reproductive system: Aside from damage to the unborn, alcohol's effect on the reproductive system may include problems with fertility. Libidos may be lower and testicles and ovaries may shrink as sperm and egg production decrease; women may undergo menopause at an earlier age.

Wernicke's encephalography is a degenerative brain syndrome that results from inflammation and hemorrhage associated with alcohol-related malnutrition.

Prevention

The evidence is overwhelming: the best way to prevent alcoholism is to avoid alcohol use in teenage and young adult years. Adolescents who have a history of alcoholism in their families or those with personal difficulties like family discord or scholastic failure are at greater risk, as are those with anxiety disorders or depression. Teens seem to respond well to educational programs, especially by peers such as Students Against Destructive Decisions (SADD—formerly, Students Against Driving Drunk). Treatment professionals recommend that educational efforts begin in elementary schools because children as young as 8 years old can form opinions about alcohol use in their given culture.

Experts suggest several ways parents can help protect children from the dangers of alcohol. Parents should teach healthy ways of dealing with life's problems so that adolescents do not rely on the false promises of alcohol to cope. Other important measures are holding forthright discussions about inappropriate uses of alcohol, setting a good example, enhancing children's self esteem and confidence, listening to children's concerns without preaching or blaming, avoiding confrontational approaches, participating in wholesome activities with children, and being willing to seek **intervention** at the first sign of trouble.

Treatment

No cure for alcoholism exists, but there are multiple paths of treatment with long-term abstinence usually the goal. The complexities of the disease usually require a combination of methods tailored to the needs of the individual alcoholic; a one-size-fits-all approach is not necessarily effective. In the early 20th century abstinence programs prevailed, but as public understanding of psychology and access to mental health treatment improved, therapies based on management of the disease through lifestyle changes and treatment of underlying conditions gained favor. As many came to reject a rigid disease model that prescribed expensive 28-day residential treatment programs and surrender to a higher power as the only route to an abstemious **recovery**, a number of secular organizations sprang up which centered their approach on personal responsibility, harm reduction, and behavior modification. Prominent among these was Rational Recovery (RR), Secular Organizations for Sobriety (SOS), Self Management and Recovery Training (SMART), and Moderation Management (MM). Some advocated abstention whereas others promoted the idea that controlled drinking could be achieved, an idea that many proponents of the disease theory vigorously reject—their view is that alcoholics are sensitized to alcohol, their brains have been changed permanently, and drinking alcohol again will trigger the same neurochemical imbalances that led to alcoholic drinking in the first place. To help address this problem, scientists have developed medications that modulate brain chemistry to reduce or eliminate the alcoholic's desire to drink. These include disulfiram (Antabuse), naltrexone (Depade, ReVia, Vivitrol), acamprosate (Campral), and topiromate (Topamax). Another drug used to help smokers stop nicotine use, varenicline (Chantix), also offers promise in the treatment of alcoholism, although a Food and Drug Administration report issued in 2008 suggests the medication may produce serious psychiatric symptoms in certain patients, which may limit its future availability. Alternative treatments are often used to supplement standard treatment and ease some of the difficulties associated with early recovery. Acupuncture and biofeedback may be helpful in relieving withdrawal symptoms. Nutritional therapy can be important, especially to address the malnutrition most alcoholics suffer. Massage and meditation may be used to relieve stress and promote relaxation.

When an alcoholic enters treatment, the first step may be detoxification, a period of withdrawal during which his or her system is purged of alcohol and its accumulated by-products; this may take several days. The next step is rehabilitation, in which the individual begins to learn to live without alcohol and rebuild his or her life. Initially, rehabilitation can be very difficult for some and is often marked by repeated relapse; for others, sobriety and resumption of normal activities occur in days, although psychological and physical healing take longer. Most programs address aspects of the alcoholic's personal development, relationships, and functioning that were neglected during his or her period of alcoholic drinking. As these are strengthened, so is the likelihood of maintaining sobriety. Because alcoholics are at risk for relapse with even one drink, many refer to themselves as "recovering" rather than "cured" to emphasize the ongoing nature of the recovery process. About 60 percent of treated alcoholics who have supportive families and stable socioeconomic backgrounds maintain sobriety for a year or more, but another 40 percent do not.

For some who begin treatment in a residential rehabilitation facility, a few week's stay in a halfway house may be recommended before the alcoholic returns to his or her former life. Since recovery is considered to be a lifelong process, the best treatment is generally a client-centered approach that combines medications, if appropriate, and therapeutic philosophies adopted from both 12-step and cognitive behavioral programs.

The families of alcoholics often develop dysfunctional patterns of coping: they may unknowingly enable the alcoholic in his or her drinking or develop a codependent relationship that helps feed the addiction without their conscious awareness. For this reason, most seek outside counseling or supportive groups like Al-Anon.

The NIDA stresses that whichever method of treatment is chosen, it is essential the alcoholic be treated for any underlying mental disorder at the same time; waiting until the individual stops drinking is placing him or her at a higher risk for relapse. Although the NIDA acknowledges that relapse is part of recovery and must not be viewed as treatment failure, neither does it ignore the psychological issues that are likely to trigger a return to drinking. In an effort to guide families through the maze of treatment options, NIDA advises they start with a family physician, especially if there are medical issues, or a psychologist. A pastor or employee assistance program may be able to direct them to counseling services or local AA groups. A few counseling sessions combined with medication, participation in organizations with a spiritual focus (such as AA), or a stay in a residential facility may prove appropriate. Most important is that the alcoholic receive individually tailored treatment early in the course of the disease. In assessing treatment, key issues that family or other responsible parties should consider include: the severity or stage of the disease and whether coexisting mental illnesses are present; how education can be continued if inpatient rehabilitation is necessary; and how involved the rest of the family will be in the short and long term. To help track compliance in alcoholics already under treatment, a new product known as sweat patches are under study; applied much like Band-Aids on the skin, they absorb alcohol residues secreted through perspiration and aid counselors and other treatment professionals in evaluating treatment effectiveness.

One approach to diagnosing alcoholism early enough for treatment to be most effective is to involve emergency room physicians; since the majority of admissions to these facilities involve alcohol, the physicians and staff are well positioned to screen for abuse of this drug. Unfortunately, most are not trained in recognizing the definitive signs of alcohol addiction and are reluctant to try to treat it because of insurance constraints.

Recently, some have given thought to the possibility of developing a safe, nonaddictive alcohol **agonist** that would block the effects of alcohol but trigger GABA release, the neurotransmitter associated with disinhibition and relaxation that alcohol causes. Giving this selective partial GABA agonist the name "synthehol," after a fictitious product featured on a popular television series, some have suggested that it could deliver the pleasurable effects of alcohol without its negative consequences such as memory loss and hangovers. To date, no such product exists.

See also Alternative Addiction Treatment; Problem Drinking.

FAQs about Alcoholism

The National Institute on Alcohol Abuse and Alcoholism (NIAAA) has posted a list of answers to frequently asked questions about alcohol use and alcoholism. It is not intended to represent diagnostic or medical advice but is general information to help readers make informed choices about alcohol use.

1. What is alcoholism? Alcoholism, also known as alcohol dependence, is a disease that includes the following four symptoms:
   • Craving—A strong need, or urge, to drink.

- Loss of control—Not being able to stop drinking once it has begun.
- Physical dependence—Withdrawal symptoms, such as nausea, sweating, shakiness, and anxiety after stopping drinking.
- Tolerance—The need to drink greater amounts of alcohol to get high.

2. Is alcoholism a disease? Yes, the craving that an alcoholic feels for alcohol can be as strong as the need for food or water. An alcoholic will continue to drink despite serious family, health, or legal problems. Like other diseases, alcoholism is chronic—meaning it lasts a person's lifetime—it usually follows a predictable course and has symptoms. The risk for developing alcoholism is influenced both by a person's genes and by his or her lifestyle.

3. Is alcoholism inherited? Research shows that the risk for developing alcoholism does run in families. The genes a person inherits partially explain this pattern, but lifestyle is also a factor. Currently, researchers are working to discover the actual genes that put people at risk for alcoholism. Friends, the amount of stress in someone's life, and how readily alcohol is available are also factors that may increase the risk of alcoholism. Its tendency to run in families does not mean a child of an alcoholic parent will automatically become an alcoholic. An individual can develop alcoholism even though no one in his or her family has a drinking problem.

4. Can alcoholism be cured? No, not at this time. Even if an alcoholic has not been drinking for a long time, he or she can still suffer a relapse. Not drinking is the safest course for most people with alcoholism.

5. Can alcoholism be treated? Yes, alcoholism treatment programs use both counseling and medications to help a person stop drinking. Treatment has helped people stop drinking and rebuild their lives.

6. Which medications treat alcoholism? There are oral medications that have been approved to treat alcohol dependence; an injectable, long-acting form of naltrexone (Vivitrol) is available. These medications have been shown to help people with dependence reduce drinking, avoid relapse to heavy drinking, and achieve and maintain abstinence.

7. Does alcoholism treatment work? Alcoholism treatment works for many people. However, like such chronic illnesses as diabetes, high blood pressure, and asthma, there are varying levels of success when it comes to treatment. Some people stop drinking and remain sober. Others have long periods of sobriety with bouts of relapse. Still others cannot stop drinking for any length of time. With treatment, the longer a person abstains from alcohol, the more likely he or she will be able to stay sober.

8. Does someone have to be an alcoholic to experience problems? No, alcoholism is only one type of an alcohol problem. Alcohol abuse can be just as harmful. A person can abuse alcohol without being an alcoholic—that is, he or she may drink too much and too often but still not be dependent on alcohol. Some of the problems linked to alcohol abuse include not being able to meet work, school, or family responsibilities; drunk-driving arrests and car crashes; and drinking-related medical conditions. Under some circumstances, social or moderate drinking can be dangerous—for example, while driving, during pregnancy, or when taking certain medications.

9. Are specific groups of people more likely to have problems? Alcohol abuse and alcoholism cut across gender (the father to son transmission of alcoholism is particularly strong; the son of an alcoholic is 9 times at greater risk compared to the general population), race, and nationality. In the United States, 17.6 million people—about 1 in every 12 adults—abuse alcohol or are alcohol dependent. In general, more men than women are alcohol dependent or have alcohol problems. Alcohol problems are highest among young adults ages 18–29 and lowest among adults ages 65 and older. People who start drinking at an early age—for example, at age 14 or younger—are at much higher risk of developing alcohol problems at some point in their lives compared to someone who starts drinking at age 21 or older.

10. Can a problem drinker simply cut down? If that person is an alcoholic, the answer is no. Alcoholics who try to cut down on drinking rarely succeed. Cutting out alcohol—that is, abstaining—is usually the best course for recovery. People who are not alcohol dependent, but who have experienced alcohol-related problems, might be able to limit the amount they drink. If they cannot stay within those limits, then they need to stop drinking completely.

11. What is a safe level of drinking? For most adults, moderate alcohol use—up to 2 drinks per day for men and 1 drink per day for women and older people—causes few, if any, problems. (One drink equals one 12-ounce bottle of beer or wine cooler, one 5-ounce glass of wine, or 1- to 3-ounces of 80-proof distilled spirits.) Certain people should not drink at all, however:
    - Women who are pregnant or trying to become pregnant
    - People who plan to drive or engage in other activities that require alertness and skill (such as driving a car)
    - People taking certain over-the-counter or prescription medications
    - People with medical conditions that can be made worse by drinking
    - Recovering alcoholics
    - People younger than age 21

12. Is it safe to drink during pregnancy? No, alcohol can harm the baby of a mother who drinks during pregnancy. Although the highest risk is to babies whose mothers drink heavily, it is not clear yet whether there is any completely safe level of alcohol during pregnancy. For this reason, the U.S. Surgeon General released advisories in 1981, and again in 2005, urging women who are pregnant or may become pregnant to abstain from alcohol. The damage caused by prenatal alcohol use includes a range of physical, behavioral, and learning problems in babies. Babies most severely affected have what is called Fetal Alcohol Syndrome (FAS).

13. Does alcohol affect older people differently? Alcohol's effects vary with age. Slower reaction times, problems with hearing and seeing, and a lower tolerance to alcohol's effects put older people at higher risk for falls, car crashes, and other types of injuries that may result from drinking. Mixing alcohol with over-the-counter or prescription medications can be very dangerous, even fatal. Alcohol also can make many medical conditions more serious.

14. Does alcohol affect women differently? Yes, alcohol affects women differently than men. Women become more impaired than men after drinking the same

amount of alcohol even when differences in body weight are taken into account. Chronic alcohol abuse also takes a heavier physical toll on women than on men. Alcohol dependence and related medical problems, such as brain, heart, and liver damage, progress more rapidly in women than in men.

15. Is alcohol good for the heart? Studies have shown that moderate drinkers are less likely to die from one form of heart disease than are people who do not drink any alcohol or who drink more. However, heavy drinking can actually increase the risk of heart failure, stroke, and high blood pressure, as well as cause other medical problems, such as liver cirrhosis.

16. When taking medications, should someone stop drinking? Possibly. More than 150 medications interact harmfully with alcohol. These interactions may result in increased risk of illness, injury, and even death. Alcohol's effects are heightened by medicines that depress the central nervous system, such as sleeping pills, antihistamines, antidepressants, anti-anxiety drugs, and some painkillers. Medicines for certain disorders, including diabetes, high blood pressure, and heart disease, also can have harmful interactions with alcohol.

17. How can a person get help for an alcohol problem? There are many national and local resources that can help. The National Drug and Alcohol Treatment Referral Routing Service provides a toll-free telephone number, 1-800-662-HELP (4357), offering information. Most people also find support groups a helpful aid to recovery. The following list includes a variety of resources:
    - Al-Anon/Alateen
    - Alcoholics Anonymous (AA)
    - National Association for Children of Alcoholics (NACOA)
    - National Clearinghouse for Alcohol and Drug Information (NCADI)

The "Alcoholism" Gene?

No alcoholism gene or group of genes has yet been shown to cause alcoholism. However, the National Institute on Drug Abuse (NIDA) has identified several chromosomal regions with "candidate genes" related to alcoholism and other addictions. Most are related to an individual's elevated risk for developing alcoholism, but some have been shown to be protective.

The increased risk for alcoholism associated with the following genetic variations is most likely to arise from the interaction among several. This interaction could be partially responsible for depression or anxiety, which the individual attempts to ease with alcohol, or it may influence alcohol metabolism in such a way that the drug has a more potent effect. In fact, variants of the CHRM2 gene are associated with depression and alcoholism, but it is not yet known how they are implicated.

Candidate Genes Associated With Alcoholism

Chromosomes 2, 5, 6, 13

- Genetic analyses have shown that hundreds of genes on these chromosomes are likely to be responsible for certain neural deficits associated with alcoholism.

- *ALDH1* encodes for aldehyde dehydrogenase that is an alcohol-metabolizing enzyme, and it seems to confer some protection. A variant in this gene often seen in Asian populations causes the enzyme to work more slowly. This is why certain members of Chinese, Japanese, or other East Asian backgrounds who consume even small amounts of alcohol may become flushed, overly warm, and develop weakness and palpitations. Although significantly milder, this biochemical reaction is identical to one elicited in individuals who mix alcohol with the drug disulfuram (Antabuse). The ALDH1 genetic variation is seen in 44 percent of Japanese, 53 percent of Vietnamese, 27 percent of Koreans, and 30 percent of Chinese, yet is rare in people of European descent. Because of the adverse reaction to alcohol the presence of this genetic variant causes, it can protect against developing the disease.
- Certain variants of the *ADH4* gene, particularly in people of European descent, increase the risk of alcoholism.
- *GABRA* variants are associated with delinquent behavior and alcohol dependence as individuals grow older.

Chromosome 7

- *CHRM2* encodes for the muscarinic acetylcholine receptor M2; it regulates neural signaling and is also linked to major depression.
- *HTAS2R16* contributes to sensitivity to bitter tastes and has been significantly linked to alcoholism.

Chromosome 8

- *OPRK1* encodes for an opioid receptor associated with regulating aversion and reward; it is also linked to the stress response and may play a role in heroin and cocaine habituation.

Chromosome 11

- *DRD2* is a dopamine receptor that regulates reward reinforcement.

Chromosome 15

- *GABRG3* encodes for a $GABA_A$ receptor subunit that regulates neural signaling.

Chromosome 20

- *PDYN*, similar to OPRK1 on chromosome 8, encodes for an opioid receptor.

"Fun" Facts

- The reason drinking alcohol causes excessive urination has nothing to do with the amount consumed but rather with alcohol's effect on the endocrine system.
- The Bureau of Alcohol, Tobacco, and Firearms (BAFT) bans the word "refreshing" to describe any alcoholic beverage.
- A person can be sent to jail for 5 years for sending a bottle of beer, wine, or spirits as a gift to a friend in Kentucky.

- Texas state law prohibits taking more than 3 sips of beer at a time while standing.
- No alcoholic beverages can be displayed within 5 feet of a cash register of any store in California that sells both alcohol and motor fuel.
- An owner or employee of an establishment in Iowa that sells alcohol cannot legally consume a drink there after closing for business.
- It is illegal in New Jersey for parents to give children under the age of 18 even a sip of alcohol.
- Nebraska state law prohibits bars from selling beer unless they are simultaneously brewing a kettle of soup.
- Ohio state law prohibits getting a fish drunk.
- Vikings used the skulls of their enemies as drinking vessels.
- McDonald's restaurants in some European countries serve alcohol because parents would otherwise be less willing to take their children there.
- Thousands of birds in Sweden became intoxicated by gorging on fermenting berries; about 50 lost their lives by flying into nearby windows.
- The United States has the strictest youth drinking laws in western civilization.
- It is illegal in Utah to advertise drink prices, alcohol brands, to show a drinking scene, to promote happy hour, to advertise free food, or for restaurants to furnish alcoholic beverage lists unless a customer specifically requests one.
- The highest price ever paid for distilled spirits at auction was $79,552 for a 50-year-old bottle of Glenfiddich whiskey in 1992.
- Abstention is much more common in the United States than in any other western country.
- The world's oldest known recipe is for beer.
- Alcoholic beverages have been produced for at least 12,000 years.
- A Chinese imperial edict of about 1116 B.C.E. asserted that the use of alcohol in moderation was required by heaven.
- During the Middle Ages, monasteries predominantly maintained the knowledge and skills necessary to produce quality alcoholic beverages.
- Distillation was developed during the Middle Ages, and the resulting alcohol was called aqua vitae or "water of life."
- The adulteration of alcoholic beverages was punishable by death in medieval Scotland.
- Drinking liqueurs was required at all treaty signings during the Middle Ages.
- It is illegal in Indiana for liquor stores to sell milk or cold soft drinks. They can, however, sell unrefrigerated soft drinks.
- An attorney general of Kansas issued the legal opinion that drinking on an airliner was forbidden by state law when the plane was in airspace over "dry" Kansas, saying that "Kansas goes all the way up and all the way down."
- The Pilgrims landed at what is now Plymouth, Massachusetts rather than continue sailing because they were running out of supplies, especially alcoholic beverages.
- Anyone under the age of 21 who takes out household trash containing even a single empty alcoholic beverage container can be charged with illegal possession of alcohol in Missouri.

- The county in Texas with the highest DWI arrests among young drivers is dry.
- The body or lightness of whiskey is primarily determined by the size of the grain from which it is made; the larger the grain, the lighter the whiskey.
- Franklin D. Roosevelt was elected President of the United States in 1932 on a pledge to end Prohibition.
- Shochu, a beverage distilled from barley, was the favorite beverage of the world's longest-living man, Shigechiyo Izumi of Japan, who lived for 120 years and 237 days.
- One glass of milk can give a person a .02 blood alcohol concentration (BAC) on a Breathalyzer test.
- Martha Washington enjoyed daily toddies. In the 1790s, happy hour began at 3:00 p.m. and cocktails continued until dinner.
- The bill for a celebration party for the 55 drafters of the U.S. Constitution was for 54 bottles of Madeira, 60 bottles of claret, 8 bottles of whiskey, 22 bottles of port, 8 bottles of hard cider, 12 beers, and 7 bowls of alcohol punch large enough that "ducks could swim in them."
- Alcohol is considered the only proper payment for teachers among the Lepcha people of Tibet.
- The U.S. national anthem, the "Star-Spangled Banner," was written to the tune of a drinking song.
- Beer was not sold in bottles until 1850; it was not sold in cans until 1935.
- The corkscrew was invented in 1860.
- The longest recorded champagne cork flight was 177 feet and 9 inches, four feet from level ground at Woodbury Vineyards in New York.
- The purpose of the indentation at the bottom of a wine bottle is to strengthen the structure of the bottle.
- Methyphobia is fear of alcohol.
- The U.S. region (commonly known as the Bible Belt) that consumes the least amount of alcohol is also known by doctors as Stroke Alley.
- Drinking lowers rather than raises the body temperature; there is an illusion of increased heat because alcohol causes the capillaries to dilate and fill with blood.
- Johnny Appleseed probably distributed apple seeds across the U.S. frontier so that people could make fermented apple juice (hard cider) rather than grow apple trees.
- White lightning is a name for illegally distilled spirits. All spirits are clear or "white" until aged in charred oak barrels.
- Temperance activists, who strongly opposed the consumption of alcohol, typically consumed patent medicines that, just like whiskey, generally contained 40 percent alcohol.
- British men have been found twice as likely to know the price of their beer as their partner's bra size.
- In Bangladesh, $5 will buy a beer or a first-class train ticket for a cross-country trip.
- The average number of grapes needed to make a bottle of wine is 600.
- The pressure in a bottle of champagne is about 90 pounds per square inch. That's about 3 times the pressure in automobile tires.

- Adolf Hitler was one of the world's best-known teetotalers or abstainers from alcohol; his adversary, Sir Winston Churchill, was one of the world's best-known heavy drinkers.
- The Puritans loaded more beer than water onto the Mayflower before they cast off for the New World.
- While there was not any cranberry sauce, mashed potatoes, sweet potatoes, or pumpkin pie to eat at the first Thanksgiving, there was beer, brandy, gin, and wine to drink.
- Colonial taverns were often required to be located near a church or meetinghouse.
- George Washington, Benjamin Franklin, and Thomas Jefferson all enjoyed brewing or distilling alcoholic beverages.
- The Colonial Army supplied its troops with a daily ration of four ounces of either rum or whiskey.
- In the 1830s, the average American aged 15 or older consumed over 5 or 6 gallons of alcohol per year.
- Whiskey and whisky both refer to alcohol distilled from grain. Whiskey is the usual American spelling, especially for beverages distilled in the United States and Ireland. Whisky is the spelling for Canadian and Scotch distilled beverages.
- There is no worm in tequila. It is actually a butterfly caterpillar, and it is in mescal, a spirit beverage distilled from a different plant.
- Bourbon takes its name from Bourbon County in Kentucky where it was first produced in 1789 by a Baptist minister.
- Alcohol is derived from the Arabic "al kohl," meaning "the essence."
- The saying "Mind your P's and Q's" comes from a time when alcoholic beverages were served in pints and quarts; to mind your P's and Q's meant to be careful how much you drank.
- In ancient Babylon, the bride's father would supply his son-in-law with all the mead (fermented honey beverage) he could drink for a month after the wedding; this period was called the "honey month," now called the "honeymoon."
- White wine is usually produced from red grapes.
- There are an estimated 49 million bubbles in a bottle of champagne.
- The strongest that any alcoholic beverage can be is 190 percent proof (or 95 percent alcohol). At higher proof, the beverage draws moisture from the air and self-dilutes.
- In Medieval England, beverage alcohol was often served with breakfast.
- Moderate consumption of alcohol does not appear to contribute to weight gain.
- Over half of the hospitals in the largest 65 metropolitan areas in the United States have reported that they offer alcoholic beverage service to their patients.
- High protein foods such as cheese and peanuts help slow the body's absorption of alcohol.
- Designated driver and similar programs have reduced drunk driving by around 25 percent over a period of 10 years.

- The body absorbs a mixed drink containing a carbonated beverage more quickly than straight shots.

Source: Adapted from Hanson, D. J. http://www.alcoholinformation.org, © 1977–2007. Courtesy of David Hanson.

Facts about Alcohol

- Children who begin smoking tobacco before the age of 13 are significantly more at risk for alcohol problems.
- Among high school seniors, alcohol use is more prevalent among Caucasian and Hispanic students than among African-American students.
- Junior, middle, and senior high school students consume 35 percent of wine coolers sold in the United States as well as 1.1 billion cans of beer.
- Thirty percent of children in grades 4 through 6 state that they have been pressured by peers to drink beer.
- The total cost of alcohol use by young people, including automobile crashes, violent crime, alcohol poisoning, burns, drowning, suicide attempts, and fetal alcohol syndrome, is more than $58 billion each year.
- Most teenagers do not know that a 12-ounce can of beer has the same amount of alcohol as a shot of whiskey or a 5-ounce glass of wine.
- The U.S. Substance Abuse and Mental Health Services Administration's (SAMHSA) National Survey on Drug Use and Health found that among full-time college students aged 18 to 20, the rates of binge drinking and heavy alcohol use in the past month remained steady from 2002 to 2005. Binge drinking is defined as 5 or more drinks on the same occasion at least one day in the past month.
- Based on combined data from the 2002 to 2005 National Surveys on Drug Use and Health, 57.8 percent of full-time college students underage for legal drinking used alcohol in the past month, 40.1 percent engaged in binge drinking, and 16.6 percent engaged in heavy drinking.
- Based on the 2002–2005 combined data of full-time college students aged 18 to 20, males were more likely than females to have used alcohol in the past month (60.4 percent vs. 55.6 percent), binge drink (46.9 percent vs. 34.4 percent), or drink heavily (22.7 percent vs. 11.5 percent).
- Asian youths were less likely to have used alcohol during the past year than Hispanic, white, or American Indian/Alaska Native youths. Filipino youths were more likely to have used alcohol during the past year than Chinese or Asian Indian youths.

Further Reading

American Psychiatric Association. *Diagnostic and Statistical Manual of Mental Disorders*, 4th Edition, Text Revision. Washington, DC: American Psychiatric Association, 2000.

Fingarette, Herbert. *Heavy Drinking: The Myth of Alcoholism as a Disease*. London: University of California Press, 1988.

Hanson, David J. *Alcohol Problems and Solutions*. August 2007. Retrieved from http://www.alcoholinformation.org

Jellinek, E. M. *The Disease Concept of Alcoholism*. New Haven: Hillhouse Press, 1960.

Johnson, Vernon E. *I'll Quit Tomorrow*. Revised edition. New York: Harper-Collins, 1980.

Ketcham, Katherine, and Asbury, William. *Beyond the Influence: Understanding and Defeating Alcoholism*. New York: Bantam Books, 2000.

Ketcham, Katherine, and Pace, Nicholas A. *Teens Under the Influence: The Truth About Kids, Alcohol, and Other Drugs*. New York: Ballantine Books, 2003.

Knapp, Caroline. *Drinking: A Love Story*. New York: The Dial Press, 1996.

McGovern, George. *Terry: My Daughter's Life-and-Death Struggle with Alcoholism*. New York: Penguin Books, 1997.

Milam, James, and Ketcham, Katherine. *Under the Influence: A Guide to the Myths and Realities of Alcoholism*. New York: Bantam Books, 1983.

Nurnberger, John I., Jr., and Bierut, Laura Jean. Seeking the Connections: Alcoholism and Our Genes. *Scientific American* April 2007: 296(4), 46–53.

Powter, Susan. *Sober . . . And Staying That Way*. New York: Simon & Schuster, 1997.

Quertemont, Etienne, and Didone, Vincent. Role of Acetaldehyde in Mediating the Pharmacological and Behavioral Effects of Alcohol. *Alcohol Research & Health* 2006: 29(4), 258–265.

Tracy, Sarah, and Acker, Caroline Jean, eds. *Altering American Consciousness: The History of Alcohol and Drug Use in the United States, 1800–2000*. Amherst and Boston: University of Massachusetts Press, 2004.

U.S. Department of Health and Human Services. *Results from the 2006 National Survey on Drug Use and Health: National Findings*. Substance Abuse and Mental Health Services Administration, Office of Applied Studies. DHHS Publication No. SMA 07-4293, 2007.

U.S. Department of Health and Human Services, Centers for Disease Control and Prevention (CDC), November 2007. Retrieved from http://www.cdc.gov

U.S. Department of Health and Human Services, National Institute of Mental Health (NIMH), March 2008. http://www.nimh.nih.gov

U.S. Department of Health and Human Services, National Institute on Alcohol Abuse and Alcoholism (NIAAA), July 2007. Retrieved from http://www.niaaa.nih.gov

U.S. Department of Health and Human Services, National Institute on Drug Abuse (NIDA), June 2007. Retrieved from http://www.nida.gov

U.S. Department of Health and Human Services, Substance Abuse and Mental Health Services Administration (SAMHSA), August 2007. Retrieved from http://www.samhsa.gov

Vaillant, George. *The Natural History of Alcoholism Revisited*. Cambridge, MA: Harvard University Press, 1995.

White, William. The Rebirth of the Disease Concept of Alcoholism in the 20th Century. *Counselor Magazine* December 2000: 1(2), 62–66.

Alpha-Ethyltryptamine (AET). *See* Psilocybin and Psilocin.

Alternative Addiction Treatment Many alcoholics and drug addicts reject the heavy emphasis on spirituality that **Alcoholics Anonymous (AA)** and the **Minnesota model** embrace; rather, they seek support through groups that meet their unique needs, or they prefer treatment options that stress the development of self-reliance and emotional maturity leading to independence from support groups. For them, and for those who find total abstinence unacceptable or impossible, alternative treatments have been developed including harm-reduction strategies that focus on the negative consequences of drug and alcohol addiction rather than on drug use. Known as tertiary levels of prevention and treatment, such strategies—needle-sharing programs to prevent HIV and other diseases, less-than-total abstinence, or the use of medical marijuana—can be controversial. Other alternative approaches that represent primary prevention efforts, which discourage the use of drugs entirely, or secondary strategies, which involve identifying and addressing the underlying sociological or psychological causes of addiction, include the following:

Moderation Management (MM)

Dedicated to helping alcoholics moderate their drinking, MM was founded in 1993. Designed primarily for those with early-stage **alcoholism**, it has been heavily criticized by mainstream treatment professionals who insist that total abstinence is the only viable treatment for any stage of alcoholism. Fueling their argument is the fact that MM's founder, Audrey Kishline, caused a fatal accident in March of 2000 that killed two people while she was driving drunk. Supporters say Kishline, already severely alcoholic when she founded the program, was not a good candidate for MM's approach, and her relapse proves that although MM can help problem drinkers control their drinking, it is not for alcoholics. After the accident, Kishline's attorney reported that Kishline herself stated that "moderation management is nothing but alcoholics covering up their problem."

Like other programs, MM proposes several steps to **recovery** that include attending meetings, examining one's reasons for and patterns of drinking, establishing priorities and goals, and periodically reviewing progress. Specific limitations that are placed on drinking behavior include:

1. Never drink and drive.
2. Never drink when it would endanger oneself or others.
3. Avoid drinking every day.
4. Limit the amount of alcohol consumed per week.

Rational Recovery (RR)

Founded in 1986, RR is a self-recovery movement that has undergone substantive changes in the 20 years since it began. The organization grew rapidly at first, but then found that its central principles began to diverge. One group broke off to form a new entity called Self Management and Recovery Training (SMART). The original RR group now places its emphasis on what it calls an "addictive voice recognition technique" (AVRT). Members believe that by learning to recognize one's addictive voice, which is any thinking that supports or suggests the use of alcohol or drugs, an addict can identify the triggers driving his or her addiction and thereby gain power over it.

RR does not involve meetings or traditional forms of therapy, one-day-at-a-time abstinence measures, or the use of medications such as naltrexone to help treat addiction. Proponents believe such methods keep the addictive voice alive, and they disdain addiction scientists who they claim are employed or funded by the for-profit treatment industry. The organization's Web site offers a crash course in self-treatment.

Secular Organizations for Sobriety (SOS)

Another organization founded in 1986 is SOS—also known as Save Our Selves. It is a network of groups that focuses on personal responsibility for addressing and recovering from addiction while relying on the support and assistance of one's chosen SOS group. The SOS Web site posts a clearinghouse that offers links to the whole network. Meetings are offered in many cities throughout the United States and in other countries.

The organization's principles are embodied in its proposed steps to recovery:

1. Acknowledge one's alcoholism/addiction.
2. Reaffirm the presence of the disease and recommit to the knowledge that, no matter what, it is not possible to drink or use again.
3. Take whichever steps are necessary to maintain sobriety.
4. Recognize that life's uncertainties cannot be used as an excuse to use or drink, and that life can be good without drugs.
5. As clean and sober individuals, be able to share thoughts and feelings with one another.
6. Maintaining sobriety should be a first priority.

Self Management and Recovery Training (SMART)

An outgrowth of the RR movement, SMART began operations in 1994 with the goal of helping addicts gain the maturity and self-reliance needed to identify and eliminate self-destructive attitudes and behaviors that result from them. Encouraging addicts to practice abstinence, develop emotional independence, and reduce their need for support groups are its three principal goals. The fundamental belief that addicts need to gain maturity and self-reliance underlie its program.

SMART meetings can be found throughout the United States and around the world and can help addicts benefit from the latest scientific approaches to addictions treatment and learn techniques for self-directed change in their lives.

Women for Sobriety (WFS)

In 1975, WFS was founded based on the perceived need for a woman-centered group that addressed the unique perspectives and problems of women suffering from alcoholism. Although its principles are similar to those of AA, it defines member's approach to recovery somewhat differently:

1. Accept responsibility for the disease and take charge of one's own life.
2. Remove negative thinking from one's life.
3. Develop a happy state of mind rather than waiting for it to just happen.
4. Understand problems so they do not become overwhelming.
5. Believe in oneself as a capable, compassionate, and caring woman.
6. Make one's life a great experience through conscious effort.
7. Embrace caring and love to change the world.
8. Focus on keeping one's priorities in order.
9. By viewing oneself as renewed, refuse to be submerged in the past.
10. Understand that love given is also returned.
11. Work to develop an enthusiasm for life.
12. Appreciate one's own competence.
13. Focus on being responsible for one's life and thoughts.

The WFS program views the treatment of alcoholism as proceeding in 6 stages, each focusing on some of the 13 principles. Level 4 of recovery, for example, embraces the concepts embedded in principles number 3, 6, and 11.

WFS groups originated in the United States, but there are also groups in Canada, Europe, Australia, and New Zealand.

See also Twelve-Step Programs.

Further Reading

Lemanski, Michael. *A History of Addiction and Recovery in the United States.* Tucson, AZ: See Sharp Press, 2001.

Marlatt, G. Alan, ed. *Harm Reduction: Pragmatic Strategies for Managing High-Risk Behaviors.* New York: The Guilford Press, 1998.

Peele, Stanton. *7 Tools to Beat Addiction.* New York: Three Rivers Press, 2004.

Schaler, Jeffrey A. Addiction Is a Choice. *Psychiatric Times* October 2002: 19(10), 54, 62.

Ambien. *See* Barbiturates.

Amino Acids. *See* Neurotransmitters.

Amphetamines Amphetamines are a group of addictive central nervous system **stimulants**. They are often prescribed to suppress appetite and treat obesity, increase concentration and focus in people with attention-deficit hyperactivity disorders, or promote wakefulness in narcoleptics, patients subject to uncontrollable sleeping patterns. Also known as "speed" or "uppers," amphetamines are listed on Schedule II of the **Controlled Substances Act (CSA)** due to their high potential for **abuse**.

In the **brain**, amphetamines act somewhat differently from **cocaine**, another potent stimulant, because they prevent the reuptake of dopamine significantly longer and thus have a prolonged effect. One of the most notorious amphetamines is **methamphetamine**, a highly addictive and destructive drug that can be easily manufactured in basement or garage laboratories. Other familiar amphetamines are well-known pharmaceuticals such as **methylphenidate** (Ritalin) and **dextroamphetamine** (Adderall), both of which are prescribed to treat attention-deficit hyperactivity disorders, usually in children. Decongestants sold over the counter often contain amphetamine-like drugs that include **ephedrine**, pseudoephedrine, and phenylpropanolamine. These are less potent than the more addictive amphetamines, but because they are used in the manufacture of much more potent drugs like methamphetamine, they are on List I of the CSA and are subject to controls mandated under the Combat Methamphetamine Epidemic Act of 2005 to monitor the accessibility and sale of products containing the drug.

An illicit **hallucinogen** that is sometimes categorized as an amphetamine is 3,4-methylenedioxymethamphetamine (MDMA), or **Ecstasy**, a so-called **designer drug**. Depending on dosage and frequency of use, drugs like Ecstasy initially produce feelings of closeness and animation that encourage social interaction and physical activity. As a type of hallucinogenic drug, it may also distort perception and sensation.

In addition to the characteristic rush of euphoria, alertness, and sense of well-being that amphetamine use produces, users may also display anxiety, repetitive behaviors, and aggressiveness. Excessive or prolonged use can result in paranoid or psychotic episodes involving delusions, violence, confusion, and hyperactivity or **hypersexuality**, which may encompass unsafe sexual practices leading to the spread of illness. Physical consequences of amphetamine abuse include irregular heartbeat, elevated blood pressure, nausea and vomiting, respiratory depression, and, potentially, seizures, coma, even death. **Withdrawal** is associated with fatigue, muscle cramps, headaches, sleep disturbances and nightmares, and severe depression, sometimes of suicidal intensity. Users who binge for days on "speed runs" ingest dose after dose of amphetamines not only to re-experience the rush but also to avoid the inevitable torment of a crash and subsequent withdrawal.

Further Reading

Califano, Joseph A., Jr. *High Society: How Substance Abuse Ravages America And What to Do About It.* New York: Perseus Books, 2007.

Hoffman, John, and Froemke, Susan, eds. *Addiction: Why Can't They Just Stop?* New York: Rodale, 2007.

Home Box Office (HBO). In partnership with the Robert Wood Johnson Foundation, the National Institute on Drug Abuse, and the National Institute on Alcohol Abuse and Alcoholism. *Addiction: Why Can't They Just Stop?* Documentary. March 2007.

Ketcham, Katherine, and Pace, Nicholas A. *Teens Under the Influence: The Truth About Kids, Alcohol, and Other Drugs.* New York: Ballantine Books, 2003.

U. S. Department of Health and Human Services, National Institute on Drug Abuse (NIDA), June 2007. Retrieved from http://www.nida.gov

U. S. Department of Health and Human Services, Substance Abuse and Mental Health Services Administration (SAMHSA), August 2007. Retrieved from http://www.samhsa.gov

U. S. Department of Justice, Drug Enforcement Administration (DEA), March 2008. Retrieved from http://www.usdoj.gov/dea

Amygdala. *See* Brain and Addiction.

Anabolic Steroids Anabolic steroids, as distinguished from other steroids, promote tissue growth. Most are more properly called anabolic-androgenic steroids because they are based on a natural androgen, testosterone. Human growth hormone (HGH), produced by the pituitary as somatotropin, is another anabolic steroid. It stimulates cellular growth and division to build muscle and strength but comes with significant side effects such as gynecomastia (breast enlargement in boys and men) and other serious disorders. Anabolic steroids are legally produced to treat conditions related to stunted growth or testosterone deficiency, but they are often illegally synthesized for an illicit market that uses them primarily to enhance athletic skills and performance. In 1991, out of concern over a growing underground market for the drugs, the U.S. Congress decided to regulate anabolic steroids by placing them on the **Controlled Substances Act (CSA)** schedule.

These testosterone-derived drugs are not addictive in the same way that alcohol or **cocaine** is addictive. However, their effects on the user can be as rewarding as the effect of a psychoactive drug. For athletes or others who yearn to have a more muscular body, who have issues with poor self-esteem, or who are driven psychologically to excel at their chosen sports, the drugs can help deliver the desired results; achieving their particular goal can give users enough of an emotional boost to keep them using the dangerous drugs despite negative consequences, a behavior that is the hallmark of **addiction**. The perceived rewards that initial use of these drugs may provide are eventually replaced by the irritability, delusions, restlessness, insomnia, and hostility they are capable of producing.

In recent years, growing reports of adolescent use of anabolic steroids has raised concerns among policymakers, the sports industry, and healthcare professionals about the dangers these drugs pose. In contrast to past use by professional athletes, the **abuse** of anabolic steroids today has grown significantly among high school and college students who want to boost muscle mass and improve athletic performance. Studies funded by the National Institute on Drug Abuse report that even 8th graders—albeit a small percentage—admit to having used steroids at least once. The Centers for Disease Control and Prevention (CDC), which also conducts surveys of high school students throughout the United States, reported in 2005 that 4.8 percent of high school students have used steroid pills or shots without a prescription.

Anabolic steroids were developed originally to treat conditions characterized by deficient levels of testosterone such as delayed puberty, or, on an experimental **treatment** basis, osteoporosis. In veterinary medicine, they are used as growth supplements or to enhance physical features such as the texture of an animal's hair or coat. Originally diverted from these legitimate uses to illicit use, steroids are now smuggled in from other countries for sale in the United States or manufactured in clandestine laboratories. Often counterfeit drugs are sold to unsuspecting users. So pervasive are illegal anabolic steroids that they can be purchased at gyms, sports competitions, or even ordered by mail.

Taken orally, administered intramuscularly by means of an injection, or rubbed on the skin, anabolic steroids are "cycled," "stacked" or "pyramided" by users to minimize side effects and avoid **tolerance**. Cycling involves periodic instances of taking multiple doses of steroids and stopping again; stacking refers to the use of several drugs simultaneously; pyramiding describes the slow escalation of dosage followed by a de-escalation. Despite these tactics, the use of anabolic steroids can cause significant side effects and serious damage, especially to the liver and cardiovascular system, and promote aggressive behavior and mood swings.

Other side effects are also daunting. Men may suffer from premature and permanent balding, impotence, breast enlargement, testicular atrophy, and high blood pressure. Women may develop more masculine features, such as facial hair or a deeper voice, as well as smaller breasts and fewer menstrual cycles. Both sexes can develop acne. Alarmingly, adolescents who take these drugs are at risk for stunted growth, and users can suffer serious damage to the heart.

Under the CSA, anabolic steroids have been placed on Schedule III with severe penalties for sale or distribution. Possession of illegal steroids carries a maximum penalty of one year in prison and a minimum $1,000 fine for a 1st offense. Those who wish to restrict or cease their use of anabolic steroids often resort to other illegal steroids such as insulin, tamoxifen, or human chorionic gonadotropin. Dietary steroids such as dehydroepiandrosterone (DHEA) are also being used to substitute for anabolic steroids, and Congress is considering adding these to the CSA's controlled substances list. In 2004, an Anabolic Steroid Control Act was passed to place additional steroids under Schedule III and expand the Drug Enforcement Administration's regulatory and enforcement authority over steroid use.

All major sports organizations, including the International Olympic Committee, National Collegiate Athletic Association, National Basketball Association, National Football League, and the National Hockey League, have banned the use of anabolic steroids by their athletes, and some organizations have also banned the steroid precursors androstenedione. They also conduct urine testing to ensure compliance.

There are over 100 different kinds of anabolic steroids, which are available only by prescription. Some are Deca-Durabolin (nandrolone decanoate), Depo-Testosterone

(testosterone cypionate), Dianabol (methandrostenolone), Durabolin (nandrolone phenylpropionate), Equipoise (boldenone undecylenate), Oxandrin (oxandrolone), Anadrol (oxymetholone), and Winstrol (stanozolol). Street names include Arnolds, Gear, Gym Candy, Juice, Pumpers, Roids, Stackers, and Weight Trainers.

See also Drug Classes; Appendix B.

Further Reading

Califano, Joseph A., Jr. *High Society: How Substance Abuse Ravages America And What to Do About It.* New York: Perseus Books, 2007.

Hoffman, John, and Froemke, Susan, eds. *Addiction: Why Can't They Just Stop?* New York: Rodale, 2007.

Home Box Office (HBO). In partnership with the Robert Wood Johnson Foundation, the National Institute on Drug Abuse, and the National Institute on Alcohol Abuse and Alcoholism. *Addiction: Why Can't They Just Stop?* Documentary. March 2007.

Ketcham, Katherine, and Pace, Nicholas, A. *Teens Under the Influence: The Truth About Kids, Alcohol, and Other Drugs.* New York: Ballantine Books, 2003.

U.S. Department of Health and Human Services, National Institute on Drug Abuse (NIDA), June 2007. Retrieved from http://www.nida.gov

U.S. Department of Health and Human Services, National Institute on Drug Abuse. *Research Report Series: Anabolic Steroid Abuse.* NIH Publication No. 06-3721, August 2006.

U.S. Department of Health and Human Services, Substance Abuse and Mental Health Services Administration (SAMHSA), August 2007. Retrieved from http://www.samhsa.gov

U.S. Department of Justice, Drug Enforcement Administration (DEA), March 2008. Retrieved from http://www.usdoj.gov/dea

Analgesics. *See* Opiates.

Analogs. *See* Designer Drugs.

Anesthesia. *See* Opiates.

Anhedonia Anhedonia is the term used to describe an inability to anticipate or to feel pleasure. In an addicted person, it is caused by the neurological changes resulting from the cumulative effects of drugs on the **brain**. When the mesolimbic dopamine reward pathway has been overstimulated by addictive drugs, the brain compensates either by reducing the number of dopamine receptors on neurons in the reward pathway or by reducing the output of dopamine. Although an addict whose neurochemistry is thus affected will often increase the amount of drugs he or she uses to compensate for his or her diminished response, the pleasure continues to lessen or ceases altogether. This leads to boredom, frustration, and other emotions that can erupt in destructive and risky behaviors as the individual tries to inject excitement into his or her life. The focus of much research, the **neuroadaptation** that gives rise to anhedonia and other symptoms of mesolimbic system dysfunction can be treated, at least to a degree, with behavioral techniques and medications. Scientists hope to discover ways in which the brain can be naturally reset to return to permanent neurochemical functioning and regain its ability to process pleasure normally.

See also Reward Deficiency Syndrome.

Further Reading

Erickson, Carlton K. *The Science of Addiction: From Neurobiology to Treatment*. New York: Nortonhym, 2007.

Hyman, S. E., and Malenka, R. C. Addiction and the Brain: The Neurobiology of Compulsion and Its Persistence. *Nature Reviews Neuroscience* 2001: 2(10), 695–703.

Kalivas, Peter, and Volkow, Nora. The Neural Basis of Addiction: A Pathology of Motivation and Choice. *American Journal of Psychiatry* August 2005: 162(8), 1403–1413.

National Institute on Drug Abuse. *The Science of Addiction: Drugs, Brains, and Behavior*. NIH Publication No. 07-5605, February 2007.

Nestler, Eric, and Malenka, Robert. The Addicted Brain. *Scientific American* September 2007. Retrieved from http://www.sciam.com/article.cfm?chanID=sa006&colID=1&articleID=0001E 632-978A-1019-978A83414B7F0101

"Anonymous" Groups. *See* Twelve-Step Programs.

Anorexia Nervosa Anorexia nervosa is a complex and very serious disease in which an individual refuses to maintain minimally normal body weight, has irrational fears about gaining weight, and, in a condition known as body dysmorphic disorder, has a significantly distorted perception of the shape or size of his or her body. Between 0.5 to 3.7 percent of females suffer from the disease, a much higher percentage than males, who have roughly one-fourth the incidence of females. Most young women with anorexia stop menstruating, which is likely due to their bodies' reduced production of estrogen.

There are two types of anorexia: the restricting type, in which a person reduces the amount of food consumed, and the bingeing/purging type, in which he or she induces vomiting or uses diuretics and laxatives to purge food from the body. **Bulimia nervosa** is a related **eating disorder** that also involves bingeing and purging, but with bulimia the individual usually maintains normal weight.

Although anorexia is categorized as an eating disorder, some aspects of the disease meet the American Psychiatric Association's ***Diagnostic and Statistical Manual of Mental Disorders*** (*DSM*) criteria for major depressive disorder, social phobia, personality disorder, or **obsessive-compulsive disorder**. How the disease is characterized is based in part on the symptoms that individual patients have. Some, particularly those who are actually starving, may have symptoms of major depression; some have an obsessive preoccupation with food; some who are socially inhibited may be fearful of eating in front of others; and some may have **impulse control disorders** (ICDs). Additional psychological symptoms include low self-esteem, inflexibility, perfectionism, and a need to tightly control one's emotions or environment.

Anorexia typically appears in adolescents or young adults. Once, it was rare in people over 40 years old, but experts now report an increasing prevalence in women over 35. Initial onset might be the result of a stressful event and might be limited to one episode, but in most cases the disorder worsens over time. As in other ICDs like pathological gambling that are associated with addictive behavior, studies of identical twins show that there is a genetic component and an elevated risk among first-degree biological relatives. Neurological studies confirm that people with substance **abuse** and addictive behaviors share common chemical imbalances, especially in serotonin levels, that seem likely to contribute to these conditions. Despite this, the disease manifests differently in each individual.

When anorectic individuals begin losing weight, they usually do so because they are actually overweight or they have started to focus critically on specific areas of their bodies, such as thighs or hips, they consider too fat. Most begin obsessive exercise regimens to

DSM Criteria for Diagnosing Anorexia Nervosa

The following criteria used for diagnosing anorexia nervosa have been adapted from the 4th edition of the American Psychiatric Association's *Diagnostic and Statistical Manual of Mental Disorders* (*DSM*).

In anorexia nervosa, the person:

1. refuses to maintain or gain any weight above 85 percent of what is considered minimally normal for someone his or her age and height;
2. has an extreme fear of gaining weight despite already being underweight;
3. is excessively concerned with weight or body shape, is in denial over the seriousness of weight loss, or evaluates self-worth in terms of body shape and weight;
4. misses 3 menstrual periods in a row, if female, and is not pregnant or taking hormones.

In the *restricting* episodes of anorexia, the person does not usually purge; in the *binge-eating/purging* episodes, he or she binges and purges on a regular basis.

Source: Adapted from American Psychiatric Association, 2000.

Symptoms

Before significant weight loss occurs, there are signs indicating a problem may be developing. The earlier the patient or concerned others can seek treatment, the more likely it is to be successful. Professional help is advisable if the person in question:

1. Shows evidence of bingeing and purging; spends time in the bathroom immediately after eating and disguises bathroom noises; smells occasionally of vomit or evidence of vomit is discovered; uses an unusual amount of breath mints; maintains a supply of laxatives, diuretics, enema preparations, or diet pills
2. Engages in fasting and/or excessive, even obsessive, exercise regimens
3. Buys and compulsively consumes large quantities of junk or non-nutritious food without any weight gain
4. Abuses substances and/or has mood or personality disorders
5. Exhibits signs of perfectionism, rigidity, or obsessive self-control
6. Shows an excessive interest in weight issues and dieting
7. Develops new eating habits such as refusing to eat with others, spreading food around the plate, or cutting food into small pieces to postpone eating
8. Has excuses to avoid eating, such as not feeling well
9. Hides food that he claims to have already eaten

speed up the weight-loss process, further stressing their depleted bodies. Gradually excluding the more caloric foods from their diet, anorectics sometimes develop highly ritualistic, secretive eating patterns to disguise the extent of the disorder.

Losing weight gives an anorectic a perception of empowerment—feelings of achievement and mastery over his or her body. These feelings drive further weight-loss efforts despite obvious undernourishment. The person interprets any weight gain or even failure to lose as proof of poor self-discipline, a deficiency of willpower, a sign of weakness. In the kind of **denial** that characterizes **addiction**, the patient cannot recognize how aberrant his or her behavior has become, and, due to body dysmorphia, may be unable to perceive the extent of emaciation.

That anorectics derive any reward from starvation is one of the more puzzling aspects of this disease, yet there is evidence that they do. Some experts believe the reward lies in the anorectic's mission—to lose weight by refusing food relieves or suppresses the tensions and anxieties that are symptoms of anxiety or mood disorders. Others believe that subjecting the body to the stress of starvation triggers the release of endogenous opioids, the brain's natural feel-good chemicals that stimulate the reward pathway and produce feelings of calm and serenity. They liken this to a runner's high that athletes can experience after sustained exercise. Whether this occurs or not, neurological imaging confirms that key activity in specific regions of anorectics' **brains** parallels that seen in pathological gamblers and substance abusers whose addictive behaviors are used, at least in part, to relieve psychological discomfort.

Prevalence and Characteristics of Anorexia Nervosa

According to the National Institute of Mental Health (NIMH), over the course of a lifetime 0.5 to 3.7 percent of girls and women will develop anorexia nervosa and 1.1 to 4.2 percent will develop bulimia nervosa. About 0.5 percent with anorexia die each year as a result of the illness, making it one of the top psychiatric illnesses leading to death.

Anorexia generally is characterized by a resistance to maintaining a healthy body weight, an intense fear of gaining weight, and extreme behaviors that result in severe weight loss. People with anorexia see themselves as overweight even when they are dangerously thin. Eating disorders involve multiple biological, behavioral, and social factors that are not well understood.

A study funded by NIMH reported in August of 2006 that Internet-based intervention programs may help some college-age, high-risk women avoid developing an eating disorder. Although it cannot be assumed that people at risk would benefit from such online approaches to prevention, the programs may serve as valuable screening tools to help susceptible individuals seek treatment before the disease has progressed.

Source: National Institute of Mental Health. http://www.nimh.nih.gov/science-news/2006/college-women-at-risk-for-eating-disorder-may-benefit-from-online-intervention.shtml

---

Once the physical symptoms of starvation or actions of alarmed family members compel the patient to seek **treatment**, a physical exam can reveal the extent of serious damage. Blood tests may show low estrogen or testosterone levels in females or males, respectively, as well as liver dysfunction and electrolyte imbalances stemming partly from purging. Often, anemia, heart rhythm abnormalities, dehydration, and thyroid irregularities are observed. More obvious symptoms of starvation can be the growth of fine, downy hair over the body (lanugo), dry and pale or yellowish skin, brittle hair or hair loss, muscle atrophy, diabetes, cold intolerance, low blood pressure, slowed heart rate, dental problems, bone thinning, and emaciation. Some statistics indicate that the overall mortality rate from anorexia in females ages 15 to 24 is 12 times higher than mortality rates from all other causes. Suicide appears to account for roughly 20 percent of these deaths.

It is critical that treatment address the psychological components of this disease, factors that may have led to the anorexia itself and those associated with the physical and emotional stress the disease has inflicted. If the disorder is caught early, outpatient therapy from specially trained counselors may be appropriate. In more severe cases, hospitalization may be necessary, both to address physical issues arising from malnutrition and starvation and to assess psychiatric complications. Individual psychotherapy is sometimes desirable prior to cognitive behavioral therapy to identify the source of a patient's distorted perception of his or her physical self and to determine some of the motivating factors for his or her behavior. An important part of treatment is to help the patient learn how to reestablish proper eating patterns by introducing small, regular meals that should be eaten under controlled supervision. Positive reinforcement is given for every pound gained, and the supportive self-help techniques that **12-step programs** or other groups offer can be helpful, especially since this disease is intimately connected to the patient's self-image and self-esteem. Most experts also strongly recommend family therapy to help members recognize and avoid triggers arising from dysfunctional family dynamics that help fuel the disease.

Further Reading

American Psychiatric Association. *Diagnostic and Statistical Manual of Mental Disorders*, 4th Edition, Text Revision. Washington, DC: American Psychiatric Association, 2000.

Davis, Caroline. Addiction and the Eating Disorders. *Psychiatric Times* February 2001. Retrieved from http://www.psychiatrictimes.com/p010259.html

Erickson, Carlton K. *The Science of Addiction: From Neurobiology to Treatment*. New York: Norton, 2007.

Grant, Jon E., and Kim, S. W. *Stop Me Because I Can't Stop Myself: Taking Control of Impulsive Behavior*. New York: McGraw-Hill, 2003.

Hyman, S. E., and Malenka, R. C. Addiction and the Brain: The Neurobiology of Compulsion and Its Persistence. *Nature Reviews Neuroscience* 2001: 2(10), 695–703.

Kalivas, Peter, and Volkow, Nora. The Neural Basis of Addiction: A Pathology of Motivation and Choice. *American Journal of Psychiatry* August 2005: 162(8), 1403–1413.

Nestler, Eric J., and Malenka, Robert. The Addicted Brain. *Scientific American* September 2007. Retrieved fromhttp://www.sciam.com/article.cfm?chanID=sa006&colID=1&articleID=0001E6 32-978A-1019-978A83414B7F0101

Neumark-Sztainer, Dianne, Eisenberg, Marla, Fulkerson, Jayne, Story, Mary, and Larson, Nicole. Family Meals and Disordered Eating in Adolescents. *Archives of Pediatrics and Adolescent Medicine* 2008: 162(1), 17–22.

Ozelli, Kristin Leutwyler. This Is Your Brain on Food. *Scientific American* September 2007: 297(3), 84–85.

Sacker, Ira, and Buff, Sheila. *Regaining Your Self: Breaking Free from the Eating Disorder Identity: A Bold New Approach*. New York: Hyperion, 2007.

Antabuse. *See* Addiction Medications.

Antagonists Antagonists inhibit or counteract the activity of other drugs or **neurotransmitters**. They do this in 1 of 3 ways: by interfering with the release of the neurotransmitter into the synapse, by preventing another drug or natural neurotransmitter from binding to receptors, or by triggering the release of the neurotransmitter into the presynaptic neuron instead of out into the synapse where it can activate the receiving cell. Alcohol is an antagonist of glutamate; **lysergic acid diethylamide** (LSD) is an antagonist of serotonin.

See also Agonists.

Anxiety Disorders Anxiety, which can range from mild to crippling, is an emotional state brought on by the anticipation of a real or imaginary threat. It is characterized by varying degrees of fear, tension, restlessness, and irritability. In more advanced cases, when extreme psychological discomfort and physical distress might include profuse sweating, tremor, nausea and vomiting, diarrhea, and/or panic, it is classified as a psychiatric condition. Untreated, such a disorder can rise to intolerably intense levels; in individuals prone to substance **abuse**, drug **addiction** frequently results from the individual's need to self-medicate as a way to alleviate symptoms. Addiction worsens anxiety as the individual struggles to reduce the substance abuse, only to experience profound discomfort which triggers increased abuse of the drug. People caught in these cycles of anxious despair and addiction are susceptible to suicide.

In addition to generalized anxiety disorder, which is not restricted to specific fears, the American Psychiatric Association's ***Diagnostic and Statistical Manual of Mental Disorders*** (*DSM*) identifies other types of anxiety: panic disorder, posttraumatic stress disorder, social phobia (or social anxiety disorder), and specific phobias (such as a fear of heights or snakes). Panic attacks may surface in the absence of any apparent triggers and can be overwhelming in their sudden and alarming symptoms which include intense feelings of impending collapse or death, sweating, heart palpitations, jitteriness, tremor, restlessness, quivering voice, breathlessness, numbness, and feeling faint. While the symptoms are dramatic, panic attacks are not life threatening. Social phobia may be manifested by sweating, trembling, inability to speak, even dizziness and faintness. Posttraumatic stress disorder is sometimes characterized by vivid **flashbacks**, terror, nightmares, and, on occasion, violent behavior.

Anxiety disorders are often associated with other mental illnesses such as depression or **obsessive-compulsive disorder**. The likelihood of a **dual diagnosis** is so great that most mental health professionals automatically screen patients with anxiety disorders for co-occurring conditions. Such people respond best to **treatment** that combines medication and psychotherapy and, in some cases, relaxation techniques. Co-occurring conditions must be treated simultaneously if treatment is to be effective.

Further Reading

Hyman, Bruce. *Anxiety Disorders*. Minneapolis, MN: Twenty-First Century Books, 2006.

Anxiolytics Used principally to treat anxiety, anxiolytics are, in most cases, **barbiturates** and **benzodiazepines**—that is, sedatives and tranquilizers—that are in the class of drugs known as **depressants**. Available by prescription only, they are most often administered for their calming effects, as tranquilizing agents prior to surgery, and to reduce muscle spasms, but they can also be used to prevent seizures. With prolonged use, barbiturates and benzodiazepines are addictive, so they are seldom used for long-term anxiety relief. Instead, a serotonin **agonist** such as buspirone may be prescribed because it can be helpful in treating generalized **anxiety disorder** and it has the added advantage of not being addictive. However, because this medication does not provide the quick relief associated with benzodiazepines, people previously treated with fast-acting tranquilizers may be dissatisfied with their response to the serotonin agonist.

Some over-the-counter herbal anxiolytics include valerian, kava, and chamomile, and research shows that **marijuana** can be effective in reducing certain forms of anxiety as well. However, the evidence for the efficacy of herbal preparations is limited, and the fact that marijuana is a controlled substance has prevented adequate research from being conducted into its potential as an anxiolytic.

There are no medications currently approved for treating **addiction** to the depressant class of anxiolytics although cognitive behavioral therapy and **12-step programs** can be helpful.

Arson. *See* Pyromania.

Ativan. *See* Benzodiazepines.

Axon. *See* Brain and Addiction.

B

"Bagging." *See* Inhalants.

Barbiturates Barbiturates are a group of central nervous system **depressants** comprising anesthetics, sedative-hypnotics, and anticonvulsants. Some have a high potential for **abuse** and fall into Schedule II of the **Controlled Substances Act (CSA)**; these include pheno-barbital (Nembutal) and secobarbital (Seconal). Others, less addictive, are listed in Schedule III or IV.

Commonly prescribed during the first half of the 1900s, barbiturates are used less frequently nowadays due to their high **addiction liability**. Of the hundreds of compounds that have been synthesized, most are still prescribed for insomnia and other sleep disorders. In smaller doses, they can produce slurred speech and impaired motor coordination, and in heavier doses they can cause coma. In combination with alcohol or other central nervous system depressants, barbiturate use can be fatal.

Available only by prescription, barbiturates have effects ranging from very short to long, especially the compounds used for anesthetic purposes. Some newer CNS depressants on the market with barbiturate-like qualities are sedative-hypnotics. Examples are zolpidem (Ambien), zaleplon (Sonata), ethchlorvynol (Placidyl), eszopiclone (Lunesta), and ramelteon (Rozerem), which are approved for the short-term **treatment** of insomnia. These drugs have many properties in common with the **benzodiazepines** and, despite advertisements touting their safety, are subject to abuse and are listed in Schedule IV of the CSA.

Further Reading

Califano, Joseph A., Jr. *High Society: How Substance Abuse Ravages America And What to Do About It.* New York: Perseus Books, 2007.

Hoffman, John, and Froemke, Susan, eds. *Addiction: Why Can't They Just Stop?* New York: Rodale, 2007.

Home Box Office (HBO). In partnership with the Robert Wood Johnson Foundation, the National Institute on Drug Abuse, and the National Institute on Alcohol Abuse and Alcoholism. *Addiction: Why Can't They Just Stop?* Documentary. March 2007.

Ketcham, Katherine, and Pace, Nicholas A. *Teens Under the Influence: The Truth About Kids, Alcohol, and Other Drugs.* New York: Ballantine Books, 2003.

U.S. Department of Health and Human Services, National Institute on Drug Abuse (NIDA), June 2007. Retrieved from http://www.nida.gov

U.S. Department of Health and Human Services, Substance Abuse and Mental Health Services Administration (SAMHSA), August 2007. Retrieved from http://www.samhsa.gov

U.S. Department of Justice, Drug Enforcement Administration (DEA), March 2008. Retrieved from http://www.usdoj.gov/dea

Begleiter, Henri (1935–2006) Before his death in 2006, Henri Begleiter was a Distinguished Professor of Psychiatry and Neuroscience at Brooklyn's State University of New York Downstate Medical Center. He was a leading neuroscientist who made significant contributions to the study of the genetics of **alcoholism** and other **addictions**. His particular insight was the discovery that neural hyperexcitability is critically involved in the genetic predisposition to addiction and certain conduct and personality disorders.

Begleiter's research demonstrated that specifically measurable **brain** deficits are inherited, and, as such, represent a genetic predisposition to addiction rather than a consequence of it, as previously thought. He conducted studies during the 1970s comparing sons of alcoholics to sons of nonalcoholics, neither group having ever been exposed to alcohol or other drugs. The neural deficits that give rise to hyperexcitability were found only in the children of alcoholics. That hyperexcitability can be relieved by the ingestion of alcohol makes it more likely that an individual will develop an addiction to the substance. Even after years of abstinence, alcoholics retain the neural deficits. Genetic analyses have shown that hundreds of genes appearing on chromosomes 2, 5, 6, and 13 are likely to be involved, encoding, among other things, glutamate and **acetylcholine** receptors.

This finding helped drive the formation of the world's largest alcoholism study, the Collaborative Study on the Genetics of Alcoholism (COGA), to identify genes associated with the disease. As part of his groundbreaking research, Begleiter introduced the concept of using biological markers called endophenotypes to study the genetics of various disorders.

Further Reading

Galanter, Marc, et al., eds. *Recent Developments in Alcoholism: Treatment Research.* New York: Plenum Press, 1989.

Behavioral Addictions Behavioral addictions are, for the most part, comprised of **impulse control disorders** manifested by an inability to control the frequency or extent of a certain behavior or the impulsive urges that cause the behavior. To some, it is debatable whether they are true **addictions** since some behaviors do not produce the pleasure or gratification associated with **substance addictions**. Those impulse control disorders that are generally acknowledged to be addictions include **compulsive computer use** (Internet addiction), **compulsive shopping**, **self-injury** (including cutting behaviors**), intermittent explosive disorder** (rage addiction), **kleptomania** (stealing), **pathological gambling**, **pyromania** (fire-starting), **sexual addiction**, and **trichotillomania** (pulling out one's hair).

Although not all these disorders are grouped as impulse control disorders in the American Psychiatric Association's ***Diagnostic and Statistical Manual of Mental Disorders (DSM)***, increasing numbers of addictions experts are coming to regard them as synonymous with behavioral addictions. Because the difference between these disorders and **compulsions** is very slight in some respects, it is helpful to highlight a key distinction: An **impulse** generally involves urges that produce a strong drive to perform the behavior, which may feel good at the time but ultimately produces regret; a compulsion usually involves obsessive, unwelcome, and intrusive thoughts that an individual can relieve only by performing an act or series of actions that he or she knows to be irrational or excessive.

There is a great deal yet to be learned about these disorders, but research is revealing that people suffering from them may be grouped into three subtypes: those who have uncontrollable urges to engage in the behavior, those who do not have urges but engage in the behavior to escape negative feelings like loneliness or depression, and those who do have urges but only when they have negative feelings—in their case, the negative feelings are triggers for the urges and ultimately the behavior. Some people have urges for no apparent reason and others respond to triggers in the environment; an example is the case of pathological gamblers' reactions to billboard advertising for casino gambling. People who enjoy the urges and behaviors are not sure they want to stop in spite of the negative consequences the addiction has; they enjoy the rush and often report that they truly feel alive only during the behavior. Others are simply compelled to complete the behavior, even though there is no longer any thrill or pleasure. They report that they do it because they have to and not because they want to. Others fear that if they receive **treatment** and learn to stop their impulsive behavior, another form, equally destructive, will take its place. There is no evidence for this fear because rewards and pleasures are processed in the same area of the **brain**; treatments that relieve one impulse control disorder are highly likely to reduce others. However, addictions to nicotine, food, and certain drugs (excluding alcohol) may be exceptions because their impact on the brain is slightly different; some have compared the urges of an impulse control disorder to the **craving** a smoker experiences when wanting a **cigarette**.

Categorizing **eating disorders** is more complicated. Although bulimia is often viewed as an impulse control disorder, **anorexia nervosa** meets some of the *DSM* criteria for major depressive disorder, social phobia, and **obsessive-compulsive disorder**; obesity, which some consider the principal symptom of **food addiction**, is viewed by the psychiatric community as a general medical condition although it can arise from psychological factors.

Most interpret a rigid obsession with exercise or an extreme and compulsive devotion to one's work as addictions. People engage in recreational activities and deal with stress, depression, and anxiety in different ways, however. Sometimes excessive behaviors like "workaholism" represent attempts to alleviate psychological distress arising from other areas of life. It is when the person is unable to control his or her level of exercise or the time he or she devotes to work, or when the activity is damaging personal relationships, ordinary functioning, or health, that his exercise regimen or work schedule might reflect symptoms of a behavioral addiction.

Although the general public is not familiar with most impulse disorders, historical evidence suggests that they have existed for centuries. Pathological gambling was reported in ancient Rome, compulsive stealing was given the formal name "kleptomania" in 1838, and medical literature from the 1900s discusses compulsive sexual behavior. Today, the disorders are more common than people realize; some estimates suggest that, excluding eating disorders, 8 to 35 million people suffer from some form of them. The total number may be much higher because most cases go unrecognized, undiagnosed, or misdiagnosed; in other cases, affected individuals may be reluctant to report what they view as shameful or deviant behavior. Often there is comorbidity (co-occurring disorders or, **dual diagnosis**) such as depression or an **anxiety disorder**, which complicates diagnosis and creates confusion about the cause of the disorder. Although it cannot always be determined whether one condition leads to another, there is convincing evidence that **mental disorders** and addictive behaviors feed off of one another, and that one disorder cannot be managed unless the other is treated as well.

Impulse control disorders afflict both males and females, although certain ones disproportionately affect one gender more than another. Pathological gambling, for example, seems to afflict men more often than women, but the data on the incidence of this disorder is not complete due primarily to misdiagnosis and the reluctance of addicts to admit to the problem.

Aside from criminal behaviors such as stealing or assaults arising out of explosive episodes of rage, behavioral addictions can be extremely destructive. Sufferers often have to lie to their employers and families and create elaborate cover-ups to hide their activities. Many face financial ruin and other deprivations before they seek treatment, or they receive inappropriate treatment from family physicians or psychiatrists who are not trained to treat these complex disorders.

Not all cases of impulse control disorder interfere with normal functioning to a substantial degree; some people manage to function fairly well. On average, the longer the interval between when symptoms first appear and treatment begins, the more severe the disorder becomes. Although it is not necessarily disabling in its milder forms, its tendency to rob people of their ability to concentrate on normal activities, and the shame, remorse, and potential legal difficulties it presents, can be very damaging. Most sufferers who attempt to control urges by avoiding the behavior often find, to their dismay, that the urges intensify. Compulsive shoppers who avoid stores may discover they are so tortured by thoughts of shopping that they are unable to cope at all, and they are driven to act on their urges simply to be able to resume normal functioning for a few hours or days.

According to the professional literature, most behavioral addictions start in childhood, although some emerge in late adolescence or adulthood and have been documented in people in their 60s. This may be due to their tendency to develop gradually, so if someone steals occasionally in childhood, it may not be until adulthood that he or she begins to experience uncontrollable urges to repeat the behavior.

Clinical and research evidence shows that impulse control disorders are similar to substance addictions in that they arise from a complex interplay of biological, genetic, and environmental causes and are seated in the area of the brain that processes reward and pleasure. Unfortunately, because of their conviction that they are bad people lacking willpower, individuals suffering from behavioral addictions often do not seek treatment. Even if they could admit the nature of their addiction, they do not know that they are suffering from a treatable psychiatric disease. Roughly 50 percent of people diagnosed with impulse control disorders also have a history of substance **abuse**; whether this is due to the abnormal brain chemistry that both groups of disorders seem to share or if the negative emotions associated with impulse control disorders cause people to seek relief from drugs is not yet known. When these disorders do occur together, it is the substance disorder that is often treated whereas the impulse control disorder is ignored. Even healthcare professionals, unaware of the prevalence or manifestations of the disease, often misdiagnose the symptoms as a manic-depressive illness (bipolar disorder), obsessive-compulsive disorder, major depressive disorder, or borderline personality disorder, and patients are frequently prescribed inappropriate medications or therapies that do little to treat the real problem. Many people suffering from impulse control disorders report they have considered suicide as the only escape from the torment their affliction causes.

Researchers are learning that impulse control disorders, contrary to what many believe, probably do not arise from a precipitating trauma or event. For years, theories abounded that parental deprivation was a principal cause, and the individual's impulsive behavior may have represented an unconscious attempt to attract parental attention. Other theories suggest that because the disorder encourages people to engage in risk-taking behavior, which in turn stimulates the brain's opioid system to release soothing neurochemicals, affected people might be suffering from a chronic state of hyperarousal that the behavior attempts to treat. These theories have not been proven, but they may have a basis in fact—or could certainly be regarded as risk factors. There also seems to be some correlation with a family history of **alcoholism**, but the relationship between the two is not clear. Even though environmental exposures may influence whether the disorder ultimately takes the form of kleptomania or gambling, and even though psychological components almost certainly affect the manifestation or severity of the disorder to some degree, it seems irrefutable that biological influences are involved in its development.

As with substance addiction, adolescents are particularly vulnerable to behavioral addictions, but they also respond well to early **interventions**. Derailing the disease immediately is important not only to reduce its severity but also to prevent the shame, guilt, and remorse that interfere with a young person's struggle to develop a healthy sense of identity. Diagnosing the disorder(s) in adolescents can be difficult because their maturing process involves a degree of rebellion, novelty seeking, risk taking, and impulsivity. It takes an alert parent or teacher to detect a subtle shift from normal expressions of teenage rebellion and psychological growing pains to aberrant or pathological behavior.

Although there are no specific treatments designed to treat impulse control disorders, experts have found, in the short term, certain medications which can be extremely helpful, particularly selective serotonin reuptake inhibitors (SSRIs), opioid **antagonists**, or mood stabilizers that tend to rebalance neurochemistry and reduce impulsive urges. Although these medications are used off-label for impulse control disorders—that is, they have not been specifically formulated to treat these particular diseases—they have demonstrated efficacy in relieving symptoms and reducing destructive behaviors. Since the origins of the disorders reside in the same complex mix of physiological and neurological factors as substance addictions, they often respond to cognitive behavioral therapy when it is targeted to the unique needs of the individual and the particular manifestations of his or her disorder. People suffering from impulse control disorders—particularly adolescents—derive great benefit from learning new strategies to overcome destructive impulses and to prevent relapse. Relaxation, habit reversal, and stimulus control techniques are among these treatment strategies.

Impulse control disorders are not symptoms of an individual's character deficiencies or choices to be destructive, immoral, or weak. Rather, like substance addictions, they reflect neurobiological abnormalities and should be regarded as serious illnesses that can respond to appropriate medical, psychological, and behavioral therapy.

Further Reading

Erickson, Carlton K. *The Science of Addiction: From Neurobiology to Treatment*. New York: Norton, 2007.

Grant, Jon E., and Kim, S. W.. *Stop Me Because I Can't Stop Myself: Taking Control of Impulsive Behavior*. New York: McGraw-Hill, 2003.

Hyman, S. E., and Malenka, R. C. Addiction and the Brain: The Neurobiology of Compulsion and Its Persistence. *Nature Reviews Neuroscience* 2001: 2(10), 695–703.

Kalivas, P. W., and Volkow, N. The Neural Basis of Addiction: A Pathology of Motivation and Choice. *American Journal of Psychiatry* August 2005: 162(8), 1403–1413.

Nestler, Eric J., and Malenka, Robert. The Addicted Brain. *Scientific American*, September 2007. Retrieved from http://www.sciam.com/article.cfm?chanID=sa006&colID=1&articleID=0001E6 32-978A-1019-978A83414B7F0101

U.S. Department of Health and Human Services, *The Science of Addiction: Drugs, Brains, and Behavior.* NIH Publication No. 07-5605, February 2007.

U.S. Department of Health and Human Services, National Institute of Mental Health (NIMH), March 2008. Retrieved from http://www.nimh.nih.gov

Behavioral Sensitization Seen in addicts and others who subject their **brains** to repeated and persistent stimuli like addictive drugs, behavioral sensitization is the development of an increased response to stimuli. Also called reverse tolerance, it is related to **long-term potentiation**, in which the synaptic strength between neurons increases. Behavioral sensitization is evident in the **neuroadaptation** seen at the cellular level, a fundamental characteristic of **addiction**, and in an individual's more intense reaction to the same amount of the addictive substance. It appears to be related to upregulation, an increase in the number or sensitivity of synaptic connections between neurons in response to the use of psychoactive drugs. The neurological changes that behavioral sensitization and upregulation produce at the synapses, scientists believe, result in a major reorganization of the brain's reward pathway and help lead to drug-seeking and other addictive behaviors.

Behavioral sensitization is the opposite of **tolerance** or behavioral habituation, in which the response to stimuli decreases. Whereas tolerance is facilitated by a transcription factor called **CREB**, another transcription factor, **Delta FosB**, is involved in the development of reverse tolerance. Both synaptic adaptations—habituation and sensitization—are the subject of intense research. In trying to determine how addictive drugs teach the brain it must have the substances to survive, scientists have valuable models for studying the way that learning and memory are built, and distorted, in the brain.

Further Reading

Hyman, S. E., and Malenka, R. C. Addiction and the Brain: The Neurobiology of Compulsion and Its Persistence. *Nature Reviews Neuroscience* 2001: 2(10), 695–703.

Kalivas, P. W., and Volkow, N. The Neural Basis of Addiction: A Pathology of Motivation and Choice. *American Journal of Psychiatry* August 2005: 162(8), 1403–1413.

Nestler, Eric J., and Malenka, Robert. The Addicted Brain. *Scientific American*, September 2007. Retrieved from http://www.sciam.com/article.cfm?chanID=sa006&colID=1&articleID=0001E6 32-978A-1019-978A83414B7F0101

U.S. Department of Health and Human Services, National Institute of Mental Health (NIMH), March 2008. Retrieved from http://www.nimh.nih.gov

U.S. Department of Health and Human Services, National Institute on Drug Abuse. *The Science of Addiction: Drugs, Brains, and Behavior.* NIH Publication No. 07-5605, February 2007.

Benzodiazepines In the United States, benzodiazepines are the most commonly prescribed drugs that affect central nervous system (CNS) function. As CNS **depressants**, their effects range from anxiety relief at low doses to mild sedation at moderate doses to hynoptic effects at higher doses.

As Schedule IV drugs, benzodiazepines have a lower **addiction liability** than **barbiturates**, although they are frequently abused by persons attempting to boost the high from other drugs or to reduce anxiety, insomnia, and shakiness associated with **hangovers** and **withdrawal** from other drugs.

Despite their lower potential for **abuse**, benzodiazepines quickly produce **tolerance**, so users may be tempted to increase the dosage. In repeated or large amounts, side effects can include irritability, memory impairment or amnesia, and physical **dependence**. They are most often obtained via prescription. To collect a large enough supply to support a drug habit, addicts usually "doctor shop" for several physicians to get multiple prescriptions, and millions of prescriptions are written for these drugs every year in the United States.

In addition to their antianxiety effect, benzodiazepines are sometimes prescribed as a muscle relaxant. Mixing these drugs with alcohol can be exceedingly dangerous. Commonly abused benzodiazepines include diazepam (Valium), alprazolam (Xanax), clonazepam (Klonopin), lorzepam (Ativan), and temazepam (Restoril), which is sometimes prescribed as a sleep aid.

One notorious benzodiazepine is **flunitrazepam** (Rohypnol), the club drug sometimes used as a date-rape agent to sedate potential victims of sexual assault. Legal in South America and Mexico as a sleep aid, Rohypnol has several street names including Circles, Mexican Valium, R-2, Roach-2, Roofies, Rope, and Rophies.

Further Reading

Califano, Joseph A., Jr. *High Society: How Substance Abuse Ravages America and What to Do About It.* New York: Perseus Books, 2007.

Hoffman, John, and Froemke, Susan, eds. *Addiction: Why Can't They Just Stop?* New York: Rodale, 2007.

Home Box Office (HBO). In partnership with the Robert Wood Johnson Foundation, the National Institute on Drug Abuse, and the National Institute on Alcohol Abuse and Alcoholism. *Addiction: Why Can't They Just Stop?* Documentary. March 2007.

Ketcham, Katherine, and Pace, Nicholas, A. *Teens Under the Influence: The Truth About Kids, Alcohol, and Other Drugs.* New York: Ballantine Books, 2003.

U.S. Department of Health and Human Services, National Institute on Drug Abuse (NIDA), June 2007. Retrieved from http://www.nida.gov

U.S. Department of Health and Human Services, Substance Abuse and Mental Health Services Administration (SAMHSA), August 2007. Retrieved from http://www.samhsa.gov

U.S. Department of Justice, Drug Enforcement Administration (DEA), March 2008. Retrieved from http://www.usdoj.gov/dea

Benzphetamine. *See* Stimulants.

Betel Quid. *See* Ghutka.

Bidis and Kreteks Both bidis and kreteks are thin, flavored **cigarettes** from India or Southeast Asia. Many adolescents are drawn to them because of their exotic appearance and the mistaken assumption that they are safer than cigarettes; in fact, they are stronger and more dangerous. Ordinarily made from inferior grades of **tobacco** and tobacco dust whose harsh taste is masked with fruity or chocolate flavorings, they are often produced in unsanitary or toxic conditions.

The tobacco in bidis, pronounced "bee-dees," is usually hand-rolled in the leaf of a native Asian plant called tendu or temburni that is tied with colored string at one or both ends. Although no domestic research on the health effects of bidis has been performed to date, research from India shows that smoking bidis increases the risk of cancers of the mouth, lung, stomach, and esophagus, and, like other tobacco products, can cause coronary and respiratory diseases.

Kreteks, pronounced "cree-teks," come primarily from Indonesia and are sometimes called clove cigarettes because their principal flavoring comes from cloves. Both bidis and kreteks deliver more **nicotine** and carcinogens—including carbon monoxide and tars—than regular cigarettes, and those who smoke bidis or kreteks are 13 to 20 times more at risk for abnormal lung function. They can cause cancer of the tongue, gums, esophagus, stomach, liver, the floor of the mouth, and the larynx.

Statistics from the U.S. Department of Health and Human Services' Centers for Disease Control and Prevention show:

- An estimated 3 percent of high school students are current bidi smokers. Bidi smoking is more than twice as common among male (4 percent) compared with female (2 percent) high school students.
- An estimated 2 percent of middle school students are current bidi smokers. Bidi smoking is more common among male (3 percent) compared with female (2 percent) middle school students.
- An estimated 3 percent of high school students are current kretek smokers. Kretek smoking is more common among male (3 percent) than female (2 percent) high school students.
- An estimated 2 percent of middle school students are current kretek smokers. Kretek use is more common among male (2 percent) compared with female (1 percent) middle school students.

In many regions of the world, bidis and kreteks are more popular than regular cigarettes. In India, the inexpensive bidis are the most widely smoked with an annual consumption of some 800 billion cigarettes. Kreteks contain a mild anesthetic, eugenol—which is also carcinogenic—that allows smokers to inhale the smoke deeply; this may help account for the widespread use of the product among young, inexperienced smokers who want to avoid the harshness associated with other types of cigarettes.

Like bidis and regular cigarettes, kreteks are dangerous products that cause coronary and respiratory diseases as well as many cancers. They generally container higher levels of nicotine, tars, and other harmful additives than conventional cigarettes, and the methods manufacturers have adopted to advertise and package them have succeeded in convincing younger users that they are fashionably desirable. With over 1 in 10 schoolchildren worldwide between the ages of 10 and 15 experimenting with products like **smokeless tobacco**, bidis, and kreteks, U.S. cigarette manufacturers have been developing and testing similar products to tap into this growing market.

Further Reading

Califano, Joseph A., Jr. *High Society: How Substance Abuse Ravages America and What to Do About It.* New York: Perseus Books, 2007.

U.S. Department of Health and Human Services, Centers for Disease Control and Prevention (CDC), January 2008. Retrieved from http://apps.nccd.cdc.gov/osh_faq

U.S. Department of Health and Human Services, Centers for Disease Control and Prevention (CDC), November 2007. Retrieved from http://www.cdc.gov/tobacco

U.S. Department of Health and Human Services. *Nicotine Addiction: A Report of the Surgeon General.* Centers for Disease Control and Prevention, Public Health Service, Center for Health Promotion and Education, Office on Smoking and Health, 1988.

U.S. Department of Health and Human Services. *Targeting Tobacco Use: The Nation's Leading Cause of Death.* Centers for Disease Control and Prevention, 2003.

U.S. Department of Health and Human Services. *The Health Consequences of Smoking: A Report of the Surgeon General.* Centers for Disease Control and Prevention, National Center for Chronic Disease Prevention and Health Promotion, Office on Smoking and Health, 2004.

U.S. Department of Health and Human Services. *Results from the 2006 National Survey on Drug Use and Health: National Findings.* Substance Abuse and Mental Health Services Administration (SAMHSA), Office of Applied Studies. DHHS Publication No. SMA 07-4293, 2007.

U.S. Department of Health and Human Services, National Cancer Institute (NCI), December 2007. Retrieved from http://www.cancer.gov/cancertopics/tobacco

U.S. Department of Health and Human Services, National Institute on Drug Abuse. *Research Report Series: Tobacco Addiction.* NIH Publication No. 06-4342, July 2006.

Binge and Heavy Drinking Binge drinking is usually defined as 5 drinks for males or 4 drinks for women on any one occasion, usually within 2 hours; heavy drinking is defined as 5 episodes of bingeing within the past 30 days.

Aside from the alcohol's effects on the body and the potential for **addiction** that consuming alcohol poses, binge and heavy drinking lead quickly to **intoxication** and result in dangerous behaviors—unsafe sex, reckless driving, and other risky activities. With young people between the ages of 12- to 20-years-old drinking nearly 20 percent of the alcohol in the United States, 90 percent of which is consumed during episodes of binge drinking, the statistics are worrisome. Intensive surveys taken in 2006 by the U.S. Department of Health and Human Services' Substance Abuse and Mental Health Services Administration reflect the incidence of this kind of drinking.

General Statistics

- More than one fifth (23 percent) of persons aged 12 or older participated in binge drinking in 2006. This is about 57 million people, similar to the estimate in 2005.

- In 2006, heavy drinking was reported by 6.9 percent of the population aged 12 or older, or 17 million people. This rate is similar to the rate of heavy drinking in 2005 (6.6 percent).

- In 2006, among young adults aged 18 to 25, the rate of binge drinking was 42.2 percent, and the rate of heavy drinking was 15.6 percent. These rates are similar to the rates in 2005.

- Underage (persons aged 12 to 20) past-month and binge drinking rates have remained essentially unchanged since 2002. In 2006, about 10.8 million persons aged 12 to 20 (28.3 percent) reported drinking alcohol in the past month. Approximately 7.2 million (19.0 percent) were binge drinkers, and 2.4 million (6.2 percent) were heavy drinkers.

- Among persons aged 12 to 20, past-month alcohol use rates were 18.6 percent among blacks, 19.7 percent among Asians, 25.3 percent among Hispanics, 27.5 percent among those reporting 2 or more races, 31.3 percent among American Indians or Alaska Natives, and 32.3 percent among whites. The 2006 rate for American Indians or Alaska Natives is higher than the 2005 rate of 21.7 percent.

- Among pregnant women aged 15 to 44, binge drinking in the 1st trimester dropped from 10.6 percent in 2003–2004 combined data to 4.6 percent in 2005–2006 combined data.
- Rates of binge alcohol use in 2006 were 1.5 percent among 12- or 13-year-olds, 8.9 percent among 14- or 15-year-olds, 20.0 percent among 16- or 17-year-olds, 36.2 percent among persons aged 18 to 20, and 46.1 percent among those aged 21 to 25. The rate peaked at ages 21 to 23 (49.3 percent at age 21, 48.9 percent at age 22, and 47.2 percent at age 23), then decreased beyond young adulthood from 34.2 percent of 26- to 34-year-olds to 18.4 percent of persons aged 35 or older.
- The rate of binge drinking was 42.2 percent for young adults aged 18 to 25. Heavy alcohol use was reported by 15.6 percent of persons aged 18 to 25. These rates are similar to the rates in 2005 (41.9 and 15.3 percent, respectively).
- The rate of current alcohol use among youths aged 12 to 17 was 16.6 percent in 2006. Youth binge and heavy drinking rates were 10.3 and 2.4 percent, respectively. These rates are essentially the same as in 2005 (16.5 percent, 9.9 percent, and 2.4 percent, respectively).

Breakdowns

Underage Drinking

- In 2006, about 10.8 million persons aged 12 to 20 (28.3 percent) reported drinking alcohol in the past month. Approximately 7.2 million (19.0 percent) were binge drinkers, and 2.4 million (6.2 percent) were heavy drinkers. These figures have remained essentially the same since the 2002 survey.

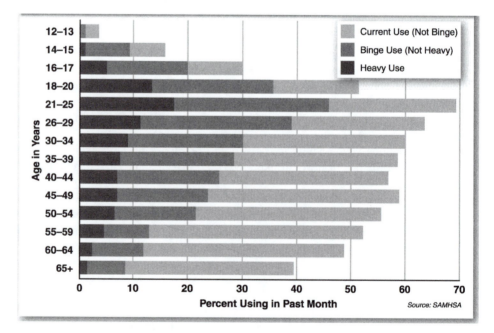

Current, Binge, and Heavy Alcohol Use among Persons Aged 12 or Older, by Age: 2006

Table 10. Alcohol Use, Binge Alcohol Use, and Heavy Alcohol Use in the Past Month among Persons Aged 12 to 20, by Demographic Characteristics: Percentages, 2005 and 2006

| Demographic Characteristic | Type of Alcohol Use | | | | | |
| | Alcohol Use | | Binge Alcohol Use | | Heavy Alcohol Use | |
	2005	2006	2005	2006	2005	2006
Total	28.2	28.3	18.8	19.0	6.0	6.2
Gender						
Male	28.9	29.2	21.3	21.3	7.6	7.9
Female	27.5	27.4	16.1	16.5	4.3	4.3
Hispanic Origin And Race						
Not Hispanic or Latino	28.7	29.0	19.0	19.5	6.4	6.5
White	32.3	32.3	22.3	22.7	7.8	8.2
Black or African American	19.0	18.6	9.1	8.6	1.8	1.3
American Indian or Alaska Native	21.7[a]	31.3	18.1	23.6	6.0	4.7
Native Hawaiian or other Pacific Islander	12.0	*	8.4	*	1.4	*
Asian	15.5	19.7	7.4[a]	11.8	1.2	1.3
Two or More Races	24.0	27.5	16.6	20.7	7.1	6.3
Hispanic or Latino	25.9	25.3	17.9	16.5	4.2	4.8
Gender/Race/Hispanic Origin						
Male, White, Not Hispanic	32.6	33.2	24.7	25.2	9.8	10.3
Female, White, Not Hispanic	31.9	31.4	19.7	20.0	5.8	5.9
Male, Black, Not Hispanic	20.4	18.7	11.4	9.7	2.5	1.5
Female, Black, Not Hispanic	17.6	18.4	6.8	7.5	1.1	1.0
Male, Hispanic	27.9	26.7	21.5	19.4	5.9	6.6
Female, Hispanic	23.7	23.8	13.9	13.2	2.5	2.7

*Low precision; no estimate reported.

Note: Binge Alcohol Use is defined as drinking 5 or more drinks on the same occasion (i.e., at the same time or within a couple of hours of each other) on at least 1 day in the past 30 days. Heavy Alcohol Use is defined as drinking five or more drinks on the same occasion on each of 5 or more days in the past 30 days; all heavy alcohol users are also binge alcohol users.

[a]Difference between estimate and 2006 estimate is statistically significant at the 0.05 level.

Source: SAMHSA.

- More males than females aged 12 to 20 reported current alcohol use (29.2 vs. 27.4 percent, respectively), binge drinking (21.3 vs. 16.5 percent), and heavy drinking (7.9 vs. 4.3 percent) in 2006.
- Among persons aged 12 to 20, binge drinking was reported by 23.6 percent of American Indians or Alaska Natives, 22.7 percent of whites, 20.7 percent of persons reporting 2 or more races, and 16.5 percent of Hispanics, but only by 11.8 percent of Asians and 8.6 percent of blacks. The 2006 rate among Asians was higher than the 2005 rate of 7.4 percent.

Drinking During Pregnancy

- Among pregnant women aged 15 to 44, an estimated 11.8 percent reported current alcohol use, 2.9 percent reported binge drinking, and 0.7 percent reported heavy drinking. These rates were significantly lower than the rates for nonpregnant women in the same age group (53 percent, 23.6 percent, and 5.4 percent, respectively).

• Binge drinking during the 1st trimester of pregnancy dropped from 10.6 percent in combined 2003–2004 data to 4.6 percent in combined 2005–2006 data. All of the current estimates for pregnant women are based on data averaged over 2005 and 2006.

Ethnic Trends

• The rate of binge alcohol use was lowest among Asians (11.8 percent). Rates for other racial/ethnic groups were 19.1 percent for blacks, 22.8 percent for persons reporting 2 or more races, 23.9 percent for Hispanics, 24.1 percent for whites, 24.1 percent for Native Hawaiians or other Pacific Islanders, and 31 percent for American Indians or Alaska Natives.

Educational Levels and Drinking

• Among adults aged 18 or older, the rate of past-month alcohol use grew with advancing levels of education. Among adults with less than a high school education, 36.5 percent were current drinkers in 2006, significantly lower than the 67.3 percent of college graduates who were current drinkers. However, among adults aged 26 or older, binge and heavy alcohol use rates were lower among college graduates (19.1 and 5.4 percent, respectively) than among those who had not completed college (22.3 vs. 6.2 percent, respectively).

• Young adults aged 18 to 22 enrolled full time in college were more likely than their peers not enrolled full time (i.e., part-time college students and persons not currently enrolled in college) to use alcohol in the past month, binge drink, and drink heavily. Past-month alcohol use was reported by 66.4 percent of full-time college

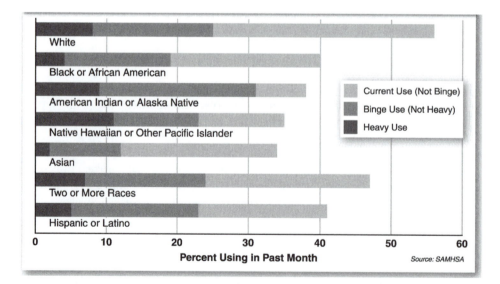

Current, Binge, and Heavy Alcohol Use among Persons Aged 12 or Older, by Race/Ethnicity: 2006

students compared with 54.1 percent of persons aged 18 to 22 who were not enrolled full time. Binge and heavy use rates for college students were 45.5 and 19 percent, respectively, compared with 38.4 and 13.3 percent, respectively, for 18- to 22-year-olds not enrolled full time in college.

- The pattern of higher rates of current alcohol use, binge alcohol use, and heavy alcohol use among full-time college students compared with rates for others aged 18 to 22 has remained consistent since 2002.

Employment and Drinking

- Rates of current alcohol use were 62 percent for full-time employed adults aged 18 or older in 2006, higher than the rate for unemployed adults (52.1 percent). However, the pattern was different for binge and heavy alcohol use. Rates of binge and heavy use for unemployed persons were 34.2 and 12.2 percent, respectively, while these rates were 29.7 and 8.9 percent for full-time employed persons.
- Most binge and heavy alcohol users were employed in 2006. Among 54 million adult binge drinkers, 42.9 million (79.4 percent) were employed either full or part time. Among 16.3 million heavy drinkers, 12.9 million (79.2 percent) were employed.

Geographic Patterns

- Among people aged 12 or older, the rate of past-month alcohol use in large metropolitan areas (53.5 percent) was higher than the 49.6 percent in small metropolitan areas and 45 percent in nonmetropolitan areas. Binge drinking was equally prevalent in small metropolitan areas (22.6 percent), large metropolitan areas (23.4 percent), and nonmetropolitan areas (22.2 percent). The rate of heavy alcohol use in large metropolitan areas increased from 6.1 percent in 2005 to 6.7 percent in 2006. The rates in small metropolitan areas and nonmetropolitan areas in 2006 were both 7.1 percent.
- The rates of binge alcohol use among youths aged 12 to 17 were 11.2 percent in nonmetropolitan areas, 9.8 percent in small metropolitan areas, and 10.3 percent in large metropolitan areas, where the rate increased from 9.3 percent in 2005. In completely rural counties of nonmetropolitan areas, 12.2 percent of youths reported binge drinking in 2006.

Drinking and the Use of Illicit Drugs and Tobacco

- The level of alcohol use was associated with illicit drug use in 2006. Among the 16.9 million heavy drinkers aged 12 or older, 32.6 percent were current illicit drug users.
- Persons who were not current alcohol users were less likely to have used illicit drugs in the past month (3.4 percent) than those who reported (a) current use of alcohol but did not meet the criteria for binge or heavy use (6.4 percent), (b) binge use but did not meet the criteria for heavy use (16.0 percent), or (c) heavy use of alcohol (32.6 percent).
- Alcohol consumption levels also were associated with **tobacco** use. Among heavy alcohol users aged 12 or older, 58.3 percent smoked **cigarettes** in the past month, while only 20.4 percent of nonbinge current drinkers and 17.2 percent of persons who did not drink alcohol in the past month were current smokers. **Smokeless tobacco** use and **cigar** use also were more prevalent among heavy drinkers (11.4 and

18.7 percent, respectively) than among nonbinge drinkers (2.1 and 4.6 percent) and nondrinkers (2.2 and 2.1 percent).

See also Alcoholism; Problem Drinking; Women, Pregnancy, and Drugs.

Further Reading

Volkmann, Chris, and Volkmann, Toren. *From Binge to Blackout: A Mother and Son Struggle with Teen Drinking*. New York: New American Library, 2006.
Wechsler, Henry, and Wuethrich, Bernice. Dying to Drink: Confronting Binge Drinking on College Campuses. Emmaus, PA: Rodale, 2002.

Binge-Eating Disorder. *See* Bulimia Nervosa.

Bingeing and Purging. *See* Eating Disorders.

Blum, Kenneth (1939–) A recognized authority in psychopharmacology and genetics, Blum is currently a Professor in the Department of Physiology and Pharmacology at North Carolina's Wake Forest University School of Medicine. While a Professor of Pharmacology at the University of Texas in the 1960s, Blum became involved in **alcoholism** research, and early experiments during the 1970s convinced him and many associates that **neurotransmitters** like serotonin, GABA, and glutamate have critical roles in alcoholism. During the 1980s, as his investigations led him more deeply into molecular genetics, his work with Ernest Noble (1929–), the former director of the National Institutes of Health's National Institute of Alcohol Abuse and Alcoholism (NIAAA), revealed the significance of the dopamine D2 allele in the disease. This confirmed the association of certain genes with alcoholism and helped launch a series of investigations within the scientific community into the **genetics of addiction**.

Although Blum's work initially raised hopes that an alcoholism gene might be identified, it has become clear that the disease arises from many causes. However, Blum is continuing to conduct research into the genetic links associated with **addiction**, but because he has been associated with marketing a line of "nutraceuticals," herbal and vitamin formulations that supposedly target the relevant genetic factors, some have discounted his work. Others regard it as groundbreaking research; highly regarded in many circles, it has been published in numerous medical and scientific journals.

Further Reading

Blum, Kenneth, and Payne, James. *Alcohol and the Addictive Brain: New Hope for Alcoholics from Biogenetic Research*. New York: The Free Press, 1991.

Body Dysmorphic Disorder. *See* Eating Disorders.

Bontril. *See* Stimulants.

Brain and Addiction The human brain consists of 3 main sections: the brain stem, where many involuntary functions like breathing and heart rate are controlled; the cerebellum,

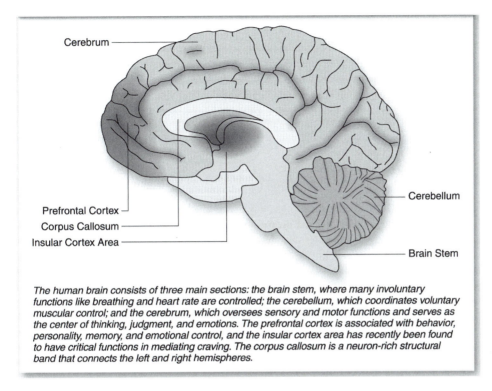

Cerebrum

Cerebellum

Prefrontal Cortex

Corpus Callosum

Insular Cortex Area

Brain Stem

The human brain consists of three main sections: the brain stem, where many involuntary functions like breathing and heart rate are controlled; the cerebellum, which coordinates voluntary muscular control; and the cerebrum, which oversees sensory and motor functions and serves as the center of thinking, judgment, and emotions. The prefrontal cortex is associated with behavior, personality, memory, and emotional control, and the insular cortex area has recently been found to have critical functions in mediating craving. The corpus callosum is a neuron-rich structural band that connects the left and right hemispheres.

Key Regions of the Brain

which coordinates voluntary muscular control; and the cerebrum, which oversees sensory and motor functions and serves as the center of thinking, judgment, and emotions. The cerebral cortex, a layer of gray matter on the cerebrum, helps integrate higher mental functions and oversees primitive areas of the brain such as the limbic system. The frontal lobe of the brain and, in particular, the prefrontal cortex are associated with behavior, personality, judgment, memory, and emotional control. The communication network that transmits information throughout the brain and spinal cord to the rest of the body is made of up billions of nerve cells called neurons. Brain cells known as glia support the functions of the neurons.

Brain Structures Involved in Addiction

Amygdala

The amygdala, a cluster of cells in the brain's limbic system, sends impulses to the ventral tegmental area and locus ceruleus to activate the release of dopamine, norepinephrine, and epinephrine. During moments of fight-or-flight arousal, it also communicates fear and panic to the prefrontal cortex. In response to feel-good stimuli such as music, food, or addictive drugs, it boosts pleasure-inducing **neurotransmitter** activity in the mesolimbic dopamine pathway traveling from the ventral tegmental area to the nucleus accumbens. The amygdala is involved in learning and processing emotions by making associations between positive stimuli and emotional reward.

Hippocampus

Another structure in the brain's limbic system, the hippocampus is sometimes called the "seat of memory" because it converts information coming into the brain into long-term memories; it is believed to help addicts recall the high that defines the dopamine reward of their drug use. It is also associated with spatial navigation. There are actually 2 hippocampi in the human brain, one in each hemisphere. In certain brain diseases and as a result of long-term drug **abuse**, the hippocampus may shrink, causing memory impairment.

Insular Cortex

A hidden region of the brain also known as the insula, the insular cortex has recently been found to have a major impact on drug-related **craving**. Studies have shown that in rats addicted to **amphetamines**, deactivation of the insula, roughly a prune-size area deep in the brain near the limbic system, completely eliminated the rats' desires for drugs. Upon reactivation of the region, the craving returned. Additional studies have shown that in long-term smokers who sustained brain injuries in the area of the insular cortex, their urge for **nicotine** disappeared entirely. Since the insula is partly responsible for monitoring and communicating the organism's needs to the prefrontal cortex where behavioral decisions are made, it is possible this region plays a significant role in drug-seeking behavior.

Limbic System

An ancient, primitive area of the brain, the limbic system is the seat of instincts, mood, and emotions, and houses the **mesolimbic dopamine system**, the reward network that produces pleasurable sensations in response to stimuli such as food, sex, or addictive drugs. Key learning and motivational circuits reside here also. In addition to the structures of the mesolimbic dopamine system, it comprises the cingulate gyrus, fornix, hypothalamus, olfactory cortex, and thalamus. Principally the origin of basic emotions, the limbic system influences other areas of the brain through a complex communications network.

Locus Ceruleus

A cluster of cells in the pons area of the brain stem that synthesizes norepinephrine, the locus ceruleus has an excitatory effect on many parts of the brain including the amygdala and hippocampus. It is highly reactive to stress, processing incoming signals through the amygdala to produce emotions of fear and panic that, in turn, affect higher thought processes in the prefrontal cortex. Although its specific role in **addiction** and the mesolimbic dopamine pathway is not clear, its intricate links to neurotransmitter activity in the limbic system give it a significant role.

Nucleus Accumbens

On the receiving end of the dopamine-regulated messages emanating from the ventral tegmental area, the nucleus accumbens links pleasure/reward responses in the mesolimbic dopamine system to environmental factors which accompany that response. This is known as incentive sensitization—the process by which the brain learns to attach significance, or salience, to these environmental cues. Most neuroscientists suggest that incentive salience can influence drug-seeking and drug-using behavior below the level of the addict's awareness. By boosting neurotransmitter activity in the dopamine pathway, the nucleus accumbens is partially responsible for the development of reverse tolerance, also known as **behavioral sensitization**. The structure helps process rewards by releasing GABA, an inhibitory neurotransmitter associated with calm and a sense of well-being.

Prefrontal Cortex

The prefrontal cortex, in the front part of the brain, is responsible for cognitive functions involving judgment, planning, and the modulation of behavior by exercising control over the more primitive **impulses** such as rage, aggression, and fear emanating from the limbic system. These higher functions are sometimes called "executive functions." The area helps determine personality traits and is involved in the formation of long-term memories. Studies of addiction focus on the mesolimbic pathways of the brain that link the limbic system to the prefrontal cortex.

Ventral Tegmental Area (VTA)

Rich in GABA- and glutamate-activating neurons, the VTA helps the brain evaluate how its needs are being met and uses dopamine as the messenger communicating this information to the nucleus accumbens. Often viewed as the starting point in the chain of events that sends dopamine coursing through the mesolimbic dopamine system, the VTA is believed to play a significant role in processing emotions and reinforcing behaviors that satisfy whatever needs the brain perceives as necessary to survival—which, in the case of addiction, are drugs. Scientists believe that, in a phenomenon known as **long-term potentiation**, synapses in the VTA strengthen over time in response to the stimulus of psychoactive drugs, and this is critical to the formation of memories.

Neurons

Although neurons with different functions have somewhat different structures—some are sensory neurons that conduct sensation to the brain, others are motor neurons that command the muscles—all have certain similarities. Every neuron consists of a cell body with a nucleus at the center. Extending from the cell body are several dendrites and a tail-like extension called an axon. At the end of the axon is the synaptic terminal. When a neuron communicates with another neuron, it produces an electric impulse that is converted into a chemical messenger called a neurotransmitter. Released at the synaptic terminal of the axon, the neurotransmitter enters the gap between neurons, called the synapse, where dendrites and other areas on the receiving cell can capture and convert it into an electrical impulse which the receiving cell uses to produce the same neurotransmitter to communicate with another cell. Since different neurons perform different functions, this "lock and key" arrangement ensures that the neurotransmitter delivers the appropriate message to the appropriate cell. The receiving cell then becomes the transmitting cell, passing the message from its axons across synapses to the receptive dendrites of other neurons.

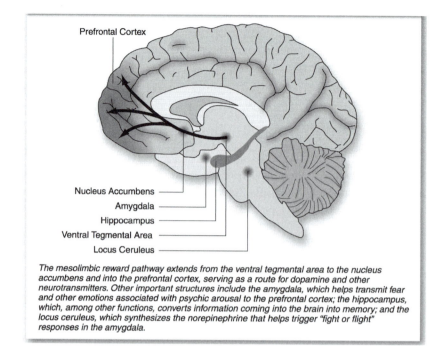

Prefrontal Cortex

Nucleus Accumbens
Amygdala
Hippocampus
Ventral Tegmental Area
Locus Ceruleus

The mesolimbic reward pathway extends from the ventral tegmental area to the nucleus accumbens and into the prefrontal cortex, serving as a route for dopamine and other neurotransmitters. Other important structures include the amygdala, which helps transmit fear and other emotions associated with psychic arousal to the prefrontal cortex; the hippocampus, which, among other functions, converts information coming into the brain into memory; and the locus ceruleus, which synthesizes the norepinephrine that helps trigger "fight or flight" responses in the amygdala.

Mesolimbic Dopamine System

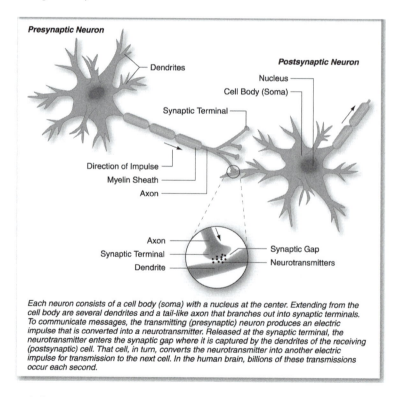

Presynaptic Neuron

Dendrites

Postsynaptic Neuron

Nucleus
Cell Body (Soma)

Synaptic Terminal

Direction of Impulse
Myelin Sheath
Axon

Axon
Synaptic Terminal
Dendrite

Synaptic Gap
Neurotransmitters

Each neuron consists of a cell body (soma) with a nucleus at the center. Extending from the cell body are several dendrites and a tail-like axon that branches out into synaptic terminals. To communicate messages, the transmitting (presynaptic) neuron produces an electric impulse that is converted into a neurotransmitter. Released at the synaptic terminal, the neurotransmitter enters the synaptic gap where it is captured by the dendrites of the receiving (postsynaptic) cell. That cell, in turn, converts the neurotransmitter into another electric impulse for transmission to the next cell. In the human brain, billions of these transmissions occur each second.

Neurotransmission

The Mesolimbic Dopamine System

Deep in the brain where instincts, mood, and emotions reside is the limbic system, whose mesolimbic dopamine system (MDS) is regarded as fundamental to addiction. It is home to the reward pathway, the circuitry that produces pleasurable sensations when an organism engages in activities that support survival, such as eating food, drinking water, or having sex. The complex neural network involved in the perception of pleasure teaches the brain to remember the activity and be motivated to repeat it, thus ensuring that the organism survives. The pathway extends from the ventral tegmental area to the nucleus accumbens and to the prefrontal cortex, serving as a route for neurotransmitters like dopamine to travel across synapses to deliver feel-good messages. Other structures in the MDS that are critically involved in addiction include the amygdala, which helps transmit fear and other emotions associated with psychic arousal to the prefrontal cortex; the hippocampus, which, among other functions, helps convert information coming into the brain into memory; and the locus ceruleus, which synthesizes norepinephrine that helps trigger fight-or-flight responses in the amygdala.

Another region of the brain called the insula, or insular cortex, has received attention in recent years. When the insula is deactivated in rats that have become addicted to amphetamines, the rats' craving for drugs appears to be eliminated. If the insula is reactivated, craving returns. Similarly, long-term smokers who sustained injuries to the area were shown to lose their desire for nicotine. These findings indicate that by communicating the brain's needs to the prefrontal cortex, the insula may have an important function in the development of drug-seeking behavior. Unfortunately, its protected position in the brain does not allow researchers to stimulate different areas to see what effects their manipulations may have on addiction.

After a neuron releases dopamine into the synapse to communicate with another neuron in the reward pathway, the dopamine is recycled by being pumped back into the transmitting cells for reuse when needed. When psychoactive drugs stimulate the reward pathway, the dopamine outpouring is more profuse, resulting in the intensely heightened pleasure known as a rush or high. Some drugs interfere with the cells' ability to recycle the neurotransmitter, so it remains in the synapse where it continues to stimulate receptors; this is why, in some cases, the high is more prolonged.

Neurotransmitters

There are three general classes of neurotransmitters: the monoamines, including dopamine, serotonin, and norepinephrine (or noradrenaline); peptides, like the endorphins,

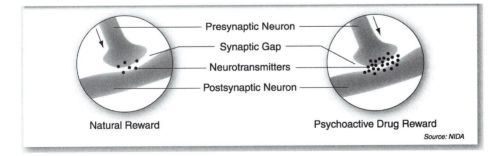

Effect of Natural Rewards vs. Psychoactive Drugs on the Mesolimbic Dopamine System

the brain's natural pain killers that are the opioids; and amino acids, which include glutamate and gamma aminobutyric acid (GABA). Along with **acetylcholine** and chemicals produced by the body's endocannabinoid system, these neurotransmitters are primarily involved in addiction. Dopamine, serotonin, and norepinephrine are the principal pleasure-giving neurotransmitters; although their interaction is complicated, their normal functioning allows individuals to experience life's natural rewards in a way that promotes learning, builds memories, and motivates behavior. Deficiencies in dopamine or serotonin can produce deteriorating behavior, heightened anxiety, deepening depression, or more serious mental illness, and too little norepinephrine leads to a lack of focus and inability to concentrate. Glutamate and GABA, respectively, represent the brain's "Go" (excitatory) and "Stop" (inhibitory) messengers and are regarded as the brain's workhorse neurotransmitters that induce a sense of well-being and reduce anxiety and depression.

When all these neurotransmitters are operating properly, the body's involuntary activities are in balance and the individual functions well, capable of rational thought, mature judgment, and appropriate reward-seeking behavior. Drugs of abuse severely upset this balance. For example, when an individual takes **heroin**, the inhibitory influence of GABA tends to suppress respiration. If the individual also consumes alcohol, which suppresses the excitatory effect of glutamate, the effect is to inhibit respiration further. This interaction can lead to respiratory difficulty or even respiratory death, due in part to the synergistic effect of drugs when they are combined. In this example, the brain, in its effort to achieve balance, or homeostasis, is likely to increase its production of glutamate to regulate breathing. If the heroin is then discontinued, the user may react to the higher brain concentrations of glutamate with extreme excitability or agitation that can be overwhelmingly uncomfortable. Relieving these **withdrawal** symptoms is precisely why addicts are driven to use the addictive substance again.

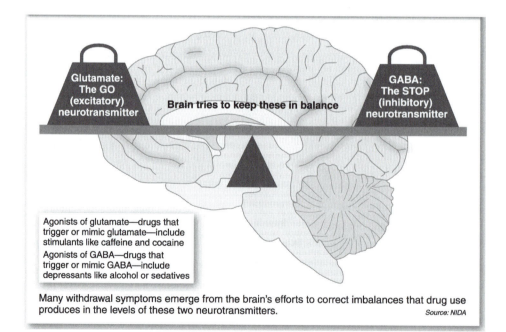

Glutamate and GABA: A Balancing Act

Drugs of abuse, by enhancing the natural tendency of neurons in the reward pathway to release dopamine, keep users coming back for more. In susceptible individuals with longer-term drug use, a homeostatic process called downregulation occurs by which the brain decreases the number of dopamine receptors available on cells. There is evidence that these cells also lose some of their ability to react to whatever level of dopamine they do receive; this is one of the mechanisms by which **tolerance** develops. The addict's capacity to feel pleasure is dulled, a condition known as **anhedonia**. Finding that he or she no longer experiences pleasure from drug use but needs it simply to feel normal, the individual ingests more. Because the strength of illegal street drugs cannot be determined, the addict could develop seizures or brain damage, or suffer a fatal overdose.

The structural changes that occur as the brain struggles to adapt to the neural disruption that drugs cause is known as **neuroadaptation**, and the imbalances are known as neurotransmitter dysregulation. Any drugs capable of causing these neurological changes have addictive potential; they ultimately damage the reward circuit, create memory and learning deficits, and produce compulsive drug-seeking or other behaviors.

Addictive drugs that enhance the action of natural neurotransmitters are **agonists**. If the natural neurotransmitter triggers activity in the receptor cell, an agonist increases that activity; if the natural neurotransmitter inhibits activity in the receptor cell, an agonist further inhibits that activity. Agonists do this 1 of 3 ways: by increasing production of the natural neurotransmitter, by interfering with the recycling or reuptake of the neurotransmitter so it stays in the synapse where it continues to activate the receptor cell, or by replacing the natural neurotransmitter and binding directly to the receptor cell. Antidepressants are agonists of serotonin, and **stimulants** like **cocaine** and **methamphetamine** are agonists of dopamine and norepinephrine.

Addictive drugs that interfere with the normal function of a natural neurotransmitter are **antagonists**. An antagonist also works in 3 ways: by interfering with the release of the neurotransmitter into the synapse, by blocking the message being communicated by preventing the natural neurotransmitter from binding to receptors, and by triggering the release of the neurotransmitter into the presynaptic neuron instead of out into the synapse where it can activate the receiving cell. Alcohol is an antagonist of glutamate; **lysergic acid diethylamide** (LSD) is an antagonist of serotonin.

Much of the processing that takes place in the reward circuitry is below the level of consciousness, and the addict is unaware of the neuroadaptation that distorts learning, memory, motivations, and urges. Because the pathway projects from the subconscious mesolimbic area to the prefrontal cortex where conscious decisions are made, it carries with it neurologically distorted messages that translate into behaviors that seem rational to the addict. This could be a reason, scientists believe, that addicts choose to engage in destructive behaviors—continuing to drink and drive despite numerous DWI citations, or gambling in spite of impending financial ruin. One study shows that, just as dopamine's pathway to the nucleus accumbens is involved in the development of addiction, the complex interplay of GABA and glutamate this activity sets off in the prefrontal cortex may play a significant role in drug-seeking behavior. The structural changes accompanying this likely transference of reward pathways from a dopamine-based pathway to a GABA/glutamate pathway seem to be enduring, providing an explanation for why most addicts retain their vulnerability to the substance despite years of sobriety, and why one drink, one snort of cocaine, one **cigarette**, or one poker game can sometimes cause a full-blown relapse.

Most researchers believe that neurotransmitter dysregulation in certain individuals arises from a combined biological, genetic, and environmental susceptibility that, in conjunction with the synaptic plasticity that defines neuroadaptation, results in addiction. Whether **behavioral addictions** fit this model is not entirely clear because it is not known if engaging in an addictive behavior sets in motion neurological changes identical to those seen in drug abuse, but what is clear is that some neurological adaptations play a significant role.

In time, due to their stimulating effects on glutamate, both addictive substances and behaviors transform the "Go" system into a hair-trigger response, a reflex so automatic that the "Stop" message cannot be issued in time. As part of its research to find ways to address dysregulation, the National Institute on Drug Abuse (NIDA) has found that cognitive behavioral therapy (CBT) can help patients recognize and avoid triggers that set off the reflex. In addition, a GABA agonist called baclofen is being developed that may allow the frontal lobe to prevent the ready activation of the "Go" switch. These measures cannot reset the chemistry of the brain. Instead, they correct for neurochemical imbalances in much the same way that insulin corrects for a diabetic's sugar imbalances. Thus, they can help restore addicts to sobriety while researchers seek new ways to teach the brain to reverse its chemical dysregulation.

See also Genetics of Addiction; Mental Disorders.

Further Reading

Biegon, Anat, and Volkow, Nora. *Sites of Drug Action in the Human Brain*. Boca Raton, FL: CRC Press, 1995.

Erickson, Carlton K. *The Science of Addiction: From Neurobiology to Treatment*. New York: Norton, 2007.

Hyman, S. E., and Malenka, R. C. Addiction and the Brain: The Neurobiology of Compulsion and Its Persistence. *Nature Reviews Neuroscience* 2001: 2(10), 695–703.

Kalivas, P. W., and Volkow, N. The Neural Basis of Addiction: A Pathology of Motivation and Choice. *American Journal of Psychiatry* August 2005: 162(8), 1403–1413.

Kauer, Julie A. Addictive Drugs and Stress Trigger a Common Change at VTA Synapses. *Neuron* February 2003: 37(4), 549–550.

Nestler, Eric J., and Malenka, Robert. The Addicted Brain. *Scientific American*, September 2007. Retrieved from http://www.sciam.com/article.cfm?chanID=sa006&colID=1&articleID=0001E6 32-978A-1019-978A83414B7F0101

U.S. Department of Health and Human Services, National Institute on Drug Abuse. *The Science of Addiction: Drugs, Brains, and Behavior*. NIH Publication No. 07-5605, February 2007.

Winters, Ken. *Adolescent Brain Development and Drug Abuse*. Philadelphia, PA: Treatment Research Institute, 2008.

Bulimia Nervosa This **eating disorder** is similar to the bingeing/purging type of **anorexia nervosa**, but people with bulimia manage to maintain their normal weight while anorectics do not. Like anorexia nervosa, a key feature of bulimia is a distorted perception of one's body weight and shape—known in psychiatric terms as body dysmorphic disorder—that drives the patient's **compulsion** to prevent weight gain. For a diagnosis of bulimia nervosa, there must be a pattern of behavior that includes 2 episodes of bingeing and purging at least twice a week for a few months.

Characteristics of Bulimia Nervosa

Bulimia nervosa is characterized by recurrent and frequent episodes of eating unusually large amounts of food (e.g., binge-eating) and a lack of control over the behavior. This is followed

---

by an activity designed to compensate for the binge, such as purging (e.g., vomiting, excessive use of laxatives or diuretics), fasting, and/or excessive exercise.

Unlike anorectics, people with bulimia can fall within normal weight ranges. However, like people with anorexia, they often fear gaining weight and are intensely unhappy with their body size and shape. Usually, bulimic behavior occurs in private and is often accompanied by feelings of disgust or shame. The binging and purging cycle usually repeats several times a week. Like anorectics, bulimics often have coexisting psychological illnesses, such as depression, anxiety, and/or substance abuse problems. Many physical conditions result from the purging aspect of the illness, including electrolyte imbalances, gastrointestinal damage, and oral or dental problems.

Other symptoms include:

- chronically inflamed and sore throat
- swollen glands in the neck and below the jaw
- worn tooth enamel and increasingly sensitive and decaying teeth as a result of exposure to stomach acids
- gastroesophageal reflux disorder
- intestinal distress and irritation from laxative abuse
- kidney problems from diuretic abuse
- severe dehydration from purging of fluids

Source: National Institute of Mental Health http://www.nimh.nih.gov/health/publications/eating-disorders/bulimia-nervosa.shtml

---

DSM Criteria for Diagnosing Bulimia Nervosa

The following criteria used for diagnosing bulimia nervosa have been adapted from the 4th edition of the American Psychiatric Association's *Diagnostic and Statistical Manual of Mental Disorders* (*DSM*).

In bulimia nervosa, the person:

1. indulges in repeated bingeing, manifested a) by eating excessive amounts of food within a 2-hour period, and b) by having no control over the amount of food he or she eats during bingeing;
2. engages in activities designed to compensate for bingeing, such as purging (vomiting or the use of laxatives, diuretics, or enemas), excessive exercise, or fasting;
3. exhibits the bingeing and compensatory behaviors shown above on an average of 2 times a week for at least 3 months;
4. evaluates his or her self-worth in terms of body shape and weight;
5. exhibits bulimic symptoms independently of symptoms of anorexia nervosa.

In the *purging* type of bulimia, the person induces vomiting or uses laxatives, diuretics, or enemas; in the *nonpurging* type, the person does not purge but engages in fasting or excessive exercise to compensate for bingeing.

Source: Adapted from American Psychiatric Association, 2000.

Unlike anorexia nervosa, which is more likely to be rooted in mood or personality disorders, bulimia is thought by most mental health experts to be an **impulse control disorder** despite evidence that other mental illnesses may be present as well. In 30 percent of bulimics, there is also likely to be a substance **abuse** problem. The person has impaired control over the quantity of food that he or she eats, consuming significantly more than would normally be appropriate (with the exception of holidays and other special occasions) in a relatively short amount of time. Primarily choosing high-calorie, sweet foods, the individual binges in response to stress, depressed moods, or negative feelings about self-image. There is evidence that sugary food might trigger feel-good neurochemical reactions in the brain's dopamine reward pathway. Bulimics typically hide bingeing from others, sometimes hoarding food in anticipation of bingeing opportunities. They eat in a frenzied manner, and sometimes report they enter a trancelike state in which they pay no attention to what they are tasting or even eating. The behavior, not the food, tends to elicit the rewarding feelings.

Bingeing episodes are followed by guilt and remorse, and the bulimic, already concerned about weight, feels compelled to compensate for the calories consumed. In a non-purging form of the disease known as binge-eating disorder, some use strategies such as fasting or extreme exercise regimens to lose weight, but most bulimics—at least 80 percent—induce vomiting by using their fingers or an object to stimulate the gag reflex; take laxatives, diuretics, or diet pills; or administer frequent enemas. Vomiting gives immediate relief from the discomfort of overeating and reduces concerns about weight gain. For some, according to the American Psychiatric Association, vomiting becomes an end in itself and some bulimics are able to vomit at will. Bulimics may use a variety of purging techniques over time.

Characteristics of Binge-Eating Disorders

Binge-eating disorder is characterized by recurrent binge-eating episodes during which a person loses control over his or her eating. Unlike bulimia, binge-eating episodes are not followed by purging, so people with binge-eating disorder often are overweight or obese. They also experience guilt, shame, and/or distress about the binge-eating, which can trigger even more frequent episodes.

Obese people with binge-eating disorder often have coexisting psychological illnesses including anxiety, depression, and personality disorders. They are also more likely to suffer from cardiovascular disease and hypertension.

Source: National Institute of Mental Health http://www.nimh.nih.gov/health/publications/eating-disorders/binge-eating-disorder.shtml

---

Since bulimics generally fall within normal weight ranges, the obvious clue to the presence of the disease—severe weight loss—is absent. Warning signs might be the presence of an anxiety or **obsessive-compulsive disorder** with behavior suggestive of bingeing, evidence of purging, or the abuse of **stimulants** to control weight.

Typically beginning in adolescence or young adulthood, the disease affects women more than men and from 1 to slightly over 4 percent of the population. Although bulimia is a different disease from anorexia nervosa, there are common characteristics, and many bulimics fit a psychological profile similar to that of anorectics: they are overly concerned with self-control and self-image, and they are driven by a need to measure up to the standards of others, a tendency that may have its origins in high parental expectations. Bulimics are also likely to be perfectionists with low self-esteem and a history of sexual or emotional abuse. The disease is more common among upper-class young women in industrialized nations, and there is some evidence that virtually no cases of bulimia were reported before the introduction of television. Experts are reluctant to draw definitive conclusions from this finding, however, since the causes of the disease are variable.

Symptoms

The earlier the patient or concerned others can seek treatment, the more likely it will be successful. Professional help is advisable if the person in question:

1. Shows evidence of bingeing and purging; spends time in the bathroom immediately after eating and disguises bathroom noises; smells occasionally of vomit or evidence of vomit is discovered; uses an unusual amount of breath mints; maintains a supply of laxatives, diuretics, enema preparations, or diet pills.
2. Engages in fasting and/or excessive, even obsessive, exercise regimens.
3. Buys and compulsively consumes large quantities of junk or non-nutritious food without any weight gain.
4. Abuses substances and/or has mood or personality disorders.
5. Exhibits signs of perfectionism, rigidity, obsessive self-control.
6. Shows an excessive interest in weight issues and dieting.

Although the extreme damage to overall health seen in anorexia does not occur to the same extent in bulimia, the disease has a significant impact. In addition to a cessation of menstruation in some women, fluid and electrolyte imbalances can have serious medical consequences. Frequent vomiting erodes tooth enamel and promotes the formation of cavities, while the excess use of laxatives can produce dehydration or even permanent intestinal dysfunction. In some cases, gastric rupture or esophageal tears can occur.

Like **treatment** for anorexia nervosa, individual psychotherapy or cognitive behavioral therapy combined with medications that address the brain's serotonin imbalances have proven to be the most effective. **Twelve-step programs** and other group approaches that target self-image issues can be particularly helpful. Family therapy is often advised to help patients and their families cope with longstanding issues that may trigger bulimic behavior.

Further Reading

American Psychiatric Association. *Diagnostic and Statistical Manual of Mental Disorders*, 4th Edition, Text Revision. Washington, DC: American Psychiatric Association, 2000.

Davis, Caroline. Addiction and the Eating Disorders. *Psychiatric Times* February 2001. Retrieved from http://www.psychiatrictimes.com/p010259.html

Erickson, Carlton K. *The Science of Addiction: From Neurobiology to Treatment*. New York: Norton, 2007.

Hyman, S. E., and Malenka, R. C. Addiction and the Brain: The Neurobiology of Compulsion and Its Persistence. *Nature Reviews Neuroscience* 2001: 2(10), 695–703.

Kalivas, P. W., and Volkow, Nora. The Neural Basis of Addiction: A Pathology of Motivation and Choice. *American Journal of Psychiatry* August 2005: 162(8), 1403–1413.

Nestler, Eric J., and Malenka, Robert. The Addicted Brain. *Scientific American*, September 2007. Retrieved from http://www.sciam.com/article.cfm?chanID=sa006&colID=1&articleID=0001E632-978A-1019-978A83414B7F0101

Neumark-Sztainer, Dianne, Eisenberg, Marla, Fulkerson, Jayne, Story, Mary, and Larson, Nicole. Family Meals and Disordered Eating in Adolescents. *Archives of Pediatrics and Adolescent Medicine* 2008: 162(1), 17–22.

Ozelli, Kristin Leutwyler. This Is Your Brain on Food. *Scientific American* September 2007: 297(3), 84–85.

Potenza, Marc N. Should Addictive Disorders Include Non-Substance-Related Conditions? *Addiction* 2006: 101(s1), 142–151.

Sacker, Ira, and Buff, Sheila. *Regaining Your Self: Breaking Free from the Eating Disorder Identity: A Bold New Approach*. New York: Hyperion, 2007.

Buprenorphine (Buprenex, Suboxone, Subutex) A partial opiate **agonist**, buprenorphine is a synthetic drug derived from thebaine which is used to treat **addictions** to **heroin** and other **opiates**. It does not produce the same level of euphoria as other opiate agonists, so its potential for **abuse** is not as great. It is available in different formulations—Buprenex, Suboxone, and Subutex. Suboxone also contains naloxone, an **antagonist** that further reduces the likelihood of abuse.

Although buprenorphine is an opioid, its maximum effects are less than those of full agonists like heroin and methadone. At low doses, it allows addicted individuals to discontinue addictive use of opiates without experiencing **withdrawal** symptoms.

Further Reading

Califano, Joseph A., Jr. *High Society: How Substance Abuse Ravages America and What to Do About It*. New York: Perseus Books, 2007.

Hoffman, John, and Froemke, Susan, eds. *Addiction: Why Can't They Just Stop?* New York: Rodale, 2007.

Home Box Office (HBO). In partnership with the Robert Wood Johnson Foundation, the National Institute on Drug Abuse, and the National Institute on Alcohol Abuse and Alcoholism. *Addiction: Why Can't They Just Stop?* Documentary. March 2007.

Ketcham, Katherine, and Pace, Nicholas A. *Teens Under the Influence: The Truth About Kids, Alcohol, and Other Drugs*. New York: Ballantine Books, 2003.

U.S. Department of Health and Human Services, National Institute on Drug Abuse (NIDA), June 2007. Retrieved from http://www.nida.gov

U.S. Department of Health and Human Services, Substance Abuse and Mental Health Services Administration (SAMHSA), August 2007. Retrieved from http://www.samhsa.gov

U.S. Department of Justice, Drug Enforcement Administration (DEA), March 2008. Retrieved from http://www.usdoj.gov/dea

Butorphanol An **opiate** that can be made from the natural **opium** derivative thebaine, butorphanol is usually manufactured synthetically. Originally available as an injectable opiate analgesic for human and veterinary use, it was eventually formulated into a nasal spray (Stadol NS). This method of delivery made the drug more accessible, and it rapidly entered circulation through illicit drug channels to users in the recreational drug market who were attracted to its convenient method of administration. As a result, in 1997 the Drug Enforcement Administration placed butorphanol on Schedule IV of the Controlled Substances Act.

Further Reading

Califano, Joseph A., Jr. *High Society: How Substance Abuse Ravages America and What to Do About It.* New York: Perseus Books, 2007.

Hoffman, John, and Froemke, Susan, eds. *Addiction: Why Can't They Just Stop?* New York: Rodale, 2007.

Home Box Office (HBO). In partnership with the Robert Wood Johnson Foundation, the National Institute on Drug Abuse, and the National Institute on Alcohol Abuse and Alcoholism. *Addiction: Why Can't They Just Stop?* Documentary. March 2007.

Ketcham, Katherine, and Pace, Nicholas A. *Teens Under the Influence: The Truth About Kids, Alcohol, and Other Drugs.* New York: Ballantine Books, 2003.

U.S. Department of Health and Human Services, National Institute on Drug Abuse (NIDA), June 2007. Retrieved from http://www.nida.gov

U.S. Department of Health and Human Services, Substance Abuse and Mental Health Services Administration (SAMHSA), August 2007. Retrieved from http://www.samhsa.gov

U.S. Department of Justice, Drug Enforcement Administration (DEA), March 2008. Retrieved from http://www.usdoj.gov/dea

C

Caffeine Addiction Caffeine is a naturally occurring central nervous system stimulant found in over 60 plants that have been harvested around the world for thousands of years. Known for its energy-boosting properties, caffeine is most commonly consumed in coffee, tea, or cocoa, as well as in cola-based soft drinks or other beverages to which synthetic caffeine has been added.

In general, most coffee consumed in the United States contains about 100 to 135 milligrams of caffeine per cup, but since coffee is derived from the seed of various types of coffee plants, the concentration of caffeine varies in different coffees. Tea, which is produced from a species of bush or tree called *Camellia sinensis*, generally contains about half the amount of caffeine that coffee contains; soft drinks have slightly less; and cocoa, derived from the cacao bean, contains very little. So-called energy drinks have about the same amount as tea.

Although many believe that coffee is addicting, it does not meet the criteria for **addiction** as spelled out in the American Psychiatric Association's ***Diagnostic and Statistical Manual of Mental Disorders*** (*DSM*). While caffeine users may look forward with great anticipation to their coffee or tea and miss the beverage if they cannot indulge—even experiencing some physical discomfort such as headaches if it is withdrawn for any length of time—the lack of control and negative consequences in one's life that characterize true addiction do not apply to caffeine.

The *DSM* does recognize other problems associated with caffeine, including caffeine **intoxication**, caffeine-induced sleep disorders, and caffeine-induced **anxiety disorder**. Caffeine intoxication occurs when someone consumes too much caffeine in a short period of time; symptoms include nervousness, restlessness, gastrointestinal distress and acid stomach, tremor, rapid heart beat, and, in extreme cases, disorientation, delusions, and possibly coma. A serious overdose—what can happen when a person takes 2 grams or more via caffeine pills—might produce fatal cardiac arrhythmias.

Caffeine-induced sleep and anxiety disorders are sometimes diagnosed in people who have a history of consuming high levels of caffeine over a long period. These conditions are manifested by persistent difficulties in sleeping or by episodes of anxiety that can easily be misdiagnosed as panic attacks, bipolar disorders, or even psychoses.

Besides contributing to gastric acidity, coffee acts as a diuretic and causes the kidneys to work harder to produce urine. Most adults can consume a moderate amount of coffee, 200 to 300 milligrams per day, without adverse effects, but pregnant women should avoid caffeine in any form—coffee, tea, soft drinks, or chocolate—because it can increase risk of miscarriage. Because of its effect on developing bone tissue, teens are advised to restrict intake to about 100 milligrams a day.

cAMP Response Element-Binding Protein. *See* CREB.

Campral. *See* Addiction Medications.

Cannabis *Cannabis* is a flowering plant sometimes called **hemp** for its fibrous product which has been used for centuries in the manufacture of paper, fuel, and industrial materials. *Cannabis* is also the "**marijuana** plant," containing delta-9-tetrahydrocannabinol (THC), the psychoactive ingredient in marijuana and hash believed to be unique to this particular genus. Two *Cannabis* subspecies or varieties—*Cannabis sativa* and *Cannabis indica*—are most closely associated with products containing THC, a drug that is often categorized as a psychedelic for the perceptual distortions it produces in higher doses. Depending on how it is administered and the user's level of tolerance, light doses of *Cannabis* produce relaxation, pleasure, and a heightened awareness of sensations; higher doses may lead to an altered perception of space and time and impaired memory; very high doses have been known to distort one's sense of identity and to trigger hallucinations. These effects make *Cannabis* a dangerous drug to use, even in small doses, when driving or in other situations requiring rapid reflexes and unimpaired motor coordination.

Cannabis is known for its tendency to stimulate appetite, relieve chronic pain, and suppress nausea. Some groups are therefore lobbying to legalize it for medical use by AIDS patients, those with persistently painful conditions, or cancer sufferers enduring the nausea and vomiting of chemotherapy. So far, these efforts have failed, but a form of synthetic THC can be prescribed by physicians via medications like Marinol or Sativex, Schedule III drugs under the Controlled Substance Act (CSA). Since they have no currently approved medical use in the United States, however, the natural forms of *Cannabis* that are derived directly from the plant and are illegally marketed in the United States—marijuana, hash, and hashish oil—are placed under Schedule I of the CSA. These illicit substances are imported from around the world via the illegal drug trade. Because *Cannabis* plants are fairly easy to cultivate under artificial conditions, hundreds of American basements and attics have been converted into clandestine growing laboratories where the plants are carefully nurtured to develop maximum concentrations of THC.

See also Drug Classes; Appendix B.

Substance/Drug	Intoxicating Effects	Potential Health Consequences
Cannabis Marijuana Hashish	Euphoria, relaxed inhibitions, increased appetite, reduced anxiety, feelings of well-being	Cough, frequent respiratory infections, impaired memory and learning, decreased motivation, anxiety, panic attacks, psychosis *Source: NIDA, DEA*

Cannabis Chart

Further Reading

Califano, Joseph A., Jr. *High Society: How Substance Abuse Ravages America And What to Do About It.* New York: Perseus Books, 2007.

Hoffman, John, and Froemke, Susan, eds. *Addiction: Why Can't They Just Stop?* New York: Rodale, 2007.

Home Box Office (HBO). In partnership with the Robert Wood Johnson Foundation, the National Institute on Drug Abuse, and the National Institute on Alcohol Abuse and Alcoholism. *Addiction: Why Can't They Just Stop?* Documentary. March 2007.

Jenkins, Richard. *Cannabis and Young People: Reviewing the Evidence.* London: Jessica Kingsley, 2006.

Ketcham, Katherine, and Pace, Nicholas A. *Teens Under the Influence: The Truth About Kids, Alcohol, and Other Drugs.* New York: Ballantine Books, 2003.

U.S. Department of Health and Human Services, National Institute on Drug Abuse (NIDA), June 2007. Retrieved from http://www.nida.gov

U.S. Department of Health and Human Services, National Institute on Drug Abuse. *Research Report Series: Marijuana Abuse.* NIH Publication No. 05-3859, July 2005.

U.S. Department of Health and Human Services, Substance Abuse and Mental Health Services Administration (SAMHSA), August 2007. Retrieved from http://www.samhsa.gov

U.S. Department of Justice, Drug Enforcement Administration (DEA), March 2008. Retrieved from http://www.usdoj.gov/dea

Carisoprodol. *See* Meprobamate.

Carpenter, Karen (1950–1983) Born in 1950, Karen Carpenter was a talented young singer who, with her brother Richard, formed one of the most successful and popular musical groups of the 1970s, selling record-breaking numbers of albums and bringing enduring new dimensions to popular music. In 1983, when she died at the peak of her career from complications of **anorexia nervosa**, America was shocked by the realization that an **eating disorder** could be so deadly. Media images had revealed the performer's increasing emaciation, but many wanted to believe that Carpenter's personal life was as radiantly happy as her vibrant stage presence and her dazzling smile seemed to suggest.

One of the first celebrities whose death was publicly known to have been caused by anorexia, Carpenter began dieting during the late 1960s to rid herself of some chubbiness present since childhood. She maintained a healthy and stable weight until the early-1970s, when she was reported to have complained that she appeared heavier in photographs than she would have liked. She became more obsessed with her appearance and adopted extreme weight-management techniques. By 1975, she was so emaciated and exhausted she was forced to cancel concert dates. By this time, her brother and fellow performer had developed an **addiction** to drugs from which he was able to recover.

Carpenter received therapy for her disease and, in its later stages, was hospitalized to undergo a procedure known as hyperalimentation, in which liquid nutrients are dripped into the body through a vein. Although this process helped her gain several pounds, her health continued to deteriorate. She gave her last performance in December of 1982, collapsing and dying of cardiac failure early in 1983.

The public nature of Carpenter's struggle with her illness focused critical media attention on anorexia nervosa and bulimia, encouraging others to

Karen and Richard Carpenter during a 1972 White House visit to then-President Richard M. Nixon. (*Official White House photo*)

publicly acknowledge their own battles with the disease and generating more research into the causes of eating disorders and better methods of treating them.

In Carpenter's memory, her family established The Carpenter Family Foundation that helps fund medical and artistic causes. Richard Carpenter is actively involved in its operations.

Further Reading

Coleman, Ray. *The Carpenters: The Untold Story.* New York: HarperCollins, 1995.

Cerebellum, Cerebral Cortex, Cerebrum. *See* Brain and Addiction.

Cesamet. *See* Medical Marijuana.

Chantix. *See* Addiction Medications.

Chemical Dependence. *See* Dependence.

Chew Tobacco, Chewing Tobacco. *See* Smokeless Tobacco.

Chloral Hydrate Like many sedative-hypnotic drugs on Schedule IV of the Controlled Substances Act, chloral hydrate has a moderate potential for **abuse**; at very high doses, it can dangerously suppress respiration and lower blood pressure. Among the oldest of central nervous system **depressants**, chloral hydrate was first synthesized in 1832 and is now marketed in syrups or soft gelatin capsules. Since the availability of numerous other drugs in this class has increased, the use of chloral hydrate to treat insomnia has lessened, but some physicians still prefer to use it in sedating children prior to medical procedures**.**

Chloral hydrate is mixed with alcohol to create the notorious "Mickey Finn" knockout drops that take effect relatively quickly. In chronic use, the drug can produce liver damage and severe symptoms when the user attempts to withdraw from it.

Further Reading

Califano, Joseph A., Jr. *High Society: How Substance Abuse Ravages America and What to Do About It.* New York: Perseus Books, 2007.
Hoffman, John, and Froemke, Susan, eds. *Addiction: Why Can't They Just Stop?* New York: Rodale, 2007.
Home Box Office (HBO). In partnership with the Robert Wood Johnson Foundation, the National Institute on Drug Abuse, and the National Institute on Alcohol Abuse and Alcoholism. *Addiction: Why Can't They Just Stop?* Documentary. March 2007.
Ketcham, Katherine, and Pace, Nicholas A. *Teens Under the Influence: The Truth About Kids, Alcohol, and Other Drugs.* New York: Ballantine Books, 2003.
U.S. Department of Health and Human Services, National Institute on Drug Abuse (NIDA), June 2007. Retrieved from http://www.nida.gov
U.S. Department of Health and Human Services, Substance Abuse and Mental Health Services Administration (SAMHSA), August 2007. Retrieved from http://www.samhsa.gov
U.S. Department of Justice, Drug Enforcement Administration (DEA), March 2008. Retrieved from http://www.usdoj.gov/dea

Chocolate Addiction. *See* Food Addiction and Obesity.

Cigarettes Twenty-five percent of Americans were cigarette smokers in 2006. Decreasing only slightly by 1 percentage point since 2002, this prevalence reveals how tenacious a cigarette **addiction** can be. In the face of its devastating effects on health, significant out-of-pocket costs, and decreasing numbers of public venues where it is permitted, cigarette smoking is a habit that millions of people adopt every day and then find, to their dismay, very difficult to quit.

In an effort to prevent children and adolescents from getting hooked on nicotine—the psychoactive drug in cigarettes—and ingesting the hundreds of dangerous chemicals that cigarettes contain, all 50 states in the United States have passed laws restricting cigarette sales to those who are at least 18 years of age. Other countries enforce similar laws.

"Cigarette" usually refers to a slim, paper-wrapped cylinder containing an addictive mixture of **tobacco** and other ingredients, but it may also refer to other products such as **marijuana** that have been rolled into cigarette paper for smoking. Although they are significantly different from **cigars**, early European cigarettes may have been modeled on the crude product that the poor created out of discarded cigar butts that the wealthy tossed into the streets. Well before that, probably as early as the 9th century, indigenous cultures in the Americas were smoking a harsh form of tobacco in reeds or other crude forms of smoking tubes.

Records show that in the 1600s, colonial settlers smoked a type of cigar as well as **pipes**, first consuming the harsh tobacco to which the Indians had introduced them before learning to cultivate a milder form that proved to be very addicting. Cigarette smoking quickly caught on during the 1800s after the British, who were exposed to the practice during the Crimean War during the mid-1800s, introduced it to the United States. As a newly developed machine able to produce 200 cigarettes a minute made them more affordable, cigarettes quickly began to outstrip the use of chewing tobacco, pipes and cigars, and snuff.

Although most people purchased tobacco and papers to roll their own cigarettes well into the 1940s and 1950s, mass production made manufactured cigarettes accessible

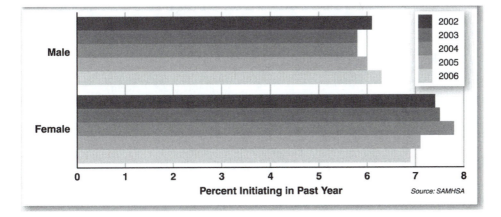

Past-Year Cigarette Initiation among Youths Aged 12 to 17 Who Had Never Smoked, by Gender: 2002–2006

everywhere. Cigarette companies spent lavishly to sell their product through print and radio ads and the newly developed medium known as television.

By the late 1950s, when nearly every household had at least one smoker living in it, disquieting news about the ill effects of smoking had become more widespread. In 1964, the U.S. Surgeon General issued a report detailing the harmful effects smoking could have on health. Almost immediately, cigarette consumption dropped by 20 percent, then rebounded quickly. Despite subsequent legislation restricting advertising and U.S. government-funded reports that verified and strengthened earlier concerns about the dangers of cigarettes and other tobacco products, high consumption has continued. The tobacco industry is now a powerful lobby that has successfully obscured the obvious dangers of their product with aggressive marketing campaigns. Nevertheless, the message has gotten through to many, and so, with fewer consumers choosing to smoke cigarettes and aware that the sooner people start smoking in life the more likely they are to be addicted for life, cigarette companies are marketing **mini cigars** and **smokeless tobacco** products more aggressively to appeal to adolescents.

According to the U.S. Department of Health and Human Services Substance Abuse and Mental Health Services Administration (SAMHSA)*:

- Among young adults 18- to 22-years-old, full-time college students were less likely to be current cigarette smokers than their peers who were not enrolled full time in college. Cigarette use in the past month in 2006 was reported by 28.4 percent of full-time college students, less than the rate of 43.5 percent for those not enrolled full time.

- Among full-time college students aged 19, current cigarette smoking increased from 24.4 percent in 2005 to 28.8 percent in 2006; however, it decreased for students aged 20 (from 32.3 to 27.2 percent) and 21 (from 36.3 to 30.2 percent). Past-month cigarette smoking also declined from 32.9 to 23.5 percent among Hispanic full-time students aged 18 to 22.

- In 2006, current cigarette smoking among youths aged 12 to 17 and young adults aged 18 to 25 was more prevalent among whites than blacks (12.4 vs. 6.0 percent for youths and 44.4 vs. 27.5 percent for young adults). Among adults aged 26 or older, however, whites and blacks used cigarettes at about the same rate (24.9 and 27.2 percent, respectively). The rates for Hispanics were 8.2 percent among youths, 28.8 percent among young adults, and 23.6 percent among those aged 26 or older.

- Among youths aged 12 to 17, the rate of current cigarette smoking in 2006 did not differ significantly for females (10.7 percent) and males (10.0 percent). The rate for both males and females declined between 2002 and 2006 (12.3 percent for males in 2002; 13.6 percent for females in 2002).

- Among youths aged 12 to 17 in 2006, 3.3 million (12.9 percent) used a tobacco product in the past month, and 2.6 million (10.4 percent) used cigarettes. The rate of past-month cigarette use among 12-to 17-year-olds declined from 13 percent in 2002 to 10.4 percent in 2006. Past-month use of smokeless tobacco, however, was higher in 2006 (2.4 percent) than in 2002 (2 percent).

- In 2006, 1.7 percent of 12- to 13-year-olds, 9.1 percent of 14- to 15-year-olds, and 19.9 percent of 16- to 17-year-olds were current cigarette smokers. The percentage of past-month cigarette smokers among 12- to 13-year-olds was lower in 2006 than in 2005 (1.7 vs. 2.4 percent). Across age groups, current cigarette use peaked at 40.2 percent among young adults aged 21 to 25. Less than a quarter (22.5 percent) of persons in the 35 or older age group in 2006 smoked cigarettes in the past month.

Table 11. Cigarette Use in Lifetime, Past Year, and Past Month among Persons Aged 12 to 17, by Demographic Characteristics: Percentages, 2005 and 2006

Demographic Characteristic	Time Period					
	Lifetime		Past Year		Past Month	
	2005	2006	2005	2006	2005	2006
Total	26.7	25.8	17.3	17.0	10.8	10.4
Gender						
Male	26.3	25.8	16.9	16.7	10.7	10.0
Female	27.2	25.9	17.8	17.4	10.8	10.7
Hispanic Origin And Race						
Not Hispanic or Latino	26.8	26.2	17.4	17.4	11.1	10.9
White	28.8	28.5	19.8	19.5	12.8	12.4
Black or African American	21.7	20.0	10.6	10.8	6.5	6.0
American Indian or Alaska Native	40.4	40.2	25.0	*	18.0	21.2
Native Hawaiian or other Pacific Islander	*	*	*	*	*	*
Asian	13.3	14.7	6.4	11.0	3.0	5.2
Two or More Races	29.2	27.2	16.7	19.2	11.0	12.7
Hispanic or Latino	26.3	24.3	16.8	15.1	9.1	8.2
Gender/Race/Hispanic Origin						
Male, White, Not Hispanic	28.3	28.1	19.1	18.9	12.5	11.8
Female, White, Not Hispanic	29.4	28.8	20.6	20.0	13.0	13.0
Male, Black, Not Hispanic	21.5	19.8	11.5	11.0	7.4	5.9
Female, Black, Not Hispanic	21.9	20.2	9.6	10.5	5.6	6.2
Male, Hispanic	26.8	25.4	16.9	15.2	9.2	8.6
Female, Hispanic	25.9	23.1	16.6	15.0	9.1	7.7

*Low precision; no estimate reported.
Source: SAMHSA.

- In 2006, the number of persons aged 12 or older who smoked cigarettes for the first time in the past 12 months was 2.4 million, which was similar to the estimate in 2005 (2.3 million) but significantly greater than the estimate for 2002 (1.9 million). Most new smokers in 2006 were under age 18 when they first smoked cigarettes (61.2 percent).
- In 2006, among recent initiates aged 12 to 49, the average age of first cigarette use was 17.1 years, similar to the average in 2005 (17.3 years).
- Of those aged 12 or older who had not smoked cigarettes prior to the past year, the past year initiation rate for cigarettes was 2.9 percent in 2006, similar to the rate in 2005 (2.7 percent). Among youths aged 12 to 17 years, incidence showed no significant changes between 2002 (6.7 percent) and 2006 (6.6 percent). This pattern was observed for both male and female youths.
- In 2006, the number of persons who had started smoking cigarettes daily within the past 12 months was 1.1 million. This estimate is similar to the estimates for 2002 (1 million), 2003 (1.1 million), 2004 (1.1 million), and 2005 (1 million). Of these new daily smokers in 2006, 44.2 percent, or 0.5 million (an average of about 1,300 initiates per day), were younger than age 18 when they started smoking daily.

Table 12. Cigarette Use in Lifetime, Past Year, and Past Month among Persons Aged 18 or Older, by Demographic Characteristics: Percentages, 2005 and 2006

Demographic Characteristic	Lifetime		Past Year		Past Month	
	2005	**2006**	**2005**	**2006**	**2005**	**2006**
Total	71.2	70.9	30.5	30.5	26.5	26.7
Gender						
Male	76.9	76.6	33.8	34.4	29.5	30.0
Female	65.9	65.6	27.4	26.9	23.8	23.6
Hispanic Origin And Race						
Not Hispanic or Latino	72.8	72.8	30.6	30.7	26.9	27.0
White	76.5	76.5	31.2	31.3	27.3	27.5
Black or African American	61.0	60.0	30.1	30.1	27.3	27.2
American Indian or Alaska Native	73.4	77.3	44.5	46.2	38.7	40.1
Native Hawaiian or other Pacific Islander	*	*	37.5	*	31.1	*
Asian	44.3	45.8	18.7	18.8	14.6	15.6
Two or More Races	67.6	75.2	38.6	36.6	34.5	33.8
Hispanic or Latino	59.9	58.4	29.7	29.4	24.2	24.7
Education						
< High School	65.7	66.2	39.1	39.4	34.8	35.6
High School Graduate	72.0	71.5	35.3	35.2	31.8	31.9
Some College	74.1	74.0	32.4	32.3	28.1	27.7
College Graduate	70.9	70.2	17.9	18.0	13.8	14.3
Current Employment						
Full-Time	73.8	73.1	32.6	33.0	28.3	28.8
Part-Time	70.3	69.7	30.2	29.9	25.2	25.4
Unemployed	72.6	72.5	49.2	51.9	43.8	47.8
Other[1]	66.3	67.0	24.3	23.6	21.5	20.9

*Low precision; no estimate reported.

[1]The Other Employment category includes retired persons, disabled persons, homemakers, students, or other persons not in the labor force.

Source: SAMHSA.

Statistics

- Cigarette smoking causes 87 percent of lung cancer deaths and is responsible for most cancers of the larynx, oral cavity and pharynx, esophagus, and bladder.
- Tobacco smoke contains thousands of chemical agents, including over 60 substances that are known to cause cancer.
- Smoking cessation has major and immediate health benefits, including decreasing the risk of lung and other cancers, heart attack, stroke, and chronic lung disease.

• The average age of first daily smoking among new daily smokers aged 12 to 49 in 2006 was 18.9 years. This was not significantly different from the average in 2005 (19.7 years).

*For more statistics, see Appendix D.

See also Nicotine.

Further Reading

Califano, Joseph A., Jr. *High Society: How Substance Abuse Ravages America and What to Do About It.* New York: Perseus Books, 2007.

Federal Trade Commission. October 2007. Retrieved from http://www.ftc.gov/opa/2007/04/cigaretterpt.shtm

U.S. Department of Health and Human Services. *Nicotine Addiction: A Report of the Surgeon General.* Centers for Disease Control and Prevention, Public Health Service, Center for Health Promotion and Education, Office on Smoking and Health, 1988.

U.S. Department of Health and Human Services. *Targeting Tobacco Use: The Nation's Leading Cause of Death.* Centers for Disease Control and Prevention, 2003.

U.S. Department of Health and Human Services. *The Health Consequences of Smoking: A Report of the Surgeon General.* Centers for Disease Control and Prevention, National Center for Chronic Disease Prevention and Health Promotion, Office on Smoking and Health, 2004.

U.S. Department of Health and Human Services. *Results from the 2006 National Survey on Drug Use and Health: National Findings.* Substance Abuse and Mental Health Services Administration (SAMHSA), Office of Applied Studies. DHHS Publication No. SMA 07-4293, 2007.

U.S. Department of Health and Human Services, Centers for Disease Control and Prevention (CDC), January 2008. Retrieved from http://apps.nccd.cdc.gov/osh_faq

U.S. Department of Health and Human Services, Centers for Disease Control and Prevention (CDC), November 2007. Retrieved from http://www.cdc.gov/tobacco

U.S. Department of Health and Human Services, National Cancer Institute (NCI), December 2007. Retrieved from http://www.cancer.gov/cancertopics/tobacco

U.S. Department of Health and Human Services, National Institute on Drug Abuse. *Research Report Series: Tobacco Addiction.* NIH Publication No. 06-4342, July 2006.

Cigarette Smoking FAQs

Tobacco use, particularly cigarette smoking, is the single most preventable cause of death in the United States. Cigarette smoking is directly responsible for approximately 30 percent of all cancer deaths annually in the United States. It also causes chronic lung disease (emphysema and chronic bronchitis), cardiovascular disease, stroke, and cataracts. Smoking during pregnancy can cause stillbirth, low birthweight, sudden infant death syndrome (SIDS), and other serious pregnancy complications. Quitting smoking greatly reduces a person's risk of developing the diseases mentioned, and can limit adverse health effects on the developing child.

1. What are the effects of cigarette smoking on cancer rates?

    Cigarette smoking causes 87 percent of lung cancer deaths. Lung cancer is the leading cause of cancer death in both men and women. Smoking is also responsible for most cancers of the larynx, oral cavity and pharynx, esophagus, and bladder. In addition, it is a cause of kidney, pancreatic, cervical, and stomach cancers, as well as acute myeloid leukemia.

2. Are there any health risks for nonsmokers?

The health risks caused by cigarette smoking are not limited to smokers. Exposure to secondhand smoke, or environmental tobacco smoke (ETS), significantly increases the risk of lung cancer and heart disease in nonsmokers as well as the risk of several respiratory illnesses in young children. The U.S. Environmental Protection Agency (EPA), the National Institute of Environmental Health Science's National Toxicology Program, and the World Health Organization's International Agency for Research on Cancer have classified secondhand smoke as a known human carcinogen—a category reserved for agents for which there is sufficient scientific evidence that they cause cancer. The U.S. EPA has estimated that exposure to secondhand smoke causes about 3,000 lung cancer deaths among nonsmokers and is responsible for up to 300,000 cases of lower respiratory tract infections in children up to 18 months of age in the United States each year.

3. What harmful chemicals are found in cigarette smoke?

Cigarette smoke contains about 4,000 chemical agents, including over 60 carcinogens. Many of these substances, such as carbon monoxide, tar, arsenic, and lead, are poisonous and toxic to the human body. Nicotine is a drug that is naturally present in the tobacco plant and is primarily responsible for a person's addiction to tobacco products, including cigarettes. During smoking, nicotine is absorbed into the bloodstream and travels to the brain in a matter of seconds. Nicotine causes an addiction to cigarettes and other tobacco products similar to the addiction produced by using heroin and cocaine.

4. How does exposure to tobacco smoke affect the cigarette smoker?

Smoking harms nearly every major organ of the body. The risk of developing smoking-related diseases, such as lung and other cancers, heart disease, stroke, and respiratory illnesses, increases with total lifetime exposure to cigarette smoke. This includes the number of cigarettes a person smokes each day, the intensity of smoking (i.e., the size and frequency of puffs), the age at which smoking began, the number of years a person has smoked, and a smoker's secondhand smoke exposure.

5. How would quitting smoking affect the risk of developing cancer and other diseases?

Smoking cessation has major and immediate health benefits for men and women of all ages. Quitting smoking decreases the risk of lung and other cancers, heart attack, stroke, and chronic lung disease. The earlier a person quits, the greater the health benefit. For example, research has shown that people who quit before age 50 reduce their risk of dying in the next 15 years by half compared with those who continue to smoke. Smoking low-yield cigarettes, as compared to cigarettes with higher tar and nicotine, provides no clear benefit to health.

Cigarillos. *See* Mini Cigars.

Cigars Unlike **cigarettes**, which are manufactured by wrapping **tobacco** in paper, cigars are made by wrapping tobacco in tobacco. The outermost leaves come from the widest part of the tobacco plant and help define the character and quality of the cigar. Cigars are produced from whole leaf tobacco while cigarettes comprise shredded and processed tobacco leaves.

Tobacco was grown in North America as early as 1610, and cigar factories proliferated during the 1800s when cigar smoking was the mark of a well-to-do man; it continued to be popular with many notable people including Winston Churchill until well into the

20th century. The increasing popularity of cigarette smoking, especially after World War II, eroded the cigar's popularity and production fell significantly. In the 1990s, however, interest in the cigar revived—especially among women. Since 1993, cigar sales in the United States have increased by about 50 percent, which marks a reversal in the 20-year decline that occurred from 1973 to 1993. Small cigar consumption has increased modestly, about 13 percent, whereas consumption of large cigars has increased nearly 70 percent. Most of the increase appears to be from teenagers and young adult males who smoke occasionally (less than daily). Smoking surveys show that the current level of cigar smoking among adolescents exceeds the use of **smokeless tobacco**. For example, one Massachusetts survey of students in grades 6 to 12 showed that cigar use (smoked a cigar in the last 30 days) ranged from 3.2 percent in 6th grade to as high as 30 percent in high school. These rates are double the use of smokeless tobacco. The same survey showed that 6 percent to 7 percent of girls in grades 9 to 11 reported they had used cigars in the past month. In general, twice as many teenage boys as girls are likely to smoke cigars.

The greatest increase in adult cigar smoking is among young and middle-aged (ages 18 to 44) white males with higher than average incomes and education. According to a 2005 article in the *American Journal of Public Health*, industry marketing of cigars and **mini cigars** directed at women and adolescents has largely been successful, and the cinnamon, grape, and other new flavorings have increased their popularity. The authors estimate that cigar consumption rose about 28 percent in the United States between 2000 and 2004, even as cigarette smoking declined.

Cigars come in various shapes and sizes—perfecto, panatela, and cheroot refer to the shape; corona (half corona, petit corona, and double corona) refer to the size. In addition, the color of the tobacco leaf may vary from light (claro) to very dark (colorado maduro), which is likely to be the strongest. Inside the wrapper are fillers, tobacco leaves that in top quality cigars are hand rolled into the wrappers to keep the tobacco moist. Most of the world's finest cigars are made in Cuba, where they probably originated, but good cigars are being machine-made around the world to satisfy a growing market. In 1962, when President John F. Kennedy instituted a trade embargo against Cuba, it became no longer possible to import Cuban cigars. Highly prized as the very best cigars made, they are frequently smuggled into the United States from Canada and other countries that can legally purchase them from Cuba.

Cigar tobacco is cured (dried) and fermented to develop taste and aroma. This process produces a high concentration of nitrates and other dangerous chemicals, making cigars significantly more toxic than cigarettes and one of the most potent delivery vehicles for nicotine. "Little cigars" look very much like cigarettes in brown paper, and many state taxing authorities are lobbying to call them cigarettes in order to generate the increased tax revenue that cigarette sales provide, but cigar manufacturers continue to resist that effort. Nevertheless, state and federal authorities as well as the American Cancer Society and other health advocacy groups are currently debating the issue.

Cigars' Harmful Ingredients

Compared to a cigarette, a large cigar emits up to 20 times more ammonia, 5 to 10 times more of the carcinogens cadmium and methylethyl nitrosamine, and up to 80 to 90 times as much of the highly carcinogenic tobacco-specific nitrosamines.

The smoke released from cigars and cigarettes contains many of the same toxic agents (carbon monoxide, nicotine, hydrogen cyanide, ammonia, and volatile aldehydes) and human carcinogens (benzene, vinyl chloride, ethylene oxide, arsenic, cadmium, nitrosamines, and polynuclear aromatic hydrocarbons). However, cigars emit significantly more of these substances for a number of reasons: the long aging and fermentation process for cigar tobacco leaves results in higher concentrations of nitrate in cigar tobaccos; the nonporous cigar wrappers make combustion of cigar tobacco less complete than that of cigarette tobacco; and the larger size of most cigars produces more smoke.

Not only can cigar smoking cause many cancers (oral cancers, including throat cancer, and cancer of the larynx, esophagus, and lung) but also chronic obstructive lung disease and coronary heart disease. There is also evidence that strongly suggests that cigar smoking is associated with cancer of the pancreas. Many of these cancers—lung, esophageal, and pancreatic—are associated with extremely low survival rates.

How Patterns of Use Affect Risk

Most cigarette smokers smoke every day and inhale. In contrast, as many as three-quarters of cigar smokers smoke only occasionally and the majority do not inhale; some may smoke only a few cigars per year. In spite of these differences, daily cigar smokers and cigarette smokers have similar levels of risk for oral (including throat), larynx, and esophageal cancers. Even among daily cigar smokers (smoking 1 or more cigars per day) who do *not* inhale, the risk of oral cancers is 7 times greater than for nonsmokers and the risk for larynx cancer is more than 10 times greater than for nonsmokers. Inhaling greatly magnifies this risk. Compared to nonsmokers, daily cigar smokers have 27 times the risk of oral cancer, 15 times the risk for esophageal cancer, and 53 times the risk of cancer of the larynx.

Cigar smokers are also at increased risk for heart and lung disease compared to nonsmokers. Regular cigar smokers who reported inhaling slightly have double the risk of chronic obstructive pulmonary (lung) disease and increase their risk of coronary heart disease by 23 percent.

Compared to cigarette smokers, cigar smokers have lower risks for cancer of the larynx and lung as well as heart and lung disease. Not inhaling probably plays a strong role in lowering these risks. However, with regular use and inhalation, the heart and lung disease risks of cigar smoking increase substantially, and, for some, disease risk may approach that seen in cigarette smokers. In fact, the lung cancer risk from inhaling moderately when smoking 5 cigars per day is comparable to that from smoking 1 pack of cigarettes per day.

The health consequences of regular cigar use, along with the increased use in teenagers, raise several concerns among public health officials. Addiction studies with cigarettes and spit tobacco clearly show that **addiction** to **nicotine** occurs almost exclusively during adolescence and young adulthood when children and teens begin using tobacco products. The high rates of adolescent cigar use may result in higher rates of nicotine **dependence** in this age group.

According to the U.S. Department of Health and Human Services' Centers for Disease Control and Prevention (CDC) and Substance Abuse and Mental Health Services Administration (SAMHSA)*:

- In 2006, past-month cigar smoking was equally common among male full-time college students aged 18 to 22 (19 percent) as among males in the same age group who were not enrolled full time in college (20.3 percent).
- In 2006, there were 3.1 million persons aged 12 or older who had used cigars for the first time in the past 12 months, similar to the number in 2005 (3.3 million). However, there was a significant increase in the number of new cigars smokers since 2003, when there were a reported 2.7 million cigar smokers.
- Among past year cigar initiates aged 12 to 49, the average age at first use was lower in 2006 (19.9 years) than in 2005 (21.2 years).
- Regular cigar smoking is associated with an increased risk for cancers of the lung, oral cavity, larynx, and esophagus.
- Heavy cigar smokers and those who inhale deeply may be at increased risk for developing coronary heart disease and chronic obstructive pulmonary disease.
- In 2005, an estimated 5.6 percent (13.6 million) of Americans 12 years of age or older were current cigar users.
- An estimated 6.9 percent of African American, 6 percent of white, 4.6 percent of Hispanic, 10.9 percent of American Indian/Alaska Native, and 1.8 percent of Asian-American adults are current cigar smokers.
- An estimated 14 percent of students in grades 9 to 12 in the United States are current cigar smokers. Cigar smoking is more common among males (19.2 percent) than females (8.7 percent) in these grades.
- An estimated 5.3 percent of middle school students in the United States are current cigar smokers. Estimates are higher for middle school boys (6.7 percent) than girls (3.8 percent).
- Marketing efforts have promoted cigars as symbols of a luxuriant and successful lifestyle. Endorsements by celebrities, development of cigar-friendly magazines, features of highly visible women smoking cigars, and product placement in movies have contributed to the increased visibility of cigar smoking in society.
- Since 2001, cigar packaging and advertisements have been required to display one of the following five health warning labels on a rotating basis.
  - SURGEON GENERAL WARNING: Cigar Smoking Can Cause Cancers Of The Mouth And Throat, Even If You Do Not Inhale.
  - SURGEON GENERAL WARNING: Cigar Smoking Can Cause Lung Cancer And Heart Disease.
  - SURGEON GENERAL WARNING: Tobacco Use Increases The Risk Of Infertility, Stillbirth And Low Birth Weight.
  - SURGEON GENERAL WARNING: Cigars Are Not A Safe Alternative To Cigarettes.
  - SURGEON GENERAL WARNING: Tobacco Smoke Increases The Risk Of Lung Cancer And Heart Disease, Even In Nonsmokers.

*For more statistics, see Appendix D.

Further Reading

Califano, Joseph A., Jr. *High Society: How Substance Abuse Ravages America and What to Do About It.* New York: Perseus Books, 2007.

Delnevo, C. D., Foulds, Jonathan, and Hrywna, Mary. Trading Tobacco: Are Youths Choosing Cigars Over Cigarettes? *American Journal of Public Health* 2005: 95, 2123.

Federal Trade Commission. October 2007. Retrieved from http://www.ftc.gov/opa/2007/04/cigaretterpt.shtm

U.S. Department of Health and Human Services. *Nicotine Addiction: A Report of the Surgeon General.* Centers for Disease Control and Prevention, Public Health Service, Center for Health Promotion and Education, Office on Smoking and Health, 1988.

U.S. Department of Health and Human Services. *Targeting Tobacco Use: The Nation's Leading Cause of Death.* Centers for Disease Control and Prevention, 2003.

U.S. Department of Health and Human Services. *The Health Consequences of Smoking: A Report of the Surgeon General.* Centers for Disease Control and Prevention, National Center for Chronic Disease Prevention and Health Promotion, Office on Smoking and Health, 2004.

U.S. Department of Health and Human Services. *Results from the 2006 National Survey on Drug Use and Health: National Findings.* Substance Abuse and Mental Health Services Administration (SAMHSA), Office of Applied Studies. DHHS Publication No. SMA 07-4293, 2007.

U.S. Department of Health and Human Services, Centers for Disease Control and Prevention (CDC), January 2008. Retrieved from http://apps.nccd.cdc.gov/osh_faq

U.S. Department of Health and Human Services, Centers for Disease Control and Prevention (CDC), November 2007. Retrieved from http://www.cdc.gov/tobacco

U.S. Department of Health and Human Services, National Cancer Institute (NCI), December 2007. Retrieved from http://www.cancer.gov/cancertopics/tobacco

U.S. Department of Health and Human Services, National Institute on Drug Abuse. *Research Report Series: Tobacco Addiction.* NIH Publication No. 06-4342, July 2006.

Questions and Answers About Cigar Smoking and Cancer

1. What are the health risks associated with cigar smoking?

Scientific evidence has shown that cancers of the oral cavity (lip, tongue, mouth, and throat), larynx, lung, and esophagus are associated with cigar smoking. Furthermore, evidence strongly suggests a link between cigar smoking and cancer of the pancreas. Daily cigar smokers, particularly those who inhale, are also at increased risk for developing heart and lung disease.

Like cigarette smoking, the risks from cigar smoking increase with more exposure. For example, compared with someone who has never smoked, smoking only 1 to 2 cigars per day doubles the risk for oral and esophageal cancers. Smoking 3 to 4 cigars daily can increase the risk of oral cancers to more than 8 times the risk for a nonsmoker, while the chance of esophageal cancer is increased to 4 times the risk for someone who has never smoked. Both cigar and cigarette smokers have similar levels of risk for oral, throat, and esophageal cancers.

The health risks associated with occasional cigar smoking (less than daily) are not known. About three-quarters of cigar smokers are occasional smokers.

2. What is the effect of inhalation on disease risk?

One of the major differences between cigar and cigarette smoking is the degree of inhalation. Almost all cigarette smokers report inhaling whereas the majority of cigar smokers do not because cigar smoke is generally more irritating. However, cigar smokers who have a history of cigarette smoking are more likely to inhale cigar smoke. Cigar smokers experience higher rates of lung cancer, coronary heart disease, and chronic obstructive lung disease than nonsmokers, but not as high as the rates for cigarette smokers. These lower rates for cigar smokers are probably related to reduced inhalation.

3. How are cigars and cigarettes different?

    Cigars and cigarettes differ in both size and the type of tobacco used. Cigarettes are generally more uniform in size and contain less than 1 gram of tobacco each. Cigars, on the other hand, can vary in size and shape and can measure more than 7 inches in length. Large cigars typically contain between 5 and 17 grams of tobacco. It is not unusual for some premium cigars to contain the tobacco equivalent of an entire pack of cigarettes. U.S. cigarettes are made from different blends of tobaccos, whereas most cigars are composed primarily of a single type of tobacco (air-cured or dried burley tobacco). Large cigars can take between 1 and 2 hours to smoke, whereas most cigarettes on the U.S. market take less than 10 minutes to smoke.

4. How are the health risks associated with cigar smoking different from those associated with smoking cigarettes?

    Health risks associated with both cigars and cigarettes are strongly linked to the degree of smoke exposure. Since smoke from cigars and cigarettes are composed of many of the same toxic and carcinogenic compounds, the differences in health risks appear to be related to differences in daily use and degree of inhalation. Most cigarette smokers smoke every day and inhale. In contrast, as many as three-quarters of cigar smokers smoke only occasionally, and the majority do not inhale.

    All cigar and cigarette smokers, whether or not they inhale, directly expose the lips, mouth, tongue, throat, and larynx to smoke and its carcinogens. Holding an unlit cigar between the lips also exposes these areas to carcinogens. In addition, when saliva containing smoke constituents is swallowed, the esophagus is exposed to carcinogens. These exposures probably account for the fact that oral and esophageal cancer risks are similar among cigar smokers and cigarette smokers.

    Cancer of the larynx occurs at lower rates among cigar smokers who do not inhale than among cigarette smokers. Lung cancer risk among daily cigar smokers who do not inhale is double that of nonsmokers, but significantly less than the risk for cigarette smokers. However, the lung cancer risk from moderately inhaling smoke from 5 cigars a day is comparable to the risk from smoking up to 1 pack of cigarettes a day.

5. What are the hazards for nonsmokers exposed to cigar smoke?

    Environmental tobacco smoke (ETS), also known as secondhand or passive smoke, is the smoke released from a lit cigar or cigarette. The ETS from cigars and cigarettes contains many of the same toxins and irritants (such as carbon monoxide, nicotine, hydrogen cyanide, and ammonia) as well as a number of known carcinogens (such as benzene, nitrosamines, vinyl chloride, arsenic, and hydrocarbons). Because cigars contain greater amounts of tobacco than cigarettes, they produce greater amounts of ETS.

There are, however, some differences between cigar and cigarette smoke due to the different ways cigars and cigarettes are made. Cigars go through a long aging and fermentation process during which high concentrations of carcinogenic compounds are produced. These compounds are released when a cigar is smoked. Cigar wrappers are less porous than cigarette wrappers, which makes the burning of cigar tobacco less complete than cigarette tobacco. As a result, the concentrations of toxins and irritants are higher in cigar smoke. Furthermore, the larger size of most cigars (more tobacco) and longer smoking time expose nonsmokers to higher levels of toxic compounds (including carbon monoxide, hydrocarbons, ammonia, cadmium, and other substances) than a cigarette. For example, measurements of the carbon monoxide (CO) concentration at a cigar party and a cigar banquet in a restaurant showed indoor CO levels comparable to those measured on a crowded California freeway. Such exposures could place nonsmoking workers attending such events at significantly increased risk for cancer as well as heart and lung diseases.

6. Are cigars addictive?

Like cigarettes and smokeless tobacco, cigars contain nicotine, an addictive drug found naturally in tobacco. If a cigar smoker inhales, the nicotine is absorbed rapidly in the lungs. If a cigar smoker does not inhale, the nicotine is absorbed more slowly through the mucous membranes in the mouth.

Nicotine is the agent in tobacco that is capable of causing addiction or dependence. Cigarettes have an average total nicotine content of about 8.4 milligrams; most popular brands of cigars contain many times that amount, so when cigar smokers inhale, they are ingesting large quantities of nicotine that is being absorbed rapidly. This has led many to believe that if cigar smokers do not inhale, the habit is not addicting. However, as demonstrated by the number of people addicted to smokeless tobacco, nicotine absorbed through the lining of the mouth is powerfully addicting.

Addiction studies of cigarettes and spit tobacco show that addiction to nicotine occurs almost exclusively during adolescence and young adulthood when young people first begin using these tobacco products. Several studies raise the concern that use of cigars predisposes individuals to the use of cigarettes. A recent survey showed that the relapse rate of former cigarette smokers who smoked cigars was twice as great as the relapse rate of former cigarette smokers who did not smoke cigars.

7. What are the benefits of quitting?

There are many health benefits to quitting cigar smoking, some immediate. Blood pressure, pulse rate, and breathing patterns start returning to normal soon after quitting. As time goes on, the likelihood of cancer begins to decrease and quitters begin to see improvement in their overall quality of life. Those who decide to quit have many options available to them; some quit all at once, while others rely on counseling or nicotine replacement products such as patches, gum, and nasal sprays to help them.

8. What are the current trends in cigar smoking?

Although cigar smoking occurs primarily among males between the ages of 35 and 64 who have higher educational backgrounds and incomes, recent studies suggest new trends. Most new cigar users today are teenagers and young adult males (ages 18 to 24) who smoke occasionally (less than daily).

Cigar use has increased nearly 5 times among women and appears to be increasing among adolescent females as well. Furthermore, a number of studies have reported high rates of use among not only teens but also preteens. Cigar use among older males (age 65 and older) has continued to decline since 1992.

9. How are current trends in cigar smoking different from past decades?

Total cigar consumption declined by about 66 percent from 1973 until 1993. Cigar use has increased more than 50 percent since 1993. The increase in cigar use in the early 1990s coincided with an increase in promotional media activities for cigars.

10. What ingredients are found in cigars?

Unlike cigarettes, mini cigars, and smokeless tobacco products, standard cigars typically do not have additives included as flavoring agents. However, in addition to nicotine, cigars contain compounds found in all processed tobacco. Some of these compounds are found in the green tobacco leaf; others are formed when the tobacco is cured, fermented, or smoked. For example, cigar tobacco has a high concentration of nitrogen compounds. During fermentation and smoking, these compounds give off several tobacco-specific nitrosamines (TSNAs), which are potent cancer-causing agents. TSNA levels found in cigar smoke are much higher than those found in cigarette smoke.

Smoke from a cigar contains many of the same toxins found in environmental tobacco smoke (secondhand smoke) from cigarettes. These elements include ammonia, carbon monoxide, benzene, and hydrogen cyanide.

Club Drugs. *See* Hallucinogens.

Cocaine and Crack Coca, the active ingredient in cocaine, is derived from the leaves of a plant in the Erythroxylaceae family native to South America where it has been used for centuries by indigenous peoples as a mild **stimulant**. Coca is concentrated into a stronger substance to become cocaine, a powerful stimulant that can be highly addictive. Its synthesis usually takes place in the country of origin, where it is neutralized by an acid to produce cocaine hydrochloride and smuggled in powder form into the United States for distribution and sale. Often diluted by having been cut with inactive ingredients to stretch the supply, when snorted it reaches the **brain** in a few minutes. It can also be dissolved in water and injected, and the user feels the effects in 15 to 30 seconds.

Crack is cocaine that has not been neutralized by hydrochloride to make a salt; instead, it is distributed as a "rock," a crystal-like chunk that, when heated, releases vapors that the user inhales. Known as "freebasing," this method of ingestion produces an immediate, intense rush that is powerfully addicting. Because it is followed by a letdown or crash, users are motivated to ingest it again. It is called "crack" for the crackling noise it makes when heated and smoked.

Cocaine's psychoactive effects include euphoria, excitation, alertness, and heightened energy. Physical effects include elevated heart rate and blood pressure, loss of appetite, insomnia, and, in high doses, hallucinations and convulsions. Localized damage can result from snorting cocaine: users may lose their sense of smell, suffer from nosebleeds, or develop hoarseness or swallowing difficulties. Sometimes reverse tolerance to cocaine develops; users become more sensitive to the drug and to the physical damage increasingly smaller doses can cause. Others develop **tolerance**, so they escalate the amount of cocaine used to toxic levels, which can produce seizures, cardiac arrest, and respiratory failure. Prolonged cocaine use is often associated with paranoia, irritability, restlessness, and even psychosis.

Cocaine acts by triggering a powerful release of the **neurotransmitter** dopamine, but the effect usually subsides in less than an hour. As the brain demands more of the drug to maintain the same level of stimulation, users binge and overdose. Chasing cocaine's intense rush and avoiding the inevitable and sometimes devastating crash that follows has been known to keep users awake for days, avoiding all other activities and following one hit of the drug after another without sleeping, eating, or interacting in any meaningful way within their environment. Crack, particularly, elicits this behavior.

Many people combine cocaine with alcohol to mediate and balance the effects of each other. Researchers at the National Institute on Drug Abuse have discovered that the liver reacts to the combination of these drugs by producing a third substance called cocaethylene, a potent chemical that increases the risk of sudden death.

A Schedule II drug under the Controlled Substances Act, cocaine was once used as an anesthetic for dental procedures and ear, nose, and throat surgeries. Sigmund Freud professed to believe it had value in treating **alcoholism** and is reputed to have used the drug himself. Common street names for cocaine include Blanca, Coca, Coke, Flake, Nieve, Perico, and Snow.

Further Reading:

Califano, Joseph A., Jr. *High Society: How Substance Abuse Ravages America and What to Do About It.* New York: Perseus Books, 2007.

Hoffman, John, and Froemke, Susan, eds. *Addiction: Why Can't They Just Stop?* New York: Rodale, 2007.

Home Box Office (HBO). In partnership with the Robert Wood Johnson Foundation, the National Institute on Drug Abuse, and the National Institute on Alcohol Abuse and Alcoholism. *Addiction: Why Can't They Just Stop?* Documentary. March 2007.

Ketcham, Katherine, and Pace, Nicholas A. *Teens Under the Influence: The Truth About Kids, Alcohol, and Other Drugs.* New York: Ballantine Books, 2003.

Kuhn, Cynthia, et al. *Buzzed: The Straight Facts About the Most Used and Abused Drugs From Alcohol to Ecstasy.* New York: Norton, 2008.

U.S. Department of Health and Human Services, National Institute on Drug Abuse (NIDA), June 2007. Retrieved from http://www.nida.gov

U.S. Department of Health and Human Services, National Institute on Drug Abuse. *Research Report Series: Cocaine Abuse and Addiction.* NIH Publication No. 99-4342, November 2004.

U.S. Department of Health and Human Services, Substance Abuse and Mental Health Services Administration (SAMHSA), August 2007. Retrieved from http://www.samhsa.gov

U.S. Department of Justice, Drug Enforcement Administration (DEA), March 2008. Retrieved from http://www.usdoj.gov/dea

Cocaine Anonymous A **12-step** organization modeled on **Alcoholics Anonymous (AA)**, Cocaine Anonymous (CA) is a free self-supporting group whose only requirement for membership is a desire to quit using cocaine and other mind-altering substances. People with addictions to other drugs are free to join to share experiences and hope in a common effort to rid themselves of drug addiction. Formed in 1983, CA has spread to Canada and Europe and estimated its membership during the 1990s as 30,000.

Like similar 12-step groups, CA does not engage in research, medical **treatment**, or drug education. Although the organization credits the origin of its 12 steps and traditions to AA, CA is not affiliated with AA. Its 12 steps and traditions can be found on the organization's Web site. Other 12-step groups dedicated to helping people who have a problem with drug addiction include All Addictions Anonymous, Crystal Meth Anonymous, Marijuana Anonymous, and Narcotics Anonymous. **Nicotine Anonymous** is a 12-step group for people addicted to **tobacco** products.

Source: Cocaine Anonymous. http://www.ca.org

Codeine Codeine is a milder version of morphine-like drugs and the basis of **hydrocodone** synthesis. Like other **opiates**, it not only relieves pain and alleviates diarrhea but it is an effective cough suppressant also found in many prescription cough medications. As an analgesic, it is often combined with acetaminophen and can be made into an injectable formulation. In tablet form, codeine is on Schedule II of the Controlled Substances Act; when combined with aspirin or other unregulated drugs, it is on Schedule III; as a cough medicine, it is on Schedule V.

Codeine is a natural component of **opium**, but the codeine currently available is usually produced from **morphine**. It is addictive, but as an oral preparation it does not produce the same level of pain relief or respiratory depression as morphine. At lower doses, codeine can produce a sense of well-being and warmth, but at higher, more dangerous doses it can lead to dizziness, confusion, cold and clammy skin, seizures, and unconsciousness.

Further Reading

Califano, Joseph A., Jr. *High Society: How Substance Abuse Ravages America and What to Do About It.* New York: Perseus Books, 2007.

Hoffman, John, and Froemke, Susan, eds. *Addiction: Why Can't They Just Stop?* New York: Rodale, 2007.

Home Box Office (HBO). In partnership with the Robert Wood Johnson Foundation, the National Institute on Drug Abuse, and the National Institute on Alcohol Abuse and Alcoholism. *Addiction: Why Can't They Just Stop?* Documentary. March 2007.

Ketcham, Katherine, and Pace, Nicholas A. *Teens Under the Influence: The Truth About Kids, Alcohol, and Other Drugs.* New York: Ballantine Books, 2003.

U.S. Department of Health and Human Services, National Institute on Drug Abuse (NIDA), June 2007. Retrieved from http://www.nida.gov

U.S. Department of Health and Human Services, Substance Abuse and Mental Health Services Administration (SAMHSA), August 2007. Retrieved from http://www.samhsa.gov

U.S. Department of Justice, Drug Enforcement Administration (DEA), March 2008. Retrieved from http://www.usdoj.gov/dea

Codependency Codependency is sometimes called **relationship addiction** because of the codependent's supposed psychological need to preserve the status quo of family relationships, however dysfunctional they may be. It is often diagnosed in families in which one or more members is an alcoholic or is addicted to other drugs or destructive behaviors. While most mental health professionals characterize this kind of relationship as a symptom of a disorder that requires treatment **intervention** and support through groups like **12-step** programs, other experts deny it even exists and claim it is a clinically meaningless term coined during the 1970s and 1980s in response to cultural trends that tended to label any dysfunction as a disease or an addiction.

Codependency refers to a pattern of behavior that one or more family members adopts to keep the peace, lessen family tensions, and smooth over difficulties by suppressing his own needs and putting the care and comfort of the addicted person first. Codependent people are thought to have low self-esteem and seek approval and validation by adopting selfless, uncomplaining roles. On a perhaps unconscious level, they are likely to fear that if the sick person becomes well again, they will no longer be needed. Rather than ask or even insist that an addict or mentally ill person seek **treatment**, codependent people often serve as enablers by overlooking destructive behavior and making excuses for it. The example frequently cited is of a codependent wife calling her husband's office to lie about why he must miss work when the truth is that he is too hung over to go. Instead of confronting him, she may also make allowances for his drinking by blaming outside pressures—work issues, family problems, financial difficulties—that "force" him to drink.

Although the 4th edition of the American Psychiatric Association's ***Diagnostic and Statistical Manual of Mental Disorders*** (*DSM*) does not recognize codependency, numerous 12-step support programs have formed to help families deal with this pattern of behavior, one that many believe can be passed to other family members. Other professionals reject this assessment, claiming that a certain amount of selflessness and sacrifice are part of any caregiving role, and to label such a person codependent—someone who is only trying to balance the care of an ill family member and running a household with meeting the needs of the rest of the family—is assigning pathology where it does not exist. On the other hand, it has been documented that children growing up in such households are often shown, later in life, to develop relationships with emotionally unstable or addicted individuals, thus perpetuating the so-called codependent cycle.

Further Reading

Beattie, Melody. *Codependent No More: How to Stop Controlling Others and Start Caring for Yourself.* Center City, MN: Hazelden Foundation, 1986.

Cognitive Behavioral Therapy. *See* Treatment.

Compulsions and Impulses A compulsion, in terms of **obsessive-compulsive** disorders, is a compelling, uncontrollable urge to perform a certain act to quiet obsessive thoughts. There is no inherent pleasure in the act and it is not likely to produce seriously negative consequences—although it is symptomatic of what can be a serious disorder. An impulse, in the context of **impulse control disorders**, is an irresistible urge to perform a certain act or behavior that gives immediate gratification or pleasure but ultimately produces negative consequences. Although impulse control disorders are frequently referred to as compulsive disorders—for example, **compulsive shopping disorder**—they are not true compulsions. Much confusion has resulted from the fact that compulsions and impulses have overlapping characteristics; compulsive behaviors can be symptomatic of impulse control disorders just as there may be impulsive components to certain compulsions. Proper diagnosis rests on identifying the critical distinction between the two behaviors: impulsive behaviors, such as pathological gambling and stealing (**kleptomania**), are consistent with the individual's wishes; compulsions, such as the need to touch a doorknob exactly 7 times before leaving the house every day, are not.

Both obsessive-compulsive and impulse control disorders arise from a complex of neurochemical and genetic factors as well as environmental influences, and they respond to **treatment** with medications and behavioral therapy.

Further Reading

American Psychiatric Association. *Diagnostic and Statistical Manual of Mental Disorder*, 4th Edition, Text Revision. Washington, DC: American Psychiatric Association, 2000.

Grant, Jon E., and Kim, S. W. *Stop Me Because I Can't Stop Myself: Taking Control of Impulsive Behavior*. New York: McGraw-Hill, 2003.

Compulsive Computer Use Compulsive has two meanings. It is a psychiatric term referring to a specific type of urge associated only with an obsessive-compulsive disorder. More generally, it applies to compelling urges and behaviors, often uncontrollable that are repetitive, excessive, and often related to **impulse control disorders**. The latter is the meaning that applies to compulsive computer use, also known as a computer addiction or Internet addiction. Some mental health professionals suggest that as many as 6 to 10 percent of Americans show symptoms of an Internet addiction, and this number is expected to rise as ever more sophisticated amusements and diversions become accessible via the Internet. Because the American Psychiatric Association in the 4th edition of its *Diagnostic and Statistical Manual* (*DSM*) does not include compulsive computer use as an impulse control disorder, many experts are lobbying for inclusion of the term in the upcoming 5th edition to be circulated in 2011 or 2012.

Excessive computer use can take many forms of online activity that would otherwise fall within normal levels of behavior: **online gaming** and gambling, virtual sexual activity (or cybersex), shopping or buying from auction sites, or chatting and messaging. Some experts feel that individuals who engage in compulsive computer activity usually fit the profile for more than one impulse control disorder. For example, they believe that those engaged in compulsive online gambling are likely to have both a **pathological gambling disorder** and an Internet addiction; others view this behavior simply as a gambling addiction.

Computer use can be considered addictive when it interferes with normal activities or the individual's ability to function appropriately; causes problems at school, work, or within the family; and has undesirable social, economic, cultural, legal, or emotional consequences. Looking for gratification or release of emotional tensions at the computer, suffering emotional discomfort if prevented from using the computer, and developing physical symptoms such as aching shoulders, carpal tunnel syndrome, and dry eyes should alert users to the possibility that their computer use might become—or has already become—addictive.

Cognitive behavioral therapy can be an effective **treatment** for this disorder if it is evaluated and treated at the same time as any other mental health problems the individual has. To help break the pattern of impulsive behavior, at least at first, medication is a helpful adjunct to counseling. Increasingly, treatment approaches will evolve as computer technology puts new temptations in front of those who are vulnerable to its attractions. Several nations have established specialized Internet addiction clinics to address this growing problem.

Compulsive Computer Use Self-Assessment Questionnaire

Like other self-assessments, this questionnaire regarding your computer use is not intended to be diagnostic, but several "yes" answers should give you concern.

1. Do you feel you spend too much time on the computer? ☐ Yes ☐ No
2. Have you unsuccessfully tried to limit the amount of time you spend online? ☐ Yes ☐ No
3. Do you try to hide from other people the type of sites you visit online? ☐ Yes ☐ No

---

4. Do your family and friends object to the amount of time you spend on the computer? □ Yes □ No
5. Do you find it hard to stay away from the computer for several days at a time? □ Yes □ No
6. Have your schoolwork and personal relationships suffered as a result of your activities on the computer? □ Yes □ No
7. Have you suffered financial difficulties or setbacks as a result of your computer activities? □ Yes □ No
8. Do you revisit particular sites, or types of sites, again and again? □ Yes □ No
9. Have you unsuccessfully tried to control your online spending? □ Yes □ No
10. Do you find yourself relying on the computer for most of your entertainment or to help control your moods? □ Yes □ No

Further Reading

Virtual Addiction Web Site. January 2008. Retrieved from http://www.virtual-addiction.com

Young, Kimberly S. *Caught in the Net: How to Recognize the Signs of Internet Addiction.* New York: John Wiley & Sons, 1998.

Compulsive Eaters Anonymous A **12-step** organization whose only requirement for membership is a desire to stop eating compulsively, Compulsive Eaters Anonymous (CEA) is today known as CEA-HOW. HOW stands for Honest, Openminded, and Willing. Like other such programs, many of its steps for **recovery** and its operating principles were adapted from Alcoholics Anonymous (AA). Its focus is the addictive properties of flour and sugar, and, although some regional differences in eating practices exist, most of the program's members are committed to abstinence from these foods. They also weigh and measure the foods that they consume.

Like AA and similar programs, CEA-HOW views compulsive eating as an illness and seeks to extend support and understanding to fellow addicts. Acceptance of the CEA eating plan is critical to recovery. The program espouses 7 tools of recovery that address members' physical, emotional, and spiritual needs:

1. Adhering to a food plan that allows no sugar or flour; portions must be weighed, measured, and reported.
2. Studying the literature and tools of AA as a guide, gaining strength from that organization's one-day-at-a-time philosophy.
3. Honoring the anonymity of fellow members.
4. Maintaining scheduled telephone contact with other members.
5. Attending a specific number of weekly meetings.
6. Being involved in the program through service, participation, and commitment.
7. Sponsoring other compulsive eaters in the group.

Like similar 12-step groups, CEA-HOW bases its 12 steps and traditions on those originally developed by AA. Other 12-step groups dedicated to helping people with **eating disorders** characterized by overeating include Eating Disorders Anonymous, Food Addicts Anonymous, GreySheeters Anonymous, and Overeaters Anonymous.

Source: Compulsive Overeaters Anonymous. http://www.ceahow.org

Compulsive Masturbation. *See* Sexual Addiction.

Compulsive Shopping or Spending Compulsive shopping is said to occur in 3 to 10 percent of the population. Along with pathological gambling, it is one of the more frequently diagnosed **impulse control disorders**. There is some evidence that Mary Todd Lincoln may have suffered from the disorder after President Lincoln's assassination, suggesting that the disease might stay dormant until later in life when stressful events allow it to emerge. Although some statistics reveal that as many as 80 percent of compulsive shoppers are women, there is evidence that males may be more affected by the disorder than previously believed. Some of the confusion lies in the fact that women, more than men, present themselves for **treatment** of this condition. Unlike other impulse control disorders such as pathological gambling, concurrent drug or alcohol **abuse** is rarely seen in people of either gender who suffer from a spending **addiction**.

Compulsive shopping is distinguished by an individual's need to purchase unneeded and unnecessary items to experience the pleasure and calm or sense of escape that shopping gives them. Although it feels good at the time to engage in the activity, the individual is left with guilt, remorse, and often high levels of debt as a result. Subsequent efforts to suppress the urges or avoid shopping only increase the level of tension, so **impulses** to shop are likely to intensify.

Often, people suffering from the disorder are themselves confused about the nature of their illness and view their symptoms as manifestations of depression or anxiety. For this reason, it is difficult to assess just how prevalent the disorder is or for doctors and other mental health professionals to treat the disorder effectively. When it is properly diagnosed, selective serotonin reuptake inhibitors or certain antipsychotic medications have been shown to be very helpful in relieving the patient's urges to shop.

Compulsive shopping does not ordinarily manifest itself until adolescence or later, when the individual first has independent access to shopping venues and the monetary means to support the **compulsion**. Teenagers who are issued their first credit card may find, to their dismay, that their enjoyment of shopping quickly escalates and the activity becomes a daily habit.

Although the American Psychiatric Association does not specifically address compulsive shopping in its ***Diagnostic and Statistical Manual of Mental Disorders*** (*DSM*), mental health experts agree that a diagnosis can be made when a patient describes an increasing preoccupation with shopping or urges to shop, spends more than he or she can afford, buys unwanted or unneeded products, and devotes more time to the activity despite its interference with normal functions. He or she may even resort to stealing to support the habit or to pay off mounting debts.

Compulsive Shopping Self-Assessment Questionnaire

The following questionnaire is designed to alert you to a potential problem you may have with compulsive shopping. Answering "yes" to more than 2 of these questions should be cause for concern.

1. Do you buy things you don't need? ☐ Yes ☐ No
2. Do you buy more than you can afford? ☐ Yes ☐ No

3. Do you have urges to shop that you have tried unsuccessfully to suppress?
□ Yes □ No
4. Has the shopping led to financial or family difficulties? □ Yes □ No
5. Do the urges or the shopping itself cause you psychological distress?
□ Yes □ No
6. Does the shopping interfere with your life in significant ways? □ Yes □ No

Further Reading

American Psychiatric Association. *Diagnostic and Statistical Manual of Mental Disorders*, 4th Edition, Text Revision. Washington, DC: American Psychiatric Association, 2000.

Arenson, Gloria. *Born To Spend: Overcoming Compulsive Shopping*. Santa Barbara, CA: Brockart Books, 2003.

Erickson, Carlton K. *The Science of Addiction: From Neurobiology to Treatment*. New York: Norton, 2007.

Grant, Jon E., and Kim, S. W. *Stop Me Because I Can't Stop Myself: Taking Control of Impulsive Behavior*. New York: McGraw-Hill, 2003.

Hyman, S. E., and Malenka, R. C. Addiction and the Brain: The Neurobiology of Compulsion and Its Persistence. *Nature Reviews Neuroscience* 2001: 2(10), 695–703.

Potenza, Marc N. Should Addictive Disorders Include Non-Substance-Related Conditions? *Addiction* 2006: 101(s1), 142–151.

Computer Addiction. *See* Compulsive Computer Use.

Concerta. *See* Methylphenidate.

Conditioning Conditioning refers to a behavioral or training technique that pairs a stimulus with a reward or reinforcement to elicit a predictable response. A frequent example given of classical conditioning is that of Ivan Pavlov, a Russian scientist who late in the 19th century conducted experiments in which he rang a bell (stimulus) just before delivering food (reinforcement) to a dog that, in anticipation of the food, was salivating. Soon the dog would salivate simply on hearing the bell even though no food was present because he had made the association between the bell and food. This is known as a conditioned response, and is often seen in drug addicts. Just as the bell became a cue, or a conditioned stimulus, other cues—such as drug **paraphernalia** or seeing the street corners where addicts used to buy drugs—can be powerful triggers to use. The National Institute on Drug Abuse has reported that the conditioned response can so intense that some **cocaine** addicts, on encountering triggers they strongly associate with cocaine use, can taste the drug in the back of their throat. Recovering addicts are often taught how to avoid such stimuli because they can be powerful triggers to relapse. The meaning that such triggers have—the desire they create in the addict—is known as incentive salience. Incentive sensitization—the process by which the **brain** learns to attach significance to these cues—is thought to occur in the nucleus accumbens region of the brain. Many neuroscientists suggest that incentive salience can influence drug-seeking and drug-using behavior below the level of the addict's awareness.

Aversive conditioning is a form of behavioral therapy that at one time was used in addictions **treatment**. By pairing a negative stimulus such as an electric shock with the ingestion of alcohol or other drugs, a negative association with use of the drug developed. Aversive conditioning as a single treatment strategy has lost favor, although the underlying principle continues to be applicable to certain behavioral therapy techniques.

Further Reading

Erickson, Carlton K. *The Science of Addiction: From Neurobiology to Treatment*. New York: Norton, 2007.

Kalivas, P. W., and Volkow, Nora. The Neural Basis of Addiction: A Pathology of Motivation and Choice. *American Journal of Psychiatry* August 2005: 162(8), 1403–1413.

Nestler, Eric J., and Malenka, Robert. The Addicted Brain. *Scientific American*, September 2007. Retrieved from http://www.sciam.com/article.cfm?chanID=sa006&colID=1&articleID=0001E6 32-978A-1019-978A83414B7F0101

U.S. Department of Health and Human Services. *The Science of Addiction: Drugs, Brains, and Behavior*. NIH Publication No. 07-5605, February 2007.

Conduct Disorders Many behaviors that are thought to be symptomatic of **impulse control disorders** or **addictions** may actually be conduct disorders, a group of behaviors that inflict harm or damage to others. Primarily diagnosed in children and adolescents who are identified by their inability to follow rules or to behave appropriately, the disorder is characterized by bullying, deceitfulness, aggression toward people or animals, theft, and damage to property.

The causes of conduct disorders are not known, but it is believed that many factors, including **brain** damage, child abuse, genetic vulnerability, school failure, and traumatic life experiences, play key roles. Interestingly, there is evidence to suggest that children of smoking mothers are more likely to develop conduct disorders and become smokers themselves. This raises the intriguing possibility that smoking and the use of other addictive drugs during pregnancy affect the child's developing brain circuitry in ways that make him or her more vulnerable to **mental disorders** or addiction later in life.

Further Reading

American Psychiatric Association. *Diagnostic and Statistical Manual of Mental Disorders*, 4th Edition, Text Revision. Washington, DC: American Psychiatric Association, 2000.

Grant, Jon E., and Kim, S. W. *Stop Me Because I Can't Stop Myself: Taking Control of Impulsive Behavior*. New York: McGraw-Hill, 2003.

Controlled Substances Act (CSA) The Controlled Substances Act (CSA) of the Comprehensive Drug Abuse Prevention and Control Act of 1970 represents the U.S. government's effort to control the manufacture and distribution of controlled substances. Because drugs of **abuse** can be synthesized in homegrown laboratories, CSA laws continue to be amended and updated to include the chemicals and equipment that are used in the drugs' manufacture. The Act outlines the regulations and penalties imposed for illicit drug trafficking and use, including personal use, as well as provisions for controlling drug-manufacturing processes. It places all regulated substances into 1 of 5 categories, or schedules, based upon the substance's medical use, potential for abuse, safety, and **addiction liability**.

See also Appendix A.

Further Reading

U.S. Department of Justice, Drug Enforcement Administration (DEA), March 2008. Retrieved from http://www.usdoj.gov/dea

Costs of Drug Abuse and Addiction According to the National Institute on Drug Abuse (NIDA), **abuse** of and **addiction** to drugs, alcohol, and nicotine cost the United States well over $500 billion per year in terms of direct and indirect costs, including those related to violence and property crimes, prison expenses, court and criminal costs, emergency room visits, healthcare utilization, child abuse and neglect, lost child support, foster care and welfare costs, reduced productivity, and unemployment. The cost to individual families in terms of human suffering and tragedy is incalculable.

The latest estimate for the costs related to illicit drug abuse, which includes **prescription drugs** used in a dosage or for a purpose other than that for which they were prescribed, is nearly $181 billion. An updated report produced in 2002 by the Office of National Drug Control Policy (ONDCP), which was charged by the White House to develop such estimates, states that healthcare costs associated with illicit drugs represented $15.8 billion of the $181 billion; lost productivity, $128.6 billion; and law enforcement and social welfare, $36.4 billion.

The estimated annual cost of alcohol-use disorders is the United States is $185 billion. Over 70 percent of this cost is attributable to lost productivity from alcohol-related illness or premature death; another 14 percent is attributable to healthcare expenditures to treat alcohol use disorders and the medical consequences of alcohol consumption; property and administrative costs associated with alcohol-related motor vehicle accidents represent almost 10 percent; and the costs associated with criminal justice and law enforcement amount to about 5 percent.

The NIDA reports that the cost to society of smoking and the use of **nicotine** products is estimated to be about $82 billion per year. When the costs of burn care from smoking-related fires, perinatal care for low-birth-weight infants of mothers who smoke, and medical care costs associated with disease caused by **secondhand smoke** are added in, total costs are estimated to be about $157 billion per year.

The costs associated with **impulse** control and **eating disorders** cannot be estimated with any degree of certainty because the incidence of the disorders is uncertain; most statistics place it at somewhere between 8 and 38 million, not including eating disorders. The total number may be higher because many cases go undiagnosed, and frequently there are co-occurring **mental disorders** that complicate cost-determination efforts.

Table 1. Cost to Society of Illicit Drug Use in the U.S.—2002

	(in Billions of Dollars)
Lost Productivity Costs:	
Premature death	$24,646
Drug abuse-related illness	33,452
Institutionalization/hospitalization	1,996
Productivity loss of victims of crime	1,800
Incarceration and crime careers	66,671
Total Lost Productivity	**$128,565**
Health Care Costs:	
Community-based specialty treatment	5,997
Federally-provided specialty treatment	217
State and local prevention & treatment efforts	2,862
Medical consequences	
Hospital and ambulatory care costs	1,454

(Continued)

Table 1. Continued

Special disease costs	
Drug-exposed infants	605
Tuberculosis	19
HIV/AIDS	3,755
Hepatitis B and C	312
Crime victim health care costs	110
Health insurance administration	513
Total Health Care	**$15,844**
Other Costs:	
Cost of goods and services lost to crime	$35,279
Private costs (legal defense, property damage for victims)	853
Social welfare	281
Total Other	**$36,413**
Total Cost of Illicit Drug Use	**$180,822**

Source: NIDA.

Table 2. Cost to Society of Alcohol Use in the U.S.—2001

	(in Billions of Dollars)
Lost Productivity Costs:	
Alcohol-related illness	$87,622
Premature death	36,499
Alcohol-related Crime	10,085
Total Lost Productivity	**$134,206**
Health Care Costs:	
Alcohol use disorders, treatment, prevention, and support	7,466
Medical consequences of alcohol consumption	18,872
Total Health Care	**$26,338**
Other Costs:	
Motor vehicle accidents	$15,744
Crime	6,328
Fire destruction	1,537
Social welfare administration	484
Total Other	**$24,093**
Total Cost of Alcohol Use	**$184,637**

Source: NIDA.

Table 3. Cost to Society of Nicotine Use in the U.S.—2006

	(in Billions of Dollars)
Direct Health Care and Associated Costs	$75,000
Lost Productivity Costs	82,000
Total Cost of Nicotine Use	**$157,000**

Source: NIDA.

Crack. *See* Cocaine and Crack.

Crank. *See* Methamphetamine.

Craving Craving is an uncontrollable desire, and, in the case of **addiction** to a substance, it is the principal motivating force responsible for drug-seeking, relapse, and other addictive behavior long past the point when the damage the substance is causing has become apparent.

For centuries, the physiology of craving has puzzled researchers even though its clear role in addiction was evident. In recent years, neurological studies have begun to reveal ways in which craving pathways are established in the **brain**. Dopamine-releasing cells in the mesolimbic reward pathway seem to learn and remember their hypersecretion of dopamine in response to addictive drugs. Called **long-term potentiation**, this cellular memory remains active for some time. Related to long-term potentiation is **behavioral sensitization**, the development of an increased response to addictive stimuli when the synaptic strength between neurons increases. The neurological changes these phenomena cause, scientists believe, result in a major reorganization of the brain that lays down pathways of learning and memory that teach the brain to need, or crave, the substance.

In addition to these findings, scientists are learning more about a deep region of the brain known as the insula, or insular cortex, which has recently been shown to have a major impact on drug-related craving. Studies have demonstrated that in rats addicted to **amphetamines**, deactivation of the insula, roughly a prune-size area near the limbic system, completely eliminated the rats' desire for the drugs. Upon reactivation of the region, the craving returned. Additional studies have shown that in long-term smokers who sustained brain injuries in the area of the insular cortex, their urge for **nicotine** disappeared entirely. Since the insula is partly responsible for monitoring and communicating the organism's needs to the prefrontal cortex where behavioral decisions are made, it is possible that it will prove to be crucial in the development and management of drug craving.

Further Reading

Santoro, Joseph, DeLetis, Robert, and Bergman, Alfred. *Kill the Craving: How to Control the Impulse to Use Drugs and Alcohol.* Oakland, CA: New Harbinger, 2001.

CREB (cAMP Response Element-Binding) Protein A transcription factor that regulates gene expression, CREB is a protein that plays a major role in the development of **tolerance**. It dampens the pleasurable effects of drugs of **abuse** and entices the user to come back for more of the drug to achieve the initial effect. When an individual consumes an addictive drug, the postsynaptic neurons affected by dopamine release a molecule called cyclic AMP (cAMP), which produces CREB. CREB in turn controls the production of dynorphins, which inhibit the dopamine-producing cells of the nucleus accumbens so that the user is unable to experience the desired level of effect. If the user abstains from the drug, the CREB concentrations in the reward pathway tend to diminish within hours or days, and the symptoms of tolerance are reduced. Paradoxically, reverse tolerance, or **behavioral sensitization**, often takes its place.

Cross-Addiction and Cross-Tolerance Substance addicts often have cross-addictions to second or third substances, which can manifest themselves in 3 ways. The user may replace the original addiction with a second one, use two drugs concurrently even though neither markedly affects the action of the other, or use them to enhance or otherwise mediate the effects of each other. Cross-tolerance occurs when someone tolerant to one drug proves to have **tolerance** to a new and different drug but one that is pharmacologically similar to the first. This can occur particularly between drugs in the same class, such as **nicotine** and caffeine, which are **stimulants**, or between various **hallucinogens**.

In cross-addiction, a user may substitute alcohol for **marijuana**, particularly when the illegality of marijuana prevents the user from getting high. In the second example of cross-addiction, alcohol and nicotine may be cross-addictions that exist concurrently without materially affecting the effect that each has on the user. In the third case, the user may **abuse cocaine** and alcohol at the same time to boost and, in some cases, mediate the effect of the other.

Cross-addictions can be exceedingly dangerous. Not only is each substance toxic on its own, the combination can produce synergistic effects—that is, the combined drugs have an even more powerful effect than the sum of effects one would expect from both drugs added together. Unintended overdoses occur regularly in people who are cross-addicted to various substances, even though the quantity of each substance, used alone, may have been relatively moderate.

Frequently, cross-addictions are referred to as multisubstance addictions or polysubstance addictions, but there are distinctions that should be made. In cross-addiction, one drug usually predominates as the addictive drug; in multisubstance or polysubstance addictions, the individual uses 3 or more drugs together in an addictive pattern, and no single drug predominates.

Cutting Behavior. *See* Self-Injury, Self-Mutilation.

Cybersex Addiction Cybersex represents any sexual activity or encounter that takes place on the Internet. It usually consists of masturbating to **pornography** or communicating with others in chat rooms about sexually explicit subjects. With a large percentage of

---

Cybersex Self-Assessment Questionnaire

Although only a mental health counselor can diagnose the disorder, a cybersex addiction should be suspected if you answer "yes" to several of the following questions.

1. Do you regularly go on the Internet to engage specifically in cybersex? □ Yes □ No
2. Do you masturbate when engaged in cybersex activities? □ Yes □ No
3. Are you preoccupied with using the Internet for cybersex? □ Yes □ No
4. Have you "graduated" from cybersex to real-life meetings with your cybersex partner(s)? □ Yes □ No
5. Do your anonymous cybersex "conversations" revolve around your unfulfilled sexual fantasies? □ Yes □ No
6. Do you look to cybersex for arousal and orgasm? □ Yes □ No
7. Are you ashamed of your cybersex activities? □ Yes □ No
8. Does cybersex replace real-life interactions with your sexual partner? □ Yes □ No

---

Internet viewing estimated to be of a sexual nature, it is a widespread practice. As technology has become more sophisticated, electronic cameras attached to the computer have allowed users to have face-to-face, real-time interaction. Some set up personal meetings or engage in online affairs, often disguising their true identity in order to indulge unusual sexual fantasies they would never act on in their real lives.

Cybersex can be a positive sexual outlet for many, such as married people separated by geography, homebound or excessively shy people unable to establish relationships outside their homes, or people with sexually transmitted diseases who must avoid intimate contact with others. However, there are sinister aspects to cybersex, such as predators roaming the Internet and targeting children or other vulnerable people. There is also a social cost—many feel that engaging in anonymous cybersex is an unfaithful act that betrays real-life relationships.

When sexual activities in cyberspace occur to the exclusion of normal interactions, are used on a regular basis to affect mood and produce a high, interfere with personal or academic responsibilities and relationships, and continue in spite of negative consequences or efforts to curtail the activity, they may be said to represent a **sexual addiction** (or cybersex addiction) in need of **treatment**.

See also Pornography Addiction.

Further Reading

American Psychiatric Association. *Diagnostic and Statistical Manual of Mental Disorders*, 4th Edition, Text Revision. Washington, DC: American Psychiatric Association, 2000.

Carnes, Patrick, Griffin, Elizabeth, and Delmonico, David. *In the Shadows of the Net: Breaking Free of Compulsive Online Sexual Behavior*. Center City, MN: Hazelden Foundation, 2001.

Grant, Jon E., and Kim, S. W. *Stop Me Because I Can't Stop Myself: Taking Control of Impulsive Behavior*. New York: McGraw-Hill, 2003.

Darvon and Darvocet. *See* Dextropropoxyphene.

Date-Rape Drugs. *See* Predatory Drugs.

Decriminalization There is considerable support for decriminalizing some if not all illegal drugs. Decriminalizing means reducing penalties to such a degree that few people suffer severe legal consequences as a result of drug possession or use; this is different from legalization, which would erase penalties. Even many law enforcement officials support decriminalization for several reasons: "victimless" drug users would no longer crowd the judicial and prison systems; an international predatory network of drug traffickers could be dismantled; drug quality and dosages could be standardized, making them safer; and society, by focusing its resources on rehabilitation, could find more effective ways of reducing or eliminating drug **abuse**. One of the most compelling reasons to decriminalize drugs is that prohibiting them simply does not work. Despite the hundreds of billions of dollars spent on law enforcement efforts, demand for drugs of abuse is staggeringly high, especially in the United States, Europe, and the Far East.

The opponents of decriminalization dispute this approach and insist that decriminalization would be perceived as encouraging drug use and lead to an epidemic of **addiction**. However, since the terrorism attacks of September 11, 2001, these sentiments may be changing. Many suggest that since drug manufacture, distribution, and sale, especially that originating from Afghanistan's **opium** industry, is proving so profitable for terrorists, it makes sense to decriminalize the opium trade in order to destroy underground networks that funnel money to terrorist organizations.

See also War on Drugs.

Further Reading

Fisher, Gary L. *Rethinking Our War on Drugs: Candid Talk about Controversial Issues.* Westport, CT: Praeger, 2006.

Delta FosB Delta FosB is a transcription factor, a protein that helps regulate gene expression. It plays a significant role in **addiction** because it causes the brain's neurons to react more strongly to the presence of an addictive drug. By accumulating in the nucleus accumbens of a chronic drug user, its effect remains active for weeks or months and thus helps foster the **behavioral sensitization** seen in the neurons of an addicted **brain**.

That these neurons continue to manifest sensitization long after drug use has stopped and delta FosB levels have returned to normal has puzzled researchers for some time. One theory holds that, because certain addictive drugs trigger the development of new dendritic spines on postsynaptic neurons, the cells are structurally more receptive to signaling and therefore overreact to drug-related stimuli. In recovering addicts, this reaction may be manifested, at least to some degree, in long-term **craving** and a lifelong vulnerability to readdiction.

In studies with mice, researchers made the fascinating discovery that nondrug rewards such as certain repetitive activities could increase delta FosB in a rodent's nucleus accumbens, raising the intriguing possibility that the protein may play as fundamental a role in the development of addictive behaviors as it seems to play in drug addiction.

Delta-9-Tetrahydrocannabinol. *See Cannabis.*

Demerol. *See* Meperidine.

Dendrite. *See* Brain and Addiction.

Denial Regarded as one of the characteristic symptoms of **addiction**, denial is an addict's inability or refusal to recognize his or her addiction for what it is. It is a largely unconscious defense mechanism that evolves gradually and can take several forms. Addicts may blame other people or events for their behavior, or they may make excuses to downplay its seriousness. Often, they minimize their symptoms, even to themselves, and avoid admitting the degree of their eagerness to use again or the severity of their **withdrawal** symptoms until their distress is so extreme it can no longer be ignored. Eventually, desperate to find solutions to their problems in external factors so they do not have to face the real issue, they resort to drastic measures such as moving to new areas of the country—the so-called geographic cure—where they somehow convince themselves "things will be different."

Because addiction causes neurological dysfunction that distorts thinking and judgment, most scientists believe that denial is a symptom of this dysregulation. Some neurological studies have shown that denial correlates with impaired "executive function"—a collection of higher thought processes that occur in the prefrontal cortex. If there is a possibility that the drug might be withdrawn, the **brain**, whose survival is now threatened because it has learned it needs the substance, finds ways to deny that the drug or drug use is a problem and allows the addict to keep the habit alive.

Depade. *See* Addiction Medications.

Dependence The use of the word "dependence" in referring to drug **abuse** or **addiction** has caused a great deal of confusion for the public and the professionals who assess and treat drug abuse. Many people use dependence and addiction interchangeably while others insist there are significant differences that should be maintained. Some of the confusion has been caused by the well-intended efforts of the American Psychiatric Association (APA).

In 1987, when the APA was about to issue the 3rd edition of its *Diagnostic and Statistical Manual III* (*DSM-III*), the classic reference used in diagnosing **mental disorders**, the APA substituted the term "dependence" for "addiction" to remove the stigma associated with the latter term and replace it with one that more accurately reflected the medical and neurological implications of chemical dependence. Carried over into the next edition, *DSM-IV-TR*, the revision began to draw comment from those who noted that traditional definitions of addiction and dependence, while similar, are different in one crucial respect: dependence does not normally refer to the loss of control that is a hallmark of addiction. Moreover, groups such as the American Society of Addiction Medicine, the American Association of Addiction Psychiatrists, and the journals *Addiction* and the *American Journal on Addictions*, have successfully used addiction for decades. A significant number of other experts, however, currently insist that addiction is a vague, clinically inaccurate term that does not properly distinguish between the medical disease that true addiction represents and abusive overindulgence in drugs or other substances. They believe that the term "dependence" remains appropriate, especially if a clear distinction is made between chemical dependence and physical dependence.

Chemical dependence is true addiction, what neuroscientists agree is a pathological condition in which **brain** function is disrupted and compromised to such an extent the addict is unable to control his or her drug-seeking and drug-using behavior. **Heroin** and **tobacco** addictions are good examples. Physical dependence refers to the body's adaptation to certain drugs; if these drugs are suddenly withdrawn, the individual may suffer some discomfort or even certain types of **withdrawal** symptoms, but at no time can the person be said to have lost control over the drug use or behavior. Antidepressants or certain beta-blockers used to control high blood pressure are examples of drugs that can cause physical dependence.

Physical dependence is similar to **pseudoaddiction**, a condition in which a patient in acute pain demands more of a pain-relieving drug. It is not a chemical dependency, nor does it necessarily occur in a patient with a history of drug addiction. It resembles true addiction in many ways: the patient displays increasing **tolerance** to the substance—known as pseudo-tolerance—and engages in drug-seeking behavior, sometimes furtively or through dishonest measures. What distinguishes pseudoaddiction from true addiction is that when the source of the pain is removed, the desire or need for the drug disappears as well. There is considerable evidence that the pain does not have to be of physical origin for pseudoaddiction to occur. Many Vietnam War veterans who used heroin to ease their psychic distress while they were in Asia were able to renounce heroin use relatively easily once they returned home.

The debate among medical professionals and addictions experts whether to use dependence versus addiction continues. Although it is not yet certain which term the APA will choose to use in the next edition of the *DSM*, there are strong indications it will revert to addiction.

Further Reading

American Psychiatric Association. *Diagnostic and Statistical Manual of Mental Disorders*, 4th Edition, Text Revision. Washington, DC: American Psychiatric Association, 2000.

Erickson, Carlton K. *The Science of Addiction: From Neurobiology to Treatment*. New York: Norton, 2007.

Hoffman, John, and Froemke, Susan, eds. *Addiction: Why Can't They Just Stop?* New York: Rodale, 2007.

Dependence Liability. *See* Addiction Liability.

Depressants By suppressing activity in the central nervous system, depressants such as alcohol, sedatives, and tranquilizers help alleviate anxiety, induce sleep, and reduce stress. They work by triggering the release of gamma aminobutyric acid (GABA), an inhibitory

Substance/Drug	Intoxicating Effects	Potential Health Consequences
Depressants Alcohol Barbiturates Benzodiazepines Flunitrazepam GHB Meprobamate Methaqualone	Slurred speech, drowsiness, mild intoxication, lowered inhibitions, poor concentration	Fatigue, confusion, dizziness, irritability, impaired memory and judgement, respiratory arrest, seizures, coma, death

Source: NIDA, DEA

Depressants Chart

neurotransmitter that, among its other effects, produces a sense of calm and lowers respiration rate. Of the hundreds of drugs that fall into the category of depressants, **alcohol** is the most widely used and abused. It is almost universally available and accessible, and although many believe it is a **stimulant** because of the levity and euphoria it initially produces, chemically it is a depressant that in large doses can dangerously suppress breathing and other vital functions. Two club drugs, **gamma hydroxybutyric acid** (GHB) and **flunitrazepam** (Rohypnol), are depressants that are sometimes categorized as **hallucinogens**. The major depressants that are subject to **abuse** are alcohol, **barbiturates** (sedative-hypnotic drugs), **benzodiazepines** (tranquilizers), **chloral hydrate**, flunitrazepam, GHB, glutethimide, **meprobamate**, methaqualone, and paraldehyde. Methaqualone was often used during the 1960s and 1970s by college students who referred to capsules containing the drug as 'Ludes, but pharmaceutical companies stopped marketing the drug in 1984.

The sudden discontinuation of depressants, such as during detoxification from **alcoholism** or barbiturate **addiction**, can lead to seizures as the **brain** tries to rebound and rebalance neurochemical levels disrupted by use of the depressants. For this reason, anyone withdrawing from abuse of depressants, especially more than one, would be advised to consult with a medical professional first.

See also Drug Classes; Appendix B.

Further Reading

Califano, Joseph A., Jr. *High Society: How Substance Abuse Ravages America and What to Do About It.* New York: Perseus Books, 2007.

Hoffman, John, and Froemke, Susan, eds. *Addiction: Why Can't They Just Stop?* New York: Rodale, 2007.

Home Box Office (HBO). In partnership with the Robert Wood Johnson Foundation, the National Institute on Drug Abuse, and the National Institute on Alcohol Abuse and Alcoholism. *Addiction: Why Can't They Just Stop?* Documentary. March 2007.

Ketcham, Katherine, and Pace, Nicholas A. *Teens Under the Influence: The Truth About Kids, Alcohol, and Other Drugs.* New York: Ballantine Books, 2003.

U.S. Department of Health and Human Services, National Institute on Drug Abuse (NIDA), June 2007. Retrieved from http://www.nida.gov

U.S. Department of Health and Human Services, Substance Abuse and Mental Health Services Administration (SAMHSA), August 2007. Retrieved from http://www.samhsa.gov

U.S. Department of Justice, Drug Enforcement Administration (DEA), March 2008. Retrieved from http://www.usdoj.gov/dea

Designer Drugs At one time, when drugs were regulated by their molecular makeup, manufacturers and others who wanted to avoid legal penalties by trafficking in illegal drugs would change the molecular structure of the drugs—they redesigned them. The newly designed drug had a similar effect on users, but since its content differed from that of the original, it was legal. **Ecstasy** is an example of a designer drug that was manufactured during the 1980s.

Known by scientists as analogs, designer drugs became very popular during the 1970s and 1980s as worldwide consumption of mind-altering drugs increased and distributors and users sought ways to avoid the legal consequences of their use. To counter this trend, new laws were introduced that regulated these drugs based on their effect on a user rather than on molecular content. Under amendments to the Controlled Substances Act in 1986, designer drugs and the chemicals that were used in their manufacture became subject to new regulations.

In response, some Internet retail distributors have begun advertising newly synthesized addictive drugs as research chemicals. Of uncertain quality and potentially deadly, these chemicals have frequently been labeled with confusing names and other terminology meant to disguise their true composition and confound legal authorities who attempt to regulate them. Because the sources of these chemicals—and the chemicals themselves—are suspect, they are highly dangerous, and their use in the manufacture of designer drugs has had sometimes tragic results.

Further Reading

Kuhn, Cynthia, et al. *Buzzed: The Straight Facts About the Most Used and Abused Drugs From Alcohol to Ecstasy*. New York: Norton, 2008.

DET. *See* Psilocybin and Psilocin.

Dexedrine. *See* Dextroamphetamine.

Dextroamphetamine (Dexedrine) Dextroamphetamine is a highly addictive **amphetamine** that was used primarily in inhalers to treat colds until the 1930s when its value as a **stimulant** surfaced. Now a Schedule II drug under the Controlled Substances Act, dextroamphetamine is the active stimulant in modern drugs used in the **treatment** of the sleeping disorder known as narcolepsy, attention-deficit disorders, obesity, and certain cases of depression.

Like other amphetamines, dextroamphetamine has a high potential for **abuse**. It must be prescribed cautiously because **tolerance** to the drug builds quickly. In moderate use it can produce nervousness, irritability and insomnia. In prolonged or excessive use, it can lead to cardiac irregularities, high blood pressure, aggression, and paranoia. Because stimulants like dextroamphetamine are associated with alertness and increased activity, many find it puzzling that it is an active ingredient in Adderall, a drug frequently prescribed to treat attention-deficit hyperactivity disorder (ADHD) whose symptoms include an inability to sit still for extended periods of time. This seeming paradox is explained by the unique combination of effects that Adderall's drug formulation has on the complex interplay of dopamine and other **neurotransmitters** in the **brain**.

Further Reading

Califano, Joseph A., Jr. *High Society: How Substance Abuse Ravages America and What to Do About It*. New York: Perseus Books, 2007.

Hoffman, John, and Froemke, Susan, eds. *Addiction: Why Can't They Just Stop?* New York: Rodale, 2007.

Home Box Office (HBO). In partnership with the Robert Wood Johnson Foundation, the National Institute on Drug Abuse, and the National Institute on Alcohol Abuse and Alcoholism. *Addiction: Why Can't They Just Stop?* Documentary. March 2007.

Ketcham, Katherine, and Pace, Nicholas A. *Teens Under the Influence: The Truth About Kids, Alcohol, and Other Drugs.* New York: Ballantine Books, 2003.

U.S. Department of Health and Human Services, National Institute on Drug Abuse (NIDA), June 2007. Retrieved from http://www.nida.gov

U.S. Department of Health and Human Services, Substance Abuse and Mental Health Services Administration (SAMHSA), August 2007. Retrieved from http://www.samhsa.gov

U.S. Department of Justice, Drug Enforcement Administration (DEA), March 2008. Retrieved from http://www.usdoj.gov/dea

Dextromethorphan (DXM) At high doses—more than 360 milligrams—the cough suppressant dextromethorphan (DXM) is a dissociative **hallucinogen** similar to **phencyclidine (PCP)** and **ketamine**. Since it can be obtained over the counter in gel cap, capsule, liquid, and tablet form, it is easily abused. Like other drugs in this class, high doses or excessive use can lead to serious consequences such as irregular heartbeat, high blood pressure, seizures, brain damage, or coma and death. It also raises the body temperature, so that individuals who consume it and engage in energetic physical activity are at risk for the dangerously high fever known as hyperthermia, which is life-threatening.

Dextromethorphan has not been scheduled under the Controlled Substances Act. The drug may be known on the street as Dex, DM, Drex, Robo, Rojo, Skittles, Triple C, or Velvet.

Further Reading

Califano, Joseph A., Jr. *High Society: How Substance Abuse Ravages America and What to Do About It.* New York: Perseus Books, 2007.

Hoffman, John, and Froemke, Susan, eds. *Addiction: Why Can't They Just Stop?* New York: Rodale, 2007.

Home Box Office (HBO). In partnership with the Robert Wood Johnson Foundation, the National Institute on Drug Abuse, and the National Institute on Alcohol Abuse and Alcoholism. *Addiction: Why Can't They Just Stop?* Documentary. March 2007.

Ketcham, Katherine, and Pace, Nicholas A. *Teens Under the Influence: The Truth About Kids, Alcohol, and Other Drugs.* New York: Ballantine Books, 2003.

U.S. Department of Health and Human Services, National Institute on Drug Abuse (NIDA), June 2007. Retrieved from http://www.nida.gov

U.S. Department of Health and Human Services, National Institute on Drug Abuse. *Research Report Series: Hallucinogens and Dissociative Drugs.* NIH Publication No. 01-4209, March 2001.

U.S. Department of Health and Human Services, Substance Abuse and Mental Health Services Administration (SAMHSA), August 2007. Retrieved from http://www.samhsa.gov

U.S. Department of Justice, Drug Enforcement Administration (DEA), March 2008. Retrieved from http://www.usdoj.gov/dea

Dextropropoxyphene (Darvon and Darvocet) More widely known as Darvon, the opiate dextropropoxyphene (propoxyphene) is a close relative of **methadone** and is used for the relief of moderate pain. Preparations containing the drug, listed on Schedule IV of the Controlled Substances Act, are available by prescription only.

Introduced in the 1950s, dextropropoxyphene was routinely prescribed as an effective pain reliever with a low **addiction liability**. However, by the 1970s it had become obvious that the drug was not only addictive but, according to the American Medical Association, might even be less effective at relieving pain than simple aspirin. In the meantime, reports of its toxicity, especially to the heart, dissuaded many physicians from prescribing it. By then, however, many users had been abusing the drug, had become addicted, or had overdosed in an effort to achieve the desired analgesic effect. Given its serious side effects, dextropropoxyphene has become a less frequently prescribed medication, particularly once statistics showed it to be among the drugs most frequently associated with drug-abuse fatalities.

Further Reading

Califano, Joseph A., Jr. *High Society: How Substance Abuse Ravages America and What to Do About It.* New York: Perseus Books, 2007.

Hoffman, John, and Froemke, Susan, eds. *Addiction: Why Can't They Just Stop?* New York: Rodale, 2007.

Home Box Office (HBO). In partnership with the Robert Wood Johnson Foundation, the National Institute on Drug Abuse, and the National Institute on Alcohol Abuse and Alcoholism. *Addiction: Why Can't They Just Stop?* Documentary. March 2007.

Ketcham, Katherine, and Pace, Nicholas A. *Teens Under the Influence: The Truth About Kids, Alcohol, and Other Drugs.* New York: Ballantine Books, 2003.

U.S. Department of Health and Human Services, National Institute on Drug Abuse (NIDA), June 2007. Retrieved from http://www.nida.gov

U.S. Department of Health and Human Services, Substance Abuse and Mental Health Services Administration (SAMHSA), August 2007. Retrieved from http://www.samhsa.gov

U.S. Department of Justice, Drug Enforcement Administration (DEA), March 2008. Retrieved from http://www.usdoj.gov/dea

Diagnostic and Statistical Manual of Mental Disorders Published by the American Psychiatric Association (APA), the *Diagnostic and Statistical Manual* (*DSM*) is the authoritative reference used among mental health professionals in the United States and elsewhere to identify and diagnose **mental disorders** based on their characteristic features. Like the World Health Organization's *International Classification of Diseases* (*ICD*) reference used around the world, the *DSM* is a valuable tool that helps ensure diagnostic precision and clarity, and it simplifies communications among the medical community, insurers, and others.

In the 1950s, the 1st edition of the *DSM* classified alcohol and drug **abuse** under Sociopathic Personality Disturbances; the 3rd edition in the 1980s was the first to distinguish abuse from **dependence**—the term it substituted for **addiction**—by stating that **tolerance** and **withdrawal** were distinguishing features of the latter. Later, the APA added the adjective "compulsive" to describe behavior associated with drug dependence. In the upcoming 5th edition scheduled for publication in 2011 or 2012, there is a good likelihood addiction will be substituted for dependence because terminology surrounding the use of chemical versus physical dependence—and even the exact meaning of dependence—has caused a great deal of confusion.

Further Reading

American Psychiatric Association. *Diagnostic and Statistical Manual of Mental Disorders*, 4th Edition, Text Revision. Washington, DC: American Psychiatric Association, 2000.

Didrex. *See* Stimulants.

Diethylpropion. *See* Stimulants.

Diethyltryptamine (DET). *See* Psilocybin and Psilocin.

Dimethyltryptamine (DMT). *See* Psilocybin and Psilocin.

Dip. *See* Smokeless Tobacco.

Disease Model of Addiction The disease model of addiction, which evolved out of a broadening understanding of neuroscience and the dynamics of **addiction**, has come to define an entire philosophy surrounding how our culture addresses the problems that addiction poses to society. This model identifies public health issues associated with addiction and seeks to define the infrastructure needed to carry out **treatment**, works to remove the stigma of addiction to increase the motivation of addicts and others to confront their disease, and clarifies the diagnostic, prognostic, and therapeutic boundaries of the various forms of the disorder.

The model embraces the view of addiction as a medical illness arising out of pathological **brain** disease that has a progressive course and characteristic symptoms. Treatment approaches are based on the 12-step model that originated with **Alcoholics Anonymous** and were later formalized to become the **Minnesota model** that, among other principles, espouses total abstinence and belief that an addict is powerless over his or her disease. The model counters those who say addiction is a choice by citing the biological components of the disease. They argue that characteristic genetic susceptibilities seen in most addicts are no different from similar vulnerabilities that give rise to other medical diseases. Finally, they argue that neurological changes seen in the brain-imaging studies of addicted individuals prove the pathology that spells disease.

Critics of the disease model reject this philosophy, saying that calling aberrant behavior a disease does not make it so—it simply allows an addict to avoid responsibility for his or her behavior and misdirects public resources. They dispute the claim that addiction follows a predictable and progressive course and cite examples of addicts who underwent spontaneous remissions with no treatment. They insist addicts can learn to control their actions with cognitive behavioral therapies and other techniques, and argue that the reason that treatments based on the Minnesota model are touted as being the best is that recovering former addicts who are graduates of **12-step programs** are the treatment counselors promoting the therapy. Critics believe that addicts offered adequate behavioral therapy can learn to use drugs moderately, and that 12-step programs are similar to religious cults that serve only to substitute one type of **dependence** for another. In addressing the question of genetic susceptibility, these same critics claim that behavior, not inheritance, determines whether drug abusers will become addicts, and that the neurological changes seen in addicted brains are the result, not the cause, of their drug-using behavior.

Although 12-step programs and the Minnesota model continue to prevail as recommended treatment approaches, a consensus is taking shape that consolidates the two views. It acknowledges the need for a broadly inclusive approach to treatment that includes personal behavior management, addresses co-occurring mental illnesses, considers relevant socioeconomic issues, and permits greater access to a variety of therapeutic resources.

Further Reading

Erickson, Carlton K. *The Science of Addiction: From Neurobiology to Treatment.* New York: Norton, 2007.

Halpern, John H.. Addiction Is a Disease. *Psychiatric Times* October 2002: 19(10), 54–55.

Schaler, Jeffrey A. Addiction Is a Choice. *Psychiatric Times* October 2002: 19(10), 54, 62.

Vaillant, George. *The Natural History of Alcoholism Revisited.* Cambridge, MA: Harvard University Press, 1995.

White, William. A Disease Concept for the 21st Century. *AddictionInfo.com.* June 2007. Retrieved from http://www.addictioninfo.org/articles/1051/1/
A-Disease-Concept-for-the-21st-Century/Page1.html

White, William. Addiction as a Disease: Birth of a Concept. *Counselor Magazine* October 2000: 1(1), 46–51, 73.

White, William. The Rebirth of the Disease Concept of Alcoholism in the 20th Century. *Counselor Magazine* December 2000: 1(2), 62–66.

White, William. Addiction Disease Concept: Advocates and Critics. *Counselor Magazine* February 2001, 2(1), 42–46.

Disulfiram. *See* Addiction Medications.

DMT. *See* Psilocybin and Psilocin.

Dopamine. *See* Neurotransmitters.

Drug Administration In terms of drug use, administration is the method by which a drug is introduced into the body, and it powerfully affects how the **brain** and the rest of the body respond to the substance. Injecting, smoking, or snorting drugs produces the fastest, most intense effect because a relatively large amount of the substance is delivered quickly to the brain. This method is also more likely to result in toxicity and possibly even fatal overdose because the addict can easily ingest too much, too fast.

Because drinking or eating the substance produces a milder effect, some addicts, seeking a quick rush or "flash," crush and snort pills that are meant to be taken orally. Such users are highly susceptible to **addiction**, as are the addicts who dissolve the tablets and inject the mixture. In addition to overdose, risks include the possibility that injecting the substance will propel insoluble fillers into the bloodstream that can result in damage to the cardiovascular system, lungs, and eyes.

Snorting and injecting drugs quickly leads to prolonged episodes of bingeing that can continue for days until delirium, psychotic behavior, or the lack of drugs forces the user to crash, a **withdrawal** period of deep depression, anxiety, **craving**, and extreme exhaustion. So great is the euphoric burst from smoked, snorted, or injected **stimulants** like crack **cocaine** that the user ignores tremors, dizziness, chest pains, vomiting, paranoia, agitation, panic, and aggression that can accompany binges. If stimulants are combined with antidepressants or cold medications containing decongestants, the user may have a life-threatening reaction to the compound effect of the drugs.

An additional danger associated with injecting drugs is that contaminated needles can transmit HIV infection and other serious diseases such as malaria, tetanus, or deadly bacterial infections, and could also lead to life-threatening blood poisoning.

Drug Classes The federal **Controlled Substances Act (CSA)** groups all drugs with the potential for **abuse** into 5 classes that are regulated by federal law to control their manufacture

Substance/Drug	Intoxicating Effects	Potential Health Consequences
Cannabis Marijuana Hashish	Euphoria, relaxed inhibitions, increased appetite, reduced anxiety, feelings of well-being	Cough, frequent respiratory infections, impaired memory and learning, decreased motivation, anxiety, panic attacks, psychosis
Depressants Alcohol Barbiturates Benzodiazepines Flunitrazepam GHB Meprobamate Methaqualone	Slurred speech, drowsiness, mild intoxication, lowered inhibitions, poor concentration	Fatigue, confusion, dizziness, irritability, impaired memory and judgement, respiratory arrest, seizures, coma, death
Hallucinogens Ketamine LSD MDMA (Ecstasy) PCP	Altered states of perception, feeling, time and distance, nausea, hallucinations, heightened senses	Flashbacks, sleeplessness, persistent mental disorders, paranoia, cardiac arrest
Inhalants Gases Aerosols Nitrites Volatile solvents	Stimulation, loss of inhibition, drunken behavior	Unconsciousness, weight loss, depression, memory impairment, cardiovascular and nervous system damage, death
Opiates Fentanyl Heroin Hydrocodone Oxycodone	Euphoria, drowsiness, sense of well-being	Nausea, constipation, vomiting, confusion, respiratory arrest, convulsions, coma, death
Stimulants Amphetamines Cocaine & crack Khat	Increased alertness, euphoria, excitation, feelings of exhilaration and mental alertness, aggression, violence, mild hallucinogenic effects	Rapid or irregular heartbeat, heart failure, insomnia, loss of coordination, anxiousness, delirium, panic, paranoia, psychosis, stroke, renal failure

Source: NIDA, DEA

Commonly Abused Drugs: Drug Classes

and distribution. How they are placed into each class, or Schedule, depends on their chemical composition, medical application, safety, and addictive potential. The groups of drugs subject to regulation include **anabolic steroids**, **depressants**, **hallucinogens** (including *Cannabis*), **opiates** (narcotics), and **stimulants**. **Inhalants** are not included in the CSA classifications because they cannot be held to the same regulatory standards.

Because many drugs produce symptoms characteristic of more than 1 of these 5 classes, there has been some confusion about this system of categorizing drugs. In terms of their effect on the body, opiates may be grouped under depressants instead of being set off in a category of their own; alcohol or *Cannabis* (**marijuana** and **hashish**) are often placed in separate categories instead of being listed, respectively, under depressants or hallucinogens; **cocaine** is treated as an opiate within the CSA system even though it does not bind to opiate receptors and does not produce morphine-like effects; and the so-called date-rape drugs

Rohypnol and GHB, considered hallucinogens, are technically depressants. To address these overlaps and resolve any confusion, many experts categorize drugs into 7 groups: anabolic steroids, *Cannabis*, depressants (including alcohol), hallucinogens, inhalants, opiates (narcotics), and stimulants.

Drug Classes: Seven Groups of Commonly Abused Drugs

Anabolic Steroids

- Boldenone undecylenate (Equipoise)
- Fluoxymesterone
- Methandriol
- Methandrostenolone (Dianabol)
- Methenolone
- Methyltestosterone
- Nandrolone decanoate (Deca-Durabolin)
- Nandrolone phenpropionate (Durabolin)
- Oxandrolone (Oxandrin)
- Oxymetholone (Anadrol)
- Stanozolol (Winstrol)
- Sten
- Sustanon
- Testosterone cypionate (Depo-Testosterone)
- Trenbolone

Cannabis

- Hashish
- Hashish Oil
- Marijuana

Depressants

- Alcohol
- Barbiturates
- Benzodiazepines
- Chloral hydrate
- Flunitrazepam
- Gamma Hydroxybutyric Acid (GHB)
- Glutethimide
- Meprobamate
- Methaqualone
- Paraldehyde
- Rohypnol

Hallucinogens

- Dextromethorphan
- Ecstasy

- Flunitrazepam (See Depressants)
- Gamma Hydroxybutyric Acid (See Depressants)
- Ibogaine
- Ketamine
- Lysergic acid diethylamide (LSD)
- Mescaline
- Phencyclidine (PCP) and similar compounds
- Psilocybin, Psilocin, other tryptamines

Inhalants

- Gases such as those found in aerosols and dispensers (whippets), lighters, and propane tanks; refrigerants; and ether, nitrous oxide, or chloroform that are used in medical settings.
- Volatile solvents, which are regular- or industrial-strength products that contain solvents; these include gasoline, glue, felt-tip markers, paint thinners, degreasers, and dry-cleaning fluids.
- Aerosols, which are widely available in most households, include hair spray, vegetable sprays, spray paint, and similar products.
- Nitrites fall into two categories: organic, such as butyl or amyl nitrites ("poppers"), and volatile, such as those found in bottles featuring products such as leather cleaner, room odorizer, or liquid aroma.

Opiates

- Buprenorphine
- Butorphanol
- Codeine (derived from opium)
- Dextropropoxyphene
- Fentanyl
- Heroin
- Hydrocodone
- Hydromorphone
- LAAM
- Meperidine
- Methadone
- Morphine
- Opium
- Oxycodone
- Oxymorphone
- Pentazocine
- Thebaine
- Tramadol

Stimulants

- Amphetamines
- Ephedrine
- Pseudoephedrine

- Caffeine
- Cocaine and Crack
- Dextroamphetamine
- Khat
- Methamphetamine
- Methcathinone
- Methylphenidate
- Nicotine

Further Reading

Califano, Joseph A., Jr. *High Society: How Substance Abuse Ravages America and What to Do About It.* New York: Perseus Books, 2007.

Hoffman, John, and Froemke, Susan, eds. *Addiction: Why Can't They Just Stop?* New York: Rodale, 2007.

Home Box Office (HBO). In partnership with the Robert Wood Johnson Foundation, the National Institute on Drug Abuse, and the National Institute on Alcohol Abuse and Alcoholism. *Addiction: Why Can't They Just Stop?* Documentary. March 2007.

U.S. Department of Health and Human Services, National Institute on Drug Abuse (NIDA), June 2007. Retrieved from http://www.nida.gov

U.S. Department of Health and Human Services, Substance Abuse and Mental Health Services Administration (SAMHSA), August 2007. Retrieved from http://www.samhsa.gov

U.S. Department of Justice, Drug Enforcement Administration (DEA), March 2008. Retrieved from http://www.usdoj.gov/dea

Drug Interactions The interactions of 2 or more drugs in the body can be dangerous; even those that are predictable in most people can affect others quite differently. Drug interactions might be antagonistic, in which one substance partially or wholly blocks the effect of the other; agonistic, in which one substance boosts the activity of the other; additive, in which the effect on the body is the sum of both agents; or synergistic, in which the action of one drug on the other produces a combined effect greater than the additive effect. Alcohol combined with other drugs frequently produces synergistic effects, sometimes with lethal results.

It is difficult if not impossible to know why some people are more sensitive to the effects of drugs or how to predict which combinations might be more dangerous for them. During the 1970s, an otherwise healthy young woman named Karen Ann Quinlan, who had been dieting for 2 or 3 days but was of normal weight, combined a few alcoholic drinks with a tranquilizer, a mix that millions of people take regularly without demonstrably ill effects. She collapsed, and the drugs—both of which were **depressants** that suppressed respiration—caused her to stop breathing. She suffered **brain** damage, lapsing into a coma and a vegetative state. She was finally permitted to die 10 years later without ever regaining consciousness. Another case is that of Heath Ledger, a promising young actor who died suddenly in 2008 from a combination of **prescription drugs**. Although his postmortem toxicology report showed several legal drugs in his system, there was reason to believe they had been consumed over a period of days rather than all at once. Nevertheless, for him, it was a deadly mix.

Most physicians do not have the time to advise each patient about potential interactions. To protect themselves, patients should consider having their prescriptions filled at the same pharmacy, one with a computerized system that can detect potential conflicts;

others may wish to research reputable Internet sites to investigate the potential risks of combining different drugs.

Drug Nomenclature Whether addictive or used in the **treatment** of **addiction**, most drugs have two names, generic and trade. The generic name represents the permanent, simplified name given to its molecular composition. The trade name, which identifies it as proprietary, or exclusive, is given by the pharmaceutical company that manufactures or markets the drug. When the patent expires, other companies may compound the generic drug into their own trade-named versions. Although the active ingredients may be identical, different formulations of trade-named drugs might have different therapeutic effects based in part on inactive ingredients and the dosage regimen. For example, even though the therapeutic compound in both is the same, one company's tablet taken twice a day might have slightly different effects from another company's sustained-release capsule taken once a day.

See also Appendix B.

Drug Nomenclature: Generic and Trade Names

The following are generic and trade names of both addictive drugs and therapeutic drugs used to treat addiction. For more complete lists of generic and trade names, see Appendix B.

Addictive Drugs, Alphabetically by Generic Names

Generic Names	Trade Names
Dextroamphetamine	Dexedrine
Diazepam	Valium
Ethchlorvynol	Placidyl
Flunitrazepam	Rohypnol
Oxycodone	OxyContin, Percocet, Percodan
Sage	Salvinorin A
Zolpidem	Ambien

Addictive Drugs, Alphabetically by Trade Names

Trade Names	Generic Names
Ambien	Zolpidem
Dexedrine	Dextroamphetamine
OxyContin	Oxycodone
Percocet	Oxycodone
Percodan	Oxycodone
Placidyl	Ethchlorvynol
Rohypnol	Flunitrazepam
Salvinorin A	Sage
Valium	Diazepam

Therapeutic Drugs, Alphabetically by Generic Names

Generic Names	Trade Names
Bupropion	Wellbutrin, Zyban
Citalopram	Celexa

Escitalopram oxalate	Lexapro
Fluoxetine	Prozac
Naltrexone	Depade, ReVia, Vivitrol
Nicotine polacrilex	Nicorette
Sertraline	Zoloft
Varenicline	Chantix
Venlafaxine	Effexor

Therapeutic Drugs, Alphabetically by Trade Names

Trade Names	**Generic Names**
Celexa	Citalopram
Chantix	Varenicline
Depade	Naltrexone
Effexor	Venlafaxine
Lexapro	Escitalopram oxalate
Nicorette	Nicotine polacrilex
Prozac	Fluoxetine
ReVia	Naltrexone
Vivitrol	Naltrexone
Wellbutrin	Bupropion
Zoloft	Sertraline
Zyban	Bupropion

Drug Screening/Testing Some schools, private-sector employers, and the federal government test students or employees for drug use. Many schools have begun to carry out random drug testing for those who participate in extracurricular activities, and they test other students if there is reasonable suspicion or cause to believe they are using drugs. Private companies may want to screen employees for drug panels—a range of predetermined drugs—based on their own internal standards.

Federally regulated drug testing was instituted decades ago to determine whether federal employees and others performing services for the U.S. government were current or former users. Five drug groups were singled out at that time for testing: **amphetamines**, cannabinoids, **cocaine**, **opiates**, and PCP. Because these groups of drugs were defined decades ago, some tests cannot detect synthetic substitutes like **oxycodone**; however, most drug-testing facilities have introduced updated laboratory procedures that allow them to do so. Nevertheless, some newer steroids can evade detection.

Drug Screening/Testing: FAQs about Drug Testing in Schools

1. What is drug testing?

   Some schools, hospitals, or places of employment screen for drugs as a means of pre-employment testing, random testing, reasonable suspicion/cause testing, post-accident testing, return-to-duty testing, and follow-up testing. This usually involves collecting urine samples to check for drugs such as marijuana, cocaine, amphetamines, PCP, and opiates.

   There are some schools that have initiated random drug testing and/or reasonable suspicion/cause testing. During random testing, schools select one or more students to undergo the test. Currently, random drug testing can only be conducted on students who participate in competitive extracurricular activities. Reasonable suspicion/cause testing requires a student to provide a urine specimen when sufficient evidence exists that the student may have used an illicit substance. Typically, this involves direct observations made by school officials that a student has used or possesses illicit substances, exhibits physical symptoms of being under the influence, and has patterns of abnormal or erratic behavior.

2. Why do some schools want to conduct random drug tests?

   Schools that have adopted random student drug testing are hoping to decrease drug abuse among students via 2 routes. First, they hope that random testing will serve as a deterrent and give students a reason to resist peer pressure to take drugs. Second, drug testing can identify adolescents who have started using drugs so that interventions can occur early, or identify adolescents who already have drug problems so they can be referred for treatment. Drug abuse not only interferes with a student's ability to learn but it can disrupt the teaching environment, affecting other students as well.

3. Is student drug testing a stand-alone solution, or do schools need other programs to prevent and reduce drug use?

   Drug testing should never be undertaken as a stand-alone response to a drug problem. If testing is done, it should be a component of broader prevention, intervention, and treatment programs, with the common goal of reducing drug use.

4. If a student tests positive for drugs, should that student face disciplinary consequences?

   The primary purpose of drug testing is not to punish students who use drugs but to prevent drug abuse and to help students already using become drug-free. The results of a positive drug test should be used to intervene with counseling and follow-up testing. For students who are diagnosed with addiction, parents and a school administrator can refer them to effective drug treatment program.

5. Why test teenagers at all?

   Teens are especially vulnerable to drug abuse, when the brain and body are still developing. In the short term, even the single use of an intoxicating drug can affect a person's judgment and decision-making—resulting in accidents, poor performance in a school or sports activity, unplanned risky behavior, and the risk of overdosing. In the long term, repeated drug abuse can lead to serious problems, such as poor academic outcomes, mood changes (depending on the drug—depression, anxiety, paranoia, psychosis), and social or family problems caused or worsened by drugs.

   Repeated drug use can also lead to addiction. Studies show that the earlier a teen begins using drugs, the more likely he or she will develop a substance abuse problem or addiction. Conversely, if teens stay away from drugs while in high school, they are less likely to develop a substance abuse problem later in life.

6. How many students actually use drugs?

   Drug use among high schools students has dropped significantly since 2001. In December, the National Institute on Drug Abuse's 2007 Monitoring the Future survey of 8th, 10th, and 12th graders showed that drug use had declined by 24 percent since 2001. Despite this marked decline, much remains to be done. Almost 50 percent of 12th graders say that they have used drugs at least once in their lifetime, and 18 percent reported using marijuana in the last month. Prescription drug abuse is high—with nearly 1 in 10 high school seniors reporting nonmedical use of the prescription painkiller Vicodin in the past year.

7. What testing methods are available?

There are several testing methods available that use urine, hair, oral fluids, and sweat (patch). These methods vary in cost, reliability, drugs detected, and detection period. Schools can determine their needs and choose the method that best suits their requirements, as long as the testing kits are from a reliable source.

8. Which drugs can be tested for?

Various testing methods normally test for a panel of drugs. Typically, a drug panel tests for marijuana, cocaine, opiates, amphetamines, and PCP. If a school has a particular problem with other drugs, such as MDMA, GHB, or steroids, they can include testing for these drugs as well.

9. What about alcohol?

Alcohol is a drug, and its use is a serious problem among young people. However, alcohol does not remain in the blood long enough for most tests to detect recent use. Breathalyzers and oral fluid tests can detect current use. Adolescents with substance abuse problems often use more than one drug, so identifying a problem with an illicit or prescription drug may also suggest an alcohol problem.

10. How accurate are drug tests? Is there a possibility a test could give a false positive?

Tests are very accurate, but not 100 percent accurate. Samples are usually divided, so if an initial test is positive, a confirmation test can be conducted. Federal guidelines are in place to ensure accuracy and fairness in drug testing programs.

11. Can students beat the tests?

Many drug-using students are aware of techniques that supposedly detoxify their systems or mask drug use. Popular magazines and Internet sites give advice on how to dilute urine samples, and there are even companies that sell clean urine or products designed to distort test results. A number of techniques and products are focused on urine tests for marijuana, but masking products are becoming increasingly available for tests of hair, oral fluids, and multiple drugs.

Most of these products do not work, are very costly, are easily identified in the testing process, and need to be on hand constantly because of the nature of random testing. Moreover, even if the specific drug is successfully masked, the product itself can be detected, in which case the student using it would become an obvious candidate for additional screening and attention. In fact, some testing programs label a test positive if a masking product is detected.

12. Is random drug testing of students legal?

In June 2002, the U.S. Supreme Court broadened the authority of public schools to test students for illegal drugs. Voting 5 to 4 in *Pottawatomie County v. Earls*, the court ruled to allow random drug tests for all middle and high school students participating in competitive extracurricular activities. The ruling greatly expanded the scope of school drug testing, which previously had been allowed only for student athletes.

13. Just because the U.S. Supreme Court said student drug testing for adolescents in competitive extracurricular activities is constitutional, does that mean it is legal in my city or state?

   A school or school district that is interested in adopting a student drug-testing program should seek legal counsel so that it complies with all federal, state, and local laws. Individual state constitutions may dictate different legal thresholds for allowing student drug testing. Communities interested in starting student drug testing programs should become familiar with the law in their respective states to ensure proper compliance.

14. What has research determined about the utility of random drug tests in schools?

   There is not very much research in this area and early research shows mixed results. One study found that student athletes who participated in randomized drug testing had overall rates of drug use similar to students who did not take part in the program, and in fact some indicators of future drug abuse increased among those participating in the drug-testing program. Because of the limited number of studies on this topic, more research is warranted.

Source: Adapted from National Institute on Drug Abuse.
http://www.nida.nih.gov/drugpages/testingfaqs.htm

Depending on the circumstances, modern drug screens can detect alcohol, amphetamines, **barbiturates**, **benzodiazepines**, cannabinoids, cocaine, opiates, nicotine, LSD, **methadone**, or PCP. Some dip-stick urine tests can be evaluated on the spot, although more accurate results are obtained from laboratory analysis. Advantages of on-site, on-the-spot urine or saliva tests are that they can be used for random drug testing and to detect immediately whether drugs were implicated in accidents or other incidents in which drug use is suspected. Alcohol is rapidly eliminated from the body, so samples should be obtained as quickly as possible, but blood, hair, urine, and sweat tests can be used to detect past drug use. Many employers require pre-employment screening, return-to-duty screening, or on-site testing that may involve random and unannounced screening. Parents find saliva tests to be an immediate and convenient tool to check for current drug use in their children, and schools may use them when there is cause to believe students are using.

Types of Drug Tests

Blood and Hair

Testing blood and hair for the presence of drug residue produces very accurate results, although they may take a few days. Body hair works as well as hair from the head, so drug users' attempts to foil the test by shaving their heads does not work, especially since hair follicles can be removed—a painful process—for testing.

Saliva Tests

A major advantage of saliva tests is that they are immediate and can be done on-site and on a random basis to detect current and past drug use. Unlike urine tests, saliva tests are virtually impossible to adulterate.

Sweat Patches

Sometimes used in the criminal justice and child protective systems, sweat patches are applied to the skin to collect sweat samples over a period of days or weeks. They cannot be removed by the user without the knowledge of the supervisory agency that conducts the test, but their reliability is questionable under some circumstances.

Urine Tests

Urine tests are very accurate, but the samples can be adulterated. Many drug users take diuretics or drink excess fluids in an attempt to dilute their urine, but most tests can screen for dilution or masking agents.

Further Reading

Lawler, Jennifer. *Drug Testing in Schools: A Pro/Con Issue*. Berkeley Heights, NJ: Enslow, 2000.
Sawvel, Patty Jo, ed. *Student Drug Testing*. Farmington Hills, MI: Greenhaven, 2006.

Drugged Driving Driving under the influence (DUI) or driving while intoxicated (DWI) means operating a motor vehicle while under the influence of any drug that alters perception, impairs reflexes or attention, skews judgment, or affects balance and coordination. Drivers using any such substance or combination of substances, even if the drugs are legal or prescribed, are dangerous on the roadways and may be subject to severe penalties if they break driving laws or are involved in accidents. According to the National Highway Traffic Safety Administration (NHTSA), car and truck accidents are the leading cause of death of teens and young adults ages 15 to 21. Drunk and drugged drivers kill over 16,000 people a year in the United States, and anywhere between 10 to 22 percent of drivers involved in accidents have been using drugs, including alcohol. Roughly 5 percent of the population over 15-years-old and 14 percent of young adults are reported to have been driving under the influence of illicit drugs in the past year. Fortunately, through the efforts of many law enforcement organizations and groups like Mothers Against Drunk Driving (MADD) and Students Against Destructive Decisions (SADD—formerly Students Against Driving Drunk), there has been a decline in fatalities and other injuries associated with drugged driving.

State laws vary regarding the penalties for driving under the influence. In 12 states (Arizona, Georgia, Indiana, Illinois, Iowa, Michigan, Minnesota, Nevada, Pennsylvania, Rhode Island, Utah, and Wisconsin), it is illegal to operate a motor vehicle with any detectable level of a prohibited drug, or its metabolites, in the driver's blood. Other state laws define drugged driving as driving when a drug "renders the driver incapable of driving safely" or "causes the driver to be impaired." Since even a small amount of **marijuana**, alcohol, or other drug—especially if 2 or more are combined—can produce significant impairment and incapacity, states are likely to interpret their penalty laws to suit the crime.

State Laws for Driving under the Influence of Alcohol

In all 50 states and the District of Columbia, the legal drunk limit for driving under the influence of alcohol is a 0.08 blood alcohol concentration (BAC), the point at which people feel euphoric and powerful despite impaired coordination, balance, and reflexes. The states differ in terms of policies regarding license suspensions, vehicle forfeiture if the driver is guilty of multiple offenses, and open containers.

States in Which Licenses Can Be Suspended for First Offense

- All states *except* Kentucky, Michigan, Montana, New Jersey, Pennsylvania, Rhode Island, South Carolina, South Dakota, Tennessee

States that Restore Driving Privileges During Suspension (when certain requirements are met):

- All states *except* Alabama, Delaware, Kansas, Massachusetts, Mississippi, Missouri, New Hampshire, Utah, Vermont, Virginia

Open Container Laws:

- *None*: Arkansas, Connecticut, Delaware, Mississippi, Missouri, Virginia, West Virginia
- *Apply to driver only*: Alaska, Kansas, Oklahoma, Rhode Island, Tennessee
- *Apply to both driver and passengers*: All other states

States that Forfeit Vehicles for Multiple Offenses:

- *Do not forfeit*: Alabama, Colorado, Connecticut, Delaware, District of Columbia, Hawaii, Idaho, Iowa, Kansas, Maryland, Nebraska, Nevada, New Hampshire, New Jersey, New Mexico, South Dakota, Utah, West Virginia, Wyoming
- *Forfeit*: All Others

Source: Insurance Institute for Highway Safety. http://www.iihs.org

---

Driving under the Influence of Drugs other than Alcohol

Determining the level of impairment of someone driving under the influence and assigning appropriate penalties is not as clear-cut a process as penalizing alcohol-related driving infractions, in part because there is no established legal limit for drugs. A driver affected by such drugs must be evaluated based on the degree of his or her **intoxication**—whether the driver lacks sober judgment or is unable to drive in a prudent manner consistent with the way an unimpaired person would drive. The evidence is of necessity partly circumstantial, based on observations of the driver's coordination and balance on sobriety tests. Blood chemical analyses may also be used to verify observed evidence. Although state motor vehicle departments are not likely to have the jurisdictional authority to suspend or revoke licenses, the courts can and do impose penalties, sometimes more severe than those imposed for similar alcohol-related offenses. Those penalties could result in suspension of driving privileges.

Teen Drivers

Motor vehicle crashes are the leading cause of death for U.S. teens, accounting for 36 percent of all deaths in this age group. However, research suggests that the most strict and comprehensive graduated drivers licensing programs are associated with reductions of 38 percent and 40 percent in fatal and injury crashes, respectively, of 16-year-old drivers.

- The risk of motor vehicle crashes is higher among 16- to 19-year-olds than among any other age group. In fact, per mile driven, teen drivers ages 16 to 19 are 4 times more likely than older drivers to crash.
- The presence of teen passengers increases the crash risk of unsupervised teen drivers; the risk increases with the number of teen passengers.
- In 2004, the motor vehicle death rate for male drivers and passengers age 16 to 19 was more than 1.5 times that of their female counterparts (19.4 per 100,000 compared with 11.1 per 100,000).
- Crash risk is particularly high during the 1st year that teenagers are eligible to drive.
- Teens are more likely than older drivers to underestimate or fail to recognize hazardous or dangerous situations.
- Teens are more likely than older drivers to speed and allow shorter distance from the front of one vehicle to the front of the next. The presence of male teenage passengers increases the likelihood of these risky driving behaviors by teen male drivers.
- Among male drivers between 15 and 20 years of age who were involved in fatal crashes in 2005, 38 percent were speeding at the time of the crash and 24 percent had been drinking.
- At all levels of blood alcohol concentration (BAC), the risk of involvement in a motor vehicle crash is greater for teens than for older drivers.
  — In 2005, 23 percent of drivers ages 15 to 20 who died in motor vehicle crashes had a BAC of 0.08 or higher.
  — In a national survey conducted in 2005, nearly 30 percent of teens reported that within the previous month, they had ridden with a driver who had been drinking alcohol. One in ten reported having driven after drinking alcohol within the same one-month period.
  — In 2005, among teen drivers who were killed in motor vehicle crashes after drinking and driving, 74 percent were unrestrained.
- In 2005, half of teen deaths from motor vehicle crashes occurred between 3 p.m. and midnight, and 54 percent occurred on Friday, Saturday, or Sunday.

Facts about Drugged Driving

- In 2005, 16,885 people died in alcohol-related motor vehicle crashes, accounting for 39 percent of all traffic-related deaths in the United States.
- An alcohol-related motor vehicle crash kills someone every 31 minutes and nonfatally injures someone every 2 minutes.

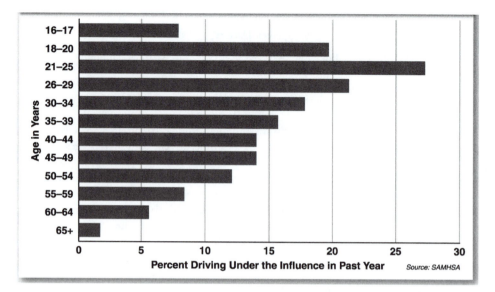

Driving under the Influence of Alcohol in the Past Year among Persons Aged 16 or Older, by Age: 2006

- Drugs other than alcohol (e.g., marijuana and cocaine) are involved in about 18 percent of motor vehicle driver deaths. These drugs are generally used in combination with alcohol.
- Each year, alcohol-related crashes in the United States cost about $51 billion.
- Most drinking and driving episodes go undetected. In 2005, nearly 1.4 million drivers were arrested for driving under the influence of alcohol or narcotics, which is less than 1 percent of the 159 million self-reported episodes of alcohol-impaired driving among U.S. adults each year.

Occurrence and Consequences

- More than half of the 414 child passengers ages 14 and younger who died in alcohol-related crashes during 2005 were riding with the drinking driver.
- In 2005, 48 children age 14 years and younger who were killed as pedestrians or pedal-cyclists were struck by impaired drivers.

Groups at Risk

- Male drivers involved in fatal motor vehicle crashes are almost twice as likely as female drivers to be intoxicated with a blood alcohol concentration (BAC) of 0.08 percent or greater. It is illegal to drive with a BAC of 0.08 percent or higher in all 50 states, the District of Columbia, and Puerto Rico.
- At all levels of blood alcohol concentration, the risk of being involved in a crash is greater for young people than for older people. In 2005, 16 percent of drivers ages 16 to 20 who died in motor vehicle crashes had been drinking alcohol.
- Young men ages 18 to 20 (under the legal drinking age) reported driving while impaired more frequently than any other age group.

- Among motorcycle drivers killed in fatal crashes, 30 percent have BACs of 0.08 percent or greater.
- Nearly half of the alcohol-impaired motorcyclists killed each year are age 40 or older, and motorcyclists ages 40 to 44 have the highest percentage of fatalities with BACs of 0.08 percent or greater.
- Of the 1,946 traffic fatalities among children ages 0 to 14 in 2005, 21 percent involved alcohol.
- Among drivers involved in fatal crashes, those with BAC levels of 0.08 percent or higher were 9 times more likely to have a prior conviction for driving while impaired (DWI) than were drivers who had not consumed alcohol.

Source: Centers for Disease Control and Prevention. http://www.cdc.gov/ncipc/duip/spotlite/3d.htm

Dual Diagnosis As many as half of all people who have mental illnesses **abuse** drugs or alcohol. Treatment specialists stress that if **treatment** is to succeed a dual diagnosis of the **addiction** and all co-occurring **mental disorders** must be made so appropriate therapy can be designed. Determining which symptoms are due to drug use and which are due to mental illness can be challenging, especially in teenagers whose moods and behavior fluctuate widely in response to emotional swings. Substance abuse can mimic, mask, or worsen mental illness, and mental illness can aggravate substance abuse. Sometimes the patient consciously uses one disorder to hide another; those who fear the stigma of having a mental illness might claim that drug abuse is responsible for their symptoms and behavior. These factors make diagnosis more difficult, and one of the many obstacles to planning effective treatment is to overcome the tendency of one disorder to lead to relapse in the other disorder.

Dual diagnoses are also referred to as comorbid disorders. The mental illnesses most frequently diagnosed with substance abuse are depression, anxiety or personality disorders,

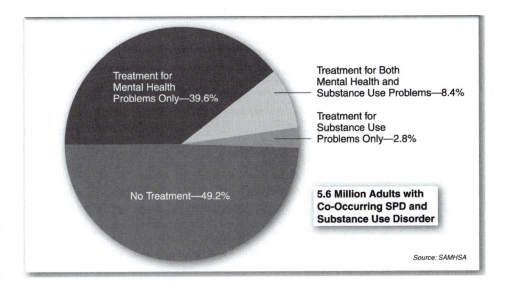

Past-Year Treatment Among Adults Aged 18 or Older with Both Serious Psychological Distress (SPD) and a Substance Use Disorder: 2006

and schizophrenia. In most cases, the individual uses the drugs to self-medicate the symptoms of the mental illness and ultimately becomes addicted. If a proper dual diagnosis is made and the mental disorders are adequately treated, the need for the drug diminishes significantly and the addiction can be arrested.

Once accurate diagnoses are made, detoxification or, in the case of severe mental illness, hospitalization may be required, followed by outpatient treatment. Other addicts might enter outpatient treatment directly. All are likely to receive psychiatric medications in addition to behavioral therapy and counseling. In many cases, **12-step programs** may not be the most effective for treating people with a dual diagnosis because the nature of their mental illnesses may prevent them from participating fully; on the other hand, group programs offer opportunities to develop new relationships and life skills. Whatever treatment approaches are used, they must be carefully evaluated and integrated into a whole program that meets the unique needs of each patient and addresses all disorders.

Further Reading

Daley, Dennis. *Dual Disorders: Counseling Clients with Chemical Dependency and Mental Illness*, 3rd Edition. Center City, MN: Hazelden Foundation, 2002.

Ortman, Dennis C. *The Dual Diagnosis Recovery Sourcebook: A Physical, Mental, and Spiritual Approach to Addiction With An Emotional Disorder*. Lincolnwood, IL: Lowell House, 2001.

Thombs, Dennis L. *Introduction to Addictive Behaviors*, 3rd Edition. New York: The Guilford Press, 2006.

Duragesic. *See* Fentanyl.

DXM. *See* Dextromethorphan.

E

Eating Disorders Eating disorders encompass a range of disturbances related to food consumption. The American Psychiatric Association, in the 4th edition of its *Diagnostic and Statistical Manual of Mental Disorders* (*DSM*), states that the two most serious eating disorders are **anorexia nervosa** and **bulimia nervosa**. In the former, the patient refuses to maintain normal weight; in the latter, he or she binges on food and controls weight gain with fasting, excessive exercise, or purging by self-induced vomiting, the use of laxatives and diuretics, or taking enemas. Both types of eating disorders are extremely serious, and anorexia, particularly, can quickly become life threatening; some statistics show that up to 15 percent of people with eating disorders die from the disease.

Prevalence and Characteristics of Anorexia Nervosa

According to the National Institute of Mental Health (NIMH), over the course of a lifetime, 0.5 to 3.7 percent of girls and women will develop anorexia nervosa and 1.1 to 4.2 percent will develop bulimia nervosa. About 0.5 percent of those with anorexia die each year as a result of their illness, making it one of the top psychiatric illnesses that lead to death.

Anorexia is characterized by a resistance to maintaining a healthy body weight, an intense fear of gaining weight, and other extreme behaviors that result in severe weight loss. People with anorexia see themselves as overweight even when they are dangerously thin. Bulimia generally is characterized by recurrent episodes of binge eating, followed by self-induced purging behaviors. People with bulimia often have normal weight, but, like those with anorexia, they are intensely dissatisfied with the appearance of their bodies. Eating disorders involve multiple biological, behavioral, and social factors that are not well understood.

A study funded by NIMH reported in August of 2006 that Internet-based intervention programs may help some college-age, high-risk women avoid developing an eating disorder. Although it cannot be assumed that all people at risk would benefit from such online approaches to prevention, the programs may serve as valuable screening tools to help susceptible individuals seek treatment before the disease has progressed.

Source: National Institute of Mental Health. http://www.nimh.nih.gov/science-news/2006/college-women-at-risk-for-eating-disorder-may-benefit-from-online-intervention.shtml

A 3rd manifestation of eating disorders is known as a bingeing and purging disorder. Unlike bulimics, the individuals eat normally, but still feel compelled to purge even though they maintain near-normal weight. Comprising a 4th type are the so-called **food addictions** (overeating **addictions**), which can often lead to obesity; a compulsive desire to gorge on sweets is a common example. Although obesity is considered by some to be an eating disorder because it involves an unhealthy relationship with food, it is not specifically characterized as such in the *DSM*; however, the manual discusses obesity within the context of a mental health disorder if there are psychological factors contributing to its cause.

The complexity of eating disorders makes many difficult to treat. Like other compulsive behaviors, proper diagnosis is critical, and the earlier a diagnosis is made, the better, but this is often complicated by the fact that shame and a distorted sense of body image, known as body dysmorphic disorder, deter patients from asking for help. This delays **treatment** until after the illness has become life-threatening, making therapeutic **interventions** more difficult.

Long associated with a low self-esteem, eating disorders stem from a complex mix of biological, environmental, and genetic causes. Although males are not exempt, the condition disproportionately affects females. At some time in their lives, anywhere from five to ten percent of girls and women suffer from eating disorders that usually appear during adolescence or early adulthood. The disease is frequently accompanied by anxiety or depression, and, in many cases, it is likely that each disorder reinforces or exacerbates the symptoms of the others.

Prevalence of Eating Disorders among Males

Although eating disorders primarily affect girls and women, boys and men are also vulnerable. One in 4 preadolescent cases of anorexia occurs in boys, and binge-eating disorder affects females and males about equally.

Like females who have eating disorders, males with the illness have a warped sense of body image and often have muscle dysmorphia, a type of disorder that is characterized by an extreme concern with becoming more muscular. Some boys with the disorder want to lose weight, while others want to gain weight or bulk up. Boys who think they are too small are at a greater risk for using steroids or other dangerous drugs to increase muscle mass.

Boys with eating disorders exhibit the same types of emotional, physical, and behavioral signs and symptoms as girls, but, for a variety of reasons, including that the disease is often considered a female disorder, boys are less likely to be diagnosed.

Source: National Institute of Mental Health. http://www.nimh.nih.gov/health/publications/eating-disorders/how-are-men-and-boys-affected.shtml

---

Eating disorders do not necessarily meet all the same diagnostic criteria. While bulimia is frequently regarded as an **impulse control disorder**, some aspects of anorexia nervosa meet the *DSM* definitions for major depressive disorder, social phobia, and **obsessive-compulsive disorder**. Nevertheless, researchers are intrigued that in people with eating disorders and in those addicted either to substances or to compulsive behaviors, key neurological activity in specific regions of the **brain** is so similar. This may help explain why eating disorders are often accompanied by a history of substance **abuse**. The progressive nature of eating disorders mirrors that of substance abuse; like drug addiction or an addiction to pathological gambling, the behavior continues in spite of negative consequences, and the individual experiences intense **craving** to repeat the behavior despite periods of abstinence.

These findings have tempered the prevailing wisdom of prior decades, which held that eating disorders arose out of psychological and family influences, particularly a history of abuse, repression of emotional expression, parental neglect or hostility, and a somewhat obsessive need to control one's environment. Nevertheless, despite the undeniable influence of biological factors, a cultural emphasis on thinness increases the possibility that a psychologically vulnerable adolescent girl or young woman will develop an eating disorder. One study reported in 2008 that girls who ate meals at the table with their families 5 or more times a week were significantly less likely to develop eating disorders than their peers. Although the same result was not shown for boys, the study authors suggest that teenage girls might be much more heavily influenced by quality time spent with families, especially in terms of developing a healthy relationship with food and in associating good eating habits with positive family interaction.

Treatment varies depending on the characteristics of the individual eating disorder and is best developed around a combined approach of cognitive behavioral therapy and medications to address contributory neurochemical imbalances; pharmaceutical approaches are particularly helpful if used early in treatment before the patient has learned new coping strategies in therapy. In some instances, family therapy is advisable to address relationship issues and interpersonal dysfunction, especially situations in which adolescent patients are still living at home. In severe cases, hospitalization may be necessary, both to institute nutritional therapy and because eating disorders of longstanding can result in serious damage to the liver and pancreas and cause heart arrhythmias and mental impairments. Death from starvation is possible.

Prevalence of Eating Disorders

Previously, eating disorders were most often seen in adolescents or young adults, but reports early in 2008 indicated that they are being diagnosed in people in their 30s and 40s as well. Women and girls are more likely to develop an eating disorder than men and boys. Males seem to account for an estimated 5 to 25 percent of patients with anorexia or bulimia, although many reports suggest they suffer the same number of binge-eating disorders as women. Eating disorders frequently co-exist with other psychiatric illnesses such as depression, substance abuse, or anxiety disorders. People with eating disorders also can suffer from numerous organic problems, such as heart disease or kidney failure, which could be fatal. Results from a large-scale national survey suggest that binge-eating disorder is more prevalent than both anorexia nervosa and bulimia nervosa.

Source: National Institute of Mental Health. http://www.nimh.nih.gov/health/publications/eating-disorders/what-are-eating-disorders.shtml; http://www.nimh.nih.gov/science-news/2007/study-tracks-prevalence-of-eating-disorders.shtml

---

FAQs about Eating Disorders

The National Institute of Mental Health has published a list of FAQs about eating disorders from which the following questions are adapted:

1. What are eating disorders?

   Eating disorders are often long-term illnesses that may require long-term treatment. They frequently occur with other mental disorders such as depression, substance abuse, and anxiety disorders. The earlier these disorders are diagnosed and treated, the better the chances are for full recovery.

2. Who has eating disorders?

   Research shows that more than 90 percent of those who have eating disorders are women between the ages of 12 and 25. However, increasing numbers of older women and men have them, and hundreds of thousands of boys are affected as well.

3. What are the symptoms of eating disorders?

   - Anorexia nervosa: People who have anorexia develop unusual eating habits such as avoiding food and meals, picking out a few foods and eating them in small amounts, weighing their food, and counting the calories of everything they eat. They may exercise excessively. A refusal to maintain normal weight is a key feature of anorexia.

   - Bulimia nervosa: People who have bulimia eat an excessive amount of food in a single episode and almost immediately make themselves vomit or use laxatives or diuretics (water pills) to get rid of the food in their bodies. This behavior often is referred to as the binge/purge cycle. Like people with anorexia, people with bulimia have an intense fear of gaining any excess weight, but generally maintain near-normal weight levels.

   - Binge-eating disorder: People with this recently recognized disorder have frequent episodes of compulsive overeating, but unlike those with bulimia, they do not purge their bodies of food. During these food binges, they often eat alone and very quickly, regardless of whether they feel hungry or full. They often feel shame or guilt over their actions. Unlike anorexia and bulimia, binge-eating disorder occurs almost as often in men as in women.

4. What medical problems can arise as a result of eating disorders?

   - Anorexia nervosa: Anorexia can slow the heart rate and lower blood pressure, increasing the chance of heart failure. Those who use drugs to stimulate vomiting, bowel movements, or urination are also at high risk for heart failure. Starvation can also result in heart failure and damage the brain. Anorexia may also cause hair and nails to grow brittle. Skin may dry out, become yellow, and develop a covering of soft hair called lanugo. Mild anemia, swollen joints, reduced muscle mass, and light-headedness also commonly occur. Severe cases of anorexia can lead to brittle bones that break easily as a result of calcium loss.

   - Bulimia nervosa: The acid in vomit can wear down the outer layer of the teeth, inflame and damage the esophagus, and enlarge the glands near the cheeks. Damage to the stomach can also occur from frequent vomiting. Irregular heartbeats, heart failure, and death may result from chemical imbalances and the loss of important minerals such as potassium. Peptic ulcers, inflammation of the pancreas, and long-term constipation are also consequences of bulimia.

   - Binge-eating disorder: Binge-eating disorder can cause high blood pressure and high cholesterol levels. Other effects of binge-eating disorder include fatigue, joint pain, Type II diabetes, gallbladder disease, and heart disease.

5. What is required for a formal diagnosis of an eating disorder?

   - Anorexia nervosa: Weighs at least 15 percent below what is considered normal for others of the same height and age; misses at least 3 consecutive menstrual cycles (if a female of childbearing age); has an intense fear of gaining weight; refuses to maintain the minimal normal body weight; and believes he or she is overweight though in reality is dangerously thin.

- Bulimia nervosa: At least 2 binge/purge cycles a week, on average, for at least 3 months; lacks control over his or her eating behavior; and seems obsessed with his or her body shape and weight.
- Binge-eating disorder: At least 2 binge-eating episodes a week, on average, for 6 months; lacks control over his or her eating behavior.

6. How are eating disorders treated?
- Anorexia nervosa: The first goal for the treatment of anorexia is to restore a healthy weight. This may require hospitalization. Once a person's physical condition is stable, treatment usually involves individual psychotherapy and family therapy during which parents help their child learn to eat again and maintain healthy eating habits on his or her own. Behavioral therapy also has been effective for helping a person return to healthy eating habits. Supportive group therapy may follow, and self-help groups within communities may provide ongoing support.
- Bulimia nervosa: Unless malnutrition is severe, any substance abuse problems that may be present at the time the eating disorder is diagnosed are usually treated first. The next goal of treatment is to reduce or eliminate the person's binge-eating and purging behavior. Behavioral therapy has proven effective in achieving this goal. Psychotherapy can help prevent the eating disorder from recurring and address issues that led to the disorder. Studies have also found that antidepressants may help. As with anorexia, family therapy is also recommended.
- Binge-eating disorder: The goals and strategies for treating binge-eating disorder are similar to those for bulimia.

Source: U.S. DHHS Substance Abuse and Mental Health Services Administration. http://mentalhealth.samhsa.gov/publications/allpubs/ken98-0047/default.asp

See also Anabolic Steroids; Food Addiction and Obesity.

Further Reading

American Psychiatric Association. *Diagnostic and Statistical Manual of Mental Disorders*, 4th Edition, Text Revision. Washington, DC: American Psychiatric Association, 2000.

Davis, Caroline. Addiction and the Eating Disorders. *Psychiatric Times* February 2001. Retrieved from http://www.psychiatrictimes.com/p010259.html

Erickson, Carlton K. *The Science of Addiction: From Neurobiology to Treatment*. New York: Norton, 2007.

Grant, Jon E., and Kim, S. W. *Stop Me Because I Can't Stop Myself: Taking Control of Impulsive Behavior*. New York: McGraw-Hill, 2003.

Hyman, S. E., and Malenka, R. C. Addiction and the Brain: The Neurobiology of Compulsion and Its Persistence. *Nature Reviews Neuroscience* 2001: 2(10), 695–703.

Kalivas, P. W., and Volkow, Nora. The Neural Basis of Addiction: A Pathology of Motivation and Choice. *American Journal of Psychiatry* August 2005: 162(8), 1403–1413.

National Institute on Drug Abuse. *The Science of Addiction: Drugs, Brains, and Behavior.* NIH Publication No. 07-5605, February 2007.

Nestler, Eric J., and Malenka, Robert. The Addicted Brain. *Scientific American*, September 2007. Retrieved from http://www.sciam.com/article.cfm?chanID=sa006&colID=1&articleID=0001E6 32-978A-1019-978A83414B7F0101

Neumark-Sztainer, Dianne, Eisenberg, Marla, Fulkerson, Jayne, Story, Mary, and Larson, Nicole. Family Meals and Disordered Eating in Adolescents. *Archives of Pediatrics and Adolescent Medicine* 2008: 162(1), 17–22.

Ozelli, Kristin Leutwyler. This Is Your Brain on Food. *Scientific American* September 2007: 297(3), 84–85.

Potenza, Marc N. Should Addictive Disorders Include Non-Substance-Related Conditions? *Addiction* 2006: 101(s1), 142–151.

Sacker, Ira, and Buff, Sheila. *Regaining Your Self: Breaking Free From the Eating Disorder Identity: A Bold New Approach.* New York: Hyperion, 2007.

Ecstasy (MDMA) Closely related to **methamphetamine** in terms of its chemical composition, 3,4-methylenedioxymethamphetamine (MDMA), or Ecstasy, is an illegal, synthetic **hallucinogen** that is very popular among young people who erroneously believe it is safe. It produces a sense of euphoria and sensual arousal and has an energizing effect that can last several hours. Marketed with colorful logos to appeal to younger users, it is often compounded with other psychoactive adulterants such as caffeine, **cocaine**, or **dextromethorphan**. By making slight modifications to its basic chemical structure, several other psychoactive chemicals can be synthesized—such as MDA (3,4-methylenedioxyamphetamine), MDEA (3,4-methylenedioxyethylamphetamine), and PMA (para-methoxyamphetamine)—that can vary considerably in potency and action. This makes them highly dangerous, particularly when users combine them with **marijuana** or alcohol, as they frequently do. The typical dosage per tablet or capsule ranges from 50 to 200 milligrams. The drug can also be snorted, but this is less common.

Synthesized in Germany in 1912, MDMA first become available as a street drug in the United States in the 1970s after the psychiatric community discovered its value in treating certain patients. It was primarily imported from clandestine European or Canadian laboratories, although a few U.S. labs have become involved in the drug's manufacture. As illegal access grew, it became a popular choice among adolescents during weekend-long raves or at nightclubs. After increasing for several years, use of MDMA has began to level off among high school students even as reports show it is increasingly used by African-Americans in their 20s and 30s and by college students. There is also evidence that gay and bisexual males are using Ecstasy to a greater degree, raising concerns that this could lead to high-risk sexual activities that increase the chances of spreading sexually transmitted diseases.

A Schedule I drug under the **Controlled Substances Act** (CSA), Ecstasy can interfere with the body's regulation of temperature, leaving users vulnerable to organ damage—or, in rare cases, death—caused by extreme increases in body heat. It may also resist metabolizing processes in the body, accumulating to toxic levels in a short period of time. Since it is chemically akin to **stimulants** like cocaine, jaw clenching and blurred vision are fairly common, and a high heart rate and elevated blood pressure are serious risks. The psychological effects include anxiety and depression that may persist long after active drug use has ceased. Research in animals indicates that MDMA is a neurotoxin that causes long-term damage to **brain** circuitry, particularly serotonin neurons. Scientists believe that it will have the same effect on human neurons. However, in very carefully regulated doses, it has been shown to have potential in treating posttraumatic stress disorder (PTSD); research and study trials are ongoing.

The drug goes by a number of street names, including Adam, Beans, Hug, Love Drug, MBDB, MDEA, "X," and XTC.

Further Reading

Califano, Joseph A., Jr. *High Society: How Substance Abuse Ravages America and What to Do About It.* New York: Perseus Books, 2007.

Hoffman, John, and Froemke, Susan, eds. *Addiction: Why Can't They Just Stop?* New York: Rodale, 2007.

Home Box Office (HBO). In partnership with the Robert Wood Johnson Foundation, the National Institute on Drug Abuse, and the National Institute on Alcohol Abuse and Alcoholism. *Addiction: Why Can't They Just Stop?* Documentary. March 2007.

Ketcham, Katherine, and Pace, Nicholas A. *Teens Under the Influence: The Truth About Kids, Alcohol, and Other Drugs.* New York: Ballantine Books, 2003.

Kuhn, Cynthia, et al. *Buzzed: The Straight Facts about the Most Used and Abused Drugs from Alcohol to Ecstasy.* New York: Norton, 2008.

U.S. Department of Health and Human Services, National Institute on Drug Abuse (NIDA), June 2007. Retrieved from http://www.nida.gov

U.S. Department of Health and Human Services, National Institute on Drug Abuse. *Research Report Series: Hallucinogens and Dissociative Drugs.* NIH Publication No. 01-4209, March 2001.

U.S. Department of Health and Human Services, National Institute on Drug Abuse. *Research Report Series: MDMA (Ecstasy) Abuse.* NIH Publication No. 06-4728, March 2006.

U.S. Department of Health and Human Services, Substance Abuse and Mental Health Services Administration (SAMHSA), August 2007. Retrieved from http://www.samhsa.gov

U.S. Department of Justice, Drug Enforcement Administration (DEA), March 2008. Retrieved from http://www.usdoj.gov/dea

Endocannabinoids. *See* Neurotransmitters.

Endogenous Opioids. *See* Opiates.

Endorphins. *See* Opiates.

Environmental Tobacco Smoke. *See* Secondhand Smoke.

Ephedrine and Pseudoephedrine Ephedrine is a central nervous system **stimulant** derived from the *Ephedra* plant, an evergreen shrub of the American Southwest, and is known primarily as a precursor drug that is critical to the manufacture of **methamphetamine**. In its natural state, it can enhance performance and improve attention span and has medical value as a decongestant. Concentrated and synthesized versions can be dangerous, especially if they are combined with either prescription or illicit drugs. It may produce anxiety, tension, excitation, insomnia, and, in larger doses, cause a dangerously elevated heart rate, high blood pressure, trouble breathing, nausea and vomiting, tremor, and dizziness. Hallucinations and paranoid psychoses have been reported at very high doses.

Because ephedrine is difficult to obtain legally, most cold medications are manufactured with pseudoephedrine as their active ingredient. However, because pseudoephedrine has been diverted from legitimate therapeutic uses to the illegal synthesis of methamphetamine, both ephedrine and pseudoephedrine are now categorized as List I chemicals under the **Controlled Substances Act (CSA)**. In order to control the manufacture of methamphetamine and similar drugs, Congress passed the Combat Methamphetamine Epidemic Act of 2005 which monitors and controls the accessibility and sale of products containing ephedrine and pseudoephedrine. These regulations require that records be kept of the names and addresses of persons purchasing the products, outline packaging and display specifications, and limit the quantities that may be purchased at any one time. Other countries have instituted similar controls.

Further Reading

Califano, Joseph A., Jr. *High Society: How Substance Abuse Ravages America and What to Do About It.* New York: Perseus Books, 2007.

Hoffman, John, and Froemke, Susan, eds. *Addiction: Why Can't They Just Stop?* New York: Rodale, 2007.

Home Box Office (HBO). In partnership with the Robert Wood Johnson Foundation, the National Institute on Drug Abuse, and the National Institute on Alcohol Abuse and Alcoholism. *Addiction: Why Can't They Just Stop?* Documentary. March 2007.

Ketcham, Katherine, and Pace, Nicholas A. *Teens Under the Influence: The Truth About Kids, Alcohol, and Other Drugs.* New York: Ballantine Books, 2003.

U.S. Department of Health and Human Services, National Institute on Drug Abuse (NIDA), June 2007. Retrieved from http://www.nida.gov

U.S. Department of Health and Human Services, Substance Abuse and Mental Health Services Administration (SAMHSA), August 2007. Retrieved from http://www.samhsa.gov

U.S. Department of Justice, Drug Enforcement Administration (DEA), March 2008. Retrieved from http://www.usdoj.gov/dea

Equanil. *See* Meprobamate.

Exercise Addiction Like excessive television viewing or workaholism, an extreme exercise regimen does not meet the American Psychiatric Association's criteria for **behavioral addictions**. However, if a workout program seems compulsive and includes an obsessive focus on rapid weight loss, it is likely to be a warning sign of an **eating disorder**. This is a serious and potentially deadly disease related to **impulse control disorders**, **obsessive-compulsive disorders**, major depression, **anxiety disorders**, and other psychiatric illnesses.

In the absence of evidence that other disorders exist, too much exercise can simply reflect the way a person chooses to respond to stress or other psychological difficulties. People experiencing brief periods of depression, anxiety, or other problems may seek relief in the healthful outlet provided by exercise. It may be symptomatic of deeper psychological problems when people avoid normal human interaction or participation in ordinary activities, when they persist in the activity despite negative consequences, and when they are unable to stop the behavior despite concerns of family and friends.

Some mental health professionals believe that the high produced by the brain's release of natural endorphins during exercise may contribute to the attraction that vigorous and sustained exercise has for some.

Further Reading

Kaminker, Laura. *Exercise Addiction: When Fitness Becomes an Obsession.* New York: The Rosen Publishing Group, 1998.

F

Famous Addicts Throughout history, people from all social and economic strata have suffered from **addictions**, but due to the stigma associated with chemical **dependence** and compulsive behaviors, these individuals were likely to have hidden their condition as long as possible. Public scrutiny of the lives of politicians, entertainers, and other famous people has exposed some of their problems just as society has become more enlightened about the causes. As a result, many public figures such as **Betty Ford** (1918–), former First Lady of the United States, have taken the courageous step of addressing **substance addictions** publicly to help heighten awareness of and prompt further research into this major public health issue.

Some of the famous people recovering from substance addictions or **impulse control disorders** include entertainers such as Robert Downey, Jr., Whitney Houston, Winona Ryder, and Robin Williams; political figures such as Mark Foley and Patrick Kennedy; and prominent public figures such as Buzz Aldrin, Annie Liebowitz, and Ted Turner. Sadly, many others have succumbed, dying prematurely of overdoses or complications of their disease; these include the talented entertainers John Belushi (1949–1982), **Karen Carpenter** (1950–1983), Chris Farley (1964–1997), Janis Joplin (1943–1970), River Phoenix (1970–1993), and Brad Renfro (1982–2008).

Fastin. *See* Stimulants.

Fentanyl Fentanyl is a synthetic **opiate** that is hundreds of times more potent than **heroin** and at least 80 times more potent than **morphine**. Its powerful pain-relieving property has led to its extensive use for anesthesia, analgesia, and the **treatment** of breakthrough cancer pain for patients who have developed a **tolerance** to other opiates.

During the 1970s, fentanyl began to be manufactured in illegal, clandestine labs. Since then, over 12 different analogs—drugs with similar functions or structures—have spread throughout the illicit market. Although drugs containing fentanyl are most often snorted or smoked, they can also be delivered via intravenous administration.

Medications containing fentanyl were first introduced during the 1960s, and today include a transdermal patch, a stick that dissolves in the mouth for transmucosal absorption, and intravenous preparations. The drug is sold in prescription form as Actiq, Duragesic, and Sublimaze. Diverted forms of the drug or synthetic formulations produced in clandestine laboratories are sometimes referred to on the street as Apache, China Girl, China White, Dance Fever, Goodfella, Jackpot, Murder 8, TNT, and Tango and Cash.

Further Reading

Califano, Joseph A., Jr. *High Society: How Substance Abuse Ravages America and What to Do About It.* New York: Perseus Books, 2007.

Hoffman, John, and Froemke, Susan, eds. *Addiction: Why Can't They Just Stop?* New York: Rodale, 2007.

Home Box Office (HBO). In partnership with the Robert Wood Johnson Foundation, the National Institute on Drug Abuse, and the National Institute on Alcohol Abuse and Alcoholism. *Addiction: Why Can't They Just Stop?* Documentary. March 2007.

Ketcham, Katherine, and Pace, Nicholas A. *Teens Under the Influence: The Truth About Kids, Alcohol, and Other Drugs.* New York: Ballantine Books, 2003.

U.S. Department of Health and Human Services, National Institute on Drug Abuse (NIDA), June 2007. Retrieved from http://www.nida.gov

U.S. Department of Health and Human Services, Substance Abuse and Mental Health Services Administration (SAMHSA), August 2007. Retrieved from http://www.samhsa.gov

U.S. Department of Justice, Drug Enforcement Administration (DEA), March 2008. Retrieved from http://www.usdoj.gov/dea

Fetal Alcohol Spectrum Disorders (FASD). *See* Women, Pregnancy, and Drugs.

Fire-Safe Cigarettes. *See* Nicotine.

Fire-Starting. *See* Pyromania.

Flashbacks People who use **hallucinogens**, particularly **lysergic acid diethylamide** (LSD), may be subject to flashbacks or hallucinations, which are perceptual distortions that emerge after the use of the drug has stopped. They may occur without warning. Why they occur in people who have used hallucinogenic drugs is not certain, although there is some evidence they might be a form of seizure or the result of neuronal destruction caused by drug use.

While flashbacks are usually transitory and tend to cease altogether over time, hallucinations are prolonged, recurrent, and likely to be unpleasant or upsetting. The latter, symptoms of a hallucinogen persisting perception disorder (HPPD), are associated with panic, anxiety, and depression—either as a result of the perceptual distortions or as triggering factors that help provoke the hallucinations. Unlike the auditory and visual hallucinations associated with psychosis, a person with HPPD is aware the altered perceptions are not real, but this does not necessarily render them any less distressing. Some anxiolytic drugs have been shown to alleviate this relatively rare syndrome.

There are experts who deny that drug-induced flashbacks or hallucinations occur at all. An LSD trip is said to be an intensely emotional experience. Psychologists have long known that any vivid experience, drug-induced or not, can later give rise to momentary memory flashes of sights or sounds from that experience; hearing the sound of the crash long after an automobile accident is an example. They suggest that flashbacks are nothing more than this same phenomenon, but there is a good deal of psychiatric literature to refute this, and the American Psychiatric Association has listed Hallucinogen Persisting Perception Disorder in its ***Diagnostic and Statistical Manual of Mental Disorders***.

Flunitrazepam (Rohypnol) Flunitrazepam, usually marketed as Rohypnol, is a depressant notorious for its use as a date-rape drug that leaves victims unable to remember events while under its influence. When mixed with alcohol, Rohypnol can incapacitate victims, putting them into a dreamlike trance or amnesiac state resembling coma so they cannot resist or remember sexual assault.

Like other **benzodiazepines**, a group of addictive central nervous system **depressants**, flunitrazepam reduces blood pressure, causes drowsiness and visual disturbances, and may lead to gastrointestinal distress. It is legal in Mexico and South America, where it is used as a sleep aid or for mild anesthesia. Smuggled or mailed into the United States, it is available in pill form but can be crushed and snorted, which increases its **addiction liability**, and is often used as a party drug. Since it is odorless, tasteless, and colorless, the tablets are sometimes impregnated with a dye so they can be seen if someone surreptitiously slips them into a beverage. Street names include Circles, Mexican Valium, R-2, Roach, Roofies, Rope, and Rophies.

The effects of the drug can last for several hours, and date-rape victims may be unable to recall the circumstances or the identity of the person who assaulted them. Because the substance is rapidly eliminated from the body, it may be very difficult to prove the drug was even involved in the attack. To address the predatory use of date-rape drugs, the United States has stiffened federal penalties for their illicit use.

Further Reading

Califano, Joseph A., Jr. *High Society: How Substance Abuse Ravages America and What to Do About It.* New York: Perseus Books, 2007.

Hoffman, John, and Froemke, Susan, eds. *Addiction: Why Can't They Just Stop?* New York: Rodale, 2007.

Home Box Office (HBO). In partnership with the Robert Wood Johnson Foundation, the National Institute on Drug Abuse, and the National Institute on Alcohol Abuse and Alcoholism. *Addiction: Why Can't They Just Stop?* Documentary. March 2007.

Ketcham, Katherine, and Pace, Nicholas A. *Teens Under the Influence: The Truth About Kids, Alcohol, and Other Drugs.* New York: Ballantine Books, 2003.

U.S. Department of Health and Human Services, National Institute on Drug Abuse (NIDA), June 2007. Retrieved from http://www.nida.gov

U.S. Department of Health and Human Services, National Institute on Drug Abuse. *Research Report Series: Hallucinogens and Dissociative Drugs.* NIH Publication No. 01-4209, March 2001.

U.S. Department of Health and Human Services, Substance Abuse and Mental Health Services Administration (SAMHSA), August 2007. Retrieved from http://www.samhsa.gov

U.S. Department of Justice, Drug Enforcement Administration (DEA), March 2008. Retrieved from http://www.usdoj.gov/dea

Food Addiction and Obesity Although there is considerable disagreement over whether or not it is possible to have a food **addiction**, most experts agree that a compulsive relationship with certain foods, especially sweets like chocolate, does meet addiction criteria established by the American Psychiatric Association in the 4th edition of its ***Diagnostic and Statistical Manual of Mental Disorders***. The consumption of the food must be impulsive, repetitive, and continue in spite of negative consequences, and the behavior must be outside of the individual's ability to control.

Like other addictions, food addictions can arise from many causes, and every individual has a unique history of contributory factors. In the past, a repetitive pattern of overeating has been regarded as a sign of weak character and poor self-discipline. However, research into the neurobiology of addiction in recent years that reveals fascinating similarities between obesity and drug addiction underscores a neurological basis for the disease. Certain foods and psychoactive drugs have been shown to activate **brain** circuits associated with pleasure and reward, particularly in the dopamine pathway. Many researchers report that, in susceptible people, food or drugs or even certain behaviors like pathological gambling increase the brain's dopamine levels, which establishes a cycle of reinforcement that triggers a repeated desire for exposure to the food, drug, or behavior. Thus, the brain develops a conditioned response to crave the substance or activity whenever it is exposed to the appropriate stimuli. In the case of food, the temptation is ever present.

The reason that food **compulsions** so frequently involve sugary or sweet foods may have its roots in human evolutionary physiology. High-calorie foods deliver quick energy, and humans may have developed a strong affinity for this source of fuel during times of famine or stress. Modern humans who do not require the same caloric intake nevertheless have the same attraction to the food, and an inability to control their intake leads to obesity and other symptoms of addiction.

Obesity has become a major health problem in America, due in part, some say, to the prevalence of high-fat fast foods. In 2001, the U.S. Surgeon General reported that obesity in the nation is increasing in all major socioeconomic and ethnic groups, including children and younger adults, and that a third of Americans are considered obese. The clinical measure used to determine obesity is the body mass index (BMI), a figure obtained by multiplying 703 times a person's weight divided by the square of their height (in inches). Thus a person who is 5 feet, 8 inches tall weighing 152 pounds has a BMI of 23. A healthy range is 19 to 24, overweight ranges from 25 to 29, and obesity begins at 30. Because the BMI formula does not measure body fat, many feel it is not necessarily a reliable indicator of obesity, but the U.S. Department of Health and Human Services' Centers for Disease Control has taken the position that it is.

The Body Mass Index

To calculate your body mass index, the clinical measure used to determine obesity, divide your weight by the square of your height and multiply by 703. Thus, if you are 5 feet, 8 inches tall (68 inches) and weigh 152 pounds:

$703 \times 152 \div 4{,}624$ [the square of 68 inches] = 23

A normal, healthy range for a person's BMI is 19 to 24; overweight ranges from 25 to 29. Obesity begins at 30 with morbid obesity beginning at 40.

The most effective **treatment** for obese individuals generally combines cognitive behavioral therapy to change conditioned behavior and medications such as serotonin reuptake inhibitors that address neurochemical imbalances. The National Institute on Drug Abuse (NIDA) has reported that there are fewer dopamine receptors in the brains of obese people and drug addicts, which helps explain why pharmaceutical approaches that address this deficit are effective. The NIDA also suggests that biofeedback techniques to reverse conditioned responses to food stimuli represent an extremely promising approach.

See also Eating Disorders.

Further Reading

American Psychiatric Association. *Diagnostic and Statistical Manual of Mental Disorders*, 4th Edition, Text Revision. Washington, DC: American Psychiatric Association, 2000.

Danowski, Debbie. *Why Can't I Stop Eating*. Center City, MN: Hazelden Foundation, 2000.

Davis, Caroline. Addiction and the Eating Disorders. *Psychiatric Times* February 2001. Retrieved from http://www.psychiatrictimes.com/p010259.html

Erickson, Carlton K. *The Science of Addiction: From Neurobiology to Treatment*. New York: Norton, 2007.

Grant, Jon E., and Kim, S. W. *Stop Me Because I Can't Stop Myself: Taking Control of Impulsive Behavior*. New York: McGraw-Hill, 2003.

Hyman, S. E., and Malenka, R. C.. Addiction and the Brain: The Neurobiology of Compulsion and Its Persistence. *Nature Reviews Neuroscience* 2001: 2(10), 695–703.

Kalivas, P. W., and Volkow, Nora. The Neural Basis of Addiction: A Pathology of Motivation and Choice. *American Journal of Psychiatry* August 2005: 162(8), 1403–1413.

National Institute on Drug Abuse. *The Science of Addiction: Drugs, Brains, and Behavior*. NIH Publication No. 07-5605, February 2007.

Nestler, Eric J., and Malenka, Robert. The Addicted Brain. *Scientific American*, September 2007. Retrieved from http://www.sciam.com/article.cfm?chanID=sa006&colID=1&articleID=0001E632-978A-1019-978A83414B7F0101

Neumark-Sztainer, Dianne, Eisenberg, Marla, Fulkerson, Jayne, Story, Mary, and Larson, Nicole. Family Meals and Disordered Eating in Adolescents. *Archives of Pediatrics and Adolescent Medicine* 2008: 162(1), 17–22.

Ozelli, Kristin Leutwyler. This Is Your Brain on Food. *Scientific American* September 2007: 297(3), 84–85.

Potenza, Marc N. Should Addictive Disorders Include Non-Substance-Related Conditions? *Addiction* 2006: 101(s1), 142–151.

Ford, Betty (1918–) Serving as First Lady of the United States from 1974 to 1977, Betty Ford, a popular and outgoing woman, began to develop a **dependence** on painkillers after they had been prescribed during the 1960s to relieve discomfort from a pinched nerve in her neck. She also drank occasional cocktails during that period, although there is little indication that she was, at that time, an alcoholic. When she and her husband moved into the White House in August of 1974, her drug use was under apparent control. However, with the increasing pressures of her position and a diagnosis of breast cancer, she again developed problems with a pinched nerve. Although she was candid with the press and the public about the mastectomy she endured that cured her cancer—a frankness that earned her the gratitude and admiration of a nation—she began to drink more heavily and rely on painkillers for the recurrent pinched nerve and related arthritis. The combined effect of the drugs became evident; she was filmed, on occasion, with slurred speech and an impaired gait.

Shortly after losing a disappointing election, the Fords left the White House and Mrs. Ford began to drink more heavily. Her alarmed family arranged an **intervention** in which they urged her to seek help. Initially devastated, she agreed to enter therapy and later credited the intervention and her subsequent **treatment** with saving her life. Soon thereafter, she founded a prestigious **alcoholism** rehabilitation center, the Betty Ford Treatment Center, in Rancho Mirage, California, which today is one of the most respected in the nation on which many others are modeled. For years, whenever possible, Mrs. Ford would personally greet incoming patients as they entered the treatment program at the Center that is based on the **Minnesota model**.

Former First Lady Betty Ford. (*Official White House photo*)

Among her other accomplishments, Mrs. Ford is highly regarded for the honesty and courage with which she faced her illnesses. She is particularly esteemed for the valuable role she has played in promoting greater openness and education about **addiction**. Until declining health related to advanced age began to curtail her activities, she remained actively involved with the board of the Betty Ford Center, spoke frequently to the public about alcoholism and other drug addiction, and worked steadily to improve treatment opportunities for all addicts.

Further Reading

Ford, Betty, with Chris Chase. *Betty, A Glad Awakening.* New York: Doubleday, 1987.

Foxy-Methoxy. *See* Psilocybin and Psilocin.

GABA. *See* Neurotransmitters.

Gamblers Anonymous A **12-step** program modeled in part on that of **Alcoholics Anonymous (AA)**, Gamblers Anonymous (GA) was formed in 1957 when two men who were struggling with compulsive gambling decided to commit to changing their behavior. Acknowledging their belief that they could control their behavior was delusional, they founded the GA organization whose only requirement for membership is a desire to stop gambling. Like AA, GA is self-supporting and is not aligned with any institution or denomination, political or religious. Originating in California, the membership has spread around the world.

Only about 10 percent of pathological gamblers seek **treatment** for their condition and, of those who join Gamblers Anonymous, less than 10 percent are able to refrain from returning to gambling after the first year. The focus of their early attendance at GA meetings tends to be on addressing the legal and financial difficulties the gambling has caused; thus, for the majority, long-term **recovery** seems to require additional forms of treatment such as cognitive behavioral therapy and, in many cases, medication.

The 12 Steps of the Gamblers Anonymous Recovery Program*

GA has developed its own 12 steps to recovery based closely on those originating with AA:

1. We admitted we were powerless over gambling—that our lives had become unmanageable.
2. Came to believe that a Power greater than ourselves could restore us to a normal way of thinking and living.
3. Made a decision to turn our will and our lives over to the care of this Power of our own understanding.
4. Made a searching and fearless moral and financial inventory of ourselves.

*Used by permission of Gamblers Anonymous

5. Admitted to ourselves and to another human being the exact nature of our wrongs.
6. Were entirely ready to have these defects of character removed.
7. Humbly asked God (of our understanding) to remove our shortcomings.
8. Made a list of all persons we had harmed and became willing to make amends to them all.
9. Made direct amends to such people wherever possible, except when to do so would injure them or others.
10. Continued to take personal inventory and when we were wrong, promptly admitted it.
11. Sought through prayer and meditation to improve our conscious contact with God as we understood Him, praying only for knowledge of His will for us and the power to carry that out.
12. Having made an effort to practice these principles in all our affairs, we tried to carry this message to other compulsive gamblers.

The Gamblers Anonymous Unity Program*

GA has developed a Unity Program that resembles the Twelve Traditions of AA. It states the principles of the organization and serves as a governing framework for fulfilling its purpose and goals.

1. Our common welfare should come first; personal recovery depends upon group unity.
2. Our leaders are but trusted servants; they do not govern.
3. The only requirement for GA membership is a desire to stop gambling.
4. Each group should be self-governing except in matters affecting other groups or GA as a whole.
5. GA has but one primary purpose—to carry its message to the compulsive gambler who still suffers.
6. GA ought never endorse, finance, or lend the GA name to any related facility or outside enterprise, lest problems of money, property, and prestige divert us from our primary purpose.
7. Every GA group ought to be fully self-supporting, declining outside contributions.
8. GA should remain forever nonprofessional, but our service centers may employ special workers.
9. GA, as such, ought never be organized, but we may create service boards or committees directly responsible to those they serve.
10. GA has no opinion on outside issues; hence the GA name ought never be drawn into public controversy.
11. Our public relations policy is based on attraction rather than promotion; we need always maintain personal anonymity at the level of press, radio, films, and television.
12. Anonymity is the spiritual foundation of the GA program, ever reminding us to place principles before personalities.

*Used by permission of Gamblers Anonymous

Self-Assessment Questionnaire

Gamblers Anonymous has a list of 20 questions to help people determine if they have a gambling problem. Most compulsive gamblers answer yes to at least 7 of these questions.

1. Did you ever lose time from work or school due to gambling?
2. Has gambling ever made your home life unhappy?
3. Did gambling affect your reputation?
4. Have you ever felt remorse after gambling?
5. Did you ever gamble to get money with which to pay debts or otherwise solve financial difficulties?
6. Did gambling cause a decrease in your ambition or efficiency?
7. After losing, did you feel you must return to gambling as soon as possible and win back your losses?
8. After a win, did you have a strong urge to return and win more?
9. Did you often gamble until your last dollar was gone?
10. Did you ever borrow to finance your gambling?
11. Have you ever sold anything to finance gambling?
12. Were you reluctant to use gambling money for normal expenditures?
13. Did gambling make you careless of the welfare of yourself or your family?
14. Did you ever gamble longer than you had planned?
15. Have you ever gambled to escape worry, trouble, boredom, or loneliness?
16. Have you ever committed, or considered committing, an illegal act to finance gambling?
17. Did gambling cause you to have difficulty in sleeping?
18. Do arguments, disappointments, or frustrations create within you an urge to gamble?
19. Did you ever have an urge to celebrate any good fortune by a few hours of gambling?
20. Have you ever considered self-destruction or suicide as a result of your gambling?

Source: Used by permission of Gamblers Anonymous. http://www.gamblersanonymous.org

Gamblers Anonymous FAQs

1. What is compulsive gambling?

    Compulsive gambling is an illness, progressive in its nature, which can never be cured but can be arrested. The GA concept is that compulsive gamblers are really very sick people who can recover if they will follow a simple program that has proved successful for thousands of men and women with a gambling or compulsive gambling problem.

2. What is the first thing a compulsive gambler ought to do in order to stop gambling?

    The compulsive gambler needs to be willing to accept the fact that he or she is in the grip of a progressive illness and has a desire to get well. Experience has shown that the GA program will always work for any person who has a desire to stop gambling. However, it will never work for the person who will not face squarely the facts about this illness.

3. How can you tell whether you are a compulsive gambler?

In GA, a compulsive gambler is described as a person whose gambling has caused growing and continuing problems in any department of life. Many members went through terrifying experiences before they were ready to accept help. Others were faced with a slow, subtle deterioration, which finally brought them to the point of admitting defeat.

4. Can a compulsive gambler ever gamble normally again?

No. The first bet to a problem gambler is like the first small drink to an alcoholic. Sooner or later he or she falls back into the same old destructive pattern. Once a person has crossed the invisible line into irresponsible uncontrolled gambling, he or she never seems to regain control.

5. Why can't a compulsive gambler simply use will power to stop gambling?

Most members recognize their lack of power to control their behavior. Many problem gamblers can abstain for long stretches, but, caught off guard and under the right set of circumstances, started gambling again without thought of the consequences.

6. I only go on gambling binges periodically. Do I need GA?

Yes. In compulsive gamblers who have periodic binges, the intervening intervals are still marked by addictive behavior and withdrawal symptoms such as nervousness, irritability, frustration, indecision, and a continued breakdown in personal relationships.

7. How does someone stop gambling through the GA program?

One does this through bringing about a progressive character change within oneself. This can be accomplished by having faith in—and following—the basic concepts of the GA Recovery Program. There are no short cuts in gaining this faith and understanding. To recover from one of the most baffling, insidious, compulsive addictions will require diligent effort. Honesty, openmindedness, and willingness are the key words in recovery.

8. Can a person recover by himself/herself by reading GA literature or medical books on the problem of compulsive gambling?

Sometimes, but not usually. The GA program works best for the individual when it is recognized and accepted as a program involving other people. Working with other compulsive gamblers in a GA group, people seem to find the necessary understanding and support. They are able to talk of their past experiences and present problems in an area where they are comfortable and accepted. Instead of feeling alone and misunderstood, they feel needed and accepted.

9. What are some characteristics of a person who is a compulsive gambler?

Personality traits frequently associated with compulsive gambling include an inability to accept reality, emotional insecurity, and immaturity. Many have the urge to avoid mature responsibility or to show off by appearing to be generous and successful winners.

10. Who can join GA?

Anyone who has a desire to stop gambling. There are no other rules or regulations concerning GA membership.

11. Why are members anonymous?

Anonymity has great value in attracting new members who initially might feel there is a stigma attached to the problem, and it represents a powerful reminder that we need always to place principles above personalities.

12. Is GA a religious society?

No. GA is composed of people from many religious faiths along with agnostics and atheists. The GA recovery program is based on acceptance of certain spiritual values, but the member is free to interpret these principles as he or she chooses.

Source: Adapted from Gamblers Anonymous. http://www.gamblersanonymous.org/qna.html

Gambling. *See* Pathological Gambling Disorder.

Gamma Aminobutyric Acid. *See* Neurotransmitters.

Gamma Hydroxybutyric Acid (GHB) Gamma hydroxybutyric acid (GHB) is a **benzodiazepine**-like drug synthesized as an odorless liquid or white powder and distributed locally. Users often mix it with alcohol but, like any other **depressant**, doing so can produce magnified and sometimes deadly results. Along with Rohypnol and **ketamine**, it is a notorious date-rape drug that is administered to victims prior to their being sexually assaulted. Because these drugs are often colorless and tasteless, they can be added to beverages and ingested without the victims' knowledge, and they leave the body so quickly it is difficult for anyone to prove the drug was involved in the assault. GHB analogs—drugs such as gamma butyrolactone (GBL) and 1,4-butanediol that are similar in function or structure—can be manufactured fairly easily from ingredients found in health food stores or on Internet sites, and they are frequently substituted for GHB.

GHB is also used for its euphoric effects; like alcohol, another CNS depressant, GHB is an **agonist** of GABA, the inhibitory **neurotransmitter** whose increased presence in the **brain** lowers anxiety levels and induces a sense of calm relaxation. Bodybuilders have also been known to **abuse** the drug for its reputed ability to promote muscle development. Since the mid-1990s, GHB use has spread to alarming levels. In 1994, 55 emergency room admissions involved GHB; 8 years later, there were 3,330, exceeded only by hospital visits involving **Ecstasy**. Statistics also show that young, mainly white males are the principal users.

GHB produces a wide range of effects depending on dosage and individual response. These include a lowered heart rate and blood pressure, nausea, dizziness, slurred speech, disorientation, clammy skin, dilated pupils, hallucinations, impaired memory, coma, and, possibly, respiratory depression and death. Normally a Schedule I drug under the **Controlled Substances Act**, GHB is a component of a Schedule III medication called Xyrem that treats symptoms of narcolepsy, a syndrome characterized by an uncontrollable desire to sleep.

Street names for this drug include Easy Lay, Georgia Home Boy, Goop, Grievous Bodily Harm, Liquid Ecstasy, Liquid X, and Scoop.

Further Reading

U.S. Department of Health and Human Services, National Institute on Drug Abuse (NIDA), June 2007. Retrieved from http://www.nida.gov

U.S. Department of Health and Human Services, National Institute on Drug Abuse. *Research Report Series: Hallucinogens and Dissociative Drugs.* NIH Publication No. 01-4209, March 2001.

U.S. Department of Health and Human Services, Substance Abuse and Mental Health Services Administration (SAMHSA), August 2007. Retrieved from http://www.samhsa.gov

U.S. Department of Justice, Drug Enforcement Administration (DEA), March 2008. Retrieved from http://www.usdoj.gov/dea

Gateway Drugs For decades, it has been assumed that the use of gateway drugs such as **alcohol** and **tobacco** escalates into the use of illicit drugs like **marijuana** and then to more addictive drugs like **cocaine** or **heroin**. However, recent studies suggest that this may not be the case.

According to a 2006 study by the American Psychiatric Association, people whose drug use escalates from alcohol to marijuana are no more likely to develop an **addiction** to drugs than those who follow a reverse pattern—using marijuana before abandoning it and substituting alcohol. Although the gateway progression is a common pattern, researchers report, it is not any more predictive of future addiction than the reverse pattern. This bears out the opinion of many scientists that drug **abuse** and addiction are based on individual biology and environmental factors; a belief supported by research into other patterns of drug use and abuse. Those factors, combined with drug availability, are the principal determinants of whether drug abuse occurs and the type of drug the individual is likely to use.

Some studies have shown, however, that the use of so-called harder drugs such as cocaine in young adulthood was strongly associated with drug use in adolescence, particularly the use of marijuana or **amphetamines**. Whether this is due to the gateway hypothesis or to the fact that the young adults involved were predisposed to drug abuse anyway is difficult to determine. As a result, some continue to argue that gateway drugs lead otherwise risk-free individuals into addiction, while others insist that teens who do not have genetic or other vulnerabilities to addiction are not likely to become addicted via exposure to gateway drugs alone. What many do agree is that in susceptible individuals, especially adolescents, gateway drugs are likely to be a route to later addiction because of the drugs' critical influences on the teens' developing **brains**.

Further Reading

Hyde, Margaret O. *Drugs 101*. Minneapolis, MN: Twenty-First Century, 2003.

Generalized Anxiety Disorder. *See* Anxiety Disorders.

Generic Names. *See* Drug Nomenclature.

Genetics of Addiction Each of roughly 20,000 genes in the human genome gives rise to proteins, and each protein has essential roles in the cellular functioning of the entire body. This makes it exceedingly complicated to determine the effect one gene can have. Partly because of this complexity, scientists seem confident that there are no **addiction** or **alcoholism** genes that specifically or directly cause chemical dependence, but they are equally confident that variations in one or more of several dozen genes contribute substantially to a given individual's risk for developing the disease. If no environmental factors associated with addiction are present, someone with a genetic predisposition may not develop an addiction. If those factors are present, that same person is at a higher risk.

Although it has been observed for centuries that alcoholism tends to run in families, factual confirmation could not be made until late in the 20th century when genetic analysis became a reality. In 1989, amid growing evidence that specific electrical activity in the **brain** is related to a risk for alcoholism, the National Institute on Alcohol Abuse and Alcoholism instituted formalized studies into the genetics of the disease. That research is embodied in the ongoing Collaborative Study on the Genetics of Alcoholism (COGA).

Armed with newly developing technologies, scientists have since launched a flurry of research into the genetic underpinnings of addiction and other diseases. The wealth of data that they have been able to mine with the sequencing of the human genome in 2003 has allowed them to locate specific chromosomes bearing "candidate genes" that can increase the likelihood of addiction. Some may affect activity in the mesolimbic dopamine pathway where the neurological basis of addiction lies; others may affect chemical metabolism in such a way that potent substances are not metabolized properly; and others have as yet unknown mechanisms of action.

People inherit 2 versions of genes (alleles)—one from the mother and one from the father—and these alleles can differ slightly from one another. Comprised of amino acids called bases, one allele may have transposed or missing bases. Even if a single base is different, in what is known as a single nucleotide polymorphism (SNP), gene expression may or may not be significantly affected. This is why an allele from one parent may contribute to disease in a way that the other allele does not. If both parents pass on the variation, the chance of their offspring developing the disease is more likely. Allelic variation is only one form of genetic variation; another form occurs when someone inherits identical variants from both parents; even though the individual's 2 alleles are the same, they can vary from most of the population's.

After the Human Genome Project announced that human beings share 99.9 percent of the same genes (although that number was revised downward slightly in 2007), the National Institutes of Health, which sought to discover what the 0.1 percent difference might mean in terms of disease, launched a number of investigations. In summarizing a study related to addiction that was conducted by its Molecular Neurobiology Branch, the National Institute on Drug Abuse announced in August 2007 that of 89 genes that have been implicated in addiction, at least 21 seem to affect the memory circuitry of the brain.

Research is continuing to reveal more genes that may contribute substantially to the development of many diseases, not just addiction, and will help scientists predict risk, identify protective genetic mechanisms, and design therapeutic targets.

Many scientists believe that someday there will be a comprehensive listing of all genetic variations associated with addiction. Although a long way from complete, the list is evolving rapidly.

Some Genetic Variations Associated with Addiction

The following findings have emerged from studies of candidate genes. Since their reward pathways are similar to those of humans', mice were used in some of these studies.

- Allele A1 of the dopamine receptor gene *DRD2* is found more frequently in **cocaine** addicts or alcoholics. This may be because people with the A1 allele have about 30 percent fewer D2 receptors than people with the A2 allele; they would likely have to consume more of the addictive substance in order to obtain or sustain the desired effect.
- Specific variations on the *CB1* gene for the *Cannabis* receptor may be related to the development of **marijuana** dependence in adolescents.

- By suppressing the action of the DAT protein in people with a specific genetic variant, cocaine inhibits the removal of dopamine from the brain, thus prolonging its effect.
- The *Mpdz* gene is associated with lessened **withdrawal** symptoms in mice addicted to barbiturates.
- Genomic analysis detected 2 sets of genes on chromosome 17 that are linked to addiction in people of European descent.
- Mice lacking the *Cnr1* cannabinoid receptor gene have a reduced reward response to **morphine**.
- Chromosome 6 may be implicated in opioid addiction.
- Allele 2 of the *CHRNA4* gene is more closely associated with addicted individuals who also have attention deficit hyperactivity disorder (ADHD).
- Nonsmokers are more likely to carry a protective variation of the *CYP2A6* gene that results in decreased **nicotine** metabolism and reduces smoking behavior.
- Mice whose *Creb* genes have been removed in the laboratory are less likely to become dependent on morphine.
- In people who have 2 specific alleles of the *ALDH*2* gene, alcoholism is rare.
- Mice with a mutated form of the *Per2* gene drink 3 times as much alcohol as other mice.

Further Reading

Erickson, Carlton K. *The Science of Addiction: From Neurobiology to Treatment.* New York: Norton, 2007.

Kauer, Julie A. Addictive Drugs and Stress Trigger a Common Change at VTA Synapses. *Neuron* February 2003: 37(4), 549–550.

Nestler, Eric J., and Malenka, Robert. The Addicted Brain. *Scientific American*, September 2007. Retrieved from http://www.sciam.com/article.cfm?chanID=sa006&colID=1&articleID=0001E6 32-978A-1019-978A83414B7F0101

U.S. Department of Health and Human Services, National Institute on Drug Abuse (NIDA), June 2007. Retrieved from http://www.nida.gov

U.S. Department of Health and Human Services, National Institute on Drug Abuse. *The Science of Addiction: Drugs, Brains, and Behavior.* NIH Publication No. 07-5605, February 2007.

GHB. *See* Gamma Hydroxybutyric Acid.

Ghutka A form of chewable, **smokeless tobacco**, ghutka—also known as gutka, gutkha, or betel quid—is a sweetish, chewable mixture combining **tobacco** with spicy and fruity ingredients. Among these are parts of the *Piper betle* plant, a spice native to India and nearby countries whose leaves are chewed for their mild stimulatory properties and contribution to oral hygiene. Ghutka also contains extracts of the areca nut and other flavorings such as cardamom, turmeric, cloves, saffron, and mustard seed. Available in tins or sachets, it is consumed in the same way Americans use moist snuff—users place a small amount between the gum and cheek and suck or chew, then swallow or spit out the saliva-laden residue.

Along with **bidis and kreteks**, which are smoked, ghutka is largely responsible for introducing most of the world's children to the use of, and ultimate **addiction** to, tobacco products. Statistics show that 30 percent of children in India's government-run school system are addicted to ghutka and among schoolchildren worldwide, the use of ghutka, bidis, and kreteks exceeds the consumption of U.S. **cigarettes**. A particular problem with ghutka is the popular perception that it is as harmless as chewing gum, a belief supported by the fact that in certain parts of Southeast Asia, a tobacco-free version of ghutka is popular. In some areas, marketing approaches that target ghutka to youth have succeeded in making this and similar chewable forms of tobacco about 3 times more popular than smokable products.

Ghutka is responsible for the same diseases that other forms of tobacco cause: oral cancers and reproductive problems including lower birth weight babies. One disorder that appears to be specifically linked to the areca nut in ghutka preparations is oral submucous fibrosis, a stiffening of oral fibrous bands that prevents the user from opening his or her mouth. The condition is irreversible and may extend into the esophagus.

Although ghutka is not currently monitored in the United States, increased globalization is making this form of smokeless tobacco and many similar products become more widespread throughout the United States.

Further Reading

Califano, Joseph A., Jr. *High Society: How Substance Abuse Ravages America and What to Do About It.* New York: Perseus Books, 2007.

U.S. Department of Health and Human Services. *Nicotine Addiction: A Report of the Surgeon General.* Centers for Disease Control and Prevention, Public Health Service, Center for Health Promotion and Education, Office on Smoking and Health, 1988.

U.S. Department of Health and Human Services. *Targeting Tobacco Use: The Nation's Leading Cause of Death.* Centers for Disease Control and Prevention, 2003.

U.S. Department of Health and Human Services. *The Health Consequences of Smoking: A Report of the Surgeon General.* Centers for Disease Control and Prevention, National Center for Chronic Disease Prevention and Health Promotion, Office on Smoking and Health, 2004.

U.S. Department of Health and Human Services, Centers for Disease Control and Prevention (CDC), January 2008. Retrieved from http://apps.nccd.cdc.gov/osh_faq

U.S. Department of Health and Human Services, Centers for Disease Control and Prevention (CDC), November 2007. Retrieved from http://www.cdc.gov/tobacco

U.S. Department of Health and Human Services, National Cancer Institute (NCI), December 2007. Retrieved from http://www.cancer.gov/cancertopics/tobacco

U.S. Department of Health and Human Services, National Institute on Drug Abuse. *Research Report Series: Tobacco Addiction.* NIH Publication No. 06-4342, July 2006.

Glia. *See* Brain and Addiction.

Glutamate. *See* Neurotransmitters.

H

Habituation. *See* Tolerance.

Hair-Pulling Addiction. *See* Trichotillomania.

Hallucinogen Persisting Perception Disorder (HPPD). *See* Flashbacks.

Hallucinogens Hallucinogenic substances, drugs that produce unreal perceptions of sight, smell, taste, touch, or hearing that do not come from external sources, have been used for centuries, especially by certain populations. Also known as psychedelics or club drugs because they are often used by people frequenting nightclubs to alter mood, they do not necessarily produce hallucinations unless they are ingested in high doses.

Hallucinogens were originally derived from plants and fungi until the means were developed to manufacture synthetic hallucinogens in a laboratory. For a long time, hallucinogens' mode of action had not been well understood, but researchers have learned relatively recently that hallucinogenic plants affect serotonin receptors in **brain** regions where mood, perception, and sensory signals are processed. Since hallucinogens at high dosages are also neurotoxins, that is, poisonous to the neurons of the brain—the long-term devastation they can cause goes well beyond the immediate dangers they pose in terms of distorted perceptions.

Common hallucinogens include **dextromethorphan**, **Ecstasy**, **ketamine**, **lysergic acid diethylamide** (LSD), **mescaline**, **phencyclidine (PCP)**, **psilocybin** and other tryptamines, salvinorin A, and **flunitrazepam** and **gamma hydroxybutyric acid** (GHB), both technically **depressants**.

Some hallucinogens that were originally developed as general anesthetics, such as PCP and ketamine, are known as dissociative hallucinogens because they cause the user to feel detached from his or her surroundings. Sometimes the cough suppressant dextromethorphan is included in this group. Some hallucinogens are regarded as **stimulants** because they elevate heart rate, blood pressure, and body temperature. It is not possible to predict how each individual will react to hallucinogens. Some experience pleasant distortions of time, space, and perceptions whereas others may have intensely disorienting and frightening experiences. Months after using hallucinogens, people may experience **flashbacks**, in which unpredictable bursts of visual or auditory memories or disorientation occur. In

Substance/Drug	Intoxicating Effects	Potential Health Consequences
Hallucinogens Ketamine LSD MDMA (Ecstasy) PCP	Altered states of perception, feeling, time and distance, nausea, hallucinations, heightened senses	Flashbacks, sleeplessness, persistent mental disorders, paranoia, cardiac arrest

Source: NIDA, DEA

Hallucinogens Chart

time, the intensity of these episodes may diminish. Psychotic-like reactions involving surreal sensations and bizarre behavior have been known to occur both during hallucinogen use and during flashbacks.

In the 1960s and 1970s, many people experimented with hallucinogens such as LSD, mescaline, and psilocybin. Hallucinogen **abuse** has declined somewhat, but **addictions** experts are concerned that a resurgence seemed to occur during the 1990s, and, by 1999, 1 out of every 6 college students reported using hallucinogens. An estimated 1 million Americans who are 12 years or older use them currently. Experts attribute this upswing to the emergence of Ecstasy as a party drug among junior and senior high school students. Initially popular as a club drug at psychedelic raves and nightclubs, Ecstasy is also increasingly seen in adults in their 20s and 30s.

A relative newcomer to the club scene is salvinorin A, also known as divinorin A, which is an extract of the mint-like herb known as salvia or sage and grown primarily in Mexico and South America. Although it has not yet been scheduled under provisions of the **Controlled Substances Act (CSA)**, it is subject to international controls and many U.S. states have outlawed its use or distribution. Its effects are similar to those of LSD or ketamine, and it is used primarily by adolescents and young adults.

Some hallucinogens can be addictive. In surveys, nearly half of the adolescents who used the drugs met diagnostic criteria for addiction, and more than half reported **withdrawal** symptoms and psychological distress when the drug was discontinued. In research studies with animals that, among other things, evaluate the addictive potential of various substances, the animals came to prefer Ecstasy to other naturally pleasurable stimuli; this response is viewed as a hallmark of addiction.

A number of phenethylamine and tryptamine analogs (2 classes of psychoactive chemical compounds that can act as **neurotransmitters** or neuromodulators with hallucinogenic properties) have entered the illegal drug market in recent years. In an effort to control their manufacture, distribution, and use, the Drug Enforcement Agency took emergency measures to place some of them on Schedule I under the CSA so that individuals trafficking in them can be prosecuted. To the concern of drug officials, more new drugs in this class continue to be synthesized.

See also Drug Classes; Appendix B.

Further Reading

Califano, Joseph A., Jr. *High Society: How Substance Abuse Ravages America and What to Do About It.* New York: Perseus Books, 2007.

Hoffman, John, and Froemke, Susan, eds. *Addiction: Why Can't They Just Stop?* New York: Rodale, 2007.

Home Box Office (HBO). In partnership with the Robert Wood Johnson Foundation, the National Institute on Drug Abuse, and the National Institute on Alcohol Abuse and Alcoholism. *Addiction: Why Can't They Just Stop?* Documentary. March 2007.

Ketcham, Katherine, and Pace, Nicholas A. *Teens Under the Influence: The Truth About Kids, Alcohol, and Other Drugs.* New York: Ballantine Books, 2003.

U.S. Department of Health and Human Services, National Institute on Drug Abuse (NIDA), June 2007. Retrieved from http://www.nida.gov

U.S. Department of Health and Human Services, National Institute on Drug Abuse. *Research Report Series: Hallucinogens and Dissociative Drugs.* NIH Publication No. 01-4209, March 2001.

U.S. Department of Health and Human Services, Substance Abuse and Mental Health Services Administration (SAMHSA), August 2007. Retrieved from http://www.samhsa.gov

U.S. Department of Justice, Drug Enforcement Administration (DEA), March 2008. Retrieved from http://www.usdoj.gov/dea

Hangovers Withdrawal from drugs takes many forms depending on the drug or drugs. Hangovers are generally considered a relatively mild form of withdrawal from alcohol. Beginning within hours of consuming the last alcoholic beverage, hangovers produce symptoms ranging from a dry mouth, sleep disturbances, and mild headaches to nausea, trembling, anxiety, depression, and sensitivity to light and sound. Severe withdrawal from alcohol entails intense **craving** and psychological discomfort, nausea and diarrhea, mental confusion, hallucinations, even seizures. If these are accompanied by an elevated heart rate, rapid breathing, disorientation, blackouts, and delirium tremens, alcohol withdrawal is a life-threatening medical emergency.

As a diuretic, alcohol increases the rate of urination, which drains essential fluids from the body, including water, and leads to dehydration, which produces many characteristic hangover symptoms. If the impurities and byproducts produced during alcohol's fermentation and distillation accumulate in the body, the symptoms may be more severe; this is particularly true if the individual drinks several different kinds of alcoholic products throughout the duration of the drinking event. Some degree of toxicity from **acetaldehyde** buildup in the body can be expected if the drinker consumes alcohol quickly or in quantities more than the liver can efficiently metabolize. The **brain** too is affected; since alcohol is a **depressant** that suppresses the excitatory **neurotransmitter** glutamate, the neurotransmitter must rebound to normal levels when the person stops drinking. The effect of rising glutamate levels interferes with sleep and produces the anxiety, tremors, and restlessness associated with hangovers. Some **addictions** experts refer to the effort on the part of the brain to normalize its chemical levels as rebound hyperexcitability.

Although people believe in hangover remedies like black coffee or fatty foods, there are no hangover cures—time is the best remedy. However, drinking large quantities of water when consuming alcohol can help prevent the buildup of toxins in the body, or drinking fruit juice or sports drinks the next day to replace the body's fluids can be helpful. Aspirin and similar compounds should be used carefully, because they can irritate an already inflamed gastrointestinal tract.

Hard Drugs vs. Soft Drugs "Hard" and "soft" are terms used to describe drugs based on addictive liability and potency. Some countries, such as the Netherlands, base drug-use legislative policies on sharp distinctions between the two groups. In the United States, the distinction is not relevant in legal terms because the laws are specific to each class of drug, or schedule, as laid out in the **Controlled Substances Act**, but many Americans apply these terms in casual usage.

Soft drugs are usually regarded as the nonaddictive or mildly addictive drugs whose penalties for use, if any, are less severe. Examples are **hallucinogens** such as LSD and **mescaline**; some countries and legislative jurisdictions also regard **marijuana** as a soft drug, but many do not. Hard drugs are highly addictive and capable of causing serious harm to the user, even death. They include **opiates** like **heroin** and **morphine** as well as **cocaine** and **methamphetamine**. Alcohol and **nicotine** are also considered hard drugs for their addictive liability and severe potential for damaging health.

Drugs that fall in the middle of these two extremes include caffeine and **Ecstasy** and, in some areas, marijuana. Although there has been some effort on the part of U.S. government and local drug officials to blur the distinction between soft and hard drugs to discourage the use of all drugs, most **addictions** experts believe the distinctions should be retained to give the public an accurate assessment of the relative risks the 2 groups pose to users.

Hard Liquor vs. Soft Liquor Some distinguish between distilled spirits like whiskey and fermented products like beer as, respectively, hard and soft liquor, but there is no difference in the active ingredient, ethyl alcohol. Regardless of how it is delivered in each beverage, a given amount of ethyl alcohol has the same effect. Confusion arises over the percentage of alcohol a given drink may contain. A 12-oz. bottle of beer, so-called soft liquor, contains 5 percent ethyl alcohol, or .6 ounces. Eighty-proof hard liquor contains 40 percent alcohol; thus, a 1-oz. shot contains .4 ounces. Whether consuming a beer or tossing down a shot of hard liquor, each drinker is consuming about half an ounce of ethyl alcohol.

In the United States, alcohol "proof" is twice the percentage of alcohol as measured by volume, so a 180-proof bottle of distilled liquor contains 90 percent alcohol. Most mixed drinks contain more than 1 ounce of alcohol, so their strength cannot accurately be determined without knowing both the number of ounces and the proof of the alcohol they contain.

Hash (Hashish) and Hashish Oil Also called hash, hashish is a potent, resinous product of the *Cannabis* plant containing a high percentage of delta-9-tetrahydrocannabinol (THC), the psychoactive component in **marijuana**. Although hashish oil comes from the same plant, it is not a product of hashish but is extracted from the plant by means of a solvent.

After flowering, female marijuana plants grow hairline projections called trichomes that are rich in resinous hashish. They are collected, dried, and compressed into various cake-like blocks or other forms of hashish, pieces of which can be crumbled and smoked in a **pipe** or baked into certain foods such as brownies or cookies. The THC content is about 5 percent, whereas that of the so-called oil is about 15 percent and varies in color and odor depending on the type of solvent used in its extraction. A drop of the oil is sometimes placed on regular **cigarettes** to create drug vehicles that are similar to marijuana joints.

Although a great deal of marijuana production occurs in North and South America, most of the hash imported into the United States comes from the Middle East, North Africa, Pakistan, and Afghanistan. Storage decreases the strength of the product and many smuggled-in drugs are several years old before they get into the hands of the average user in the United States. Many secret growing laboratories have been established in the United States where cultivation of high-grade marijuana and hashish under tightly controlled conditions is possible.

Hashish and hashish oil are on Schedule I of the **Controlled Substances Act**. Although they have no legally accepted medical uses, they are known to be effective antiemetics and are sometimes used illegally by cancer patients suffering from nausea and vomiting of chemotherapy. Overdosing on hashish can produce excessive fatigue, hallucinations, paranoia, or other symptoms of psychosis.

Further Reading

Califano, Joseph A., Jr. *High Society: How Substance Abuse Ravages America and What to Do About It.* New York: Perseus Books, 2007.

Hoffman, John, and Froemke, Susan, eds. *Addiction: Why Can't They Just Stop?* New York: Rodale, 2007.

Home Box Office (HBO). In partnership with the Robert Wood Johnson Foundation, the National Institute on Drug Abuse, and the National Institute on Alcohol Abuse and Alcoholism. *Addiction: Why Can't They Just Stop?* Documentary. March 2007.

Ketcham, Katherine, and Pace, Nicholas A. *Teens Under the Influence: The Truth About Kids, Alcohol, and Other Drugs.* New York: Ballantine Books, 2003.

U.S. Department of Health and Human Services, National Institute on Drug Abuse (NIDA), June 2007. Retrieved from http://www.nida.gov

U.S. Department of Health and Human Services, Substance Abuse and Mental Health Services Administration (SAMHSA), August 2007. Retrieved from http://www.samhsa.gov

U.S. Department of Justice, Drug Enforcement Administration (DEA), March 2008. Retrieved from http://www.usdoj.gov/dea

Hazelden Foundation. *See* Minnesota Model.

Hemp Hemp, the fibrous product of ***Cannabis*** whose name is sometimes used as a synonym for the marijuana-producing plant, is one of the world's oldest sources of fiber and was widely used for paper and textiles until the Industrial Revolution. In World War II, U.S. farmers were encouraged to grow the plant to replace supplies no longer available through Japanese-controlled agricultural sources. Since then, because hemp is viewed as the "**marijuana** plant," there are prohibitions against cultivating it in the United States even though it can be used for food or fuel and its seed oils are of value in the production of paints and other materials. Environmentalists are working to change U.S. law because hemp is easy to cultivate, grows quickly, requires no pesticides, and is fully biodegradable. It could replace other materials now used in industrial manufacturing that produce a high degree of waste and have significantly negative environmental impacts.

Aware of its value, many European countries and Canada issue licenses to grow the plant, exempting it from international drug laws in recognition that certain agricultural conditions and breeding practices can yield plants of high-quality fiber with little or no concentrations of THC. As global pressures mount to produce more green products, it is likely that hemp cultivation will once again be permitted in the United States to meet demand for this versatile raw material.

Further Reading

Robinson, Rowan. *The Great Book of Hemp: The Complete Guide to the Environmental, Commercial, and Medicinal Uses of the World's Most Extraordinary Plant.* Rochester, VT: Park Street, 1995.

Heroin A powerful, highly addictive **opiate** synthesized from **morphine**, heroin is a Schedule I drug under the **Controlled Substances Act**. Although it can be imported from Southeast Asia (Afghanistan in particular), Mexico and South America are primary sources.

South American heroin is usually the white-to-dark brown variety most often seen on the East Coast, while the Mexican black tar variety is seen more on the West Coast. The difference in color and texture of the heroin product depends on manufacturing processes and additives.

Although heroin was initially used as a pain medication in the early 20th century and developed to treat morphine **addiction**, it turned out to be somewhere between 2 to 10 times more addictive than the drug it was designed to replace. By 1914, heroin had become subject to legal controls and soon all use was pronounced illegal. Today, despite its powerful analgesic properties, it is considered to have no medical value even though other **opium** derivatives are widely used in medicine.

Heroin is a popular recreational drug, and there is some concern that newer manufacturing processes that allow the smoking or snorting of heroin have increased its use by those who reject intravenous administration, which has the potential for spreading HIV, hepatitis, or other diseases. Although users of the Mexican variety must dissolve and inject the drug, those who purchase the powder tend to avoid IV use. Believing they are buying high-quality heroin when they purchase the drug on the street, users are often buying a product cut with sugar, starch, acetaminophen, or a number of other ingredients. Nevertheless, the purity of heroin sold today has increased; in the past, a "bag"—a specific unit of heroin—routinely contained 1 to 10 percent pure heroin; today it is more likely to contain 10 to 70 percent. This level of purity has contributed to increased addiction, especially among young adults who mistakenly believe that smoking or snorting the drug is less addicting than IV injections and thus start using the drug less cautiously. Overall, heroin use nationwide appears to be decreasing, although some coastal cities report higher use.

Like that of many other opiates, the short-term effect of heroin is a sudden rush of euphoria and relaxation followed quickly by intermittent periods of dozing known as nodding off. An overdose may include respiratory depression, clammy skin, seizures, and, ultimately, coma and death. Longer-term use can lead to heart or liver disease and a variety of pulmonary disorders based in part on the overall physical debilitation that accompanies drug use. Among intravenous users, collapsed veins and serious infections can arise. **Tolerance** to the drug mounts quickly, and **withdrawal**, which can begin as soon as a few hours after the last dose, are notorious for the high degree of misery they cause, including diarrhea and vomiting, muscle and bone pain, agitation, and intense **craving**. Sudden withdrawal from heroin can be dangerously traumatic to the body, even fatal.

In 1997, recognizing that opiate addictions must be treated as a public health problem, the National Institutes of Health (NIH) convened a panel to address heroin addiction and **treatment**. In acknowledging the tremendous value of drugs like **methadone** or **buprenorphine** that block the effect of the heroin on the brain's opiate receptors, the NIH panel stressed the importance of removing legal barriers to such treatments. It also recommended that supportive behavioral therapies be made broadly available since research has shown that cognitive behavioral therapy can be very useful in treating opiate addiction.

Street names for heroin include Black Tar (or Negra), H, Horse, Junk, Skag, and Smack.

Further Reading

Califano, Joseph A., Jr. *High Society: How Substance Abuse Ravages America and What to Do About It.* New York: Perseus Books, 2007.

Hoffman, John, and Froemke, Susan, eds. *Addiction: Why Can't They Just Stop?* New York: Rodale, 2007.

Home Box Office (HBO). In partnership with the Robert Wood Johnson Foundation, the National Institute on Drug Abuse, and the National Institute on Alcohol Abuse and Alcoholism. *Addiction: Why Can't They Just Stop?* Documentary. March 2007.

Ketcham, Katherine, and Pace, Nicholas A. *Teens Under the Influence: The Truth About Kids, Alcohol, and Other Drugs.* New York: Ballantine Books, 2003.

U.S. Department of Health and Human Services, National Institute on Drug Abuse (NIDA), June 2007. Retrieved from http://www.nida.gov

U.S. Department of Health and Human Services, National Institute on Drug Abuse. *Research Report Series: Heroin Abuse and Addiction.* NIH Publication No. 05-4165, May 2005.

U.S. Department of Health and Human Services, Substance Abuse and Mental Health Services Administration (SAMHSA), August 2007. Retrieved from http://www.samhsa.gov

U.S. Department of Justice, Drug Enforcement Administration (DEA), March 2008. Retrieved from http://www.usdoj.gov/dea

Hippocampus. *See* Brain and Addiction.

Hookah Also known as a waterpipe, a hookah is a Middle Eastern device used for smoking **tobacco** or fruity, tobacco-like substances whose smoke is filtered through water or other liquid held in the base. The smoking material is placed in a small bowl at the top, and, as it burns, smoke circulates through the liquid to pick up moisture and temper the harshness of the smoke. Smokers inhale from 1 or more of several small, flexible hoses projecting from the sides of the hookah. In some cultures, smoking a hookah with others is a social ritual that may occupy 30 to 45 minutes. In other cultures, some use hookahs for smoking marijuana or other psychoactive drugs.

An increase in the Arab-American population in the United States has helped fuel the increasing popularity of smoking hookahs, a practice now spreading to other cultures in urban areas and university settings. Hookah bars and cafes are growing in number, creating concern among health professionals about the widening trend of younger people to be attracted to using fashionable hookahs to consume **nicotine** or other noxious substances. Given the variables involved in using a waterpipe—the nature of the material smoked, the liquid through which it is filtered, or the temperature at which it is burned, for example—the health effects of smoking tobacco through a hookah have not been definitively ascertained. Some suggest that the extended ritual delivers more toxins than an entire pack of **cigarettes**, while others claim that tobacco smoked through a hookah is filtered in a way that it cannot deliver the same level of carcinogens or produce as much carbon monoxide as cigarettes and **cigars**.

Jurisdictions concerned about the adverse health effects of smoking hookahs have banned their use. Consequently, hookah cafes, which are sometimes known as **shisha** bars for a popular type of sweetened tobacco frequently smoked in hookahs, are prohibited in many cities unless their managers have obtained special permits. In some areas, "shisha" is used as a synonym for "hookah."

Harmful Effects

A hookah pipe is traditionally used to smoke a tobacco mixture called shisha, which contains tobacco and flavorings such as fruit pulp, molasses, and honey. The hookah pipe uses coals to heat the shisha, and the smoke that is created passes through tubes and water so it is cooled before it is inhaled.

According to the American Cancer Society, several types of cancer as well as other negative health effects have been linked to smoking a hookah pipe. Passing the smoke through water may remove some compounds, but research shows that many toxins remain in the water-filtered smoke. These toxins include nicotine, which is the highly addictive compound in tobacco smoke; thus, hookah users suffer the same effects of nicotine use (e.g., increase in blood pressure and heart rate and change in dopamine production in the brain) that occur in cigarette smokers.

When smoking shisha, a person not only inhales tobacco smoke but also inhales smoke from the burning flavorings. Because hookah smoking is a relatively new activity in the United States, very limited research has been conducted on the health effects of inhaling smoke from the flavored substances.

Further Reading

U.S. Department of Health and Human Services, Centers for Disease Control and Prevention (CDC), November 2007. Retrieved from http://www.cdc.gov/tobacco

"Huffing." *See* Inhalants.

Hycomine. *See* Hydrocodone.

Hydrocodone Formulated as cough suppressants and analgesics that share properties with **codeine** and **morphine**, hydrocodone-containing products are among the most frequently prescribed **opiates** in the United States. A semi-synthetic opioid, hydrocodone is an active ingredient in a broad array of medications. Lortab ASA contains hydrocodone and aspirin, Vicoprofen contains hydrocodone and ibuprofen, and Hycomine contains hydrocodone and an antihistamine. Hydrocodone acetaminophen combinations such as Vicodin or Lorcet, which represent about 80 percent of all hydrocodone prescriptions, are associated with liver damage if used excessively.

With analgesic potency equivalent to or exceeding that of oral morphine, hydrocodone products are widely abused. Given their wide availability as prescribed oral pharmaceuticals, no underground industry seems to exist for manufacturing them. Instead, addicts usually obtain the drugs by doctor shopping, theft, fraudulent Internet purchases, or from friends or acquaintances. The drug is being abused in ever-greater numbers even by children; so alarming is the escalation, as evidenced by hydrocodone-associated emergency room admissions and deaths, regulatory agencies are considering tightening restrictions on its use. Currently, all products marketed in the United States are either Schedule III combination products primarily intended for pain management or Schedule V antitussive medications often marketed in liquid formulations to control coughing under the **Controlled Substances Act**. These schedules may change to reflect the risks of using these addictive and dangerous drugs.

Street names for hydrocodone and its products include Hydro, Norco, and Vikes.

Further Reading

Califano, Joseph A., Jr. *High Society: How Substance Abuse Ravages America and What to Do About It.* New York: Perseus Books, 2007.

Hoffman, John, and Froemke, Susan, eds. *Addiction: Why Can't They Just Stop?* New York: Rodale, 2007.

Home Box Office (HBO). In partnership with the Robert Wood Johnson Foundation, the National Institute on Drug Abuse, and the National Institute on Alcohol Abuse and Alcoholism. *Addiction: Why Can't They Just Stop?* Documentary. March 2007.

Ketcham, Katherine, and Pace, Nicholas A. *Teens Under the Influence: The Truth About Kids, Alcohol, and Other Drugs.* New York: Ballantine Books, 2003.

U.S. Department of Health and Human Services, National Institute on Drug Abuse (NIDA), June 2007. Retrieved from http://www.nida.gov

U.S. Department of Health and Human Services, Substance Abuse and Mental Health Services Administration (SAMHSA), August 2007. Retrieved from http://www.samhsa.gov

U.S. Department of Justice, Drug Enforcement Administration (DEA), March 2008. Retrieved from http://www.usdoj.gov/dea

Hydromorphone A Schedule II drug under provisions of the **Controlled Substances Act**, hydromorphone is an opioid analgesic 2 to 8 times more potent than **morphine**. It can be obtained in tablets, which are dissolved and injected much like **heroin**, as a suppository, or in multiple-dose vials. Highly addictive, hydromorphone is the active ingredient in Palladone, which was approved by the Food and Drug Administration in September 2004 for managing persistent pain. Later findings showing Palladone could alter other drug levels in the body led to the suspension of marketing in September 2005, but other prescription pain relievers that contain hydromorphone continue to be diverted to the illicit market.

Like other **opiates**, hydromorphone produces relaxation, euphoria, sleepiness, and constipation; in high or toxic doses, it can result in respiratory depression, reduced blood pressure, coma, and death. Opioid **antagonists** such as naloxone are not only used in the **treatment** of **addiction** to hydromorphone but can be specific antidotes for overdose by binding to the brain's receptors for the drug. Used legitimately for medical purposes under the trade name Dilaudid, hydromorphone has also been given various street names such as D, Dillies, Dust, Footballs, Juice, and Smack.

Further Reading

Califano, Joseph A., Jr. *High Society: How Substance Abuse Ravages America and What to Do About It.* New York: Perseus Books, 2007.

Hoffman, John, and Froemke, Susan, eds. *Addiction: Why Can't They Just Stop?* New York: Rodale, 2007.

Home Box Office (HBO). In partnership with the Robert Wood Johnson Foundation, the National Institute on Drug Abuse, and the National Institute on Alcohol Abuse and Alcoholism. *Addiction: Why Can't They Just Stop?* Documentary. March 2007.

Ketcham, Katherine, and Pace, Nicholas A. *Teens Under the Influence: The Truth About Kids, Alcohol, and Other Drugs.* New York: Ballantine Books, 2003.

U.S. Department of Health and Human Services, National Institute on Drug Abuse (NIDA), June 2007. Retrieved from http://www.nida.gov

U.S. Department of Health and Human Services, Substance Abuse and Mental Health Services Administration (SAMHSA), August 2007. Retrieved from http://www.samhsa.gov

U.S. Department of Justice, Drug Enforcement Administration (DEA), March 2008. Retrieved from http://www.usdoj.gov/dea

Hypersexuality Strictly defined, hypersexuality is a very high rate of sexual activity that is of a compulsive nature and suggests the presence of other disorders. In some people suffering from bipolar disease, hypersexuality may be a symptom of the manic phase of their illness. It can also be a sign of certain **brain** injuries or disease. Thus it is not synonymous with a **sexual addiction** nor is it necessarily a symptom.

Whatever its cause, hypersexuality can take many forms: pronounced obsessions or sexual encounters with other people, compulsive masturbation, or an excessive exposure to **pornography**. Diagnosis depends both on the degree of sexual activity as well as on the underlying causes. A healthy libido and vigorous sex drive alone are not symptomatic of hypersexuality. Instead, experts agree that disrupted functioning and other negative consequences must be present before a diagnosis of hypersexuality should be made, and the disorder must be assessed in terms of its origins in bipolar disease, **impulse control disorder** and sexual addiction, or relevant brain pathology.

In the past, female hypersexuality was known as nymphomania; in males, the same symptoms were called satyriasis. Hypersexuality has replaced both of these in mental health terminology.

I

Ibogaine Ibogaine is a hallucinogenic drug derived from the African shrub *Tabernanthe iboga*. Used by indigenous groups as a **stimulant** in healing and initiation ceremonies, in high doses it is a powerful psychedelic. It is slowly gathering mainstream attention as an antiaddiction drug. Since the 1960s, when an addict accidentally discovered the drug's efficacy in reducing his symptoms of **withdrawal** and **craving** associated with **heroin** use, there has been intense interest in learning how the drug works in the **brain**. Studies have shown that ibogaine metabolism in the body produces another substance, noribogaine, which evidently blocks the brain receptors that control craving; it also tends to boost levels of serotonin and dopamine, which enhances a user's overall sense of well-being and relieves withdrawal symptoms. The research suggests it can be effective in treating nicotine, alcohol, **methamphetamine**, and **cocaine** addictions, and perhaps even compulsive behaviors.

Despite significant excitement over the drug's potential, many are dissuaded by its daunting side effects. Even at therapeutic doses, it can produce nausea, vomiting, unco-ordinated movements, and exhausting psychedelic experiences that last for a day or more; at higher doses, it can be toxic and produce cardiac arrhythmias. Although the U.S. Food and Drug Administration approved trials of the drug in 1993, the National Institute on Drug Abuse (NIDA) elected not to fund it, partly because of these side effects. Nevertheless, many countries allow drug **addiction** clinics to conduct **treatment** using ibogaine as an experimental drug, and evidence is building that it can be effective with even a single dose, especially if the treatment is followed by counseling. Although not funding studies directly, the NIDA is supporting ibogaine research with indirect grants, and Canada recently approved a case study of people seeking ibogaine-based treatment for **opiate** addiction.

In 1967, along with other **hallucinogens** such as LSD, ibogaine was classified as a Schedule I controlled substance under the **Controlled Substances Act** in the United States.

Further Reading

Alper, Kenneth R., and Glick, Stanley, eds. *Ibogaine: Proceedings from the First International Congress.* San Diego: Academic Press, 2001.

U.S. Department of Health and Human Services, National Institute on Drug Abuse. *Research Report Series: Hallucinogens and Dissociative Drugs.* NIH Publication No. 01-4209, March 2001.

Impulse Control Disorders (ICDs) Also known as **behavioral addictions**, impulse control disorders are defined by compelling urges to perform acts that may give immediate pleasure but have negative consequences and cause remorse later. They are similar to **obsessive-compulsive disorders** (OCDs), but the latter represent an anxiety-driven need to quiet repetitive and troublesome thoughts by performing compulsive, irrational, ritualized acts. Impulsive behaviors like suddenly deciding to buy unneeded items, on the other hand, are usually associated with gratification of some kind, at least temporarily. When they become pathological—occurring to such a degree that an individual's ability to function or behave appropriately is impaired—they are considered impulse control disorders. Like those with obsessive-compulsive disorders or **conduct disorders**, people with impulse control disorders are likely to have an **anxiety disorder** or depression, and are usually more susceptible to substance abuse.

In the 4th edition of its *Diagnostic and Statistical Manual of Mental Disorders*, the American Psychiatric Association (APA) describes individuals suffering from impulse control disorders as unable to resist impulsive behaviors that may be harmful to themselves or others. Their acts are usually not premeditated and can seldom be controlled by willpower because they are performed to relieve the increasing tensions or arousal which typically precede it.

Most experts agree that 9 disorders meet appropriate criteria: **compulsive computer use** (Internet addiction), **compulsive shopping**, **self-injury** (including cutting behaviors), **intermittent explosive disorder** (rage addiction), **kleptomania** (stealing), pathological gambling, **pyromania** (fire-starting), **sexual addiction**, and **trichotillomania** (pulling out one's hair). Some mental health professionals do not agree that these behaviors are **addictions** even though they meet a principal diagnostic criteria—they are characterized by a repeated **compulsion** to engage in an activity despite the adverse consequences of doing so.

Some impulse control disorders that are not associated with addiction include attention-seeking behaviors or antisocial and narcissistic disorders. **Eating disorders**, including so-called **food addictions**, are complex and cannot be easily categorized; many experts feel they should be classified as anxiety or depressive disorders, although one form, **bulimia nervosa**, is regarded by some mental health professionals as an impulse control disorder. Some experts regard novelty-seeking (or risk-taking) as an impulse control disorder in which the individual engages in high-risk behaviors like bungee-jumping or extreme sports for the rush they deliver. Kleptomania and other thrill-seeking behaviors are frequently seen in the same individual, and there is speculation that the **neurotransmitter** norepinephrine may be partly responsible. However, the APA has yet to include risky behavior or novelty-seeking as symptoms of the **mental disorders** it has identified.

Most behavioral addictions start in childhood, although some emerge in late adolescence or adulthood. Even if children experience urges to steal, it is not until later that the urges become compelling and the older or grown children have the independent means to act on them. Despite earlier beliefs to the contrary, researchers are learning that impulse control disorders are not likely to have originated with a precipitating trauma or parental neglect or abuse. Instead, increasing evidence points to a combination of neurobiological factors that combine with genetic and environmental influences, and there is a clinically significant correlation between many of these disorders and **alcoholism** or other substance abuse.

Diagnosis can be difficult, principally because of patient reluctance to admit to certain behaviors. Furthermore, in adolescents, their youth already predisposes them to risky and impulsive behaviors that are part of the maturing process, and this can lead to misdiagnosis. Parents can help by being attuned to significant deviations from so-called normal levels of teenage behavior. Another factor complicating diagnosis is the fact that many healthcare professionals, unaware of the prevalence or manifestations of the diseases, view the symptoms as diagnostic of a manic-depressive illness (bipolar disorder), obsessive-compulsive disorder, major depressive disorder, or borderline personality disorder, and patients are frequently prescribed inappropriate medications or therapies that do little to treat the real problem. This has caused a significant portion of people to consider suicide as the only way to end the torment their disease has caused them and the people who care about them.

FAQs about Impulse Control Disorders

1. What causes impulse control disorders?

   There is no single cause; impulse control disorders are complicated illnesses that arise from biology, genes, and/or environment.

2. Are impulse control disorders chronic?

   Although impulse control disorders do not simply disappear, the behavior may be arrested for long periods. After treatment ends and impulses have stopped, however, those afflicted must remain vigilant to avoid things that might trigger new urges. Most people resume the behavior at some point if the illness is not managed.

3. Is there a genetic component to impulse control disorders?

   There is evidence to suggest that it is common to find several members of the same family with similar disorders.

4. Once the disorder is treated, will another one take its place?

   Some people do shift from one addiction to another. Education, treatment, and counseling help control this tendency.

5. Does an impulse control disorder indicate a failing of character?

   No, people do not lack willpower or moral character just because they suffer from an impulse control disorder. They are psychiatric illnesses of the brain and can be treated.

6. How can someone with an impulse control disorder be helped?

   Most people with impulse control disorders do not think they need treatment and may need to suffer serious consequences of their behavior before they find or accept treatment. Presenting education and treatment options to the afflicted person can make a difference. Also, support groups for family and friends of those afflicted by impulse control disorders may have suggestions for urging the person into treatment.

Source: Adapted from: Grant, 2003.

Impulse control disorders are associated with the area of the **brain** that processes reward and pleasure. Research findings suggest that they may be related to low levels of serotonin, and the effectiveness of serotonin reuptake inhibitors and opioid **antagonists** in treating them tends to confirm this. Evidence for a genetic basis is also supported by studies showing that pathological gambling is more common in the identical twin of someone suffering from the disease than it is in unaffected identical twins. Unfortunately, even if patients can admit the nature of their addiction to others, many do not know that they are suffering from a treatable psychiatric disease.

Although some impulse control disorders are relatively uncommon, anywhere from 8 to 35 million Americans are afflicted with some form of them, and they create major problems for families. Once the disorders are properly diagnosed and assessed to determine the variables that apply in individual cases, they can be treated effectively with appropriate combinations of medication and cognitive behavioral therapy. Adolescents, whose developing brains leave them particularly susceptible to the influences that help foster impulse control disorders, respond well to early **treatment**. Since about half of the people diagnosed also have a history of substance abuse, it is essential that both disorders be treated at the same time.

Further Reading

American Psychiatric Association. *Diagnostic and Statistical Manual of Mental Disorders*, 4th Edition, Text Revision. Washington, DC: American Psychiatric Association, 2000.

Davis, Caroline. Addiction and the Eating Disorders. *Psychiatric Times* February 2001. Retrieved from http://www.psychiatrictimes.com/p010259.html

Grant, Jon E., and Kim, S. W.. *Stop Me Because I Can't Stop Myself: Taking Control of Impulsive Behavior.* New York: McGraw-Hill, 2003.

Hyman, S. E., and Malenka, R. C. Addiction and the Brain: The Neurobiology of Compulsion and Its Persistence. *Nature Reviews Neuroscience* 2001: 2(10), 695–703.

Peele, Stanton. Is Gambling an Addiction Like Drug and Alcohol Addiction? *Electronic Journal of Gambling Issues* February 2001. Retrieved from http://www.camh.net/egambling/issue3/feature/index.html

Potenza, Marc N. Should Addictive Disorders Include Non-Substance-Related Conditions? *Addiction* 2006: 101(s1), 142–151.

Young, Kimberly S. *Caught in the Net: How to Recognize the Signs of Internet Addiction.* New York: John Wiley, 1998.

Impulses. *See* Compulsions and Impulses.

Incentive Salience. *See* Conditioning.

Inhalants Over 1,000 substances fall into the category of inhalants. Unregulated under the **Controlled Substances Act**, they are abused primarily by children and adolescents with serious and often tragic consequences. As a result, most states have adopted stringent laws to discourage minors from the purchase or possession of these products. Although **withdrawal** from inhalants does not usually produce clinically significant symptoms, these substances are subject to compulsive and repeated use despite the associated negative consequences, thus meriting inclusion into studies of addictive drugs. Inhalants include:

- Gases such as those found in aerosols and dispensers, lighters, and propane tanks; refrigerants; and the ether, nitrous oxide, and chloroform that are used in medical settings.
- Volatile solvents, which are regular- or industrial-strength products that contain solvents, which include gasoline, glue, felt-tip markers, paint thinners, degreasers, and dry-cleaning fluids.
- Aerosols, which are widely available in most households, including hair spray, vegetable sprays, spray paint, and similar products.
- Nitrites, which fall into 2 categories: organic, such as butyl or amyl nitrites (poppers), and volatile, brown-bottle products such as leather cleaner, room odorizer, or liquid aroma.

Substance/Drug	Intoxicating Effects	Potential Health Consequences
Inhalants Gases Aerosols Nitrites Volatile solvents	Stimulation, loss of inhibition, drunken behavior	Unconsciousness, weight loss, depression, memory impairment, cardiovascular and nervous system damage, death *Source: NIDA, DEA*

Inhalant Chart

Inhalants produce intoxicating effects similar to those of alcohol when they are sniffed, snorted, bagged, or huffed. They are particularly insidious because they are legal, inexpensive, and readily available in every household. It is easy to hide their presence in plain sight and conceal their use since the products are everywhere and the symptoms of use are not always easy to recognize. Their ready availability deceives younger users into thinking they are safe when, in fact, they can be extraordinarily dangerous.

Statistics show that the highest level of use is by 10- to 12-year-old children, with use declining as they get older. According to a national news report delivered in the spring of 2007, over a half a million adolescents engaged in huffing in the previous year; in 2003, almost 23 million people ages 12 and older reported using an inhalant at least once in their lifetime.

Huffing involves holding a cloth soaked with the substance to the face so the user can inhale it, or the cloth is placed into an open container. Some users paint the chemicals onto their skin, clothing, or fingernails so they can inhale the fumes without detection. When bagging, users place objects like felt-tipped markers containing appropriate chemicals into paper or plastic bags, crush the bags, and then inhale the fumes. There is a seemingly endless variety of ways someone can **abuse** inhalants, and the drugs act rapidly by constricting the user's blood vessels. Since the effect is short-lived, users repeat the process, which deepens the **intoxication**, leads to disinhibition and loss of control, and can cause them to lose consciousness.

Inhalants share characteristics with other classes of drugs; they are **depressants** because they suppress the central nervous system and lower respiration and blood pressure; they resemble **hallucinogens** because they distort perceptions of time and space. They can induce slurred speech, nausea, and headaches; impair motor coordination; trigger excitable or unpredictable behavior; and produce physical evidence of use such as watery eyes or a rash around the mouth. Longer-term, more serious effects may include bone marrow, kidney, or liver damage from the chemicals contained in inhalants as well as memory and intellectual impairment. Some of the psychological and neurological damage caused by inhalants is extreme and tragic. An immediate and deadly consequence of use can be asphyxiation or heart failure, sometimes known as the sudden sniffing death syndrome seen in first-time users. Using a paper bag to concentrate the fumes is responsible for suffocation deaths due to displacement of oxygen in the lungs.

Reflecting the wide variety of products that can be abused as inhalants, many street names have emerged: Air Blast, Ames, Amys, Bang, Bolt, Boppers, Bullet, Bullet Bolt, Buzz Bomb, Discorama, Highball, Hippie Crack, Huff, Kick, Laughing Gas, Locker Room, Medusa, Moon Gas, Oz, Pearls, Poor Man's Pot, Poppers, Quicksilver, Rush, Satan's Secret, Shoot the Breeze, Snappers, Snotballs, Spray, Texas Shoe Shine, Thrust, Toilet Water, and Whippets.

See also Drug Classes; Appendix B.

Further Reading

Califano, Joseph A., Jr. *High Society: How Substance Abuse Ravages America and What to Do About It.* New York: Perseus Books, 2007.

Hoffman, John, and Froemke, Susan, eds. *Addiction: Why Can't They Just Stop?* New York: Rodale, 2007.

Home Box Office (HBO). In partnership with the Robert Wood Johnson Foundation, the National Institute on Drug Abuse, and the National Institute on Alcohol Abuse and Alcoholism. *Addiction: Why Can't They Just Stop?* Documentary. March 2007.

Ketcham, Katherine, and Pace, Nicholas A. *Teens Under the Influence: The Truth About Kids, Alcohol, and Other Drugs.* New York: Ballantine Books, 2003.

U.S. Department of Health and Human Services, National Institute on Drug Abuse (NIDA), June 2007. Retrieved from http://www.nida.gov

U.S. Department of Health and Human Services, National Institute on Drug Abuse. *Research Report Series: Inhalant Abuse.* NIH Publication No. 05-3818, March 2005.

U.S. Department of Health and Human Services, Substance Abuse and Mental Health Services Administration (SAMHSA), August 2007. Retrieved from http://www.samhsa.gov

U.S. Department of Justice, Drug Enforcement Administration (DEA), March 2008. Retrieved from http://www.usdoj.gov/dea

Insular Cortex. *See* Brain and Addiction.

Insurance Coverage and Addiction The provision of insurance coverage for addiction **treatment** is a controversial issue. For several decades during the second half of the 20th century, few insurance companies offered any coverage; they might have paid for acute treatment such as in-hospital detoxification but it was frequently disguised as treatment for physical symptoms such as exhaustion or malnutrition. However, as it has become clear that society must acknowledge and appropriately treat **addiction** as a serious public health issue, pressure has been brought to bear on the insurance industry to cover necessary treatments. As the **Minnesota model** of inpatient, 28-day rehabilitation became the standard of care during the 1970s and 1980s, some large employers began to insure employees for treatment. Until then, addicts had recourse only to **12-step** groups such as **Alcoholics Anonymous** or, for those who could afford it, to private medical or psychological counseling that produced limited results.

Opportunities for treatment covered by insurance did not extend to the rest of the population. In large part, this was because insurance company underwriters, even after they began to view addiction as a disease rather than a moral issue, believed that patients were resistant to treatment and prone to relapse, and thus would be an enormous economic drain on the industry. Since this same attitude has often prevailed in treating mental illnesses, many local, state, and federal laws were passed during the 1980s and 1990s attempting to legislate equity in insurance coverage. Nevertheless, substance **abuse** was excluded, even from coverage mandated by the Mental Health Parity Act that the U.S. federal government enacted in 1998.

Although many states attempted to address this gap, significant exclusions in coverage for any kind of **substance addiction** continued to exist. In 1992, to raise awareness of these inequities, the American Psychiatric Association adopted the position that all substance-related disorders were mental illnesses that responded readily to treatment. With the organization's official opposition to excluding addiction and substance-related disorders from insurance coverage, and with mounting evidence from federal, state, and private-sector studies that addiction treatment is cost-effective in both the short- and long-term, the pressure on the insurance industry to provide comprehensive addiction treatment continued to build. Nevertheless, due to the already out-of-control escalating cost of health care in the United States, about 50 million people are excluded from any type of coverage, so it is unlikely that affordable ways of providing addiction treatment coverage to the people who need it most can be found. Political pressure for universal coverage that covers all Americans is growing to address this rapidly mounting healthcare crisis. It is possible that in a few years, entirely new forms of coverage will be offered that will extend quality care, including comprehensive addiction treatment, to all.

Intermittent Explosive Disorder People suffering from intermittent explosive disorder, sometimes referred to as rage **addiction**, are repeatedly unable to resist aggressive actions such as destruction of property or personal assault. Some forms of domestic violence may fall into this category, but the aggression must be unprovoked to be diagnostic of a true explosive disorder. Although some would define road rage as an intermittent explosive disorder, the degree of aggression must be significantly out of proportion to any precipitating event. For this reason, the mutually aggressive behavior often seen in angry drivers on the highway does not necessarily fit the diagnostic profile.

Many experts claim that the high rate of murders and other serious assaults in the United States is due, in part, to the easy access that people with intermittent explosive disorders have to guns. The immediacy of firearms produces lethal results when violence-prone individuals act impulsively on their rage whereas, in a society in which guns are restricted, such assaults would be far less likely to result in fatalities. However, there are no statistics to support the assertion that individuals who suffer from this disorder commit a disproportionately large percentage of firearm-related crimes.

DSM Criteria for Diagnosing Intermittent Explosive Disorder

The following criteria used for diagnosing intermittent explosive disorder have been adapted from the 4th edition of the American Psychiatric Association's *Diagnostic and Statistical Manual of Mental Disorders* (*DSM*).

In intermittent explosive disorder:

1. the person has episodes of aggressive outbursts involving assaults on people or damage to property;
2. the person's degree of anger or aggressiveness is out of proportion to the provocation;
3. the aggression is not symptomatic of or the result of other mental disorders such as borderline personality disorder, psychosis, or conduct disorder; or the result of substance abuse or intoxication; or symptoms of a head injury or other medical condition.

Source: Adapted from American Psychiatric Association, 2000.

Treatment for this disorder, similar to that recommended for treating other **impulse control disorders**, is usually a combination of medication and cognitive behavioral therapy.

Further Reading

Cohen, Jeffrey, and Fish, Marian. *Handbook of School-based Interventions: Resolving Student Problems and Promoting Healthy Educational Environments*. New York: Wiley, 1993.

Grant, Jon E., and Kim, S. W. *Stop Me Because I Can't Stop Myself: Taking Control of Impulsive Behavior*. New York: McGraw-Hill, 2003.

Internet Addiction. *See* Compulsive Computer Use.

Intervention An intervention is a systematic attempt to encourage an addicted person to get help. It generally takes the form of a face-to-face conversation and is conducted in a nonjudgmental atmosphere when the addicted person is not under the influence of drugs and the person who conducts the intervention is able to maintain calm. Sometimes it is advisable to ask a trusted friend or a professional counselor to conduct the intervention, which should occur before the **addiction** has progressed too far and the addict has hit bottom. For many addicts, early intervention and prompt **treatment** are critical determinants of treatment success.

Informal interventions may consist of having a one-on-one personal talk about the addiction. More formal interventions involve a third party leading discussions, and family members and friends may be present to reveal how the addicted person's behavior has affected them.

An important goal of an intervention is to make it clear the addict must commit to a specific plan of treatment; a promise to stop or change behavior is not enough. Participants should be specific about how the addiction has negatively affected their lives in the past, why the addiction must end, and what the future consequences will be if the addict refuses to go for or participate in the necessary treatment.

Intervention saves lives, but it can be a very difficult, emotional, and painful process for everyone concerned. Most treatment centers and specialists recommend that families enlist the aid of trained professional counselors to guide them through the process and deal with the aftermath.

Further Reading

Jay, Jeff, and Jay, Debra. *Love First: A New Approach to Intervention for Alcoholism & Drug Addiction*. Center City, MN: Hazelden Foundation, 2000.

Monti, Peter M., Colby, Suzanne, and O'Leary, Tracy, eds. *Adolescents, Alcohol, and Substance Abuse: Reaching Teens through Brief Interventions*. New York: The Guilford Press, 2001.

Intoxication A temporary state that is not itself evidence of **addiction**, intoxication refers to the direct effects that a psychoactive substance has on the central nervous system. Although most would define intoxication in terms of how it makes them feel, in a literal context, intoxication means toxicity or poisoning.

Symptoms of intoxication vary depending on the substance and how it affects the **brain**, but they frequently include perceptual difficulties, impaired coordination and reflexes, changes in personality, blurred vision, slurred speech, dizziness, and impaired judgment. One psychoactive drug that does not produce a sense of intoxication is nicotine.

Acute intoxication is associated with recent or continuing use of the psychoactive substance. In substance-induced psychotic intoxication, symptoms may appear during long-term **withdrawal**, days or weeks after use of the substance has stopped and the drug has been metabolized. Physiological intoxication represents the heart palpitations or other physical symptoms that drugs like caffeine might produce.

Although intoxication is usually a manifestation of substance **abuse**, not addiction, it can be an early warning sign of addiction if even a few episodes of intoxication are seen in a young person between the ages of 15 to 25. Further, repeated episodes of intoxication in people of all ages are frequently associated with addiction.

J

Jellinek, Elvin Morton (1890–1963) A biostatistician and physiologist with degrees from several international universities, E. M. Jellinek became one of the nation's foremost **alcoholism** researchers, and he was among the first to call it a disease. In 1960, he published *The Disease Concept of Alcoholism*, a work that legitimized that position and was influential in helping to transform society's attitude toward compulsive drinking from one of disdain to one of compassion.

During the 1940s, Jellinek was a Professor of Applied Physiology at Yale University where he founded the Yale Center of Alcohol Studies and the Yale Plan Clinic for the **treatment** of alcoholism. He joined forces with **Marty Mann** (1904–1980), the first woman to join **Alcoholics Anonymous** (AA) and a fierce public advocate for humane alcoholism treatment, to create the National Committee for Education on Alcoholism (NCEA), now the National Council on Alcoholism and Drug Dependence (NCADD). Through their involvement with NCEA, Mann and Jellinek as well as AA's **Bill Wilson**, an advisor to the NCEA, promoted the disease model of alcoholism and the value of AA as a treatment approach. For a time, Mann and Jellinek enjoyed the prestige afforded by their association with Yale University, but this relationship ended in 1949 when the new director of Yale's Center of Alcohol Studies objected to some of the data that Jellinek and Mann used to support the disease model.

In 1952, Jellinek was recruited by the World Health Organization in Geneva, Switzerland, to be a consultant on alcoholism. After leaving that organization a few years later, he worked with the University of Toronto and the University of Alberta, moving in 1962 to Stanford University in California where he remained until his death.

In *The Disease Concept of Alcoholism*, Jellinek identified several manifestations, or types, of the disorder, noting that many alcoholics might easily fit more than one category:

- Alpha alcoholics, or Type I, drank heavily to relieve anxiety or depression but did not exhibit signs of **withdrawal** or loss of control.
- Beta alcoholics, or Type II, showed none of the mental obsession or physical **dependence** associated with drinking but developed organic damage in the form of cirrhosis of the liver, or pancreatitis.
- Gamma alcoholics, Type III, were those who could abstain for days or weeks but quickly lost control again once they began to drink; they exhibited the progressive form of the disease.

- Delta alcoholics, Type IV, drank day and night, topping off as necessary; while they seldom became acutely intoxicated and could withdraw from alcohol entirely for a day or two, they were seldom completely sober.
- Epsilon alcoholics, Type V, engaged in intense binges, during which they might inflict considerable damage on themselves or others.

In the United States today, alcoholism experts and also AA view gamma alcoholism as the embodiment of all 5 types.

Further Reading

Jellinek, E. M. *The Disease Concept of Alcoholism*. New Haven: Hillhouse Press, 1960.

Jung, Carl Gustav (1875–1961) An eminent and widely respected Swiss psychiatrist and former student of Sigmund Freud, Carl Jung had an indirect but profound effect on **Bill Wilson**, the founder of **Alcoholics Anonymous** (AA), and on the fundamental principles of the organization.

During the 1930s, treating a patient whose **alcoholism** refused to respond to other therapy and believing that nothing else could help the man recover, Jung advised the patient to seek a spiritual conversion that might rescue him from his **addiction**. Following Jung's advice, the patient joined the U.S. evangelical group known as the Oxford Group to which Bill Wilson also belonged. Following its principles of service to others combined with meditation and prayer as avenues to **recovery**, he subsequently underwent a religious experience that relieved his **compulsion** to drink.

In 1934, as Wilson was in the midst of a desperate, life-or-death battle with his own alcoholism, another Oxford Group member who was acquainted with Jung's patient suggested that Wilson seek a spiritual awakening too. During a period of hospitalization and detoxification, Wilson appealed to God for help and reported that he was immediately suffused with a sense of peace and hope, an experience so profound that he felt a new confidence in his ability to recover, as indeed he began to do. With the encouragement of his physician, **William Silkworth** (1873–1951), Wilson subsequently wove into AA's philosophy the importance of spirituality and of surrendering one's will over to one's personal conception of God.

Before Jung's death in 1961, Wilson wrote to him to thank the psychiatrist for providing a concept that had "proved to be the foundation of such success as Alcoholics Anonymous has since achieved."

Further Reading

Bair, Deirdre. *Jung: A Biography*. Boston: Little, Brown & Company, 2004.
Hoffman, Edward. *The Wisdom of Carl Jung*. New York: Kensington, 2003.

❖ K

Ketamine An anesthetic that causes patients to feel detached from pain or their environment, ketamine is 1 of 3 **hallucinogens** that are also known as date-rape drugs. Originally an animal tranquilizer and anesthetic, ketamine has become popular at rave dance clubs. It acts quickly at low doses to cause dizziness and euphoria, but at higher doses causes the amnesia and coma that make users vulnerable to sexual predators. It can also cause delirium, high blood pressure, and depression.

Produced for many years in laboratories for the legitimate veterinary market, ketamine has been increasingly diverted in recent years for illicit recreational use. Robberies of U.S. veterinary clinics have increased, and importation of the drug from Mexican pharmacies is on the rise. By removing the liquid from the pharmaceutical product, users can orally consume the powder that remains or snort, inject, or sprinkle it on **marijuana** and smoke it. The method of administration determines how quickly users experience its effects.

On Schedule III of the **Controlled Substances Act**, ketamine has numerous street names including Bump, Cat Valium, Green, Honey Oil, Jet, K, Purple, Special K, Special La Coke, Super Acid, Super C, Vitamin K. Large doses that cause users to feel dissociated from their environment are sometimes referred to as out-of-body or near-death experiences, or K-Hole.

Further Reading

Califano, Joseph A., Jr. *High Society: How Substance Abuse Ravages America and What to Do About It.* New York: Perseus Books, 2007.

Hoffman, John, and Froemke, Susan, eds. *Addiction: Why Can't They Just Stop?* New York: Rodale, 2007.

Home Box Office (HBO). In partnership with the Robert Wood Johnson Foundation, the National Institute on Drug Abuse, and the National Institute on Alcohol Abuse and Alcoholism. *Addiction: Why Can't They Just Stop?* Documentary. March 2007.

Ketcham, Katherine, and Pace, Nicholas A. *Teens Under the Influence: The Truth About Kids, Alcohol, and Other Drugs.* New York: Ballantine Books, 2003.

U.S. Department of Health and Human Services, National Institute on Drug Abuse (NIDA), June 2007. Retrieved from http://www.nida.gov

U.S. Department of Health and Human Services, National Institute on Drug Abuse. *Research Report Series: Hallucinogens and Dissociative Drugs.* NIH Publication No. 01-4209, March 2001.

U.S. Department of Health and Human Services, Substance Abuse and Mental Health Services Administration (SAMHSA), August 2007. Retrieved from http://www.samhsa.gov

U.S. Department of Justice, Drug Enforcement Administration (DEA), March 2008. Retrieved from http://www.usdoj.gov/dea

Khat Pronounced "cot," khat is a **stimulant** derived from the East African shrub *Catha edulis* and has been used socially for centuries by indigenous cultures to reduce fatigue and suppress appetite. The leaves and other parts of the plant are chewed like **tobacco** or dried to make a tea, paste, or flaky material that can be smoked. With excessive use, it is capable of producing manic behavior, hallucinations, grandiose delusions, increased heart rate and exhaustion, hyperactivity, insomnia, and gastric disorders.

Prohibited in the United States, khat is legal in much of Europe as well as on the Arabian Peninsula and East Africa where it is grown and smuggled to the West. Two of its ingredients are regulated under the **Controlled Substances Act**—cathinone on Schedule I and cathine on Schedule IV.

Although several million people use khat throughout the world—primarily in the Middle East—it has been known to induce psychosis in some. Among its street names are Abyssinian Tea, African Salad, Catha, Chat, Kat, and Oat. In Yemen, it is called Qat.

Further Reading

Califano, Joseph A., Jr. *High Society: How Substance Abuse Ravages America and What to Do About It.* New York: Perseus Books, 2007.

Hoffman, John, and Froemke, Susan, eds. *Addiction: Why Can't They Just Stop?* New York: Rodale, 2007.

Home Box Office (HBO). In partnership with the Robert Wood Johnson Foundation, the National Institute on Drug Abuse, and the National Institute on Alcohol Abuse and Alcoholism. *Addiction: Why Can't They Just Stop?* Documentary. March 2007.

Ketcham, Katherine, and Pace, Nicholas A. *Teens Under the Influence: The Truth About Kids, Alcohol, and Other Drugs.* New York: Ballantine Books, 2003.

U.S. Department of Health and Human Services, National Institute on Drug Abuse (NIDA), June 2007. Retrieved from http://www.nida.gov

U.S. Department of Health and Human Services, Substance Abuse and Mental Health Services Administration (SAMHSA), August 2007. Retrieved from http://www.samhsa.gov

U.S. Department of Justice, Drug Enforcement Administration (DEA), March 2008. Retrieved from http://www.usdoj.gov/dea

Kleptomania Like other **impulse control disorders**, kleptomania—compulsive stealing—is driven by an urge to seek a high and the release of tension that precedes the act. It is not associated with revenge, anger, or the need to acquire the merchandise or property being stolen. Often, the goods that are taken are of little monetary value and of no use to the thief, who may even return them at a later date. More than twice as many women as men seem to suffer from the disorder, although the data may be distorted by the fact that women seek **treatment** more often than men. Kleptomania tends to first appear in late adolescence and is characterized by solitary thievery with virtually no premeditation and little concern at the time for being caught. Most kleptomaniacs shoplift from stores, although they may also steal from friends and relatives, and over half tend to hoard the stolen items for what the individuals report is the sense of comfort they give. Remorseful because of their behavior, most kleptomaniacs try to repress their urges to steal again only to find that doing so produces rising tensions that fuel more of the behavior.

Although its causes are not known, kleptomania has been reported in people with dementia, with certain types of **brain** tumors, or with cortical atrophy. This suggests that changes in brain structure or function associated with injury, illness, or aging may contribute to the disorder in some people, particularly those with late onset.

There is not a wealth of data available on the treatment of kleptomania, but experts note that it is often associated with substance **abuse** and anxiety or other **mental disorders** that must be treated concurrently if treatment is to be effective. Impulse control disorders like kleptomania are associated with a lower than normal expression of serotonin in the brain, and drugs that address this deficit have shown positive results. Cognitive behavioral therapy has also been effective, and many patients treated with a combination of behavioral therapy and medication have responded well. As is the case with other mental disorders, the sooner treatment is started, the more positive the outcome is likely to be.

DSM Criteria for Diagnosing Kleptomania

The following criteria used for diagnosing kleptomania have been adapted from the 4th edition of the American Psychiatric Association's *Diagnostic and Statistical Manual of Mental Disorders (DSM)*.

In kleptomania, the person:

1. is repeatedly unable to resist stealing objects regardless of the items' monetary value or any need for them on his or her part;
2. feels a sense of tension or anticipation before stealing;
3. experiences pleasure or gratification with stealing and does not steal for revenge, vengeance, out of anger, or as a symptom of a psychosis or mental illness such as a conduct or manic disorder.

Source: Adapted from American Psychiatric Association, 2000.

Kleptomania Self-Assessment Questionnaire

The following questionnaire can help determine whether you might be suffering from kleptomania. Answering "yes" to 2 or more of these questions should be cause for concern.

1. Do you have urges to steal or do you actually commit theft? □ Yes □ No
2. Does stealing relieve feelings of tension or anxiety? □ Yes □ No
3. Has stealing interfered with your normal activities, functioning, or relationships? □ Yes □ No
4. Has stealing caused you legal difficulties? □ Yes □ No
5. Do urges to steal or stealing itself cause you psychological distress? □ Yes □ No

---

Further Reading

Goldman, Marcus J. *Kleptomania: The Compulsion to Steal—What Can Be Done?* Far Hills, NJ: New Horizon Press, 1997.

Grant, Jon E., and Kim, S. W. *Stop Me Because I Can't Stop Myself: Taking Control of Impulsive Behavior.* New York: McGraw-Hill, 2003.

Klonopin. *See* Benzodiazepines.

Kreteks. *See* Bidis and Kreteks.

L

LAAM. *See* Levo-alpha-acetyl-methadol.

Legalization of Drugs. *See* Decriminalization.

Levo-alpha-acetyl-methadol (LAAM) Levo-alpha-acetyl-methadol is a synthetic compound similar to **methadone** used to treat an **addiction** to **opiates**, especially to **heroin**. Approved in 1994 as a Schedule II drug under the Controlled Substances Act, LAMM offers some advantages over methadone; its effects last longer, from 48 to 72 hours compared to methadone's 24 hours, so it only needs to be administered every few days rather than daily. This can significantly affect **treatmen**t compliance of addicts who find it burdensome to have to make daily trips to clinics for treatment. Amid evidence that LAMM can create serious cardiac disruptions, however, some experts advise caution and recommend continued testing before relying on the drug as a first-line treatment for opiate addiction.

Further Reading

Califano, Joseph A., Jr. *High Society: How Substance Abuse Ravages America and What to Do About It.* New York: Perseus Books, 2007.

Hoffman, John, and Froemke, Susan, eds. *Addiction: Why Can't They Just Stop?* New York: Rodale, 2007.

Home Box Office (HBO). In partnership with the Robert Wood Johnson Foundation, the National Institute on Drug Abuse, and the National Institute on Alcohol Abuse and Alcoholism. *Addiction: Why Can't They Just Stop?* Documentary. March 2007.

Ketcham, Katherine, and Pace, Nicholas A. *Teens Under the Influence: The Truth About Kids, Alcohol, and Other Drugs.* New York: Ballantine Books, 2003.

U.S. Department of Health and Human Services, National Institute on Drug Abuse (NIDA), June 2007. Retrieved from http://www.nida.gov

U.S. Department of Health and Human Services, Substance Abuse and Mental Health Services Administration (SAMHSA), August 2007. Retrieved from http://www.samhsa.gov

U.S. Department of Justice, Drug Enforcement Administration (DEA), March 2008. Retrieved from http://www.usdoj.gov/dea

Light Cigarettes. *See* Nicotine.

Limbic System. *See* Brain and Addiction.

Little Cigars. *See* Mini Cigars.

Locus Ceruleus. *See* Brain and Addiction.

Lonamin. *See* Stimulants.

Long-Term Depression. *See* Long-Term Potentiation.

Long-Term Potentiation First recognized and identified in 1966, long-term potentiation describes the strengthening of synapses in the brain's ventral tegmental area in response to specific stimuli. Addictive drugs, despite differences in their molecular structure, appear to share a capacity for inducing long-term potentiation; nonaddictive drugs do not. Scientists believe that long-term potentiation and its opposite, long-term depression, or a weakening of synaptic strength, are fundamental to **behavioral sensitization** and the formation of memories. The variability of its effect on cells and the length of time it continues to exert that effect—sometimes for years—depends in part on where it is taking place in the **brain** and the specificity of the **neurotransmitters** and receptors involved.

In the ventral tegmental area, addictive drugs stimulate neurons to release glutamate that in turn causes dopamine-producing cells to increase their output into the reward pathway. The strengthened synaptic activity, known as potentiation, primes the cell so that it remembers its level of response. When the brain becomes primed to respond to drug cues, the likelihood of eventual relapse increases. Each time an individual consumes drugs, the intensity and duration of his or her response tend to increase and, as the dopaminergic effect lingers in the synapses for a longer period of time, the cells become sensitized. They are said to display synaptic plasticity, the characteristic **neuroadaptation** associated with **addiction** that may be part of the basis for **craving**.

Researchers have found that stress triggers long-term potentiation the same way that addictive drugs do, perhaps because it reawakens the memory of strengthened synaptic connections and cells. Why is not yet clear, but it may help explain why stress can so powerfully threaten years of abstinence.

Further Reading

Erickson, Carlton K. *The Science of Addiction: From Neurobiology to Treatment*. New York: Norton, 2007.

Kalivas, P. W., and Volkow, Nora. The Neural Basis of Addiction: A Pathology of Motivation and Choice. *American Journal of Psychiatry* August 2005: 162(8), 1403–1413.

Kauer, Julie A. Addictive Drugs and Stress Trigger a Common Change at VTA Synapses. *Neuron* February 2003: 37(4), 549–550.

Nestler, Eric J., and Malenka, Robert. The Addicted Brain. *Scientific American*, September 2007. Retrieved from http://www.sciam.com/article.cfm?chanID=sa006&colID=1&articleID=0001E6 32-978A-1019-978A83414B7F0101

U.S. Department of Health and Human Services, National Institute on Drug Abuse. *The Science of Addiction: Drugs, Brains, and Behavior*. NIH Publication No. 07-5605, February 2007.

Love Addiction. *See* Relationship Addiction.

Low-Tar Cigarettes. *See* Nicotine.

LSD. *See* Lysergic Acid Diethylamide.

Lunesta. *See* Barbiturates.

Lysergic Acid Diethylamide (LSD) One of the most potent **hallucinogens**, LSD was first synthesized in 1938 by Swiss scientists seeking to discover the medical potential of certain fungi. A few years later, after accidentally ingesting one of the compounds, one scientist experienced the first known LSD trip involving frightening hallucinations, dissociation from time and place, distorted perceptions, and a seeming dissolution of his ego.

Because of its structural similarity to certain **brain** chemicals, LSD was later used as a research tool in the study of mental illness and then became popular as a recreational drug during the 1960s after its use was heavily encouraged by popular members of the counterculture like Timothy Leary (1920–1996). Although early research indicated that LSD showed promise as a psychotherapeutic tool or might have other medical value, its popularity in the 1960's drug culture led to its ban for any purpose, including medical research. This ban has lifted in recent years, and one group of researchers has received permission to conduct experiments with the drug. Some studies have shown it may have therapeutic value in the **treatment** of **alcoholism**.

Usually produced in a crystalline form in laboratories in the United States and elsewhere, LSD is crushed into a powder and formulated into tablets or thin squares of gelatin, dissolved and diluted to be applied to colorfully printed paper or pressed into sugar cubes. Blotter acid represents small, single-dose squares of paper impregnated with the drug for individual use. Once ingested, its effects can be felt within 30 to 90 minutes and typically last several hours.

Researchers are learning that hallucinogenic drugs like LSD target certain serotonin receptors to produce their psychoactive effects principally in the cerebral cortex, where mood and perception are processed, and in the locus ceruleus, which detects sensory signals from external stimuli and other parts of the body. Initial effects of the drug include elevated temperature, increased heart rate and blood pressure, insomnia, and tremors. Some users may experience crossover sensations in which they can "see" sounds and "hear" colors. Aside from its neurotoxic effect in the brain, LSD can lead to bizarre and dangerous behaviors that can injure the self or others. Other users experience despair and fear of insanity as impaired perceptions produce overwhelming hallucinations and panic. Personal injury is also possible, especially during **flashbacks**. A negative experience or bad trip while under the influence of LSD can haunt users for days or months. The effect LSD will have on each user is unpredictable; some may even develop psychoses or severe depression.

LSD use has varied over the years—decreasing in recent years despite its popularity at nightclubs, concert venues, and raves—but it remains a significant drug of **abuse**. Although the hallucinogen is not addictive and most people can stop its use without much difficulty, it does produce **tolerance**, so users may find themselves ingesting more, a practice that can lead to the death of brain cells and permanent neurological damage. It is a Schedule I substance under the **Controlled Substances Act**.

LSD goes by numerous street names, including Acid, Blotter, Blotter Acid, Dots, Mellow Yellow, Microdot, Pane, Paper Acid, Sugar, Sugar Cubes, Trip, Window Glass, Window Pane, and Zen.

Further Reading

Califano, Joseph A., Jr. *High Society: How Substance Abuse Ravages America and What to Do About It.* New York: Perseus Books, 2007.

Hoffman, John, and Froemke, Susan, eds. *Addiction: Why Can't They Just Stop?* New York: Rodale, 2007.

Home Box Office (HBO). In partnership with the Robert Wood Johnson Foundation, the National Institute on Drug Abuse, and the National Institute on Alcohol Abuse and Alcoholism. *Addiction: Why Can't They Just Stop?* Documentary. March 2007.

Ketcham, Katherine, and Pace, Nicholas A. *Teens Under the Influence: The Truth About Kids, Alcohol, and Other Drugs.* New York: Ballantine Books, 2003.

U.S. Department of Health and Human Services, National Institute on Drug Abuse (NIDA), June 2007. Retrieved from http://www.nida.gov

U.S. Department of Health and Human Services, National Institute on Drug Abuse. *Research Report Series: Hallucinogens and Dissociative Drugs.* NIH Publication No. 01-4209, March 2001.

U.S. Department of Health and Human Services, Substance Abuse and Mental Health Services Administration (SAMHSA), August 2007. Retrieved from http://www.samhsa.gov

U.S. Department of Justice, Drug Enforcement Administration (DEA), March 2008. Retrieved from http://www.usdoj.gov/dea

M

Mann, Marty (1904–1980) In 1939, as a desperate alcoholic, Marty Mann was introduced to the newly formed organization known as **Alcoholics Anonymous** (AA) by her psychiatrist, **Harry Tiebout** (1896–1966). AA meetings had just begun to form, and at that time they were held in the home of **Bill Wilson** (1895–1971), AA's principal founder. Mann became the first female member of the organization. Despite some early relapses, she was ultimately able to remain abstinent and subsequently became one of the most influential and dynamic spokespersons for humane alcoholism **treatment** in the nation.

Five years after she joined AA and with a prolonged period of abstinence, she became determined to try to remove the stigma of **alcoholism** by defining it as the serious disease she believed it to be. She was involved in alcoholism research at the Yale Center of Alcohol Studies where, with **E. M. Jellinek** (1890–1963), she cofounded the National Committee for Education on Alcoholism (NCEA), now the National Council on Alcoholism and Drug Dependence (NCADD). NCADD is today one of America's foremost educational resources for information on alcoholism and for raising public awareness of drug **dependence**.

For 24 years, Mann was director of the NCEA and traveled the country, giving as many as 200 speeches a year to Congress as well as to private and public groups to spread the message that alcoholics were sick people deserving of help. In the early 1950s, Edward R. Murrow (1908–1965), a distinguished journalist of the time, named Mann one of the 10 greatest living Americans.

Despite a life of poor health—alcoholism, cancer, and severe depression—Mann, with her remarkable charisma and dynamic ability to engage her audiences, carved a distinguished career advocating for the medical issues facing alcoholics and the need for better treatment. Although she retired from the NCEA at age 65, she continued her lecture tours, dying in 1980 at age 75 just 2 weeks after speaking before one of AA's international conventions.

Further Reading

Alcoholics Anonymous. *Alcoholics Anonymous (The Big Book)*, 3rd Edition. New York: Alcoholics Anonymous World Services, 1976.

Brown, Sally, and Brown, David. *A Biography of Mrs. Marty Mann, The First Lady of Alcoholics Anonymous*. Center City, MN: Hazelden Foundation, 2001.

Marijuana The most commonly abused illicit drug in the United States, marijuana is sometimes categorized as a **hallucinogen** because delta-9-tetrahydrocannabinol (THC), its psychoactive ingredient, can produce altered sensations and perceptions at higher doses. It is also known for its ability to relax users, relieve pain or nausea, and aid sleep.

Marijuana has a long history of use around the world. Documentation shows it was consumed in China in 2737 B.C.E., and there is evidence showing use by other cultures for centuries before that. In the United States in the 1800s, it was a popular legal drug used for treating the pain of migraine headaches and for insomnia. One report states that until its use was prohibited in 1937, marijuana was 1 of the 3 most prescribed medicines in the United States, and when alcohol was prohibited in 1920, its use increased. Despite the lessons learned from the failures of **Prohibition**, the U.S. Temperance Movement and other groups succeeded in enacting laws prohibiting marijuana, and a 1936 propaganda movie, *Reefer Madness,* portraying marijuana as a drug that triggered psychotic behavior, supported that agenda. Early antimarijuana legislative measures included the Marijuana Tax Act of 1937 that levied taxes on its use. Decades later, the Comprehensive Drug Abuse Prevention and Control Act of 1970 classified marijuana as a Schedule I drug, and its importation, cultivation, possession, use, sale, and distribution is now illegal under federal law in the United States. Most states set the penalties for infractions, however, and these vary from nonexistent for a small amount being used "on the advice of a physician" to more severe sentences that include incarceration and fines.

Although criminalizing marijuana led to decreased consumption during the middle of the 1900s, use surged again during the Vietnam War when returning soldiers who began using the drug in Asia continued the practice in the United States. Its use has continued to expand. Despite eradicative efforts and increased enforcement of drug trafficking laws, marijuana production has grown dramatically on the domestic front, in Mexico, and especially in Canada where Asian groups are beginning to dominate high-potency marijuana wholesale distribution systems.

The average content of THC in marijuana was less than 1 percent in 1974; today it is 4 to 6 percent, and can be as high as 25 percent. Because many factors affect potency, the strength of street marijuana varies considerably. Most of the drug available today is 15 to 20 times more potent than what was used 40 years ago. This is one reason addictions experts are concerned about marijuana use; it is a different drug from the one that was outlawed during the early part of the 20th century.

Marijuana is usually harvested as a combination of dried leaves, stems, and seeds; a resinous product that can be scraped from the leaves is a more concentrated form called **hashish**; other extracts in the form of a sticky black liquid are known as hash oil. The dried marijuana is usually rolled in **cigarette** papers to form a joint, layered into a hollowed-out **cigar** and smoked as a blunt, or sprinkled into the bowl of a **pipe** or bong from which its smoke can be inhaled. It may also be brewed in a tea or baked into edibles like cookies or brownies, although its effects are not as great as those resulting from smoking the drug. It acts on the same dopamine reward pathway as other drugs of **abuse** and, like some of them, seems to affect each individual differently based in part on genetic heritage.

The use of marijuana, particularly for medical purposes, is the subject of ongoing and fierce debate. Many reputable medical authorities believe the drug has significant value in relieving pain and reducing the symptoms of certain diseases; they cite convincing evidence that a legal drug like alcohol has far more damaging effects than marijuana. They also suggest that much of the resistance against legalizing *Cannabis* products comes from the manufacturing industry, which is fearful that increased use of **hemp** might prove too competitive for their plastics, petroleum, and textile products. Others argue that marijuana, especially in a smokable form, has dangerous health consequences and that legalizing the drug will only increase its use among adolescents whose developing **brains** should not be exposed to psychoactive drugs. They also fear that marijuana is a **gateway drug** to more dangerous substances. In spite of this controversy, the Drug Enforcement Administration has approved, and affirms that it will continue to approve, ongoing research into the medicinal value of THC.

Depending on dosage, THC produces relaxation, hunger, enjoyment, dissociation from and relief of pain, heightened sensations, and altered perceptions. In higher doses, it can produce hallucinations and paranoia. Long-term smoking of the drug is often associated with respiratory problems. Other issues related to regular use over time include learning and memory impairments, infertility, depression, anxiety, and personality disturbances. Immediately after marijuana use, one study has shown a user's risk of heart attack more than quadruples, and the high levels of hydrocarbons in marijuana smoke have convinced many researchers that it may be more harmful to the lungs than smoking **tobacco**. Some studies have indicated that marijuana smoking significantly increases the risk of cancer of the head or neck, in some cases doubling or tripling the risk.

There is some debate about whether marijuana is truly addictive, but evidence shows that some people who use the drug—but by no means a majority—meet criteria that define **addiction**: They use the drug compulsively and they continue to do so despite negative consequences. Heavy users also exhibit signs of **withdrawal** including irritability, anxiety, and insomnia. According to some statistics, 10 percent of the 25 million Americans who use marijuana are addicted. Although there are currently no medications to treat marijuana addiction, researchers are studying drugs that might block THC from binding to cannabinoid receptors in the brain, thus preventing marijuana from producing its psychoactive effect.

Depending on its source, method of administration, or other factors, marijuana goes by a wide range of street names. Some include Aunt Mary, Boom, Bud, Dope, Gangster, Ganja, Grass, Grifa, Hemp, Herb, Hydro, Joint, Kif, Mary Jane, MJ, Mota, Pot, Reefer, Roach, Sinsemilla, Skunk, Smoke, Thai Sticks, Weed, Widow, and Yerba.

See also Appendix C.

Marijuana Facts

- The main active chemical in marijuana is THC (delta-9-tetrahydrocannabinol). The membranes of certain nerve cells in the brain contain protein receptors that bind to THC. Once securely in place, THC kicks off a series of cellular reactions that ultimately lead to the high that users experience when they smoke marijuana.
- Marijuana smoke contains 50 to 70 percent more carcinogenic hydrocarbons than tobacco smoke.
- Someone who smokes marijuana daily may be functioning at a reduced intellectual level all the time.
- Long-term marijuana abuse can lead to addiction for some people; a warning sign is if they abuse the drug compulsively even though it interferes with family, school, work, and recreational activities.
- An estimated 2.4 million Americans used marijuana for the first time in 2000. The annual number of new marijuana users has varied considerably since 1965 when there were an estimated 0.6 million new users. The number of new marijuana users reached a peak in 1976 and 1977 at around 3.2 million.

Between 1990 and 1996, the estimated number of new users increased from 1.4 million to 2.5 million and has remained at this level.

- As of 2000, marijuana was the most common illicit drug, used by 76 percent of illicit drug users. Approximately 59 percent consumed only marijuana, 17 percent used marijuana and another illicit drug, and the remaining 24 percent used an illicit drug but not marijuana in the past month.
- Marijuana users may have the same respiratory problems that tobacco smokers have, such as chronic cough and more frequent chest colds.
- Marijuana smoking affects the brain and leads to impaired short-term memory, perception, judgment, and motor skills.
- Marijuana has adverse effects on many of the skills required for driving a car. Driving while high can lead to car accidents. Users often have delayed responses to sights and sounds that drivers need to notice.
- Most teenagers do not use marijuana. Fewer than 1 in 4 high school seniors is a current marijuana user.
- Marijuana may play a role in car accidents. In one study, researchers found that, of 150 reckless drivers who were tested for drugs at an arrest scene, 33 percent tested positive for marijuana, and 12 percent tested positive for both marijuana and cocaine. Data have also shown that while smoking marijuana, people show the same lack of coordination on standard drunk driver tests as those who have had too much to drink.

Source: National Institute on Drug Abuse. http://www.nida.gov

FAQs about Marijuana

1. What is marijuana?

Marijuana is a green, brown, or gray mixture of dried, shredded leaves, stems, seeds, and flowers of the hemp plant. Street names include pot, herb, weed, grass, boom, Mary Jane, gangster, or chronic. Sinsemilla, hashish (hash), and hash oil are stronger forms of marijuana. All forms are mind-altering because they contain THC (delta-9-tetrahydrocannabinol), the main active ingredient. They also contain more than 400 other chemicals. Marijuana's effects on the user depend on its strength, which is related to the amount of THC it contains. The THC content of marijuana has been increasing since the 1970s.

2. How is marijuana used?

Marijuana is usually smoked as a cigarette (called a joint or a nail), or in a pipe, or a bong. It also appears in cigar wrappers called blunts, in which it is often combined with another drug, such as crack cocaine.

3. How long does marijuana stay in the user's body?

THC in marijuana is rapidly absorbed by fatty tissues in various organs. Generally, traces (metabolites) of THC can be detected by standard urine testing methods several days after a smoking session. However, traces can sometimes be detected in chronic heavy users for weeks after they have stopped using marijuana.

4. How many teens smoke marijuana?

Contrary to popular belief, most teenagers do not use marijuana. Among students surveyed in an annual national survey, only about one in six 10th graders report they are current marijuana users (i.e., used marijuana within the past month). Fewer than 1 in 4 high school seniors is a current marijuana user.

5. Why do young people use marijuana?

There are many reasons why some young people start smoking marijuana. Many smoke because they see their brothers, sisters, friends, or even older family members using it. Some use marijuana because of peer pressure. Others may think it's cool because they hear songs about it and see it on TV and in movies. Some teens may feel they need marijuana and other drugs to help them escape from problems at home, at school, or with friends.

6. What happens if you smoke marijuana?

The way the drug affects each person depends on many factors, including:
- the user's previous experience with the drug;
- how strong the marijuana is (how much THC it has);
- what the user expects to happen;
- where the drug is used;
- how it is administered; and
- whether the user is drinking alcohol or using other drugs.

Some people feel nothing when they smoke marijuana. Others may feel relaxed or high. Sometimes marijuana makes users feel thirsty and very hungry—a reaction often called "the munchies." Some users experience negative effects—sudden feelings of anxiety and paranoid thoughts. This is likely to happen when a more potent variety of marijuana is used.

7. What are the short-term effects of marijuana use?

The short-term effects of marijuana include:
- problems with memory and learning;
- distorted perception (sights, sounds, time, touch);
- trouble with thinking and problem-solving;
- loss of motor coordination; and
- increased heart rate.

These effects are even greater when other drugs are mixed with marijuana; this is dangerous because people may not always know what drugs they are ingesting.

8. Does marijuana affect school, sports, or other activities?

It can. Marijuana affects memory, judgment, and perception in school, in sports or clubs, or in social settings. Heavy use could cause you to lose interest in your appearance and school or work performance. Athletes could find their performance is off: timing, movements, and coordination are all affected by THC. Also, because marijuana can affect judgment and decision-making, its use can lead to risky sexual behavior, resulting in exposure to sexually transmitted diseases like HIV, the virus that causes AIDS.

9. What are the long-term effects of marijuana use?

Findings show that regular use of marijuana or THC may play a role in some kinds of cancer and in problems with the respiratory and immune systems.
- Cancer: Although it is not known whether regular marijuana use causes cancer, it contains some of the same cancer-causing chemicals found in tobacco smoke, in some cases in higher concentrations. Studies show that someone who smokes 5 joints per day may be taking in as many cancer-causing chemicals as someone who smokes a full pack of cigarettes every day.
- Lungs and airways: People who smoke marijuana often develop the same kinds of breathing problems that cigarette smokers have: coughing and wheezing.

They tend to have more chest colds than nonusers and are at greater risk of getting lung infections like pneumonia.

- Immune system: Animal studies have found that THC can damage the cells and tissues in the body that help protect against disease.
- Gum disease.

10. Does marijuana lead to the use of other drugs?

It could. Long-term studies of high school students and their patterns of drug use show that few young people use other illegal drugs without first trying marijuana. For example, the risk of using cocaine may be greater for those who have tried marijuana than for those who never have. Using marijuana puts children and teens in contact with people who are users and sellers of other drugs. Scientists are examining the possibility that long-term marijuana use may create changes in the brain that make a person more at risk of becoming addicted to other drugs, such as alcohol or cocaine.

11. How can you tell if someone has been using marijuana?

If someone is high on marijuana, he or she might:
- seem dizzy and have trouble walking;
- have very red, bloodshot eyes; and
- have a hard time remembering things that just happened.

When the early effects fade, over a few hours, the user can become very sleepy.

12. Can marijuana be used as a medicine?

THC, the active chemical in marijuana, is manufactured into a pill available by prescription that can be used to treat the nausea and vomiting that occur with certain cancer treatments and to help AIDS patients regain their appetite. According to scientists, more research needs to be done on THC's side effects and other potential medical uses. Under U.S. law, marijuana is a Schedule I controlled substance. This means that the drug, at least in its smoked form, has no commonly accepted medical use.

13. How does marijuana affect driving?

Marijuana has serious harmful effects on the skills required to drive safely: alertness, concentration, coordination, and reaction time. Marijuana use can make it difficult to judge distances and react to signals and sounds on the road.

14. If a woman is pregnant and smokes marijuana, will it hurt the baby?

Doctors advise pregnant women not to use any drugs because they could harm the growing fetus. Although one animal study has linked marijuana use to loss of the fetus early in pregnancy, 2 studies in humans found no association between marijuana use and early pregnancy loss. More research is necessary to understand fully the effects of marijuana use on pregnancy outcome. Studies in children born to mothers who used marijuana have shown increased behavioral problems during infancy and preschool years. In school, these children are more likely to have problems with decision-making, memory, and the ability to remain attentive. Since some parts of the brain continue to develop throughout adolescence, it is also possible that certain kinds of problems may appear as the child matures.

15. What does marijuana do to the brain?

Some studies show that long-term, regular users have impaired mental functions. Heavy use of marijuana affects parts of the brain that control memory, attention, and learning; these changes are similar to those caused by cocaine, heroin, and alcohol.

16. Can people become addicted to marijuana?

    Yes. Long-term marijuana use can lead to addiction. According to one study, marijuana use by teenagers who have prior antisocial problems can quickly lead to addiction. Some frequent heavy marijuana users develop tolerance to its effects, so they need larger amounts of marijuana to get the same effect.

17. What if a person wants to quit using the drug?

    Researchers are testing different ways to help marijuana users abstain from use. There are currently no medications for treating marijuana addiction. Treatment programs focus on counseling and a number of programs are designed especially to help teenagers who are abusers. Family doctors can be a good source for information and can help in dealing with adolescent marijuana problems.

Source: National Institute on Drug Abuse. http://www.nida.gov

Further Reading

Califano, Joseph A., Jr. *High Society: How Substance Abuse Ravages America and What to Do About It.* New York: Perseus Books, 2007.

Hoffman, John, and Froemke, Susan, eds. *Addiction: Why Can't They Just Stop?* New York: Rodale, 2007.

Home Box Office (HBO). In partnership with the Robert Wood Johnson Foundation, the National Institute on Drug Abuse, and the National Institute on Alcohol Abuse and Alcoholism. *Addiction: Why Can't They Just Stop?* Documentary. March 2007.

Ketcham, Katherine, and Pace, Nicholas A. *Teens Under the Influence: The Truth About Kids, Alcohol, and Other Drugs.* New York: Ballantine Books, 2003.

U.S. Department of Health and Human Services, National Institute on Drug Abuse (NIDA), June 2007. Retrieved from http://www.nida.gov

U.S. Department of Health and Human Services, National Institute on Drug Abuse. *Research Report Series: Hallucinogens and Dissociative Drugs.* NIH Publication No. 01-4209, March 2001.

U.S. Department of Health and Human Services, Substance Abuse and Mental Health Services Administration (SAMHSA), August 2007. Retrieved from http://www.samhsa.gov

U.S. Department of Justice, Drug Enforcement Administration (DEA), March 2008. Retrieved from http://www.usdoj.gov/dea

Marijuana Laws. *See* Appendix C.

Marinol. *See* Medical Marijuana.

Mazanor. *See* Stimulants.

Mazindol. *See* Stimulants.

MDMA. *See* Ecstasy.

Medical Marijuana Although U.S. federal law prohibits the use of **marijuana** for any reason, law enforcement has recognized that the active ingredient in marijuana, delta-9-tetrahydrocannabinol (THC), has significant value in relieving pain and reducing the symptoms of certain diseases. Among other things, it can alleviate the nausea and vomiting of cancer chemotherapy, ease the spasticity associated with multiple sclerosis, and is said to relieve the intraocular pressure caused by glaucoma. Citing the dangers of smoking—the usual method of marijuana administration—and the presence of potentially harmful additives and other compounds in marijuana, the federal government has refused to permit the use of marijuana for these purposes, but drugs containing a synthetic form of THC have been approved.

The first of these, marketed under the trade name Marinol, binds to the brain's cannabinoid receptors to produce its pain relieving and antinausea effects. It can also stimulate the appetite of AIDS patients or others suffering from weight-loss diseases. Although many attest to Marinol's efficacy, others claim that it does not produce the same pain relief or alleviation of symptoms that marijuana does, and that its negative side effects cause many patients to prefer THC in its natural form. Marinol's side effects can include rapid heartbeat, dizziness, confusion, and gastrointestinal distress.

With the view that preventing ill people from receiving medication that can help them is unnecessarily cruel, several states have decriminalized possession and use of marijuana in its natural form for medical purposes and sought to make it available through state-supported channels. These include Alaska, California, Colorado, Maine, Montana, Nevada, Oregon, Vermont, and Washington as well as the District of Columbia. Nevertheless, federal law can override state laws, and, although research into the benefits and uses of marijuana in medical applications can proceed in FDA-approved research studies, pharmaceuticals with synthetic THC are the only legal means of treating illnesses responsive to the drug. Since the introduction of Marinol, other synthetic and partially synthetic cannabinoids that have been developed include Cesamet and Sativex. Acomplia is a cannabinoid **antagonist** that is used in treating obesity and helps with smoking cessation.

Further Reading

Califano, Joseph A., Jr. *High Society: How Substance Abuse Ravages America and What to Do About It.* New York: Perseus Books, 2007.

Hoffman, John, and Froemke, Susan, eds. *Addiction: Why Can't They Just Stop?* New York: Rodale, 2007.

Home Box Office (HBO). In partnership with the Robert Wood Johnson Foundation, the National Institute on Drug Abuse, and the National Institute on Alcohol Abuse and Alcoholism. *Addiction: Why Can't They Just Stop?* Documentary. March 2007.

Ketcham, Katherine, and Pace, Nicholas A. *Teens Under the Influence: The Truth About Kids, Alcohol, and Other Drugs.* New York: Ballantine Books, 2003.

U.S. Department of Health and Human Services, National Institute on Drug Abuse (NIDA), June 2007. Retrieved from http://www.nida.gov

U.S. Department of Health and Human Services, Substance Abuse and Mental Health Services Administration (SAMHSA), August 2007. Retrieved from http://www.samhsa.gov

U.S. Department of Justice, Drug Enforcement Administration (DEA), March 2008. Retrieved from http://www.usdoj.gov/dea

Mental Disorders The American Psychiatric Association's ***Diagnostic and Statistical Manual of Mental Disorders*** (***DSM***) defines a mental disorder as a group of behavioral or psychological symptoms that cause distress, disability, or an increased risk of suffering, pain, disability, death, or the loss of freedom. This is of necessity a broad definition because many disorders are manifested in behaviors that appear, on the surface, to be voluntary, harmless, and pleasurable, particularly if they do not directly affect others. A victimless sexual paraphilia such as fantasizing is an example, and for this reason there has been some discussion among mental health professionals about excluding some of the paraphilias from the forthcoming edition of the *DSM* due to be published in 2011 or early in 2012. However, by influencing the afflicted person's attitudes, personality, and relationships with others, most mental disorders do have a negative, although perhaps indirect, effect on others. They are frequently associated with drug abuse or may mimic or worsen some of the symptoms of impulse control disorders, the behavioral addictions.

Prevalence of Various Disorders

The most prevalent lifetime mental disorders are anxiety disorders (29 percent), mood disorders (21 percent), impulse control disorders (25 percent), and substance use disorders (15 percent).

Source: National Institute of Mental Health. http://www.nimh.nih.gov/health/statistics/ncsr-study/questions-and-answers-about-the-national-comorbidity-survey-replication-ncsr-study.shtml

---

Warning Signs of Teen Mental Health Problems

Some of the following signs point to potential mental health problems. Teens suffering from any of these symptoms are advised to discuss them with a parent, teacher, or mental health counselor.

If you are troubled by feeling:

- very angry most of the time, and you cry frequently or overreact to things;
- worthless or guilty much of the time;
- anxious or worried more than other young people;
- grief for a long time after a loss or death;
- extremely fearful—you have unexplained fears or more fears than most of your friends;
- constantly concerned about physical problems or appearance;
- frightened that your mind is controlled or is out of control.

You experience big changes, for example:

- do much worse in school;
- lose interest in things you used to enjoy;
- have unexplained changes in sleeping or eating habits;
- avoid friends or family and want to be alone all the time;
- daydream too much and can't get things done;
- feel life is too hard to handle or you think about suicide;
- hear voices that cannot be explained.

You are limited by:

- poor concentration; you can't make decisions;
- an inability to sit still or focus attention;
- worry about being harmed, hurting others, or about doing something bad;

- anxiety that prevents you from participating in normal activities that your friends engage in without undue difficulty;
- the need to wash, clean things, or perform certain routines dozens of times a day;
- thoughts that race almost too fast to follow;
- persistent nightmares.

You behave in ways that cause problems, for example:

- use alcohol or other drugs;
- eat large amounts of food and then force yourself to vomit, abuse laxatives, or take enemas to avoid weight gain;
- continue to diet or exercise obsessively although you are already very thin;
- often hurt other people, destroy property, or break the law;
- do things that can be life threatening.

Source: Adapted from U.S. DHHS Substance Abuse and Mental Health Services Administration. http://mentalhealth.samhsa.gov/publications/allpubs/Ca-0023/default.asp

See also Dual Diagnosis.

Mepergan. *See* Meperidine.

Meperidine A synthetic **opiate**, meperidine is commercially known by the brand names Demerol and Mepergan and was originally introduced as a pain reliever in the 1930s. As an opiate, its effects are similar to those of **morphine**, and it is listed on Schedule II of the Controlled Substances Act.

Because it is a synthetic drug, several analogs—drugs that are similar in structure or function—have also been produced in the laboratory. One of these is 1-methyl-4-proprionoxypiperidine, MPPP; another similar drug—1-methyl-4- phenyl-1,2,3,6, tetrahydropyridine or MPTP—proved after synthesizing to be a powerful neurotoxin that kills the same neurons in the **brain** area affected by Parkinson's disease. When addicts abuse this drug, they develop irreversible Parkinson-like symptoms that included tremor, freezing immobility, and difficulty moving. This is an example of the unexpected and tragic damage that can occur when psychoactive drugs are formulated in clandestine labs with no regulatory control or scientific oversight.

Further Reading

Califano, Joseph A., Jr. *High Society: How Substance Abuse Ravages America and What to Do About It.* New York: Perseus Books, 2007.

Hoffman, John, and Froemke, Susan, eds. *Addiction: Why Can't They Just Stop?* New York: Rodale, 2007.

Home Box Office (HBO). In partnership with the Robert Wood Johnson Foundation, the National Institute on Drug Abuse, and the National Institute on Alcohol Abuse and Alcoholism. *Addiction: Why Can't They Just Stop?* Documentary. March 2007.

Ketcham, Katherine, and Pace, Nicholas A. *Teens Under the Influence: The Truth About Kids, Alcohol, and Other Drugs.* New York: Ballantine Books, 2003.

U.S. Department of Health and Human Services, National Institute on Drug Abuse (NIDA), June 2007. Retrieved from http://www.nida.gov

U.S. Department of Health and Human Services, Substance Abuse and Mental Health Services Administration (SAMHSA), August 2007. Retrieved from http://www.samhsa.gov

U.S. Department of Justice, Drug Enforcement Administration (DEA), March 2008. Retrieved from http://www.usdoj.gov/dea

Meprobamate A central nervous system **depressant**, meprobamate is an antianxiety drug first introduced in the middle of the 20th century. Although its effects are much like those of the **barbiturates**, it is associated with lower levels of toxicity and sedation. Popularly regarded as a type of tranquilizer in the 1950s, it was marketed under such names as Miltown and Equanil. A Schedule IV drug under the **Controlled Substances Act (CSA)**, meprobamate is not as addicting as other barbiturates, although excessive use can produce physical **dependence**. Carisoprodol, marketed as Soma as a muscle relaxant, is not on the CSA's schedule, but its metabolism in the body produces meprobamate and is sometimes regarded as a drug of **abuse**.

Further Reading

Califano, Joseph A., Jr. *High Society: How Substance Abuse Ravages America and What to Do About It.* New York: Perseus Books, 2007.

Hoffman, John, and Froemke, Susan, eds. *Addiction: Why Can't They Just Stop?* New York: Rodale, 2007.

Home Box Office (HBO). In partnership with the Robert Wood Johnson Foundation, the National Institute on Drug Abuse, and the National Institute on Alcohol Abuse and Alcoholism. *Addiction: Why Can't They Just Stop?* Documentary. March 2007.

Ketcham, Katherine, and Pace, Nicholas A. *Teens Under the Influence: The Truth About Kids, Alcohol, and Other Drugs.* New York: Ballantine Books, 2003.

U.S. Department of Health and Human Services, National Institute on Drug Abuse (NIDA), June 2007. Retrieved from http://www.nida.gov

U.S. Department of Health and Human Services, Substance Abuse and Mental Health Services Administration (SAMHSA), August 2007. Retrieved from http://www.samhsa.gov

U.S. Department of Justice, Drug Enforcement Administration (DEA), March 2008. Retrieved from http://www.usdoj.gov/dea

Mescaline One of the oldest psychedelics known, mescaline (3, 4, 5-trimethoxyphenethylamine) is a powerful drug found in peyote and other varieties of small cacti. Mescaline has traditionally been featured in Native American religious and ceremonial rites, and it became widely known as a recreational **hallucinogen** in the 1950s and 1960s. Peyote buttons removed from the plant's crown are dried and eaten, or soaked in water to produce a liquid that can be mixed with beverages or injected. Like LSD, mescaline is not addicting in the usual sense, but chronic or prolonged use can result in cognitive disruption and permanent **mental disorders**. Users may also develop a cross-tolerance to other hallucinogens.

A Schedule I substance under the **Controlled Substances Act**, mescaline is not as potent as LSD but the trips it produces can be positive or negative depending on dosage. The drug's effects include a distorted sense of time and place, restlessness, **flashbacks**, vivid and sometimes terrifying hallucinations, disorganized thoughts, and potentially psychotic behaviors.

Mescaline can be produced synthetically, with the result that a number of variations on the chemical formula of the natural substance have entered the market masquerading as

Ecstasy. These include 4-methyl-2,5-dimethoxyamphetamine (DOM), 4-bromo-2,5-dimethoxyamphetamine (DOB), 4-bromo-2,5-dimethoxyphenethylamine (2C-B or Nexus), para-methoxyamphetamine (PMA,) and para-methoxymethamphetamine (PMMA). PMA, which first appeared on the illicit market briefly in the early 1970s, is associated with a number of deaths in both the United States and Europe.

Street names for mescaline and peyote include Big Chief, Buttons, Cactus, and Mes.

Further Reading

Califano, Joseph A., Jr. *High Society: How Substance Abuse Ravages America and What to Do About It.* New York: Perseus Books, 2007.

Hoffman, John, and Froemke, Susan, eds. *Addiction: Why Can't They Just Stop?* New York: Rodale, 2007.

Home Box Office (HBO). In partnership with the Robert Wood Johnson Foundation, the National Institute on Drug Abuse, and the National Institute on Alcohol Abuse and Alcoholism. *Addiction: Why Can't They Just Stop?* Documentary. March 2007.

U.S. Department of Health and Human Services, National Institute on Drug Abuse (NIDA), June 2007. Retrieved from http://www.nida.gov

U.S. Department of Health and Human Services, Substance Abuse and Mental Health Services Administration (SAMHSA), August 2007. Retrieved from http://www.samhsa.gov

U.S. Department of Justice, Drug Enforcement Administration (DEA), March 2008. Retrieved from http://www.usdoj.gov/dea

Mesolimbic Dopamine System Part of the limbic system is the mesolimbic dopamine system, which houses the reward pathway that is responsible for the pleasurable emotions that drugs and other natural stimuli such as food or sex produce. The pathway extends from the **ventral tegmental area** to the nucleus accumbens and into the prefrontal cortex, serving as a route for **neurotransmitters** like dopamine to travel across synapses to deliver feel-good messages. Other structures important to the mesolimbic dopamine system include the amygdala, which helps transmit fear and other emotions associated with psychic arousal to the prefrontal cortex; the hippocampus, which, among other functions, helps convert information coming into the **brain** into memory; and the locus ceruleus, which synthesizes norepinephrine that helps trigger fight or flight responses in the amygdala.

See also Brain and Addiction.

Metadate. *See* Methylphenidate.

Methadone For more than 50 years, methadone, a synthetic narcotic first developed to address a **morphine** shortage during World War II, has been shown to be an effective **treatment** for people addicted to opiates, particularly **heroin**, by binding to the brain's opioid receptors. First introduced into the United States in 1947 as a pain reliever, methadone today is primarily associated with addictions treatment. It is a Schedule II drug in oral, tablet, or injectable formulations under the **Controlled Substances Act**.

Methadone can produce a physical dependence, but since it does not provide the euphoric rush of other opiates, people treated with the drug do not engage in the uncontrolled and compulsive drug-seeking behaviors associated with opiate **addiction**. When methadone is administered daily under carefully controlled conditions, it does not impair emotional, cognitive, or motor functioning, so addicts can engage in normal activities such as attending school, driving a car, or keeping a job. By suppressing **cravings** and eliminating **withdrawal** symptoms, more stabilized addicts are thus able to change their behavior and transform their lifestyle in ways that will sustain **recovery**.

For decades, federal regulations and state laws have governed the clinics and hospitals that manage methadone programs, which currently treat 150,000 to 200,000 estimated heroin addicts, but in 1999 proposals were made to give individual physicians greater latitude in prescribing methadone. This could help make the treatment more accessible to an estimated half a million additional heroin addicts, although the Drug Enforcement Administration would continue to oversee the drug's distribution.

Like any other opiate, methadone can cause health problems if it is abused, but under medical supervision it is considered a safe drug, especially in view of the alternative. At proper dosages, it can produce minor symptoms like drowsiness, excessive sweating, and constipation, but these symptoms usually subside as the body adjusts to the drug.

In terms of the cost, statistics show that methadone maintenance programs, at about $13 per addict per day, produce significant savings over incarceration or other control measures. Additional economies are realized by preventing the spread of diseases like HIV, AIDS, tuberculosis, and hepatitis through the use of infected needles.

Further Reading

Califano, Joseph A., Jr. *High Society: How Substance Abuse Ravages America and What to Do About It.* New York: Perseus Books, 2007.

Hoffman, John, and Froemke, Susan, eds. *Addiction: Why Can't They Just Stop?* New York: Rodale, 2007.

Home Box Office (HBO). In partnership with the Robert Wood Johnson Foundation, the National Institute on Drug Abuse, and the National Institute on Alcohol Abuse and Alcoholism. *Addiction: Why Can't They Just Stop?* Documentary. March 2007.

Ketcham, Katherine, and Pace, Nicholas A. *Teens Under the Influence: The Truth About Kids, Alcohol, and Other Drugs.* New York: Ballantine Books, 2003.

U.S. Department of Health and Human Services, National Institute on Drug Abuse (NIDA), June 2007. Retrieved from http://www.nida.gov

U.S. Department of Health and Human Services, Substance Abuse and Mental Health Services Administration (SAMHSA), August 2007. Retrieved from http://www.samhsa.gov

U.S. Department of Justice, Drug Enforcement Administration (DEA), March 2008. Retrieved from http://www.usdoj.gov/dea

Methamphetamine Methamphetamine belongs to the phenethylamine family, a class of **stimulant** and hallucinogenic chemicals. It is a powerfully addicting drug that has brought devastation and heartbreak to many U.S. communities and other areas of the world. Next to alcohol and marijuana, it is the most frequently abused drug in the western United States, but it is rapidly moving east as increasing numbers of drug trafficking organizations open up new smuggling routes.

Synthesized in laboratories, methamphetamine was diverted from pharmaceutical purposes in the 1960s and 1970s to make the rounds of college campuses as a recreational drug, which is any legal or illegal psychoactive drug that is used for recreational purposes. It was popular because it increased alertness, social extroversion, and concentration. However, its highly addictive qualities frightened off many users, and when the Drug Enforcement Administration placed it on Schedule II under the **Controlled Substances Act**, its use as a recreational drug dropped. It continued to be prescribed for certain conditions—such as the sleep disorder narcolepsy—and resurged again as a recreational drug in the 1980s as home-grown labs began manufacturing the drug cheaply with easily obtained ingredients. In an effort to reduce the number of clandestine labs synthesizing the drug, federal legislation was enacted to restrict the accessibility and sale of the precursor chemicals that go into its production. These chemicals include ephedrine and pseudoephedrine, the active ingredient in many decongestants and cold medications. Tighter controls on access to these ingredients appears to have driven methamphetamine production into Mexico where larger organized groups of criminal drug traffickers are developing sophisticated manufacturing and smuggling operations.

Unlike other stimulants such as cocaine, methamphetamine produces a long-lasting high. After the immediate and profuse outpouring of dopamine that is produced by an initial dose of the illegal stimulant, the neurotransmitter remains active because methamphetamine also inhibits its reabsorption back into the neurons. This extended effect accounts for some of the popularity of the drug, but it is also one of the reasons it is so destructive. Extremely high levels of dopamine have been shown to damage the dopamine cells themselves and lead to symptoms similar to those seen in Parkinson's disease. If the user is able to achieve long-term abstinence, some of these symptoms may be reversed, but in most cases they are permanent.

The drug is available in several forms. "Crystal" or "ice" is a powerfully addicting form that can be diluted and injected, or rocks can be smoked to achieve a more intense rush. A Thai version of meth called "ya ba" (or "yaba") is sold in a pill form that can be ingested or crushed and snorted. Taking the drug orally results in a less intense but more sustained reaction that lasts for several hours. In small amounts, meth produces wakefulness, gregariousness, heightened physical activity, and sense of well-being, but the drug is so addicting that users quickly develop a chemical and psychological dependence and rapidly escalate use. As the high dissipates and the inevitable crash begins, users dose again and again to avoid the depression and anxiety associated with coming down off a high. This sets up a cycle of binge and crash that in some cases will continue for several days, during which the user does not eat or sleep. Such an episode is referred to as a run and may result in tweaking, a meth-induced psychosis that is characterized by auditory and visual hallucinations, extreme anxiety, irritability, paranoia, and a capacity for sudden violence. So severe are the symptoms that law enforcement personnel who must approach people they suspect of tweaking are advised to do so with extreme caution and with backup personnel. Over half of all meth users are said to tweak.

Chronic long-term use of methamphetamine can be more ruinous than alcoholism or an **addiction** to opiates. Aside from hallucinations, paranoia, obsessive picking of the skin, bizarre or violent behavior, and potentially irreversible damage to the brain's neurons that chronic methamphetamine use causes, its detrimental impact on others can be devastating. Methamphetamine addicts neglect their responsibilities, jobs, even their children, for days at a time, in effect abandoning them. They are likely to engage in risky sexual behavior, share dirty needles, and participate in other dangerous activities. The drug's effects on cardiac rhythm and blood pressure can lead to heart attacks and stroke. Although **withdrawal** from methamphetamines does not produce noticeable physical symptoms, the craving for the drug and the psychological crash are intense, and unseen but persistent changes in the brain are profound. Because of these lingering effects, many therapists believe that a standard inpatient 4-week rehabilitation period might not be long enough. They suggest that it could take a good deal longer before meth addicts are psychologically prepared for outpatient treatment.

There are, to date, no medications available to treat addiction to methamphetamines. Although it is particularly difficult to recover from a meth addiction, carefully tailored behavioral therapy, positive reinforcement, and drug testing to ensure and maintain compliance can be successful. The National Institute on Drug Abuse is actively pursuing research based on an immunization strategy for methamphetamine overdose.

Statistics show that almost 5 percent of the population over 12-years old has tried methamphetamine at least once, and that most users are Caucasians in their 20s and 30s with a high school education or better. They are almost equally divided by gender with a broad variety of occupations. Fortunately, use among high school students has declined since 2001, but the World Health Organization estimates that there are 35 million methamphetamine users worldwide, compared to 15 million cocaine and 7 million heroin users. In the United States, meth addiction is at epidemic levels in many states, and drug enforcement officials, in virtual panic over its rapid spread into other areas of the country, say it is the number one drug problem. Some localities claim that 100 percent of the crime in their areas is directly related to methamphetamine.

Methamphetamine addicts are very likely to relapse a few times because of the drug's high addictive liability and the intense psychological craving users suffer during withdrawal. The matrix model, a cognitive behavioral technique using family therapy, positive reinforcement, and behavioral conditioning, has shown some promise in this area. In part, the therapy teaches recovering addicts to avoid drug cues and to learn to channel their habitual reaction to negative feelings like anger or disappointment into a more positive direction. In time, this builds new and healthier patterns of behavior. Rewards for clean urine tests in the form of tangible goods like cash seem helpful in keeping addicts abstinent. Because the dopamine system of a meth addict is depleted, treatment with the Parkinson's disease medication levodopa (L-dopa) has also shown some benefit, although its effects diminish over time.

The enormous costs to society that meth addiction imposes are also environmental; every pound of methamphetamine that is manufactured produces about 6 pounds of toxic waste that is usually dumped into fields and streams across the United States and finds its way into the food and water supply.

Street names for methamphetamine include Bikers Coffee, Black Beauties, Chalk, Chicken Feed, Crank, Crystal, Crystal (or Krystal) Meth, Gak, Glass, Go-Fast, Ice, Lith, Methlies Quick, Poor Man's Cocaine, Shabu, Speed, Stove Top, Tina, Tweak, Uppers, Yaba, and Yellow Bam.

Further Reading

Califano, Joseph A., Jr. *High Society: How Substance Abuse Ravages America and What to Do About It.* New York: Perseus Books, 2007.

Hoffman, John, and Froemke, Susan, eds. *Addiction: Why Can't They Just Stop?* New York: Rodale, 2007.

Home Box Office (HBO). In partnership with the Robert Wood Johnson Foundation, the National Institute on Drug Abuse, and the National Institute on Alcohol Abuse and Alcoholism. *Addiction: Why Can't They Just Stop?* Documentary. March 2007.

Sheff, David. *Beautiful Boy: A Father's Journey Through His Son's Addiction.* Boston: Houghton Mifflin, 2008.

Sheff, Nicholas. *Tweak: Growing Up on Amphetamines.* New York: Atheneum Books, 2007.

U.S. Department of Health and Human Services, National Institute on Drug Abuse (NIDA), June 2007. Retrieved from http://www.nida.gov

U.S. Department of Health and Human Services, National Institute on Drug Abuse. *Research Report Series: Methamphetamine Abuse and Addiction.* NIH Publication No. 06-4210, September 2006.

U.S. Department of Health and Human Services, Substance Abuse and Mental Health Services Administration (SAMHSA), August 2007. Retrieved from http://www.samhsa.gov

U.S. Department of Justice, Drug Enforcement Administration (DEA), March 2008. Retrieved from http://www.usdoj.gov/dea

Methaqualone. *See* Depressants.

Methcathinone A derivative of **khat**, a **stimulant** that is popularly known as Cat, methcathinone is similar to **methamphetamine** manufactured in clandestine labs. It is addictive and is usually snorted, although it can be diluted in water and injected. In other countries, it may be available in gel form.

A Schedule I drug under the **Controlled Substances Act**, methcathinone is not difficult to synthesize. Although once used as an antidepressant in the former Soviet Union because it can act as a serotonin reuptake inhibitor, it is currently considered a recreational drug in most parts of the world and routinely marketed for this purpose.

Like methamphetamine, methcathinone synthesis requires **ephedrine**; in efforts to control its manufacture, federal laws have been passed in recent years to monitor and regulate the access and sale of ephedrine to the public.

Other street names include Bathtub Speed, Kitty, Meth's Cat, Meth's Kitten, and Wannabe-Speed.

Further Reading

Califano, Joseph A., Jr. *High Society: How Substance Abuse Ravages America and What to Do About It.* New York: Perseus Books, 2007.

Hoffman, John, and Froemke, Susan, eds. *Addiction: Why Can't They Just Stop?* New York: Rodale, 2007.

Home Box Office (HBO). In partnership with the Robert Wood Johnson Foundation, the National Institute on Drug Abuse, and the National Institute on Alcohol Abuse and Alcoholism. *Addiction: Why Can't They Just Stop?* Documentary. March 2007.

Ketcham, Katherine, and Pace, Nicholas A. *Teens Under the Influence: The Truth About Kids, Alcohol, and Other Drugs.* New York: Ballantine Books, 2003.

U.S. Department of Health and Human Services, National Institute on Drug Abuse (NIDA), June 2007. Retrieved from http://www.nida.gov

U.S. Department of Health and Human Services, Substance Abuse and Mental Health Services Administration (SAMHSA), August 2007. Retrieved from http://www.samhsa.gov

U.S. Department of Justice, Drug Enforcement Administration (DEA), March 2008. Retrieved from http://www.usdoj.gov/dea

Methylphenidate Methylphenidate is a **stimulant** used in several pharmaceuticals prescribed to treat attention-deficit hyperactivity disorder (ADHD) including Ritalin, Concerta, and Metadate. Like other drugs used to treat ADHD, it seems to have a calming and focusing effect on children despite its categorization as a stimulant. It may also be used to treat narcolepsy, a sleep disorder.

Although methylphenidate is not as strong as **amphetamines**, stimulants that are frequently abused, it raises dopamine levels in the **brain** to such a degree that it has been adopted as a recreational drug. Using the medication at proper dosages for ADHD does not lead to **chemical dependence**, but those who abuse the drug crush and snort the pills to produce a quick rush similar to that of cocaine, and these users are highly susceptible to addiction. Another method of administration, dissolving the tablets and injecting the mixture, propels insoluble fillers into the bloodstream that can result in damage to the cardiovascular system, lungs, and eyes. The drug also can trigger the same kind of bingeing and psychotic episodes that abuse of other stimulants produces. The Drug Enforcement Administration has placed methylphenidate on Schedule II of the Controlled Substances Act, but authorities are very concerned that adolescents and others have easy access to the substance through friends taking prescription forms of the drug.

See also Drug Administration.

Further Reading

Califano, Joseph A., Jr. *High Society: How Substance Abuse Ravages America and What to Do About It.* New York: Perseus Books, 2007.

Hoffman, John, and Froemke, Susan, eds. *Addiction: Why Can't They Just Stop?* New York: Rodale, 2007.

Home Box Office (HBO). In partnership with the Robert Wood Johnson Foundation, the National Institute on Drug Abuse, and the National Institute on Alcohol Abuse and Alcoholism. *Addiction: Why Can't They Just Stop?* Documentary. March 2007.

Ketcham, Katherine, and Pace, Nicholas A. *Teens Under the Influence: The Truth About Kids, Alcohol, and Other Drugs.* New York: Ballantine Books, 2003.

U.S. Department of Health and Human Services, National Institute on Drug Abuse (NIDA), June 2007. Retrieved from http://www.nida.gov

U.S. Department of Health and Human Services, Substance Abuse and Mental Health Services Administration (SAMHSA), August 2007. Retrieved from http://www.samhsa.gov

U.S. Department of Justice, Drug Enforcement Administration (DEA), March 2008. Retrieved from http://www.usdoj.gov/dea

Miltown. *See* Meprobamate.

Mini Cigars Mini cigars or miniatures are relatively new terms collectively given to the small, cigar-like products formerly known as cigarillos or little **cigars**. Although many view cigarillos and little cigars as the same product, some purists make distinctions. Little cigars are often filtered and marketed in packs of 20 and frequently advertised as alternatives to **cigarettes**. Cigarillos are more likely to be manufactured without a filter and packaged in tins or 5-pack packages. Both products resemble brown cigarettes, but they are technically considered to be cigars because their outer wrappers are made of **tobacco** leaves.

These products have become alarmingly popular among young people. Filtered and unfiltered, they are flavored to appeal to a wide range of tastes, and may be inhaled or not depending on the user's preference. They are stronger than cigarettes, contain many more additives, and are highly addictive, thus proving to be even more harmful than cigarettes despite the widespread misconception that they are safer. A little cigar or cigarillo generally contains about 3 times the tobacco in a cigarette and is slightly smaller. Many times little cigars are used as blunts—the tobacco is removed and replaced with **marijuana**.

Two groups within the U.S. Department of Health and Human Services—the Centers for Disease Control and Prevention and the Substance Abuse and Mental Health Services Administration—report the following statistics. Although this information applies to regular cigars, much of the data could be extrapolated to apply to mini cigars as well.

- Regular cigar smoking is associated with an increased risk for cancers of the lung, oral cavity, larynx, and esophagus.
- Heavy cigar smokers and those who inhale deeply may be at increased risk for developing coronary heart disease and chronic obstructive pulmonary disease.
- In 2005, an estimated 5.6 percent, or 13.6 million Americans, 12 years of age or older were current cigar users.
- An estimated 6.9 percent of African American, 6.0 percent of white, 4.6 percent of Hispanic, 10.9 percent of American Indian/Alaska Native, and 1.8 percent of Asian-American adults are current cigar smokers.
- An estimated 14 percent of students in grades 9 to 12 in the United States are current cigar smokers. Cigar smoking is more common among males (19.2 percent) than females (8.7 percent) in these grades.
- An estimated 5.3 percent of middle school students in the United States are current cigar smokers. Estimates are higher for middle school boys (6.7 percent) than girls (3.8 percent).
- Marketing efforts have promoted cigars as symbols of a luxuriant and successful lifestyle. Endorsements by celebrities, development of cigar-friendly magazines featuring very attractive women smoking cigars, and product placement in movies have contributed to the increased visibility of cigar smoking in society.
- Since 2001, cigar packaging and advertisements have been required to display one of the following 5 health warning labels on a rotating basis.
  - SURGEON GENERAL WARNING: Cigar Smoking Can Cause Cancers Of The Mouth And Throat, Even If You Do Not Inhale.
  - SURGEON GENERAL WARNING: Cigar Smoking Can Cause Lung Cancer And Heart Disease.
  - SURGEON GENERAL WARNING: Tobacco Use Increases The Risk Of Infertility, Stillbirth And Low Birth Weight.
  - SURGEON GENERAL WARNING: Cigars Are Not A Safe Alternative To Cigarettes.
  - SURGEON GENERAL WARNING: Tobacco Smoke Increases The Risk Of Lung Cancer And Heart Disease, Even In Nonsmokers.

Although mini cigars meet the Federal Trade Commission's definition of a cigar—as a roll of tobacco that is wrapped in leaf tobacco or in a substance that contains tobacco—there is considerable pressure from federal and state tax agencies to classify mini cigars as cigarettes, which generate far greater tax revenues. Health advocacy organizations such as the American Lung Association and the American Heart Association also support this move, not only to subject cigars to greater regulatory control but also to raise their cost to children and adolescents who would be less likely to purchase the more expensive product.

See also Nicotine.

Further Reading

Califano, Joseph A., Jr. *High Society: How Substance Abuse Ravages America and What to Do About It.* New York: Perseus Books, 2007.

Delnevo, C.D., Foulds, Jonathan, and Hrywna, Mary. Trading Tobacco: Are Youths Choosing Cigars over Cigarettes? *American Journal of Public Health* 2005: 95, 2123.

Federal Trade Commission. October 2007. Retrieved from http://www.ftc.gov/opa/2007/04/cigaretterpt.shtm

U.S. Department of Health and Human Services. *Nicotine Addiction: A Report of the Surgeon General.* Centers for Disease Control and Prevention, Public Health Service, Center for Health Promotion and Education, Office on Smoking and Health, 1988.

U.S. Department of Health and Human Services. *Targeting Tobacco Use: The Nation's Leading Cause of Death.* Centers for Disease Control and Prevention, 2003.

U.S. Department of Health and Human Services. *The Health Consequences of Smoking: A Report of the Surgeon General.* Centers for Disease Control and Prevention, National Center for Chronic Disease Prevention and Health Promotion, Office on Smoking and Health, 2004.

U.S. Department of Health and Human Services. *Results from the 2006 National Survey on Drug Use and Health: National Findings.* Substance Abuse and Mental Health Services Administration (SAMHSA), Office of Applied Studies. DHHS Publication No. SMA 07-4293, 2007.

U.S. Department of Health and Human Services, Centers for Disease Control and Prevention (CDC), January 2008. Retrieved from http://apps.nccd.cdc.gov/osh_faq

U.S. Department of Health and Human Services, Centers for Disease Control and Prevention (CDC), November 2007. Retrieved from http://www.cdc.gov/tobacco

U.S. Department of Health and Human Services, National Cancer Institute (NCI), December 2007. Retrieved from http://www.cancer.gov/cancertopics/tobacco

U.S. Department of Health and Human Services, National Institute on Drug Abuse. *Research Report Series: Tobacco Addiction.* NIH Publication No. 06-4342, July 2006.

Miniatures. *See* Mini Cigars.

Minnesota Model Developed during the late 1940s and 1950s by therapists at a Minnesota state hospital, the Minnesota model is an addiction treatment method based on the principles of **Alcoholics Anonymous (AA).** It is a multidisciplinary approach that brings professionals and nonprofessionals into the **treatment** program to educate patients about the disease and offer intensive counseling, group therapy, and guidance in lifestyle and behavioral issues. In the 1950s, the model was adopted by the Hazelden Foundation, a prestigious **addiction** treatment facility, and it has since become a treatment standard worldwide.

Originally structured as a 28-day inpatient treatment program that required follow-up membership in AA or other **12-step programs**, the Minnesota model has evolved to meet the realities of a managed care economy; the length of inpatient stays has become more flexible and outpatient treatment is now frequently offered. Nevertheless, the core principles of the Minnesota model have remained unchanged. They reflect the firm belief that **alcoholism** and drug addiction are diseases that destroy the whole person—physically, mentally, and spiritually. Individualized treatment programs developed by professional and nonprofessional counselors help the addict address the different dimensions of his illness. Total abstinence, inclusion of the family in the treatment plan, and continued care after discharge are core elements of the model.

Principles of The Minnesota Model

Several fundamental principles are the basis of the Minnesota model treatment approach. Although originally developed to treat alcoholism, they apply to all forms of chemical dependence.

1. Alcoholism is an involuntary, primary disease that is diagnosable.
2. Because it is a progressive, chronic disease, untreated alcoholism will worsen without treatment.

---

3. Although it cannot be cured, alcoholism can be arrested.
4. Treatment outcome cannot necessarily be predicted by the alcoholic's motivations for seeking treatment.
5. Successful alcoholism treatment must address physical, psychological, social, and spiritual dimensions.
6. Alcoholics should be treated with respect and dignity in a supportive environment if treatment is to succeed.
7. Alcoholics and other addicts are vulnerable to the abuse of other drugs; treatment for these addictions can be addressed as chemical dependence.
8. Alcoholism and chemical dependency are best treated with a multidisciplinary approach and individualized treatment plans.
9. A primary counselor, usually a recovering addict, is the best person to organize and implement an addict's treatment plan.
10. Recommended treatment combines 12-step work such as that found in AA, lectures, and individualized counseling.
11. The best follow-up group support structure for recovering addicts is AA.

The Minnesota model, which banished earlier methods of treatment such as punitive incarceration or commitment to insane asylums, represented a compassionate revolution in how society addressed addiction. Although it is still incorporated into many treatment programs today, cognitive behavioral therapy and newer medications that treat the **cravings** and symptoms of addiction are supplementing this form of treatment or, in some cases, replacing it.

Further Reading

Spicer, Jerry. *The Minnesota Model: The Evolution of the Multidisciplinary Approach to Addiction Recovery*. Center City, MN: Hazelden Foundation, 1993.

Moderation Management. *See* Alternative Addiction Treatment.

Monitoring the Future Monitoring the Future (MTF) is a long-term, ongoing survey project funded by the National Institute on Drug Abuse and conducted by the University of Michigan. The survey regularly queries representative samples of high school and college students and young adults about their attitudes, values, and behaviors to form a fuller understanding of the lifestyles of contemporary youth in the United States. Part of the survey focuses on drug use among high school students—in particular, past-month, past-year, and lifetime* drug use

---

*"Lifetime" refers to use at least once during a respondent's lifetime. "Past year" refers to use at least once during the year preceding an individual's response to the survey. "Past month" refers to use at least once during the 30 days preceding an individual's response to the survey. "Daily" refers to an individual's drug use 20 or more times in the 30 days prior to the survey, except for cigarettes, where the definition is one or more cigarettes per day in the 30 days prior to the survey.

among 8th, 10th, and 12th graders. The 33rd annual study was conducted during 2007.** Its findings follow.

Positive Trends

- **Any illicit drug**—From 2006 to 2007, 8th graders reporting lifetime use of any illicit drug declined from 20.9 percent to 190 percent and past-year use declined from 14.8 percent to 13.2 percent. Since 2001, annual prevalence has fallen by 32 percent among 8th graders, nearly 25 percent among 10th graders, and 13 percent among 12th graders. Since the peak year in 1996, past-year prevalence has fallen by 44 percent among 8th graders. The peak year for past-year **abuse** among 10th and 12th graders was 1997; since then, past-year prevalence has fallen by 27 percent among 10th graders and by 15 percent among 12th graders.

- **Marijuana**—Past-year use of **marijuana** among 8th graders significantly declined from 11.7 percent in 2006 to 10.3 percent in 2007, and is down from its 1996 peak of 18.3 percent. Annual prevalence of marijuana use has fallen by 33 percent among 8th graders, 25 percent among 10th graders, and 14 percent among 12th graders since 2001. Disapproval of trying marijuana once or twice, smoking marijuana occasionally, or smoking marijuana regularly*** increased significantly among 8th graders from 2006 to 2007, and remained stable for 10th and 12th graders for the same period.

- **Methamphetamine**—Lifetime and past-year **methamphetamine** use decreased among 8th and 12th graders between 2006 and 2007; lifetime use among 8th graders declined from 2.7 percent to 1.8 percent, and lifetime use among 12th graders declined from 4.4 percent to 3.0 percent. Past-year methamphetamine use was reported by 1.1 percent of 8th graders in 2007 (a decline from 1.8 percent in 2006), 1.6 percent of 10th graders, and 1.7 percent of 12th graders (a decline from 2.5 percent in 2006).

- **Sedatives/Barbiturates**—There has been a decline in the lifetime use of sedatives from a peak of 10.5 percent in 2005 to 9.3 percent in 2007. Past-year use of sedatives or **barbiturates** declined from a peak of 7.2 percent in 2005 to 6.2 percent in 2007. (This question was asked only of 12th graders.)

- **Inhalants**—After some increases in recent years, there were no significant changes from 2006 to 2007 in the proportion of students in the 8th, 10th, and 12th grades reporting lifetime, past-year, or past-month abuse of **inhalants**.

- **Cigarettes/Nicotine**—Among 8th graders, **cigarette** use declined between 2006 and 2007 in most categories; lifetime use dropped from 24.6 percent to 22.1 percent and

**For the 2007 MTF, 48,025 students in a nationally representative sample of 403 public and private schools were surveyed about lifetime, past-year, past-month, and daily use of drugs, alcohol, and cigarettes and smokeless tobacco. The latest data are online at www.drugabuse.gov.

***In addition to studying drug use among 8th, 10th, and 12th graders, MTF collects information on 3 attitudinal indicators related to drug use. These indicators are perceived risk of harm in taking a drug, disapproval of others who take drugs, and perceived availability of drugs.

past-month use fell from 8.7 percent to 7.1 percent. Daily cigarette smoking among 8th graders dropped from 4.0 percent to 3.0 percent, down from its 10.4 percent peak in 1996. Lifetime cigarette use was reported by 34.6 percent of 10th graders and 46.2 percent of 12th graders, and smoking half a pack or more a day was reported by 1.1 percent of 8th graders, 2.7 percent of 10th graders, and 5.7 percent of 12th graders in 2007.

- **Crack Cocaine**—Past-month abuse of crack among 10th graders declined from 0.7 percent in 2006 to 0.5 percent in 2007. From 2001 to 2007, students in 8th and 10th grades showed declines of crack use of 29.6 percent and 58.0 percent, respectively. Past-month abuse of **cocaine** (powder) among 12th graders declined from 2.4 percent in 2006 to 1.7 percent in 2007. Disapproval of trying cocaine once or twice increased among 8th graders from 86.5 percent in 2006 to 88.2 percent in 2007, and disapproval of trying crack once or twice increased from 87.2 percent to 88.6 percent. Disapproval did not change among 10th or 12th graders for the same period.
- **Anabolic Steroids**—Perceived availability of **anabolic steroids** dropped among 10th graders, from 30.2 percent in 2006 to 27.7 percent in 2007, but remained stable among 8th and 12th graders. Steroid use in all 3 grade levels remained unchanged from 2006 to 2007.
- **Alcohol**—Tenth-graders reported a modest decline in past-year use of flavored alcoholic beverages, from 48.8 percent in 2006 to 45.9 percent in 2007. Eighth-graders reporting disapproval of trying "one or two drinks of an alcoholic beverage" increased from 51.3 percent in 2006 to 54.0 percent in 2007. Disapproval of having "five or more drinks once or twice each weekend" increased from 82.0 percent in 2006 to 83.8 percent in 2007.****

Negative Trends

- **Prescription Drugs**—**Prescription drug** use remains unacceptably high with virtually no drop in nonmedical use of most individual prescription drugs. This year, for the first time, researchers pulled together data for all prescription drugs as a measurable group (including **amphetamines**, sedatives/barbiturates, tranquilizers, and **opiates** other than **heroin** such as Vicodin and OxyContin) and found that 15.4 percent of high school seniors reported nonmedical use of at least one prescription medication within the past year.*****
- **MDMA (Ecstasy)**—The 2007 results represent the 3rd year in a row showing a weakening of attitudes among the youngest students regarding MDMA. Among 8th graders, the perceived harmfulness of taking MDMA occasionally decreased from 52.0 percent to 48.6 percent from 2006 to 2007. Among 10th graders, the perceived harmfulness decreased from 71.3 percent to 68.2 percent. Perceived risk of MDMA use remained unchanged for 12th graders from 2006 to 2007. Concurrently, between 2004 and 2007, past-year use of MDMA increased in 10th graders from 2.4

****For information on the health effects of alcohol, visit the Web site of the National Institute on Alcohol Abuse and Alcoholism at www.niaaa.nih.gov.

*****For more information on the misuse or nonmedical use of pain medications or other prescription drugs, visit www.drugabuse.gov and click on Prescription Medications under Drugs of Abuse.

Table 4. Trends in Prevalence of Various Drugs for 8th, 10th, and 12th Graders, 2004–2007

	8th Graders				10th Graders				12th Graders			
	2004	2005	2006	2007	2004	2005	2006	2007	2004	2005	2006	2007
Any Illicit Drug Use												
lifetime	21.5	21.4	20.9	19.0	39.8	38.2	36.1	35.6	51.1	50.4	48.2	46.8
past year	15.2	15.5	14.8	13.2	31.1	29.8	28.7	28.1	38.8	38.4	36.5	35.9
past month	8.4	8.5	8.1	7.4	18.3	17.3	16.8	16.9	23.4	23.1	21.5	21.9
Marijuana/Hashish												
lifetime	16.3	16.5	15.7	14.2	35.1	34.1	31.8	31.0	45.7	44.8	42.3	41.8
past year	11.8	12.2	11.7	10.3	27.5	26.6	25.2	24.6	34.3	33.6	31.5	31.7
past month	6.4	6.6	6.5	5.7	15.9	15.2	14.2	14.2	19.9	19.8	18.3	18.8
daily	0.8	1.0	1.0	0.8	3.2	3.1	2.8	2.8	5.6	5.0	5.0	5.1
Inhalants												
Lifetime	17.3	17.1	16.1	15.6	12.4	13.1	13.3	13.6	10.9	11.4	11.1	10.5
past year	9.6	9.5	9.1	8.3	5.9	6.0	6.5	6.6	4.2	5.0	4.5	3.7
past month	4.5	4.2	4.1	3.9	2.4	2.2	2.3	2.5	1.5	2.0	1.5	1.2
Hallucinogens												
Lifetime	3.5	3.8	3.4	3.1	6.4	5.8	6.1	6.4	9.7	8.8	8.3	8.4
past year	2.2	2.4	2.1	1.9	4.1	4.0	4.1	4.4	6.2	5.5	4.9	5.4
past month	1.0	1.1	0.9	1.0	1.6	1.5	1.5	1.7	1.9	1.9	1.5	1.7
LSD												
lifetime	1.8	1.9	1.6	1.6	2.8	2.5	2.7	3.0	4.6	3.5	3.3	3.4
past year	1.1	1.2	0.9	1.1	1.6	1.5	1.7	1.9	2.2	1.8	1.7	2.1
past month	0.5	0.5	0.4	0.5	0.6	0.6	0.7	0.7	0.7	0.7	0.6	0.6
Cocaine												
lifetime	3.4	3.7	3.4	3.1	5.4	5.2	4.8	5.3	8.1	8.0	8.5	7.8
past year	2.0	2.2	2.0	2.0	3.7	3.5	3.2	3.4	5.3	5.1	5.7	5.2
past month	0.9	1.0	1.0	0.9	1.7	1.5	1.5	1.3	2.3	2.3	2.5	2.0
Crack Cocaine												
lifetime	2.4	2.4	2.3	2.1	2.6	2.5	2.2	2.3	3.9	3.5	3.5	3.2

(*Continued*)

Table 4. Continued

	8th Graders				10th Graders				12th Graders			
	2004	2005	2006	2007	2004	2005	2006	2007	2004	2005	2006	2007
past year	1.3	1.4	1.3	1.3	1.7	1.7	1.3	1.3	2.3	1.9	2.1	1.9
past month	0.6	0.6	0.6	0.6	0.8	0.7	0.7	0.5	1.0	1.0	0.9	0.9
Heroin												
lifetime	1.6	1.5	1.4	1.3	1.5	1.5	1.4	1.5	1.5	1.5	1.4	1.5
past year	1.0	0.8	0.8	0.8	0.9	0.9	0.9	0.8	0.9	0.8	0.8	0.9
past month	0.5	0.5	0.3	0.4	0.5	0.5	0.5	0.4	0.5	0.5	0.4	0.4
Tranquilizers												
lifetime	4.0	4.1	4.3	3.9	7.3	7.1	7.2	7.4	10.6	9.9	10.3	9.5
past year	2.5	2.8	2.6	2.4	5.1	4.8	5.2	5.3	7.3	6.8	6.6	6.2
past month	1.2	1.3	1.3	1.1	2.3	2.3	2.4	2.6	3.1	2.9	2.7	2.6
Alcohol												
Lifetime	43.9	41.0	40.5	38.9	64.2	63.2	61.5	61.7	76.8	75.1	72.7	72.2
past year	36.7	33.9	33.6	31.8	58.2	56.7	55.8	56.3	70.6	68.6	66.5	66.4
past month	18.6	17.1	17.2	15.9	35.2	33.2	33.8	33.4	48.0	47.0	45.3	44.4
daily	0.6	0.5	0.5	0.6	1.3	1.3	1.4	1.4	2.8	3.1	3.0	3.1
Cigarettes (any use)												
lifetime	27.9	25.9	24.6	22.1	40.7	38.9	36.1	34.6	52.8	50.0	47.1	46.2
past month	9.2	9.3	8.7	7.1	16.0	14.9	14.5	14.0	25.0	23.2	21.6	21.6
daily	4.4	4.0	4.0	3.0	8.3	7.5	7.6	7.2	15.6	13.6	12.2	12.3
1/2 pack+/day	1.7	1.7	1.5	1.1	3.3	3.1	3.3	2.7	8.0	6.9	5.9	5.7
Smokeless Tobacco												
lifetime	11.0	10.1	10.2	9.1	13.8	14.5	15.0	15.1	16.7	17.5	15.2	15.1
past month	4.1	3.3	3.7	3.2	4.9	5.6	5.7	6.1	6.7	7.6	6.1	6.6
daily	1.0	0.7	0.7	0.8	1.6	1.9	1.7	1.6	2.8	2.5	2.2	2.8
Steroids												
lifetime	1.9	1.7	1.6	1.5	2.4	2.0	1.8	1.8	3.4	2.6	2.7	2.2

	1	2	3	4	5	6	7	8	9	10	11	12
past year	1.1	1.1	0.9	0.8	1.5	1.3	1.2	1.1	2.5	1.5	1.8	1.4
past month	0.5	0.5	0.5	0.4	0.8	0.6	0.6	0.5	1.6	0.9	1.1	1.0
MDMA												
lifetime	2.8	2.8	2.5	2.3	4.3	4.0	4.5	5.2	7.5	5.4	6.5	6.5
past year	1.7	1.7	1.4	1.5	2.4	2.6	2.8	3.5	4.0	3.0	4.1	4.5
past month	0.8	0.6	0.7	0.6	0.8	1.0	1.2	1.2	1.2	1.0	1.3	1.6
Methamphetamine												
lifetime	2.5	3.1	2.7	1.8	5.3	4.1	3.2	2.8	6.2	4.5	4.4	3.0
past year	1.5	1.8	1.8	1.1	3.0	2.9	1.8	1.6	3.4	2.5	2.5	1.7
past month	0.6	0.7	0.6	0.6	1.3	1.1	0.7	0.4	1.4	0.9	0.9	0.6
Vicodin												
past year	2.5	2.6	3.0	2.7	6.2	5.9	7.0	7.2	9.3	9.5	9.7	9.6
OxyContin												
past year	1.7	1.8	2.6	1.8	3.5	3.2	3.8	3.9	5.0	5.5	4.3	5.2

Source: NIDA.

to 3.5 percent, and between 2005 and 2007, past-year use of MDMA increased among 12th graders from 3.0 to 4.5 percent.

- **Hallucinogens**—Among 10th graders, the perceived harmfulness of taking **LSD** once or twice decreased from 38.8 percent in 2006 to 35.4 percent in 2007. The perceived harm of taking LSD regularly decreased from 60.7 percent in 2006 to 56.8 percent in 2007. Disapproval of using LSD once or twice significantly decreased for 10th graders from 71.2 percent in 2006 to 67.7 percent in 2007; disapproval of taking LSD regularly dropped from 74.9 percent in 2006 to 71.5 percent in 2007.

- **Heroin/Opiates**—Among 8th graders, past-month use of injecting heroin increased from 0.2 percent in 2006 to 0.3 percent in 2007. Past-year heroin use without a needle increased among 12th graders from 0.6 percent in 2006 to 1.0 percent in 2007. OxyContin use in the past year was reported by 1.8 percent of 8th graders, 3.9 percent of 10th graders, and 5.2 percent of 12th graders. Vicodin use in the past year was reported by 2.7 percent of 8th graders, 7.2 percent of 10th graders, and 9.6 percent of 12th graders, remaining stable at relatively high levels for each grade.

See also Appendix D.

Further Reading

Johnston, L. D., O'Malley, Patrick, Bachman, Jerald, and Schulenberg, John. *Monitoring the Future. National Results on Adolescent Drug Use: Overview of Key Findings, 2006.* NIH Publication No. 07-6202, May 2007.

Monoamines. *See* Neurotransmitters.

Morphine A derivative of **opium**, morphine is one of the most powerful natural pain relievers known and has become the standard against which other **opiates**, natural and synthetic, are judged.

The drug was first extracted from opium in 1803 and became a legal analgesic that most were able to use safely. It was only after the later introduction of the hypodermic needle, which made intravenous injection possible, that morphine became commonly associated with abuse and addiction. During the Civil War, returning soldiers brought home morphine kits for alleviating the pain of battle injuries, and women learned to inject the drug. By the late 1800s, there were over 150,000 morphine addicts and roughly 400,000 users in the United States. Today, morphine is available in an oral form, suppositories, and injectable preparations. Because synthetic and semi-synthetic morphine-like drugs are widely available both by prescription and through illicit channels, **addiction** to natural morphine is not as widespread as it once was even though opiate addiction in general continues to be a significant problem.

Like other pain-relievers such as **codeine** and **heroin**, morphine powerfully engages the dopamine reward pathway. Synthetic derivatives such as **hydromorphone** that have been manufactured in the laboratory are even more potent than morphine and are extremely addicting. Not only do drug abusers pay the consequences but babies born to morphine-addicted women must endure the notoriously agonizing process of **withdrawal** as well.

Morphine is a Schedule II drug under the **Controlled Substances Act** and can be treated with substances like naloxone and naltrexone that block its effect.

Further Reading

Califano, Joseph A., Jr. *High Society: How Substance Abuse Ravages America and What to Do About It.* New York: Perseus Books, 2007.

Hoffman, John, and Froemke, Susan, eds. *Addiction: Why Can't They Just Stop?* New York: Rodale, 2007.

Home Box Office (HBO). In partnership with the Robert Wood Johnson Foundation, the National Institute on Drug Abuse, and the National Institute on Alcohol Abuse and Alcoholism. *Addiction: Why Can't They Just Stop?* Documentary. March 2007.

Ketcham, Katherine, and Pace, Nicholas A. *Teens Under the Influence: The Truth About Kids, Alcohol, and Other Drugs.* New York: Ballantine Books, 2003.

U.S. Department of Health and Human Services, National Institute on Drug Abuse (NIDA), June 2007. Retrieved from http://www.nida.gov

U.S. Department of Health and Human Services, Substance Abuse and Mental Health Services Administration (SAMHSA), August 2007. Retrieved from http://www.samhsa.gov

U.S. Department of Justice, Drug Enforcement Administration (DEA), March 2008. Retrieved from http://www.usdoj.gov/dea

Motivational Enhancement Therapy. *See* Treatment.

Multisubstance Addiction. *See* Cross-Addiction and Cross-Tolerance.

Muscle Dysmorphia. *See* Eating Disorders.

---❖ N

Naltrexone. *See* Addiction Medications.

Narcotics. *See* Opiates.

Narcotics Anonymous. *See* Twelve-Step Programs.

Nation, Carrie Amelia (1846–1911) Carrie Amelia Nation was a fierce advocate for temperance during the late 1800s and early 1900s. Born in 1846, she married a hard-drinking physician whom she eventually left, later marrying a man 19 years her senior named David Nation. A devoutly religious woman who became involved in the growing temperance movement that sought to ban the use of alcohol, she is reported to have changed the spelling of her name to "Carry" in the belief that she was foreordained by God to "carry a nation" to sobriety. In Medicine Lodge, Kansas, where she lived for a time, she formed a local chapter of the Women's Christian Temperance Union (WCTU).

As her religious fervor and convictions about the evils of alcohol and other social ills grew, she began to attack liquor-selling establishments in her home state. At first, she threw rocks and bricks at them, later wielding a hatchet with which to splinter their doors and furniture. At six feet tall, she was an imposing woman, and her efforts to close down local saloons attracted the attention of citizens from other jurisdictions who asked her to launch assaults on similar businesses in their towns. As her fervor swept her from state to state, Nation's behavior landed her in jail on several occasions. She paid her fines by using the profits from her speaking tours and by selling miniature souvenir hatchets, and her speeches, considered inspirational by some, became increasingly popular. With a formidable personality and strong convictions that she was divinely inspired, she was a considerable nuisance to the patrons and owners of saloons where she sang hymns, chastised drinkers, and smashed bottles of liquor. Many drinking establishments are reported to have posted slogans reading, "All Nations Welcome But Carrie."

Nation never lived to see **Prohibition** become law in 1920. She died in 1911 after collapsing on stage during what would be her final public oration, and she was buried in Missouri where the WCTU inscribed a stone reading, "Faithful to the Cause of Prohibition, She Hath Done What She Could."

Carrie Nation.

Further Reading

Grace, Fran. *Carry A. Nation: Retelling the Life*. Bloomington, IN: Indiana University Press, 2001.

Nembutal. *See* Barbiturates.

Neuroadaptation Neuroadaptation, also known as synaptic plasticity, is the biological event by which pathways in the **brain** become more or less active over time due to repeated exposure to certain stimuli. The phenomenon is integral to learning and memory, and is one of the defining features of **addiction** to drugs and to certain behaviors such as pathological gambling.

   Addictive drugs and certain behaviors trigger neurochemical changes in the brain that stimulate the reward pathway in susceptible people. As the brain is repeatedly exposed to the stimuli, the neurochemical changes lead to dysregulation of the **mesolimbic dopamine system**, the reward center of the brain originating in the ventral tegmental area of the brain and extending to the prefrontal cortex. When this transformation takes place, the individual is no longer able to experience the normal pleasures of life, and addictive behavior—along with lack of control and impaired judgment associated with it—results. Addictions experts are studying biochemical and behavioral methods that they hope will help reset or rebalance the brain to its normal neurological state so the individual can respond to naturally pleasurable stimuli and be free of addictive **compulsions**.

Neurons. *See* Brain and Addiction.

Neurotransmitters The chemicals that are responsible for regulating **brain** function by sending, receiving, modulating, and amplifying messages are known as neurotransmitters. When a neurotransmitter such as dopamine binds to (or attaches to) dopamine receptors on the dendrites of a receiving cell (the postsynaptic cell), that cell produces an electric impulse that triggers the manufacture of the same neurotransmitter—in this case, dopamine. Now a **presynaptic cell**, the neuron sends the dopamine via its axon into the synaptic gap where it binds to and stimulates the next receiving neuron. As that cell (the postsynaptic cell) fires, the cycle continues. Once the dopamine has stimulated receptors on a postsynaptic cell, it either breaks down in the synaptic cleft or is reabsorbed into the presynaptic neuron for later use. Some drugs like Prozac that treat depression associated with low serotonin levels in the brain are known as serotonin reuptake inhibitors because they inhibit the reabsorption (reuptake) of serotonin from the synaptic cleft back into the cell; this allows the neurotransmitter to remain active in the brain for a longer period of time.

The effect a neurotransmitter has depends on the receptors activated on the postsynaptic cell. Combined input from several synapses usually ignites neuronal impulses, and it is simplistic to imagine that a single neurotransmitter triggers a specific action in a receiving cell. Neuromodulators, which many regard as neurotransmitters in their own right, affect the activity of other neurotransmitters by boosting or slowing their activity.

The principal neurotransmitters involved in **addiction** are those that act directly on the reward pathway and result in the **neuroadaptation** that is the hallmark of addiction. Most of these neurotransmitters fall into 3 categories: the monoamines, peptides known as opioids, and amino acids. A 4th type, **acetylcholine**, is known both as a "small molecule neurotransmitter" and as a neuromodulator; a 5th group is comprised of the endocannabinoids, the receptors for which were not discovered until the late 1980s.

Monoamines

The monoamines associated with addiction are dopamine, serotonin, and norepinephrine.

Dopamine

As the principal neurotransmitter in the reward pathway that produces a pleasurable high, dopamine plays a central role in addiction. In proper proportions with other neurochemicals, it produces a sense of well-being and contributes to alertness, sexual excitement, mental relaxation, and helps balance aggressive tendencies. **Stimulants** like **methamphetamine** and **cocaine** are **agonists** of dopamine.

Dopamine receptors are like docking stations in the brain for dopamine. When receptors are more plentiful, the brain seems more sensitive to natural reinforcers that promote social closeness and positive life goals, and thus allows the individual to balance these with pleasure-giving activities in a healthy way. Sometimes the brain tries to compensate for the flood of dopamine that drug use creates by reducing the number of dopamine receptors on neurons. Also known as downregulation, this decrease means the addict no longer feels the pleasure that drug use once produced and begins to lose the ability to experience any pleasure at all. Called **anhedonia**, this condition is often the result of prolonged drug addiction. One arm of current research into addiction is focusing on how to increase dopamine receptors in individuals with low levels.

The principal dopamine receptors associated with drug addiction are the D1 (excitatory) and D2 (inhibitory) receptors. According to brain studies conducted by the National Institutes of Health's National Institute on Drug Abuse, higher levels of dopamine receptors in the brain help protect against an individual's succumbing to obesity, drug **abuse**, or addiction, while lower levels leave the individual more vulnerable. What alarms researchers and addictions specialists is the fact that the increased dopamine deficits that result from drug abuse in individuals who already lack sufficient dopamine receptors may lead to serious neurological diseases as the individual grows older.

Dopamine is also present in 3 other important pathways in the brain; although they do not play as large a role in addiction as the mesolimbic (reward) pathway, they are nevertheless important components of the brain's dopamine system. They are the nigrostriatal pathway, where dopamine functions in motor control and neuronal death or damage is involved in Parkinson's disease; the tuberoinfundibular pathway, which includes the hypothalamus and pituitary gland and is involved in learning and hormonal regulation; and the mesocortical pathway, which projects from the ventral tegmental area (VTA) to the prefrontal cortex of the brain and may play a role in producing the symptoms of schizophrenia. Drug use that disrupts the reward pathway also affects these pathways in ways that are not yet understood.

Norepinephrine

Both a hormone and a neurotransmitter, norepinephrine—also called noradrenaline—is synthesized from dopamine inside neurons of the central nervous system. Sometimes referred to as the fight or flight hormone that primes the body to respond to stress or alarming stimuli, it is involved in regulation of blood pressure and other actions peripheral to the central nervous system.

In the brain, norepinephrine acts as a neurotransmitter that contributes to a sense of well-being and a reduction in compulsive behavior. Like serotonin reuptake inhibitors (SRIs) that help keep serotonin active in the synapse where it can continue to exert its influence on postsynaptic neurons, norepinephrine reuptake inhibitors (NRIs) are used in a similar way to treat depression, often by combining them with SRIs to produce serotonin-norepinephrine reuptake inhibitors (SNRIs). Some evidence suggests that NRIs may help prevent the reabsorption of dopamine into neurons, permitting more of the neurotransmitter to remain in the synapses where it can enhance the individual's pleasurable feelings.

Just as low levels of norepinephrine can result in depression, levels that are too high produce anxiety and an elevated heart rate and blood pressure. Agonists of norepinephrine such as cocaine have the same effects.

Serotonin

Often associated with antidepressants, serotonin is manufactured in the brain by the amino acid tryptophan and is located in the raphé nuclei, a group of neural fibers and cells in the brain stem. Although it elevates an individual's pain threshold and can enhance one's sense of well-being, serotonin does not produce the pleasure associated with dopamine. A deficit of the neurotransmitter may contribute to aggressive and compulsive behavior and is strongly associated with depression. The National Institute of Mental Health reports that in the brains of many people who commit suicide, serotonin levels are found to be nearly depleted. Chronic alcohol abuse also drains the brain's supply of serotonin by reducing its activity at the synapse. Antidepressants are agonists of serotonin because they boost its effect in the brain. **Lysergic acid diethylamide** (LSD) is an **antagonist**.

As a modulator of the stress hormones epinephrine and norepinephrine, serotonin is also found throughout the body. Its concentrations in the brain can be positively affected by diet—particularly, it is believed, by carbohydrates.

Opioids

Morphine-like substances the body makes are known as endogenous opioids: endorphins, enkephalins, and dynorphins. Alpha-endorphin, beta-endorphin, and gamma-endorphine—especially beta-endorphin—relieve pain and promote a sense of relaxation and peace. The enkephalins inhibit neurochemical transmissions in pain pathways, thus reducing the perception of emotional and physical discomfort. Both opioid groups activate receptors in the **mesolimbic dopamine system** to produce rewarding effects. The dynorphins, on the other hand, activate different receptors in the pathway. Produced by the cAMP response element-binding (**CREB**) protein that plays a key role in gene expression, the dynorphins reduce the amount of dopamine released in the nucleus accumbens. As the pleasurable effects of dopamine are tamped down, **tolerance** builds, which in turn compels the user to consume more of the addictive substance to obtain the desired effect.

Opiate drugs like **morphine** and **heroin** bind readily to receptors for endogenous opioids, which helps account for the highly addictive nature of these drugs. Opioid antagonists like naloxone and naltrexone have been developed to help in the **treatment** of addiction to opiates.

Amino Acids

Glutamate

The most common of the brain's neurotransmitters, glutamate is the excitatory neurotransmitter often paired with GABA as the workhorses of the central nervous system because the number of synapses involving these amino acids in the brain is much greater than that of other neurotransmitters. Glutamate's function throughout the brain is widespread and critical to overall brain biochemistry and cognitive processes. Because the neurotransmitter is believed to facilitate synaptic plasticity, it has crucial roles in learning and memory.

Researchers have conducted numerous studies using **amphetamines**, cocaine, **morphine**, nicotine, and alcohol as the stimuli to determine how each drug affects certain glutamate receptors. They compared the dopamine levels produced in response to each stimulus to dopamine levels produced at a later date in response to the same stimulus, and found the latter to be a stronger response. This suggested that when the brain learned that it experienced pleasure for the first time, it strengthened its synaptic connections. Known as **long-term potentiation**, this phenomenon has a powerful impact on learning and behavior and is a highly significant factor in the course that addictive disease is likely to follow.

Alcohol and other **depressants** are antagonists of glutamate; stimulants are agonists.

Gamma Aminobutyric Acid (GABA)

GABA, as the other workhorse neurotransmitter in the brain, has a very different effect from its partner workhorse, glutamate. It inhibits neuron's postsynaptic response and, if allowed to remain in the synaptic cleft, induces a sense of calm. It is associated with a reduction in compulsive behavior, lower levels of anxiety, heart rate, and blood pressure, and a relaxed state. In alcohol abuse and **alcoholism**, prolonged drinking modifies GABA receptors such that they cease to function properly.

Two GABA receptors in particular are involved in addiction: GABA$_A$ and GABA$_B$, whose difference lies in the speed with which they trigger the inhibition of the postsynaptic neuron. Interestingly, although GABA is an inhibitory neurotransmitter, it is excitatory in the immature mammalian brain, and in the adult brain it is synthesized from glutamate, an excitatory neurotransmitter.

Common agonists of GABA are the **benzodiazepines**, which are tranquilizers such as Valium. These drugs, as well as alcohol and **barbiturates**, enhance the effect of GABA on GABA$_A$ receptors. As use of these substances reduces the sensitivity or number of the brain's GABA$_A$ receptors, a process called downregulation, an individual may require more of the drugs to achieve the desired effect. This is known as tolerance. Because GABA and glutamate balance each other exquisitely in a normal brain, a significant disruption of one can result in neurological dysfunction and a wide spectrum of distressing **withdrawal** symptoms.

Acetylcholine

Acetylcholine affects the activities of surrounding neurons, not just the pre- and postsynaptic neurons, and has a broad range of effects throughout the nervous system. Although its primary role is to modulate the body's voluntary muscular activity, it also plays an important role in addiction by activating dopamine receptors on postsynaptic neurons in the reward pathway. One type of receptor for acetylcholine is particularly sensitive to nicotine, and its activation by acetylcholine enhances cycles of learning and reinforcement in the dopamine pathway that contribute to addiction.

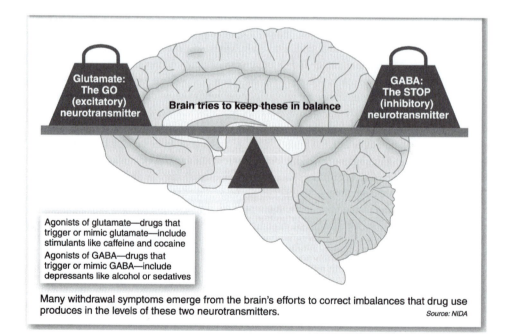

Glutamate: The GO (excitatory) neurotransmitter

Brain tries to keep these in balance

GABA: The STOP (inhibitory) neurotransmitter

Agonists of glutamate—drugs that trigger or mimic glutamate—include stimulants like caffeine and cocaine

Agonists of GABA—drugs that trigger or mimic GABA—include depressants like alcohol or sedatives

Many withdrawal symptoms emerge from the brain's efforts to correct imbalances that drug use produces in the levels of these two neurotransmitters.

Source: NIDA

Glutamate and GABA: A Balancing Act

Acetylcholine is considered a peripheral neurotransmitter because of the critical role it plays in the major muscle groups of the body outside of the brain and spinal cord. There is only one other peripheral neurotransmitter, norepinephrine, whose primary function outside the central nervous system is to help regulate blood pressure.

Endocannabinoids

Also known as endogenous cannabinoids, meaning they are naturally produced by the body, the endocannabinoids represent a group of chemical messengers involved in long-term potentiation and memory. One such chemical is anandamide, discovered in 1992, that shares some of the pharmaceutical properties of tetrahydrocannabinol (THC), the active ingredient in **marijuana**. This may explain its role in motivation, pleasure, appetite and food intake, and pain relief.

In the brain, endocannabinoids bind to a specific cannabinoid receptor known as CB1, the same receptor to which THC binds, and at one time it was thought that the endocannabinoids might be the body's marijuana. The human body does not produce THC, however, so the purpose of the CB1 receptor is not completely understood.

Another cannabinoid receptor, CB2, is primarily involved in immune system functions. Since the cannabinoid receptors were not discovered until 1988, the role of the endocannabinoids is still not completely understood. Ongoing research has revealed that they may have complex roles in learning, eating behaviors, sleeping patterns, and analgesia.

Further Reading

Kauer, Julie A. Addictive Drugs and Stress Trigger a Common Change at VTA Synapses. *Neuron* February 2003: 37(4), 549–550.

Nicotine An alkaloid of the *Nicotiana tabacum* plant that is native to South America, nicotine is a colorless, poisonous, highly addictive **stimulant**. It is consumed in **tobacco** products such as **pipes**, **cigars** and **cigarettes**, or in smokeless substances such as snuff or chewing tobacco. In the United States, about 70 million people—about half of whom are girls and women—use tobacco in one form or another, making it second only to alcohol as the most widely abused addictive drug. Although the incidence of smoking has declined in the last 30 years, it remains the leading preventable cause of death, killing nearly half a million people in the United States every year. About 9 million smokers have a chronic disease associated with smoking, and **secondhand smoke** kills about 70,000 Americans annually. Thousands of dangerous chemicals other than nicotine—tars, carbon monoxide, and **acetaldehyde**—that are in tobacco products and the smoke they emit compound the harm. Tars, which represent the particulate matter in smoke other than water and alkaloid compounds such as nicotine, are associated with an increased risk of lung cancer, emphysema,

---

Statistics

More Americans die in a single day from smoking than died in 2005 in Iraq and Afghanistan combined.

Source: Califano, 2007.

---

and other respiratory disorders, while carbon monoxide increases the risk of cardiovascular disease. Smoking contributes to cancers of all kinds, not just lung cancer, and smokers die from various types of cancer at 2 to 4 times the rate of nonsmokers depending on how heavily they use tobacco products.

Cigarette Ingredients

Nicotine is an addictive drug found naturally in tobacco. Other chemicals in tobacco plants may come from fertilizers or insecticides used in the growing process or from contaminants in air, soil, or water. Some chemicals are added when tobacco is cured; others are added in the manufacturing process.

Hundreds of ingredients are added to cigarettes to make them more acceptable to the consumer; they make cigarettes milder and easier to inhale, improve taste, prolong burning, and increase shelf life. Laboratory analyses have shown that tobacco smoke contains more than 4,000 chemicals. Of these, at least 250 are toxic and more than 60 are known carcinogens (capable of causing cancer).

Cigarette Brand Statistics

- Ninety-nine percent of all cigarettes sold in the United States are filtered.
- Cigarette brands that yield approximately 1–6 mg of tar by machine testing conducted by the Federal Trade Commission are generally called "ultralight." Those with approximately 6–15 mg of tar are called "light," and brands yielding more than 15 mg of tar are called "regular" or "full flavor." Of all cigarettes sold in the United States, 84 percent are either light or ultralight (i.e., low-tar) brands.
- Twenty-seven percent of all cigarettes sold in the United States are mentholated brands.
- National survey data for 2005 revealed that Marlboro is preferred by 48 percent of cigarette smokers aged 12–17 years, 51 percent of smokers aged 18–25 years, and 40 percent of smokers aged 26 years or older.
- Use of mentholated brands varies widely by race and ethnicity. Among smokers aged 12 years or older, roughly 3 times as many African Americans reported using mentholated brands as white or Hispanic smokers. Fifty-five percent of African-American middle school students who smoke and 64 percent of African-American high school students who smoke reported using mentholated brands.

Cigarette Advertising Statistics

- In 2005, cigarette companies are reported to have spent over $35,000,000 *per day* on advertising and promotion; this is over $40 per day for every man, woman, and child in the United States.
- Cigarette companies spent $31,000,000 on the sponsorship of sports teams or individual athletes in 2005.

Only a drop or two of pure nicotine—about 50 mg—can be fatal. One cigarette contains anywhere from .5 to 15 mg of nicotine, so someone who ingests a whole cigarette or cigar could become seriously ill. Smoking delivers only 1 to 2 milligrams of nicotine, but even that amount powerfully triggers the adrenal glands to release the stimulatory hormone epinephrine that raises the body's blood pressure, respiration, heart rate, and glucose levels. Nicotine's immediate kick abates within a few minutes, causing smokers to reach for the cigarettes again. Nonsmokers subjected to secondary smoke, or cigar and pipe smokers who do not inhale, absorb nicotine and other chemicals through their mucosal membranes; although the effect of these substances on the **brain** and body accumulate more slowly, they are every bit as toxic and habituating. Recent studies show that nicotine, while considered less dangerous than **heroin** or **cocaine**, is more harmful than many other illegal drugs such as **marijuana** and **Ecstasy**, and adolescents who chew tobacco are statistically much more likely to take up smoking as a substitute nicotine habit than quit the drug altogether.

Nicotine has an affinity for the brain's **acetylcholine** receptors, specifically those carrying subunit proteins known as alpha$_4$ and beta$_2$. By mimicking the action of acetylcholine and binding to these receptors, nicotine triggers the strong responses in the dopamine pathway that are so powerfully related to **addiction**. Moreover, it is not broken down in the synapse because some of the other chemicals in tobacco block acetylcholinesterase, the enzyme that normally performs this function. Without the enzyme to metabolize it, nicotine continues to stimulate the neurons to fire and release large amounts of dopamine. Studies with mice in which the alpha$_4$ or beta$_2$ subunit proteins have been removed or enhanced confirm that these particular receptors heavily influence addiction. This may explain why some individuals—those with a large number of these specific receptors—become addicted to nicotine after exposure to only 3 or 4 cigarettes.

Nicotine addiction often accompanies the **abuse** of other drugs, especially alcohol. Interestingly, one of the new drugs developed for nicotine addiction, varenicline (Chantix), also seems to be effective in treating **alcoholism**, a finding that offers further clues into the nature of addiction and how it can best be treated. In 2008, however, this drug was reported to produce serious psychiatric symptoms in some patients, so its future availability is questionable.

The healthcare costs directly associated with tobacco use amount to over $75 billion annually in the United States, and this figure does not include costs associated with the illness and death caused by secondhand smoke, burns, or the perinatal and infant care that smoking mothers and their low-birth weight babies require. Lost productivity from smoking-related disease amounts to about $82 billion a year, so estimates of total costs to society exceed $150 billion a year.

Smoking is a dirty habit leaving pervasive and stale odors that cling for days in furniture and clothing. Ashes of smokable materials or spit-out chew are annoying, even repulsive, to many. Yellow teeth, bad breath, and stained fingertips mark users who are frequently plagued by coughing and a buildup of phlegm in the airways long before signs of active disease set in. For these reasons alone, many smokers try to quit, but today less than 10 percent prove successful for more than a month despite the assistance of quit-smoking aids like nicotine substitutes. Members of previous generations who quit cold-turkey had even lower quit rates because nicotine **withdrawal** symptoms, which include intense **craving**, irritability, and decreased concentration and cognitive function, sent many back to smoking within a few hours or days.

Seeking help in quitting, many smokers have joined support groups and other organizations such as Nicotine Anonymous. Modeled on **Alcoholics Anonymous**, the self-help group was formed in the early 1980s and is one of the largest national organizations today committed to providing a supportive network to smokers and ex-smokers. Many local groups and regional or state mental health facilities offer quit-smoking assistance as well. These may be found through Internet referral sources such as the American Cancer Society and related organizations.

In addition to self-help groups, recent decades have witnessed the development of several nicotine substitutes and medications that, combined with behavioral therapy, have helped millions quit more easily. Although some of the substances are sold over the counter (OTC), experts strongly recommend that they be used with the advice or supervision of a healthcare professional.

History

Tobacco use in the West probably originated with Native Americans who chewed the leaves and smoked Indian weed in a peace pipe known as a calumet. Spanish conquerors and others introduced tobacco to Europe as the American colonies began to discover its value as a cash crop in England. Once harvested in a more potent form, tobacco was cultivated by the Europeans and colonial settlers to produce a milder plant, but it retained its powerful potential to addict. In 1662, records show, settlers were reported to be "so given up" to abuse of nicotine that they needed to smoke several pipes of tobacco a day. By this time, tobacco had become highly significant to the colonial economy despite its already negative reputation as a noxious-smelling and harmful drug.

The taste for tobacco products spread rapidly throughout the world, taking different forms based on cultural and regional practices. The Spanish enjoyed cigar smoking while the French indulged in flavored snuff they kept in fashionable, pocket-sized snuff boxes. As slavery increased in the colonies, tobacco production skyrocketed to supply a growing market that had spread to Asia. A machine patented in the early 1800s that produced 200 cigarettes a minute made this more affordable means of ingesting nicotine popular, and by the early 1900s cigarettes began to replace chewing tobacco, pipes and cigars, and snuff. World Wars I and II fueled an even greater demand; widespread contact among soldiers spread the habit around the world, and women began smoking in vastly greater numbers as they entered the workforce to fill jobs vacated by the nation's men fighting overseas. Although antismoking leagues had proliferated in the United States, smoking and the use of tobacco products in most urban and suburban areas of the country were regarded as socially acceptable, even sophisticated habits, and the tobacco industry continued to explode. Cigarette production grew by the billions year after year.

By 1957, however, when the negative health effects of smoking had become undeniable, U.S. Surgeon General Leroy E. Burney officially confirmed the relationship between smoking and lung cancer, a position underscored by 1964's *Report of the Surgeon General's Advisory Committee on Smoking and Health*. In a country in which nearly half of all Americans smoked in virtually every home, restaurant, or office, this was startling news that, for a time, caused cigarette consumption to drop by 20 percent. It accelerated again, however, and in 1966 President Lyndon Johnson signed a bill requiring cautionary statements to be printed on cigarette packages stating, "Caution: Cigarette smoking may be hazardous to your health." Cigarette advertising on radio and TV was banned in 1971, and subsequent public health messages were disseminated by the government that raised increasing concerns not only about the relationship between smoking and cancer but also about the harmful effects of secondhand smoke. In the 1980s, it was confirmed that nicotine was indeed the addictive agent in tobacco, something science had until then been unable to verify. U.S. Surgeon General C. Everett Koop issued a report entitled *The Health Consequences of Involuntary Smoking* that definitely identified secondhand smoking as a health risk, leading to tighter legislation to restrict smoking on airline flights, broader regulations on print advertising and sale to minors, and ultimately to a general ban on smoking in public places.

Incidence of Nicotine Use and Addiction

Nicotine, along with alcohol and marijuana, is one of the most heavily abused drugs in the United States. Fortunately, the use of tobacco products has declined significantly from peak numbers in 1965, reflecting the success of public service and educational messages about its dangers. Especially encouraging are statistics showing that adolescents and young adults are heeding the warnings in greater numbers than ever before, although children are experimenting with smoking at ever-younger ages. Over 20 percent of high school students smoke, and statistics show that the earlier a person starts to smoke, the greater the likelihood he or she will become addicted. There is also some concern that the rate of decline in smoking by women has lessened. This is of concern partly because many women continue smoking while pregnant, inflicting health problems on their unborn children and producing low birth weight babies.

Tobacco Use Statistics*

- In 2006, an estimated 72.9 million Americans aged 12 or older used a tobacco product. This represents 29.6 percent of the population in that age range. In addition, 61.6 million persons (25 percent of the population) were current cigarette smokers; 13.7 million (5.6 percent) smoked cigars; 8.2 million (3.3 percent) used smokeless tobacco; and 2.3 million (0.9 percent) smoked tobacco in pipes.
- The rates of current use of cigarettes, smokeless tobacco, cigars, and pipe tobacco were unchanged between 2005 and 2006 among persons aged 12 or older. However, between 2002 and 2006, past-month cigarette use decreased from 26 to 25 percent. Rates of past-month use of cigars, smokeless tobacco, and pipe tobacco were similar in 2002 and 2006.
- The rate of past-month cigarette use among 12- to 17-year-olds declined from 13 percent in 2002 to 10.4 percent in 2006. However, past-month smokeless tobacco use was higher in 2006 (2.4 percent) than in 2002 (2 percent).
- Among pregnant women aged 15 to 44, combined data for 2005 and 2006 indicated that the rate of past-month cigarette use was 16.5 percent. The rate was higher among women in that age group who were not pregnant (29.5 percent).

*For more statistics, see Appendix D.

Experts express concern about the relentless onslaught of advertising from cigarette companies and are especially dismayed that many tobacco companies deliberately market products designed to appeal to and entice young people to smoke. The industry produces flavored cigars and other materials to make them more attractive to teens, and secretly increased the percentage of nicotine in cigarettes from 1998 to 2004 to make them more addictive. It also promotes low-yield and cigarette-like products, advertising them as a reduced-risk tobacco product to encourage adolescents to try them. They also sell flavored cigarettes in pastel colors for girls and young women or the complete line of light-to-regular cigarettes and small flavored cigars with names like "Buffalo" and "Smokin Joe" that are deliberately targeted to young Native Americans. An adolescent's susceptibility to tobacco as well as to other drugs lies in part in the effect drugs have on learning, memory, and motivation in the developing brain. There is also evidence that other chemicals in tobacco products may be addictive for adolescents in not-yet-understood ways that do not seem to affect adults. To counteract the powerful influences of the tobacco lobby, some public health advisors believe that more vigorous educational campaigns to discourage tobacco use among adolescents and young adults are needed.

Statistics

- In general, young people who smoke are not as healthy as their peers. Smoking by children and adolescents impairs lung growth and reduces lung function. Teenage smokers suffer from shortness of breath almost 3 times as often as teens who don't smoke, and they produce phlegm more than twice as often. Early smoking is also related to respiratory infections, chronic cough, wheezing, periodontal problems, tooth loss, vision problems, and headaches.
- Smoking at a young age increases the risk for lung cancer, and because most people who begin smoking in adolescence continue to smoke as adults, they have an increased risk for many types of cancer that continues to escalate over time. Studies also have shown that early signs of heart disease and stroke can be found in adolescents who smoke.
- Certain tobacco products are advertised and promoted disproportionately to members of racial/minority communities. For example, marketing toward Hispanics and American Indians/Alaska Natives has included advertising and promotion of cigarette brands with names such as Rio, Dorado, and American Spirit, and the tobacco industry has sponsored Tet festivals and activities related to Asian-American Heritage Month.
- Research suggests that African-American publications receive proportionately higher revenues from tobacco companies than do mainstream publications.
- American Indians/Alaska Natives (AI/AN) have the greatest cigarette smoking prevalence (23.1 percent), followed by non-Hispanic whites (14.9 percent), Hispanics (9.3 percent), non-Hispanic blacks (6.5 percent), and Asians (4.3 percent).
- Among Asian subpopulations, smoking prevalence ranges from 2.2 percent for Vietnamese to 6.8 percent for Koreans; among Hispanic populations, prevalence ranges from 7.3 percent for Central and South Americans to 11.2 percent for Cubans.

- A wide range in likelihood of starting smoking has been observed among youth who have never smoked. Overall, 22.2 percent of youth aged 12 to 17 years are likely to start smoking.
- Mexican youth (28.8 percent) are significantly more likely to start smoking than non-Hispanic white (20.8 percent), non-Hispanic black (23 percent), Cuban (16.4 percent), Asian Indian (15.4 percent), Chinese (15.3 percent), and Vietnamese (13.8 percent) youth.

Source: Centers for Disease Control and Prevention.

There is some good news, however. Statistics for 2005 show that although 25.9 percent of 8th graders, 38.9 percent of 10th graders, and 50 percent of 12th graders had smoked at some point, these figures were lower than figures for 2004.

Health Effects of Nicotine and the Use of Tobacco Products

As the single most avoidable cause of disease, disability, and death in the United States, smoking and the use of other tobacco products are responsible for a broad range of serious health issues from cataracts to miscarriage. While the majority of the serious problems are related to cancer and cardiovascular disease, smoking can harm every organ in the body and trigger serious illnesses in nonsmokers exposed to secondhand smoke or in unborn children whose mothers smoke.

Given the hundreds of chemicals in tobacco products and the wide spectrum of problems they cause, it is difficult to isolate each ingredient and assign a direct cause and effect relationship to its impact on health. However, nicotine primarily affects the bronchial and cardiovascular systems principally by constricting veins and arteries, impeding blood circulation, promoting congestive heart failure, and creating clots and blockages in legs and other appendages that can lead to gangrene. Carbon monoxide is implicated in displacing oxygen in the body, contributing to emphysema and other pulmonary dysfunction. The buildup of tars and other debris in lung membranes makes the smoker more vulnerable to pneumonia and chronic obstructive pulmonary disease (COPD).

Cancer is most closely associated with diseases that arise from smoking. Although most people think specifically of lung cancer in this connection, many other malignancies, including bladder, head and neck, brain, and pancreatic cancers, are attributable at least in part to smoking. This is because the same toxins that enter the brain and the lungs through smoking enter the rest of the body via the bloodstream and thus affect cells in every organ.

Cigars and pipes do not necessarily harm other organs to the same extent that cigarettes do, but they are heavily associated with oral cancers of the lip, tongue, and mouth, as well as many other diseases.

Effects of Nicotine on Health

Consuming nicotine and related chemicals from smoking and the use of smokeless tobacco products harms every organ of the body, some more than others. Not only can tobacco use be linked directly to specific diseases, it significantly reduces the user's quality of life by causing bad breath and yellow teeth; a dirty, smelly car, home, and workplace; persistent coughing and phlegm-filled throat; a gravelly voice; impaired lung function resulting in shortness of breath and reduced athletic stamina; more frequent colds and sinus infections; limited participation in or attendance at nonsmoking events; and disapproval and criticism from family and friends.

Among the more serious health effects smoking and other tobacco products cause are cancer, cardiovascular disease, and respiratory disorders.

Cancer

- Smoking causes about 90 percent of lung cancer deaths in women and almost 80 percent of lung cancer deaths in men. The risk of dying from lung cancer is more than 23 times higher among men who smoke cigarettes, and about 13 times higher among women who smoke cigarettes compared with never-smokers.
- Smoking causes cancers of the bladder, oral cavity, pharynx, larynx (voice box), esophagus, cervix, kidney, lung, pancreas, and stomach, and causes acute myeloid leukemia.
- Rates of cancers related to cigarette smoking vary widely in members of racial/ethnic groups but are highest in African-American men.

Heart Disease and Stroke

- Smoking causes coronary heart disease, the leading cause of death in the United States. Cigarette smokers are 2 to 4 times more likely to develop coronary heart disease than nonsmokers.
- Cigarette smoking approximately doubles a person's risk for stroke.
- Cigarette smoking causes reduced circulation by narrowing the blood vessels (arteries). Smokers are more than 10 times as likely as nonsmokers to develop peripheral vascular disease.
- Smoking causes abdominal aortic aneurysm.

Respiratory Health

- Cigarette smoking is associated with a tenfold increase in the risk of dying from chronic obstructive lung disease (COPD). About 90 percent of all deaths from COPD are attributable to cigarette smoking.
- Cigarette smoking has many adverse reproductive and early childhood effects, including an increased risk for infertility, preterm delivery, stillbirth, low birth weight, and sudden infant death syndrome (SIDS).
- Postmenopausal women who smoke have lower bone density than women who never smoked. Women who smoke have an increased risk for hip fracture than those who never smoked.

What Happens the Moment Someone Quits Smoking?

Within minutes after a person smokes his or her last cigarette, the body begins to change for the better:

- 20 minutes after quitting, heart rate drops.
- 12 hours after quitting, carbon monoxide level in the blood drops to normal.

- 2 weeks to 3 months after quitting, heart attack risk begins to drop and lung function begins to improve.
- 1 to 9 months after quitting, coughing and shortness of breath decrease.
- 1 year after quitting, the added risk of coronary heart disease is half that of a smoker's.
- 5 years after quitting, the risk of stroke is reduced to that of a nonsmoker's.
- 10 years after quitting, lung cancer death rate is about half that of a smoker's and the risk of cancers of the mouth, throat, esophagus, bladder, kidney, and pancreas decreases.
- 15 years after quitting, the risk of coronary heart disease is back to that of a nonsmoker's.

Tobacco and Smoking

- Nicotine in cigarettes, cigars, and spit tobacco is addictive.
- Nicotine narrows blood vessels and puts added strain on the heart.
- Smoking can destroy lungs and reduce oxygen available for muscles used during sports.
- Smokers suffer shortness of breath almost 3 times more often than nonsmokers.
- Smokers run slower and can't run as far, affecting overall athletic performance.
- Tobacco smoke can make hair and clothes stink.
- Tobacco stains teeth and causes bad breath.
- Short-term use of spit tobacco can cause cracked lips, white spots, sores, and bleeding in the mouth.
- Surgery to remove oral cancers caused by tobacco use can lead to serious changes in the face.
- Despite all the tobacco use on TV and in movies, music videos, billboards and magazines, most teens, adults, and athletes don't use tobacco.
- Adolescents who use tobacco may cough and have asthma attacks more often and develop respiratory problems, leading to more sick days, more doctor bills, and poorer athletic performance; be more likely to use alcohol and other drugs such as cocaine and marijuana; become addicted to tobacco and find it extremely hard to quit.
- Spit tobacco and cigars are not safe alternatives to cigarettes; low-tar and additive-free cigarettes are not safe either.
- Many children start using tobacco by age 11, and many are addicted by age 14.

"Safe" Cigarettes

Despite the advertising claims of marketers, there is no safe cigarette or tobacco product, even those whose nicotine or chemical content has been drastically reduced. First introduced in the 1960s, cigarettes with reduced volumes of certain chemicals now represent a large majority of the cigarette market and are most frequently marketed as light, ultra-light, or low-tar cigarettes. Recently, newer products dubbed PREPs (potentially reduced exposure products) or reduced-risk products have been introduced that also claim to lower the harmful effects of smoking. These include the very light cigarettes such as Eclipse as well as lozenges and snuff. Given that nicotine is a toxin, however, even these products— and the smoke they produce if they are burnable—pose a serious health risk. Critics also point out that many users, in an attempt to override the nicotine-reduction properties that cigarette manufacturers build into some lighter cigarettes, pinch the ends of filters to block the excess air inhaled with each puff. Other evidence shows that smokers simply use more of the lighter tobacco products to compensate for the lesser amount of nicotine delivered with each cigarette.

Low-Tar Cigarettes

- Filter vents are placed just millimeters from where smokers put their lips or fingers when smoking. As a result, many smokers block the vents, which actually turns the light cigarette into a regular cigarette. Some cigarette makers increase the length of the paper wrap covering the outside of the cigarette filter. Although tobacco under the wrap is still available to the smoker, this tobacco is not burned during the machine test. The result is that the machine measures less tar and nicotine levels than is available to the smoker.
- Use of low-tar products increases dramatically as age, education level, and income level increase, and is higher among women than men.
- Many smokers of low-tar cigarettes may have switched to such brands instead of quitting. Smokers may be misled by the implied promise of reduced toxicity underlying the marketing of such brands.

The so-called natural and herbal cigarettes, some of which are no longer marketed because their claims of safety were effectively debunked, have also been shown to be dangerous. Two imported types of cigarettes—**bidis and kreteks**—are falsely reputed to be safer alternatives to regular cigarettes but, in fact, have higher concentrations of nicotine and other toxic chemicals than regular cigarettes sold in the United States.

Health experts and others emphasize that because it is not known exactly how much tar, nicotine, carbon monoxide, or other chemicals it takes to cause disease, and because it takes many years for some of these illnesses to appear, it is impossible, even irresponsible, to claim that any product containing these ingredients is safe. A 2007 health study revealed that smoking so-called ultralight and light cigarettes is just as harmful to the heart and cardiovascular system as smoking regular cigarettes. Because more than a third of the people who smoke these products believe they are somehow protecting their health, they are less likely to quit smoking or they continue to smoke for a longer period of time, significantly worsening their health.

Efforts by the tobacco industry and others to market nicotine water as a safe way to ingest nicotine when smoking is not permitted, such as on airplanes, were shut down in recent years by the Food and Drug Administration (FDA), which denied claims from its manufacturer that the adulterated water should be considered a dietary supplement instead of a drug. Other tobacco industry efforts to market substitute nicotine products have also been rejected by the FDA.

Withdrawal

The symptoms of nicotine withdrawal vary from individual to individual, but most people, after 24 hours without cigarettes, show signs of hostility, impatience, irritability, or aggression, and they are less tolerant of stress. Nearly all those who quit experience repeated episodes of craving, sometimes intense, which can last for weeks but slowly diminish over time. Many find this craving intolerable and cite it as the primary reason they return to smoking. Cognitive and motor functions can suffer in the first days and weeks after quitting, and **anhedonia**, an inability to experience normal pleasures, is a frequent symptom, with a duration and intensity similar to that experienced with other drugs like cocaine or alcohol.

Although prescription nicotine products designed to treat addiction have low levels of nicotine and are free of carcinogens and other toxic chemicals, they should be used judiciously because nicotine is a toxic substance. Used in conjunction with behavioral therapy, however, these nicotine replacement therapies (NRTs) are extremely helpful in easing the craving and discomfort of withdrawal. Another significant benefit is that they provide an opportunity for the addict to focus on breaking psychological **dependence** on cigarettes without being distracted by nicotine cravings. This kind of dependence is often characterized by habits such as reaching for a cigarette when the telephone rings, smoking with morning coffee and after every meal, holding a cigarette to occupy one's hands during social encounters, or taking cigarette breaks to relieve moments of stress. The smell, sight, and feel of cigarettes and the rituals involved in handling and smoking them become powerfully associated with reward in the brains of smokers. This contributes significantly to the discomfort of withdrawal, which is already notoriously difficult due to the craving it produces.

Withdrawal and Quitting

Nicotine withdrawal symptoms usually peak about 1 to 3 weeks after quitting tobacco. People who have successfully quit have found a number of ways to help them cope with withdrawal symptoms, techniques that are especially important in the first week when symptoms are strongest and the chance of relapse is greatest. When people quit smoking or using smokeless tobacco, they often report one or more of the following symptoms:

- Experiencing a strong urge to smoke, dip, or chew
- Feeling angry or frustrated
- Feeling anxious or depressed
- Finding it hard to concentrate
- Feeling headachy, restless, or tired
- Being hungry or gaining weight
- Having trouble sleeping

These symptoms are temporary, but cravings or urges to use tobacco may last much longer than other symptoms.

After quitting, tobacco users should:

- Drink a lot of water and fruit juice. Avoid drinks that contain caffeine or alcohol.
- Play with a pencil, paper clip, or other item to occupy the hands.

- Try sugar-free gum or hard candies, sunflower seeds, carrots, or celery sticks to replace the oral habit of smoking.
- Stay busy. Enjoy activities that are hard to combine with smoking. Go to places where smoking is not allowed.
- Change habits. Get up from the table immediately after eating and take a walk. If driving a car is a trigger to smoke, use public transportation or ride with a nonsmoker.
- Brush teeth often to appreciate the feeling of a clean mouth.
- Avoid situations and places strongly associated with the pleasure of smoking.
- Take advantage of resources that offer support.

Treatment

Millions of people successfully quit smoking every year, although some have more difficulty than others. A generation ago, little was available in the way of **treatment** except programs that focused on a measured and gradual reduction in cigarette use or cold-turkey approaches that require the sudden cessation of smoking and lead to withdrawal symptoms lasting for several days or weeks. Many would-be quitters make several attempts to quit before they can quit for good—75 to 80 percent of people who try to quit relapse, sometimes several times. Mark Twain (1835–1910), the prominent American humorist and writer, made a famous comment summing it up: Quitting smoking, he said, was the easiest thing he'd ever done because he'd done it a thousand times.

For some, simple economics have proven to be sufficient incentive to quit. Statistics reveal that when New York City raised taxes to over $7 a pack, smoking decreased by 36 percent among 12- to 17-year-olds; in the same age group, evidence shows that a 10 percent rise in the cost of cigarettes produces a 12 percent decline in use. In recent decades, several techniques involving nicotine replacement substances, medications, and behavioral therapies that combine psychological support with skills training to help instill long-term coping strategies have proven very useful. Although many people have claimed success with alternative treatments such as hypnosis, acupuncture, laser therapy, herbal supplements, or electrostimulation, there is no scientific evidence to support the efficacy of these methods. When smokers find an approach that does work for them, they usually discover that once they have passed the 3-month mark of no smoking, they are able to remain smoke-free.

Genetic research is yielding clues to inborn factors related to nicotine addiction just as it is to other addictions. People with a certain variation of the *CYP2A6* gene have reduced levels of an enzyme that metabolizes nicotine; this reduction slows the drug's breakdown and relieves those individuals' craving and need for nicotine. Theoretically, medications could be developed to inhibit the function of the enzyme in people who do not have the *CYP2A6* variation.

Behavioral Therapy

Traditionally, behavioral therapies for nicotine addiction have been available through quit-smoking clinics or other forms of face-to-face counseling. In recent years, electronic communications have made many of these services available via telephone and the Internet, which have greatly broadened their access. Nevertheless, most experts stress that active involvement in individual or group counseling in a supportive environment yields the maximum benefit in recovering from an addiction to nicotine or any other substance. Combining these approaches with nicotine replacements or medications can produce even more positive results.

Nicotine Replacement Therapies

Nicotine replacement therapies (NRTs) include transdermal patches, gum, lozenges, inhalers, and nasal sprays. Many are available over the counter, have a lower level of nicotine than tobacco products, and are generally used with behavioral therapy. They do not provide the pleasurable kick of tobacco products so the impetus to use them addictively is greatly reduced, but their ability to reduce craving and other symptoms of withdrawal make them valuable treatment tools.

One of the earliest of these products to reach the commercial market was Nicorette gum, which was made available by prescription in 1984. Many who disliked the flavor of the gum turned to the transdermal patches that physicians began prescribing in the early 1990s. Although these can now be purchased over the counter, a nicotine inhaler and a spray were also introduced in the early 1990s that are available only by prescription. All of these NRTs seem to have similar levels of success, and the choice smokers make between them is driven primarily by personal preference.

Medication

For several years, Zyban was the only FDA-approved medicine available to help smokers quit. Zyban is a low-dose formulation of bupropion, an antidepressant; by rebalancing neurotransmitters in the brain, it relieves some of the intense craving quitters experience and allows them to manage withdrawal discomfort with greater ease and control. With a success rate of 15 to 20 percent one year after use, Zyban does come with some side effects; the most frequently reported include dizziness, insomnia, dry mouth, and constipation. The drug is usually taken for several weeks.

Recently, another antismoking drug has become available. Varenicline (Chantix) partially activates the nicotine receptors in the brain so they are blocked from responding to nicotine; it also helps rebalance glutamate levels to reduce the discomfort of withdrawal and seems to tamp down the dopamine reward system. Early results show that if the drug is taken for the prescribed full course of 12 weeks or longer, it helps about 25 percent of users succeed in quitting permanently. It too has side effects, some significant: headache, vomiting, strange dreams, and changes in the sense of taste, and a 2008 Food and Drug Administration report stated that it can cause some patients to develop serious depression.

An unexpected benefit of Chantix is its effect on alcoholics—it reduces their craving and desire to drink. This is a significant finding because drinking and smoking often go together; some studies suggest that as many as 85 percent of smokers drink heavily, and those who take varenicline to quit smoking may also be able to reduce or quit their drinking as well. An added advantage is that the drug is not metabolized in the liver, an organ likely to be damaged in chronic alcoholics, so it can be used without fear of inflicting further damage.

Another drug showing promise in helping smokers quit is rimonabant (Acomplia), a weight-loss drug that works by binding to the brain's CB1 cannabinoid receptor. The FDA is studying the drug prior to approval of its use in the United States.

Researchers continue to investigate other medications to treat nicotine addiction including hypertensives and agonists like varenicline that target the brain's nicotine receptors. They are also trying to develop vaccines that would stimulate the production of antibodies that could block nicotine's access to the brain.

Clinical Guidelines for Treatment

In 2000, the United States Department of Health and Human Services convened a panel of experts to study existing treatment approaches to tobacco addiction and prepare a set of guidelines to most effectively address the problem. The key findings are summarized here.

1. Tobacco dependence is a chronic condition that often requires repeated intervention. However, effective treatments exist that can produce long-term or even permanent abstinence.

2. Because effective tobacco dependence treatments are available, every patient who uses tobacco should be offered at least one of these treatments:
   - Patients willing to try to quit tobacco use should be provided with treatments of demonstrable effectiveness.
   - Patients unwilling to try to quit should be provided with a brief intervention that is designed to increase their motivation to quit.

3. It is essential that clinicians and healthcare delivery systems keep detailed records.

4. Brief tobacco dependence treatment is effective, and every patient who uses tobacco should be offered at least brief treatment.

5. There is a strong dose-response relationship between the intensity of tobacco dependence counseling and its effectiveness. Treatments involving person-to-person contact (via individual, group, or proactive telephone counseling) are consistently effective, and their effectiveness increases with treatment intensity (e.g., minutes of contact).

6. Three types of counseling and behavioral therapies were found to be especially effective and should be used with all patients who are attempting tobacco cessation:
   - Provision of practical counseling (problem solving/skills training).
   - Provision of social support as part of treatment (intra-treatment social support).
   - Help in securing social support outside of treatment (extra-treatment social support).

7. Numerous effective pharmacotherapies for smoking cessation now exist. Except in the presence of contraindications, these should be used with all patients who are attempting to quit smoking.
   - Five 1st-line pharmacotherapies were identified that reliably increased long-term smoking abstinence rates:
     - Bupropion SR
     - Nicotine gum (or lozenge)
     - Nicotine inhaler
     - Nicotine nasal spray
     - Nicotine patch
   - Two 2nd-line pharmacotherapies were identified as efficacious and may be considered by clinicians if 1st-line pharmacotherapies are not effective:
     - Clonidine (a drug used to treat high blood pressure)
     - Nortriptyline (a tricyclic antidepressant)
   - Over-the-counter nicotine patches are effective relative to placebo, and their use should be encouraged.

FAQs about Smoking and Health

1. What are the health effects of smoking?

    Smoking causes many chronic diseases, such as lung cancer and many other forms of cancer; heart disease; and respiratory diseases, including emphysema, chronic bronchitis, and pneumonia. Each year in the United States, about 1 in every 5 deaths is attributable to smoking.

    Overall, smokers are less healthy than nonsmokers. Smoking affects the immune system, which increases a person's risk for infections. Smoking also increases the risk for fractures, dental diseases, sexual problems, eye diseases, and peptic ulcers.

    When people quit smoking, their bodies begin to recover, and the risk for smoking-related diseases decreases over time. Although people who smoke will never be as healthy as they would have been had they never smoked at all, risks continue to decrease the longer they stay smoke free.

2. How does smoking affect the risk for respiratory disease?

    Smoking injures lung tissue and affects the lungs' ability to fight infections. Tissue damage from smoking can lead to chronic obstructive pulmonary disease (COPD), which is sometimes called emphysema. COPD is the 4th leading cause of death in the United States.

    Smokers are more likely than nonsmokers to have upper and lower respiratory tract infections, perhaps because smoking suppresses immune function. Smokers' lung function also declines more quickly than that of nonsmokers.

3. How does smoking affect the risk for cardiovascular disease?

    Heart disease and stroke are cardiovascular (heart and blood vessel) diseases that result from smoking and, respectively, are the 1st and 3rd leading causes of death in the United States. Most cases of these diseases are related to atherosclerosis, a hardening and narrowing of the arteries. Smoking speeds up this process, even in young smokers. Cigarette smoke damages the cells lining the blood vessels and heart, creating swelling that prevents the flow of blood and oxygen to the heart. Smoking also increases a person's risk of dangerous blood clots, which can also cause a heart attack or stroke.

    Fortunately, risks for heart disease and stroke decrease steadily after a person quits. One year after a person quits, the excess risk for coronary heart disease is half that of a smoker, and after 15 years, the risk for coronary heart disease returns to that of a nonsmoker. After 5 to 15 years, a former smoker's risk for stroke decreases to that of a nonsmoker.

4. How does smoking cause emphysema?

    Smoking can lead to chronic obstructive pulmonary disease (COPD), in which the airways and air sacs lose their elasticity and the walls between many of the air sacs are destroyed. The walls of the airways also become inflamed and swollen and more mucous is formed. As a result it becomes very difficult to get air in and out of the lungs. Because these changes happen slowly over a number of years, a person may not notice the changes until it's too late.

5. Is there a cure for emphysema?

    There is no cure for emphysema, but the risk of developing this disease decreases when a person quits smoking.

6. How does smoking affect the risk for cancer?

Certain agents in tobacco smoke can damage important genes that control the growth of cells, which increases a person's risk for many types of cancer.

Lung cancer is the leading cause of cancer death. About 87 percent of lung cancer cases are caused by smoking. Smokers are about 20 times more likely to develop lung cancer than nonsmokers. Smoking also causes cancers of the mouth, throat, larynx (voice box), and esophagus, and it increases a person's risk of developing cancer of the pancreas, kidney, bladder, cervix, and stomach. Smoking may also contribute to the development of acute myeloid leukemia, which is a cancer of the blood.

For smoking-attributable cancers, the risk generally increases with the number of cigarettes smoked and the number of years of smoking. Risks decrease after a person quits completely. Ten years after quitting, the risk of developing lung cancer decreases by as much as half.

7. How does smoking affect reproductive health in women?

Women who smoke have more difficulty becoming pregnant and have a greater risk of never becoming pregnant. Those who smoke during pregnancy also have a greater chance of complications, including placenta previa, a condition in which the placenta grows too close to the opening of the uterus, and placental abruption, a condition in which the placenta prematurely separates from the wall of the uterus.

In addition to complications, women who smoke during pregnancy are at higher risk for premature birth, a low birth weight infant, stillbirth, and infant mortality.

8. How does smoking affect reproductive health in men?

Although only a small number of studies have looked at the relationship between smoking and erectile dysfunction, research findings suggest that smoking may be associated with an increased risk for this condition. More studies are needed before researchers can conclude that smoking is causally related to erectile dysfunction.

Research also suggests that cigarette smoking may affect the amount of semen and sperm produced and adversely affect sperm quality.

9. How long does nicotine stay in the body, and what mechanisms are used to test for nicotine in the body?

The amount of nicotine, cotinine, carbon monoxide, or other components found in the body varies with the amount of tobacco used, the type of product used, and a person's smoking behavior (e.g., how deeply the person inhales). However, within 3 to 4 days of quitting, any byproducts found in the body should be at levels low enough to indicate that the person is no longer actively smoking.

Measuring concentrations of nicotine or its breakdown products (e.g., cotinine) in body fluids such as blood, urine, or saliva can reveal whether a person currently smokes and about how much the person smokes. Other tests for tobacco use measure concentrations of carbon monoxide or other gases in a person's breath.

People exposed to secondhand smoke may have a measurable level of nicotine or nicotine byproducts in their bodies, but the level is the result of passive inhalation rather than active tobacco use. Anyone scheduled for testing may want to avoid closed areas where people are smoking for a day or two before the test is given.

10. What is nicotine addiction?

Nicotine is the highly addictive drug found naturally in tobacco. Nicotine is found in cigarettes, cigars, smokeless tobacco, shisha (the flavored tobacco smoked in a hookah or water pipe), bidis, and kreteks (clove cigarettes). Even if a tobacco product is marketed as all natural, it is still addictive because of its nicotine content.

Nicotine meets the following criteria for an addictive substance:

1. The user's behavior is largely controlled by a substance that causes mood change, primarily because of the substance's effects on the brain.
2. The individual will continue to use the substance, often putting it before other priorities.
3. The person develops a tolerance for the drug, so increasing amounts are needed to create the same effect.
4. Withdrawal symptoms occur if the person does not use the drug.
5. A strong tendency for relapse exists after quitting.

11. How does nicotine affect the body?

Nicotine reaches the brain within 10 seconds after smoke enters the lungs and raises the heart and breathing rates. Nicotine also causes more glucose (blood sugar) to be released into the blood, which may explain why smokers say they feel more alert after smoking.

Nicotine also causes the brain cells to release an unusually large amount of dopamine, which stimulates pleasure centers in the brain and makes the smoker feel good.

The effects of nicotine do not last very long. When the effects wear off, the smoker feels a strong urge to smoke again to get more nicotine.

Repeated doses of nicotine alter the brain's activities. The brain reduces the amount of dopamine that it produces and the number of receptors that carry dopamine to the cells. When this happens, the smoker needs nicotine just to have normal levels of dopamine in the brain. If the level of dopamine drops, the smoker feels irritable and depressed.

Both young and older smokers can become addicted to nicotine. In adults, nicotine addiction is linked to the amount and frequency of tobacco used. In teens, nicotine addiction appears to be linked to the length of time they have been regular tobacco users. Teens who only smoke small amounts but who smoke daily are still at high risk of becoming addicted to nicotine.

12. What are the health effects of casual/light smoking?

Some people believe that smoking only in social situations or smoking only a few cigarettes a day is not harmful. Although health risks related to smoking increase with the amount smoked and the length of time a person smokes, there is no safe amount to smoke.

Any time that tobacco smoke touches a living cell, some damage is done. When a person inhales cigarette smoke, the smoke enters the lungs and damages lung tissue. Nicotine in the smoke is then rapidly absorbed into the blood and within 10 seconds, it starts affecting the brain. It quickly increases heart rate and blood pressure and restricts blood flow to the heart. It also lowers skin temperature and reduces blood flow in the legs and feet.

A major concern is that most people who start as casual smokers think they can stop whenever they choose. However, studies show that many of them become regular smokers.

13. What are the health effects of smoking a hookah pipe?

    A hookah pipe is used to smoke a tobacco mixture called shisha. Shisha contains itobacco and flavorings such as fruit pulp, molasses, and honey. The hookah pipe uses coals to heat the shisha, and the smoke that is created passes through tubes and water so it is cooled before it is inhaled.

    When smoking shisha, a person not only inhales tobacco smoke but also inhales smoke from the burning flavorings. Because hookah smoking is a relatively new activity in the United States, no research is available on the health effects of inhaling smoke from the substance.

    According to the American Cancer Society, several types of cancer, as well as other negative health effects, have been linked to smoking a hookah pipe. Passing the smoke through water may remove some compounds, but research shows that many toxins remain in the water-filtered smoke. These toxins include nicotine, which is the highly addictive compound in tobacco smoke. Consequently, hookah users suffer the same effects of nicotine use (e.g., increases in blood pressure and heart rate and changes in dopamine production in the brain) that occur in cigarette smokers.

14. What are the health effects of using smokeless tobacco?

    Smokeless tobacco products are not a safe replacement for smoking. These products have significant health risks and generally deliver more nicotine than cigarettes. Youth who use smokeless tobacco also are more likely to become cigarette smokers. Smokeless tobacco contains more than 25 cancer-causing compounds, including arsenic and formaldehyde. People who use these products have an increased risk of developing cancers of the mouth and throat.

    Smokeless tobacco use also is strongly associated with the formation of skin lesions in the mouth. These include leukoplakia, which are white patches that can turn into cancer over time, and erythroplakia, which are red patches that have a high potential for becoming cancerous.

    Smokeless tobacco also is strongly associated with gum recession. Gum recession not only is unsightly but it also increases one's risk of getting cavities on the tooth roots and can make teeth sensitive.

15. How does smoking affect infants born to mothers who smoke?

    Smoking during pregnancy increases the risk for pregnancy complications, premature delivery, a low birth weight infant, and stillbirth.

    Babies whose mothers smoke while pregnant and babies who are exposed to secondhand smoke after birth are more likely to die from sudden infant death syndrome (SIDS) than babies who are not exposed to cigarette smoke. These babies also have weaker lungs than other babies, which increases their risk for many health problems.

16. What are "fire-safe" cigarettes?

    Fire-safe or self-extinguishing cigarettes are cigarettes designed to stop burning if they are not puffed on regularly. Fire-safe cigarettes were developed to help prevent fires and fire-related injuries resulting from improper disposal of smoking materials. In the United States, smoking materials are the leading cause of fire-related deaths, accounting for more than 1 of every 4 fire deaths.

FAQs about Light Cigarettes

Many smokers choose low-tar, mild, light, or ultralight cigarettes because they think that these cigarettes may be less harmful to their health than regular or full-flavor cigarettes. Although smoke from light cigarettes may feel smoother and lighter on the throat and chest, light cigarettes are not healthier than regular cigarettes. The truth is that light cigarettes do not reduce the health risks of smoking. The only way to reduce a smoker's risk, and the risk to others, is to stop smoking completely.

1. What about the lower tar and nicotine numbers on light and ultralight cigarette packs and in ads for these products?

   These numbers come from smoking machines, which "smoke" every brand of cigarettes exactly the same way.

   These numbers do not really tell how much tar and nicotine a particular smoker may get because people do not smoke cigarettes the same way machines do. And no 2 people smoke the same way.

2. How do light cigarettes trick the smoking machines?

   Tobacco companies designed light cigarettes with tiny pinholes on the filters. These filter vents dilute cigarette smoke with air when light cigarettes are puffed by smoking machines, causing the machines to measure artificially low tar and nicotine levels.

   Many smokers do not know that their cigarette filters have vent holes. The filter vents are uncovered when cigarettes are smoked on smoking machines. However, filter vents are placed just millimeters from where smokers put their lips or fingers when smoking. As a result, many smokers block the vents—which actually turns the light cigarette into a regular cigarette.

   Some cigarette makers increased the length of the paper wrap covering the outside of the cigarette filter, which decreases the number of puffs that occur during the machine test. Although tobacco under the wrap is still available to the smoker, this tobacco is not burned during the machine test. The result is that the machine measures less tar and nicotine levels than is available to the smoker.

   Because smokers, unlike machines, crave nicotine, they may inhale more deeply; take larger, more rapid, or more frequent puffs; or smoke a few extra cigarettes each day to get enough nicotine to satisfy their craving. This is called "compensating," and it means that smokers end up inhaling more tar, nicotine, and other harmful chemicals than the machine-based numbers suggest.

3. What is the scientific evidence about the health effects of light cigarettes?

   The National Cancer Institute (NCI) has concluded that light cigarettes provide no benefit to smokers' health.

   According to the NCI, people who switch to light cigarettes from regular cigarettes are likely to inhale the same amount of hazardous chemicals, and they remain at high risk for developing smoking-related cancers and other diseases.

   Researchers also found that the strategies used by the tobacco industry to advertise and promote light cigarettes are intended to reassure smokers, to discourage them from quitting, and to lead consumers to perceive filtered and light cigarettes as safer alternatives to regular cigarettes.

There is also no evidence that switching to light or ultralight cigarettes actually helps smokers quit.

4. Have the tobacco companies conducted research on the amount of tar and nicotine people actually inhale while smoking light cigarettes?

The tobacco industry's own documents show that companies are aware that smokers of light cigarettes compensate by taking bigger puffs.

Industry documents also show that the companies are aware of the difference between machine-measured yields of tar and nicotine and what the smoker actually inhales.

5. What is the bottom line for smokers who want to protect their health?

There is no such thing as a safe cigarette. The only proven way to reduce the risk of smoking-related disease is to quit smoking completely.

Smokers who quit live longer than those who continue to smoke. The earlier smokers quit, the greater the health benefit. Research has shown that people who quit before age 30 eliminate almost all of their risk of developing a tobacco-related disease. Even smokers who quit at age 50 reduce their risk of dying from a tobacco-related disease.

Quitting also decreases the risk of lung cancer, heart attacks, stroke, and chronic lung disease.

Nicotine: FAQs about Quitting

Key Points

- Quitting smoking reduces the health risks of many types of cancer, including cancers of the lung, esophagus, larynx (voice box), mouth, throat, kidney, bladder, pancreas, stomach, and cervix, as well as acute myeloid leukemia. It also substantially reduces the risk of developing and dying from cancer.
- Strong and consistent evidence shows that nicotine replacement products can help people quit smoking. These products are available in 5 forms: patch, gum, lozenge, nasal spray, and inhaler.
- Bupropion and varenicline are prescription medications that can also help smokers quit.

1. What health problems are caused by smoking?

Smoking harms nearly every organ of the body and diminishes a person's overall health. Smoking is a leading cause of cancer and of death from cancer.

Smoking also causes heart disease, stroke, lung disease (chronic bronchitis and emphysema), hip fractures, and cataracts. Smokers are at higher risk of developing pneumonia and other airway infections.

A pregnant smoker is at higher risk of having her baby born too early and with an abnormally low weight. A woman who smokes during or after pregnancy increases her infant's risk of death from sudden infant death syndrome (SIDS).

Millions of Americans have health problems caused by smoking. Cigarette smoking and exposure to tobacco smoke cause nearly 500,000 premature deaths each year in the United States. Of these premature deaths, about

40 percent are from cancer, 35 percent are from heart disease and stroke, and 25 percent are from lung disease. Regardless of their age, smokers can substantially reduce their risk of disease, including cancer, by quitting.

2. Does tobacco smoke contain harmful chemicals?

Yes. Tobacco smoke contains chemicals that are harmful to both smokers and nonsmokers. Breathing even a little tobacco smoke can be harmful. Of the 4,000 chemicals in tobacco smoke, at least 250 are known to be harmful. The toxic chemicals found in smoke include hydrogen cyanide (used in chemical weapons), carbon monoxide (found in car exhaust), formaldehyde (used as an embalming fluid), ammonia (used in household cleaners), and toluene (found in paint thinners).

Of the 250 known harmful chemicals in tobacco smoke, more than 50 have been found to cause cancer. These chemicals include:

- arsenic (a heavy metal toxin)
- benzene (a chemical found in gasoline)
- beryllium (a toxic metal)
- cadmium (a metal used in batteries)
- chromium (a metallic element)
- ethylene oxide (a chemical used to sterilize medical devices)
- nickel (a metallic element)
- polonium-210 (a chemical element that gives off radiation)
- vinyl chloride (a toxic substance used in plastics manufacture)

3. What are the immediate benefits of quitting smoking?

The immediate health benefits of quitting smoking are substantial. Heart rate and blood pressure, which were abnormally high while smoking, begin to return to normal. Within a few hours, the level of carbon monoxide in the blood begins to decline. (Carbon monoxide, a colorless, odorless gas found in cigarette smoke, reduces the blood's ability to carry oxygen.) Within a few weeks, people who quit smoking have improved circulation, don't produce as much phlegm, and don't cough or wheeze as often. Within several months of quitting, people can expect significant improvements in lung function.

4. What are the long-term benefits of quitting smoking?

Quitting reduces the risk of cancer and other diseases, such as heart disease and lung disease, caused by smoking. People who quit smoking, regardless of their age, are less likely than those who continue to smoke to die from smoking-related illness. Studies have shown that quitting at about age 30 reduces the chance of dying from smoking-related diseases by more than 90 percent. People who quit at about age 50 reduce their risk of dying prematurely by 50 percent compared with those who continue to smoke. Even people who quit at about age 60 or older live longer than those who continue to smoke.

5. Does quitting smoking lower the risk of cancer?

Quitting smoking substantially reduces the risk of developing and dying from cancer, and this benefit increases the longer a person remains smoke free. However, even after many years of not smoking, the risk of lung cancer in former smokers remains higher than in people who have never smoked. Risk depends on a number of factors, including the number of years of smoking, the number of cigarettes smoked per day, the age at which smoking began, and the presence or absence of illness at the time of quitting.

6. Should someone already diagnosed with cancer bother to quit smoking?

People diagnosed with cancer should definitely quit smoking because their immune systems will fight the disease more efficiently, their bodies will heal more readily, and their chance of the cancer recurring will lessen.

7. What are some of the challenges associated with quitting smoking?

Quitting smoking may cause short-term withdrawal symptoms, especially for those who have smoked a large number of cigarettes for a long period of time:

- Feeling sad or anxious: Nicotine withdrawal usually entails some depression, anxiety, and agitation or restlessness, and, for many, nicotine replacement products help relieve these symptoms. However, even without medication, withdrawal symptoms and other problems do subside over time. It helps to keep in mind that people who kick the smoking habit have the opportunity for a healthier future.
- Gaining weight: Some people who quit smoking gain an average of 6 to 8 pounds, but for many this is temporary and in any case is far less of a threat to health than smoking. Regular physical activity can help people maintain a healthy weight.

8. Can a doctor, dentist, or pharmacist help a person quit smoking?

Doctors, dentists, and pharmacists can be good sources of information about the health risks of smoking and the benefits of quitting. They can describe the proper use and potential side effects of nicotine replacement therapy and other medicines, and they can help people find local quit-smoking resources.

9. How should someone help another person quit smoking?

It is important to find out if the person wants to quit smoking. Most smokers say they want to quit. If they don't, try to find out why.

- Express concerns in terms of the smoker's health.
- Acknowledge that the smoker may get something out of smoking and may find it difficult to quit.
- Be encouraging and express faith that the smoker can quit for good.
- Suggest a specific action, such as calling a smoking quitline, for help in quitting smoking.
- Ask the smoker what sort of help he or she would find supportive.
- Avoid sending quit-smoking materials to smokers unless they ask for them.
- Avoid criticizing, nagging, or reminding the smoker about past failures.

10. What are nicotine replacement products?

Nicotine replacement products deliver small, measured doses of nicotine into the body, which helps to relieve the cravings and withdrawal symptoms often felt by people trying to quit smoking. It's far less harmful for a person to get nicotine from a nicotine replacement product than from cigarettes because tobacco smoke contains many toxic and cancer-causing substances.

All nicotine replacement products, which are approved by the U.S. Food and Drug Administration (FDA) and available in the following 5 forms, appear to be equally effective:

- The nicotine patch is available over the counter (without a prescription). A new patch is worn on the skin each day, supplying a small but steady amount of nicotine to the body. The nicotine patch is sold in varying strengths as an 8-week quit-smoking treatment. Nicotine doses are gradually lowered as the treatment progresses. The nicotine patch may not be a good choice for people with skin problems or allergies to adhesive tape. Also, people who experience the side effect of vivid dreams may opt to wear the patch only during the daytime.

- Nicotine gum is available over the counter in 2- and 4-mg strengths. When a person chews nicotine gum and then places the chewed product between the cheek and gum tissue, nicotine is released into the bloodstream through the lining of the mouth. To keep a steady amount of nicotine in the body, a new piece of gum can be chewed every 1 or 2 hours. Nicotine gum might not be appropriate for people with temporomandibular joint (TMJ) disease or for those with dentures or other dental work such as bridges. The gum releases nicotine more effectively when coffee, juice, and other acidic beverages are not consumed at the same time.

- The nicotine lozenge is also available over the counter in 2- and 4-mg strengths. The use of the lozenge is similar to that of nicotine gum; it is placed between the cheek and gum tissue and allowed to dissolve. Nicotine is released into the bloodstream through the lining of the mouth. The lozenge works best when used every 1 or 2 hours and when coffee, juice, and other acidic beverages are not consumed at the same time.

- Nicotine nasal spray is available by prescription only. The spray comes in a pump bottle containing nicotine that tobacco users can inhale when they have an urge to smoke. Absorption of nicotine via the spray is faster than that achieved with any of the other types of nicotine replacement. This product is not recommended for people with nasal or sinus conditions, allergies, or asthma, nor is it recommended for young tobacco users. Side effects from the spray include sneezing, coughing, and watering eyes, but these problems usually go away with continued use of the spray.

- A nicotine inhaler, also available only by prescription, delivers a vaporized form of nicotine to the mouth through a mouthpiece attached to a plastic cartridge. Even though it is called an inhaler, the device does not deliver nicotine to the lungs the way a cigarette does. Most of the nicotine only travels to the mouth and throat, where it is absorbed through the mucous membranes. Common side effects include throat and mouth irritation and coughing. Anyone with a bronchial problem such as asthma should use it with caution.

Experts recommend combining nicotine replacement therapy with advice or counseling from a doctor, dentist, pharmacist, or other healthcare provider, and they suggest smokers avoid using tobacco when they begin using nicotine replacement products because too much nicotine can cause nausea, vomiting, dizziness, diarrhea, weakness, or rapid heartbeat

11. Are there products to help people quit smoking that do not contain nicotine?

Bupropion, a prescription antidepressant marketed as Zyban, was approved by the FDA in 1997 to treat nicotine addiction by easing the craving and discomfort of withdrawal. Some common side effects of bupropion are dry mouth, difficulty sleeping, headache, dizziness, and skin rash. People should not use this drug if they have a seizure condition such as epilepsy or an eating disorder such as anorexia nervosa or bulimia, or if they are taking other medicines that contain bupropion hydrochloride. Also, people should avoid using alcohol while taking buproprion because alcohol consumption increases the risk of having a seizure.

Varenicline, a prescription medicine marketed as Chantix, was approved by the FDA in 2006 to help smokers who wish to quit by easing their withdrawal symptoms and by blocking the effects of nicotine from cigarettes if they resume smoking. Some common side effects of varenicline are nausea, changes in dreaming, constipation, gas, and vomiting, and a 2008 FDA report stated that it may cause serious symptoms of depression in some patients. The healthcare provider should determine whether the smoker is pregnant, breastfeeding, or suffering from certain disorders before prescribing this medication.

12. What about combining medications?

In some cases, it may be advisable to combine 2 nicotine replacement therapies or 2 other medications for best results, but this decision should be made by a healthcare provider.

13. Are there alternative methods to help people quit smoking?

Some people claim that alternative approaches such as hypnosis, herbal therapies, or acupuncture helped them quit smoking, but there is as yet no concrete scientific data to support this approach.

14. What if a person smokes again after quitting?

Many smokers find it difficult to quit. People commonly quit smoking and then find themselves smoking again, especially in the first few weeks or months after quitting. People who smoke after quitting should try again to quit. Most people find that they need to persist in their attempts to quit smoking before they quit for good. Like other addictions, nicotine addiction is characterized by relapse, but those who can stop smoking for 3 months usually have an excellent prognosis.

15. What about weight gain after quitting smoking?

Weight gain is a particular concern for some people. Although it is not uncommon for people to gain some weight when they quit smoking, studies show that the average weight gain is only 6 to 8 pounds, and many people lose at least part of this weight after a period of time.

16. Is there a shot to help people quit smoking/tobacco?

At this time, there is no medication available that is given as a shot that is approved as a safe and effective way to help people quit smoking or using smokeless tobacco. However, researchers are working on several vaccines that might be helpful in the future. These vaccines cause the body's immune system to produce antibodies that stop nicotine from reaching the brain.

It will be a few years before the clinical trials are completed and a vaccine can be submitted to the FDA for possible approval, so smokers should be wary of Web sites or clinics that claim to have a stop-smoking shot or vaccine.

Further Reading

Califano, Joseph A., Jr. *High Society: How Substance Abuse Ravages America and What to Do About It.* New York: Perseus Books, 2007.

Delnevo, C. D., Foulds, Jonathan, and Hrywna, Mary. Trading Tobacco: Are Youths Choosing Cigars over Cigarettes? *American Journal of Public Health* 2005: 95, 2123.

Federal Trade Commission. October 2007. Retrieved from http://www.ftc.gov/opa/2007/04/cigaretterpt.shtm

U.S. Department of Health and Human Services. *Nicotine Addiction: A Report of the Surgeon General.* Centers for Disease Control and Prevention, Public Health Service, Center for Health Promotion and Education, Office on Smoking and Health, 1988.

U.S. Department of Health and Human Services. *Targeting Tobacco Use: The Nation's Leading Cause of Death.* Centers for Disease Control and Prevention, 2003.

U.S. Department of Health and Human Services, *The Health Consequences of Involuntary Exposure to Tobacco Smoke: A Report of the Surgeon General.* Centers for Disease Control and Prevention, National Center for Chronic Disease Prevention and Health Promotion, Office on Smoking and Health, 2006.

U.S. Department of Health and Human Services. *Results from the 2006 National Survey on Drug Use and Health: National Findings.* Substance Abuse and Mental Health Services Administration (SAMHSA), Office of Applied Studies. DHHS Publication No. SMA 07-4293, 2007.

U.S. Department of Health and Human Services, Centers for Disease Control and Prevention (CDC), January 2008. Retrieved from http://apps.nccd.cdc.gov/osh_faq

U.S. Department of Health and Human Services, Centers for Disease Control and Prevention (CDC), November 2007. Retrieved from http://www.cdc.gov/tobacco

U.S. Department of Health and Human Services, National Cancer Institute (NCI), December 2007. Retrieved from http://www.cancer.gov/cancertopics/tobacco

U.S. Department of Health and Human Services, National Institute on Drug Abuse. *Research Report Series: Tobacco Addiction.* NIH Publication No. 06-4342, July 2006.

U.S. Environmental Protection Agency. *Respiratory Health Effects of Passive Smoking: Lung Cancer and Other Disorders.* Washington, DC: U.S. Environmental Protection Agency, 1992.

Nicotine Anonymous. *See* Twelve-Step Programs.

N, N-diisopropyl-5-methoxytryptamine. *See* Psilocybin and Psilocin.

Noradrenaline, Norepinephrine. *See* Neurotransmitters.

Nucleus Accumbens. *See* Brain and Addiction.

Numorphan. *See* Oxymorphone.

Nymphomania. *See* Hypersexuality.